THE POLITICS OF RACE
Canada, the United States, and Australia

Second Edition

The Politics of Race is an excellent resource for students and general readers seeking to learn about race policies and legislation. Arguing that 'states make race,' it provides a unique comparison of the development and construction of race in three White settler societies – Canada, the United States, and Australia.

This timely new edition focuses on the politics of race after 9/11 and Barack Obama's election as president of the United States. Jill Vickers and Annette Isaac explore how state-sanctioned race discrimination has intensified in the wake of heightened security. It also explains the new race formation of Islamophobia in all three countries and the shifts in how Hispanics and Asian Americans are being treated in the United States. As race and politics become increasingly intertwined in both academic and popular discourse, *The Politics of Race* aids readers in evaluating different approaches for promoting racial justice and transforming states.

JILL VICKERS is Distinguished Research Professor and Emeritus Chancellor's Professor in the Department of Political Science at Carleton University.

ANNETTE ISAAC is a faculty lecturer in the Department of Political Science at Carleton University and a former international development specialist.

JILL VICKERS AND ANNETTE ISAAC

The Politics of Race

Canada, the United States,
and Australia

Second Edition

UNIVERSITY OF TORONTO PRESS
Toronto Buffalo London

©University of Toronto Press 2012
Toronto Buffalo London
www.utppublishing.com
Printed in Canada

ISBN 978-1-4426-4242-3 (cloth)
ISBN 978-1-4426-1131-3 (paper)

∞

Printed on acid-free, 100% post-consumer recycled paper with vegetable-based inks.

Library and Archives Canada Cataloguing in Publication

Vickers, Jill, 1942–
The politics of race : Canada, the United States, and Australia / Jill Vickers and Annette Isaac. – 2nd ed.

Includes bibliographical references and index.
ISBN 978-1-4426-4242-3 (bound). – ISBN 978-1-4426-1131-3 (pbk.)

1. Race relations – Political aspects.   2. Canada – Race relations.   3. United States – Race relations.   4. Australia – Race relations.   I. Isaac, Annette, 1951–   II. Title.

HT1521.V52 2012   305.8   C2012-901581-4

University of Toronto Press acknowledges the financial assistance to its publishing program of the Canada Council for the Arts and the Ontario Arts Council.

 Canada Council   Conseil des Arts
for the Arts   du Canada

 ONTARIO ARTS COUNCIL
CONSEIL DES ARTS DE L'ONTARIO

University of Toronto Press acknowledges the financial support of the Government of Canada through the Canada Book Fund for its publishing activities.

Contents

Preface to the Second Edition

This new edition offers an updated comparative analysis of 'the politics of race' in Australia, Canada, and the United States. Our focus remains on how governments use state institutions and laws to 'make race.' Governments create, administer, and remake the founding race regimes that characterize these three federal democracies. Increasingly, however, new race formations such as Islamophobia are developing that reflect international conflicts, real and imagined. This edition highlights several new race formations as well as key events since the first edition.

Most significant in this regard are the terrorist attacks on the United States of 11 September 2001 – the '9/11 attacks' – which happened just before the first edition appeared. While acknowledging those events, the first edition did not consider how they would affect the politics of race. The United States suffered most profoundly and responded most fiercely. But though many Australians were killed in a 2002 nightclub attack in Bali, Indonesia, there have been no attacks on Australian soil; and Canadians have largely escaped attacks. Another significant event was the 2008 election of a U.S. president with African heritage – a potential game changer in American politics, and in its foreign policy. Also between the two editions, a Conservative prime minister officially apologized to Canada's Indigenous people for past federal governments' harmful policies and established remedial programs and compensation funds for those damaged by their experiences in residential schools. Also, Asian Americans became the 'poster children' of U.S. immigration policy because of their high educational achievements; but at the same time, the dramatic growth of the Asian economies is now being perceived as a threat, and local Asians are often accused of being *too* successful.

Do such events disprove the claims we made in the first edition that governments use state institutions and discourses to privilege many White citizens and disadvantage most of their non-White counterparts? Our findings are mixed: some things improved between the two editions; but White privilege persists.[1] Many legal practices and ideas that sustained these countries' founding race regimes have been replaced with new ones. For example, Prime Minister John Howard's 'intervention' in Australia's Northern Territory denied Aboriginal communities self-government on arguably flimsy grounds. Foundational race regimes are hard to dismantle, mainly because the categories they have created persist. New studies of how the U.S. Census Bureau perpetuates old race categories have revealed the mechanisms whereby successive governments 'make race.' Democratic racism, which developed in the latter half of the twentieth century, and which we discussed in the first edition, still blocks efforts to eradicate or transform old race regimes. Meanwhile, governments' security preoccupations during the post-9/11 'war on terror' have generated new forms of racialization, which we discuss in one of this edition's three new chapters.

As in the first edition, the text's approach to the politics of race is comparative and state focused. But in this edition, we discuss our historical institutionalist (HI) framework in more depth. Instead of focusing on 'race relations' among individuals or groups, HI compares the roles played by governments, state institutions, institutionalized discourses, and various historical legacies in the making of race. Despite important differences, the three states studied share *federal architectures that divide power between central and state governments;* and all three have *hard-to-amend written constitutions* that are interpreted and arbitrated by independent High or Supreme Courts. All three White settler societies reflect British colonial initiatives and share a *common law system* as well as other institutional features, including *similar electoral systems*. In this edition we have added a chapter that compares how federalism and other similar institutional arrangements shape 'the politics of race' in the three countries.

In this edition, we also focus more on how institutionalized discourses help governments and state institutions create, reproduce, and maintain race regimes and other race formations. We have expanded the discussion of democratic racism in the Introduction; and in chapter 6 we introduce the idea of 'democratic responsiveness,' which shows how *democratic theory and practice actually can inhibit change if democratic majorities remain White*. The new chapter 3 focuses on migration and refugee policies in the context of the politics of race and includes an expanded discussion of multiculturalism. In chapter 6 we show how the key values in multiculturalism differ from those promoted by anti-racism theories. We focus on discourses that governments and state officials use to legitimize race regimes and their consequences. We focus less on ideologies advanced by movements, whether they seek to mobilize non-Whites against racialism or to mobilize Whites. An example of the latter is the Tea Party movement in the United States, which opposes health care reform as well as other reforms that they believe will benefit non-Whites and disadvantage Whites. This doesn't mean we consider such movements or the ideas they promote to be unimportant. A complete 'comparative politics of race' would include both levels. Our focus on states challenges the long-established belief that states and governments are above the fray and that they merely 'manage' race-based conflicts.

In the first edition we focused on Anthony Marx's proposition that 'states make race.' In this second edition, we also focus on *how* states make race, and we identify the institutional and discursive mechanisms used by each state, including the mechanisms that all three share. We focus more explicitly on comparing how institutions of governance, such as the police, the courts, immigration departments, census bureaux, and prison systems, make and perpetuate historical race categories and regimes, and on how they recycle ideas that sustain race hatred and conflict. Many present-day state institutions remain marked by legacies dating back to when those institutions were founded; ideas the founders resorted to when legitimizing the exclusion of non-Whites (and women) from citizenship persist in tangible forms. (The U.S. Electoral College is an example.) We conceptualize political institutions as highly stable patterns of behaviour and ideas intermixed. While they are creations of specific individuals and groups, each generation experiences them as bigger than itself; and when we participate in them as citizens, legislators, bureaucrats, or judges, our behaviour is moulded by each institution's norms of appropriateness.

Some studies of 'race relations' focus on the ideas, attitudes, and behaviour of individuals, not on race relations as something shaped by state institutions and their norms of appropriateness. Approaches characterized by individualism assume that racism involves individuals and that institutions and states are merely the current aggregations of individuals' preferences. In such approaches, what happened in the past is deemed irrelevant once old laws have been repealed. This fosters the belief that educating individuals is sufficient to end race-based prejudice. The idea is that once individuals are persuaded or compelled by law to change their preferences, racism simply will end. By contrast, we theorize that although state and political institutions were created by some human actors and regularly are modified by others, human institutions persist over time and are more durable than just the sum of each generation's individual actions and preferences. In technical HI terms, institutions are path dependent in that when founders set them along a particular path, they continue down it until they encounter a roadblock or experience shocks. When this happens, the individuals who then constitute them try either to bring the institution back to its original path or to restructure it so that it can continue along a somewhat altered path. A comparative institutionalist approach allows us to compare how the governments in Canada, Australia, and the United States responded to the significant challenges they faced as the politics of race changed. For example, U.S. political elites responded to the end of slavery and victory or defeat in the Civil War by reshaping institutions and restructuring discourses. Ultimately, they fostered a Whites-only nationalism that helped rebuild solidarity among Whites and that placed governments back on the path of racialism in the context of segregation. An HI approach shows how governments and elites borrowed policies, ideas, and practices such as residential schools from one another in order to sustain White rule. Chappell, Chesterman, and Hill (2009, chapter 8) demonstrate the similar ways in which all three governments have responded to what they have perceived to be a greater security threat since 9/11. In each case, the balancing act between providing security for citizens and their property, and protecting citizens' civil and human rights, reveals fault lines between White majorities and non-White minorities, as we discuss in chapter 7 in relation to Islamophobia.

If states 'make race,' why don't most political scientists study the politics of race? In his 1993 presidential address to the Canadian Political Science Association, Vince Wilson claimed that a 'willful silence' exists about race – a silence that reflects Canadians' conception of Canada as a 'kinder, gentler nation' than the United States. 'Wilful ignorance' also describes political scientists' neglect of 'the politics of race'; in this regard, Thompson (2008, 521) shows that 'analyses concerning the relationship(s) between race and politics have been ... tangential in mainstream English Canadian political science.' In Australia, the state's role in the history of the politics of race has been subject to bitter interpretive wars among historians and in partisan politics. But not in political science. In the United States, where there is more open debate and conflict about race issues, 'the study of race and ethnicity ... [is] a feature of several fields within ... political science' (Hanchard and Chung 2004, 329). But the dominance of the rational choice approach characterized by methodological individualism hampers comparative work on the politics of race, and 'race garner[s] little attention in ... comparative politics,' though the politics of race involves issues of concern to comparative politics, including sovereignty, territoriality, citizenship, nation building, political culture, and comparative federalism.

The status of the United States as a superpower means it is *sui generis* and to be treated as an exception in important ways. But there also are significant similarities in how the three states make, develop, and sustain race regimes, because of federalism, a shared common law system, and liberal conceptions of politics – enough similarities to make comparative work worthwhile. Moreover, state actors have often borrowed ideas, policies, and practices from one another, making comparison even more feasible. Two of this volume's new chapters focus on such comparisons, while the new chapter 7 focuses on other important ways in which the politics of race in the United States has differed because of that country's greater power on the international scene relative to Australia and Canada.

This book provides a framework that undergraduate students and general readers can use to understand how systematic racism and race conflict originate in state formation and development. It explains how each state constructed race categories and regimes somewhat differently. The concept of *race regimes* identifies complex combinations of laws, practices, and ideas through which White elites have governed non-White minorities in the three federal democracies. In each, non-Whites are demanding inclusion, racial justice, and 'a fair share.' This book's framework should help students and readers assess how each government responds to such movements as well as the approaches each government takes to transforming its state – or resisting transformation. We also show readers how race oppression and White privilege were part of the construction and operations of state institutions, practices, and ideas in these three highly affluent democracies, and we identify the ongoing negative effects on non-Whites of past race regimes. By exploring 'Whiteness' and how groups fall into and out of Whiteness, we show that people don't need to have non-White skins in order to experience racialization. Hispanics, Catholic Irish, Jewish Americans, and – more recently – Middle Easterners have been racialized even though their states may categorize them as 'White.' 'Race' is the idiom through which states oppress and discriminate against people whom the dominant majority consider different or inferior. It also is used to justify denying them rights, resources, and opportunities.

The affluence and democracy enjoyed by the current descendants of the original White settlers in these three countries, and later by White immigrants, are the result of free or cheap land that had been seized from Indigenous peoples, and of the exploitation of coerced, unpaid, or poorly paid non-White (and racialized) labour. All three states acted in the interests of dominant Whites; and police, militaries, courts, legal systems, federalism, nationalism, electoral systems, bureaucracies, executives, and legislatures all helped create and maintain the race regimes that governed non-Whites in each country (or kept non-Whites out). Democracy, in the form of elections and majority rule, has been a tool of White supremacy and racialism. Long disadvantaged minorities struggle not against authoritarian governments in these countries but against racial democracies.

Acknowledgments

Jill Vickers wishes to thank those who supported the production of this text through two editions. Professor Vince Wilson, former chair of Carleton University's Political Science Department, promoted the idea of 'politics of race' courses; and the late Professor Edward Osei Kwadwo Prempeh helped conceptualize the first edition and co-taught the first course. Keira Ladner and Carla Lam, subsequent course assistants, helped her add insights from First Nations' and mixed-race perspectives. Carla Lam researched 'the facts of the matter' for the first edition, and Barbara Loh prepared the text. Former Dean and Vice President (Academic) Dennis Forcese published the first edition through his small press when the premature death of Edward Kwadwo Prempeh made it seem that the planned, larger textbook would languish unfinished.

Annette Isaac brought a new perspective and field-tested critiques to the revision of the first edition. Having grown up in a Black-majority Caribbean context before immigrating to 'multicultural' Canada, Annette provided fresh insights to this second edition, challenging many of Jill's oversimplifications. Research assistants Nancy El-Gindy and Janna Ferguson updated the statistical profiles and undertook some copy editing. Nancy provided new insights on the politics of race from a Middle Eastern, Muslim perspective; while Janna's U.S. residence provided useful insights on the exciting Obama era. Jill's former student Ikram Jama provided valuable insights into Somali experiences.

Jill Vickers also wishes to thank Keith Johnson – husband and best friend – for his support and contagious historian's respect for evidence. She also thanks her son Michael Vickers for scanning the first edition.

Annette Isaac is indebted to the late Edward Osei Kwadwo Prempeh, with whom she co-taught a 'race and ethnicity' course. His ideas live on in the curiosity and frank questioning that students bring to the classroom. She also wishes to thank Jill Vickers, who accepted her ideas for this edition. Our work together has been lively and enriching. Special thanks to Henry Cudjoe for being a sounding board about African Americans' experiences in the U.S. and Canadian diasporas. And a personal note of appreciation to Gerald Saper, Annette's husband, who listened patiently to her constant monologue about what is unquestionably one of the most unresolved issues of our times: who matters, when, how, and why.

Finally, we thank University of Toronto Press editors Daniel Quinlan, who carefully guided us through the remaking of the second edition, and Wayne Herrington, who ushered the project to its final conclusion. We also thank Marie Gabe, indexer of the second edition, for her patience and support throughout the entire process.

THE POLITICS OF RACE
Canada, the United States, and Australia

Second Edition

Introduction: The Politics of Race in Three Settler States

The purpose of this book is to explore the politics of race[1] in Canada, Australia, and the United States. All three countries were colonies created by Britain, and White descendants of British colonists have dominated them politically and economically for centuries. Accounts of their settlement usually stress the hard lives and heroic efforts of pioneers who 'won' the land from the 'wilderness' and who tamed anarchic frontiers; so claims each country's founding myth. But they also are referred to as 'supplanting' societies because, far from being empty wilderness, the lands on which these countries were built had been home to Indigenous peoples for thousands of years. The idea of a supplanting society highlights the often violent invasions and brutal massacres of Indigenous peoples, which happened to some extent in all three countries. But the process did vary. For example, in North America, competition among colonizing states – especially Spain, France, and Britain – and the cooperation required by the fur trade resulted in quite varied relationships between Indigenous peoples and colonizers, including – at times – extensive cooperation in the form of commercial and military alliances and treaties. Such things were not part of Australia's colonial history. The three countries are also referred to as settler societies, a concept used by Stasiulis and Yuval-Davis (1995) to capture both territory that was seized by invading colonizers and the planted settlements. We will use *supplanting* when referring to invasion and dispossession and *settlement* when referring to settler pioneering. Both these concepts were central to colonialism in all three countries.

Our main focus in this book is the role that states and state institutions have played in dispossession, colonization, and governing as each relates to the politics of race. Though the histories of the three countries differ in some ways, there are important common elements in how state institutions and political systems functioned and in how they created the large, prosperous federations that exist today. An important difference is that each of these three states was established during a specific stage of development in Britain's colonial project. The United States was an early colony of settlement, and the colonists' relations with Indigenous peoples – then the majority – were at first on a nation-to-nation basis. Australia was founded later in Britain's colonial history as a place to send and incarcerate convicts. The British governors declared it an empty continent – *terra nullius*. This established the legal fiction that there had been no prior settlements or organized Indigenous governments. Consequently, no treaties were negotiated, as they sometimes were in North America. In the thirteen American colonies, British settlers – often refugees from religious oppression – rebelled against colonial rule and established a new nation, which they mythologized as a beacon of liberty for the world. The myth of ***manifest destiny*** conveyed their belief that God had ordained their conquest of the continent to secure individual freedom; yet the myth and the nation's founding documents 'forgot' the slave system and the dispossession of the Indigenous nations on whose land the new White nation was to be built. In this book we explore how the three settler states and the governance institutions created during colonization and subsequent nation building shaped the politics of race in ways that differ from what occurred in Europe and from how race functions in settler societies where Whites are a minority, as in South Africa and Brazil.

Though their histories were different, these White settler states shared many common experiences. Settler governments established political regimes that to varying degrees were based on racialism. Racialism is an ideology with three main pillars: first, that the human species is composed of separate entities called races; second, that race determines the abilities of human groups (races) and that such abilities are inherited along with physical features such as skin colour; and third, that it is legitimate for one 'race' to rule over another because the dominant race always has superior abilities. Each of these pillars has since been discredited scientifically, but together, at the time, they formed the ideological foundations of each state, and they explain how the supplanting societies dispossessed the original owners of their territories. As a consequence, racialist ideas have been embedded in the institutions and practices of government and continue to influence politics in significant ways. In this book we show how these racialist ideas have been embedded in the institutions of governance in all three states.[2]

In each country, the British colonizers established basic laws and government structures; then as the colonies developed, they maintained some of these structures while changing others. Still later, when the colonies achieved independence or self-government (home rule), they modified the form of government even more. In each case, the colonies came together to form federations. The states created and contained race regimes – that is, legal and political institutions and practices based on racialism. Beliefs in race superiority, which the founders of these federations used to justify systems of White privilege and dominance, paralleled systems of oppression, exploitation, dispossession, and marginalization. Each race regime was embedded in constitutions and institutions of governance. In each case, those who created these governance arrangements helped create and maintain the founding race regimes.

The involvement of settler governments in creating race regimes and promoting racialism was neither casual nor incidental. All of the main institutions of government played a role in establishing and maintaining race regimes, as we will show. Legislatures and executives authorized the dispossession of Indigenous peoples to provide free or cheap land for settlers, to open access to natural resources, and to provide for roads and railways. Judges often administered two sets of laws, one for Black slaves or Indigenous peoples, the other for White settlers and colonial officials. Police incarcerated surviving Indigenous peoples on reservations, returned fleeing slaves to their owners, and punished those who resisted. Public servants directed and managed the removal of generations of children to residential schools to be 'civilized,' supposedly for their own good. Indeed, church men and women made sure that Indigenous languages and spiritual practices were beaten out of these children to eliminate resistance. The military drove Indigenous peoples off their lands and sometimes waged war against them. They also protected those White settlers who took vigilante action against Indigenous people who resisted. Other White institutions, including churches, schools, and the media, also were involved in maintaining race regimes, especially by transmitting race ideologies to reassure settlers that their dominance was legitimate because they were superior and to prove to non-Whites that they were inferior. These institutions hid overt oppression from White citizens. Without the use of force by Britain and by the settler governments, without the police and the military, and without state powers and institutions such as the courts, the foundational race regimes couldn't have been established and legitimized.

States Make Race

The principal theme of this book is that 'states make race.'[3] White settler states in these supplanting societies differed from the European states that initiated colonialism. From the outset, they maintained at least two different legal and governance regimes – one for White citizens, the other for non-Whites. And they used racialist ideas to legitimize that fact. The political theories used to explain the nature of European nation-states assume there is a single legal and governance regime within each society. This was not always the case, but it was the theory that the settlers transferred to the new societies, one that hid the actual practices of racialist settler states.

All three states are federal in architecture, with governance powers divided between two levels: federal, and state or provincial. There also are local governments, but in all three states, these are creatures of the state/provincial governments and have no powers guaranteed in the constitution. The practices and governance arrangements of the three states, including the vertical division of powers and how various interests are to be represented in governance institutions, are enumerated in written constitutions, which are hard to change but are also subject to judicial interpretation. The workings of these federal governments bear little similarity to European theories of politics based on unitary states. The politics of race is intertwined with the structures of federalism in the maintenance of race regimes. Later, in a separate chapter, we will discuss federalism and the politics of race.

In all three countries the foundational race regime was internal colonialism, which specifically governed Indigenous or Aboriginal peoples. In the United States, slavery was also a foundational race regime, one that mainly governed slaves imported from Africa and the Caribbean but also some Indigenous slaves. These founding race regimes formed the basis for subsequent race regimes. In the United States, for example, the very first census had three categories: 'free,' 'slave,' and 'Indians.' Quickly, however, the main race categories became 'White' and 'non-

White.' All three states built legal regimes of segregation to separate those who were included and privileged from those who were oppressed and excluded by the race regimes. They also created race regimes to govern immigration – regimes that excluded the Chinese and others categorized as non-White (non-Whites already present were denied most civil and political rights). Each state also mobilized a Whites-only nationalism that was based on racialist ideologies and that helped consolidate changes in race regimes. The habits of mind that developed in each country became deeply rooted in its national myths so that the dominant Whites believed they had prospered and now ruled because non-Whites were inferior, lazy, and ignorant. In fact, they had prospered *because of* White privilege and supremacy. Race regimes ultimately were naturalized and made invisible, most of the time, especially to Whites and even to many non-Whites.

That's All Ancient History!
What Does It Have to Do with Things Now?

The *Sydney Morning Herald* reported on 27 May 2000 that Aborigines and Torres Strait Islanders were 'the poorest, unhealthiest, least-employed, worst-housed and most imprisoned Australians.'[4] The report also showed that only half the White Australians polled believed that Aborigines are worse off than other Australians. Yet 60 per cent maintained that Aborigines got 'too much' special government assistance. There are two things to note here. First, though by the time of this survey most of the legal elements of Australia's repressive race regime had been repealed, its impact was ongoing, as was evident in the life situations and chances of Aboriginal people in 2000, and as continues to be evident more than a decade later. Second, a large number of 'ordinary' Australians don't recognize that several centuries of dispossession and state-administered race discrimination have privileged White Australians and disadvantaged Aborigines. But White Australians' overwhelming electoral strength enables them to resist governments' attempts to redress centuries of race-based disadvantage. A somewhat similar situation exists in Canada, though as we will show, there has been more progress in deconstructing race regimes.

In the United States, the impact of slavery, civil war, and long periods of legal segregation and exclusion have made the problem more complex. The election as president of a man of mixed race with an African father doesn't signal that racialism is dead. For example, 'birthers' believe that President Obama isn't eligible to be president because he wasn't born in the United States, which the U.S. constitution requires. (He was born in Hawaii, which is part of the United States.) Other groups believe he is a Muslim. There is no factual basis for these (and similar) claims, yet T-shirts, buttons, and bumper stickers that make them are sold at Republican Party conventions and right-wing events. It is worth noting that in Australia, the election of an Aboriginal prime minister is incomprehensible in the present day. Indeed, even the election of Aborigines to a state or federal legislature is rare.

In all three countries, the data we present show that Whites are wealthier, healthier, better employed, and better housed and that they have better access to better education, besides being much less likely to be incarcerated. Indigenous or Aboriginal peoples are the most disadvantaged, but African Americans, Blacks, and Hispanics also experience disadvantage. Asians and Middle Easterners experience racialized discrimination. Yet in all three countries in 2012, despite commissions, studies, protests, exposés, and international disapproval, many Whites – who demonstrably are dominant and privileged – refuse to believe any of this. This is so much the case that we theorize that a new race regime – *democratic racism* – exists in all three countries and is obstructing significant change.

What We Can and Cannot Compare: Race Regimes in Three Settler States

Much of this book reports findings from a systematic comparison of the *founding* race regimes in Australia, Canada, and the United States. Such cross-country comparisons can pose problems. Though the official data that governments report may seem comparable, often they are not. For example, in chapter 7 we explore the contemporary experiences of 'Asians' – a category that is used by all three governments but is defined differently by each. The Canadian government uses 'Asia' as a geographic term, thus categorizing people from all Asian countries as 'Asians.' Yet the U.S. Bureau of the Census treats 'Asians' as a racial category, thus excluding people from West and Central Asia and from Siberia, all of whom they consider 'Caucasian.' The Australian government seems to follow the U.S. approach; however, it reports 'ancestry,' not race, and it excludes fewer countries. Consequently, we cannot accurately compare the *current* circumstances of 'Asians' in the three countries, though we can compare the founding race regimes, which excluded and discriminated against the Chinese from the late nineteenth century until after the Second World War. We also can compare the current experiences of 'Asians' with those of other racialized minorities.

Hispanics are the largest minority in the United States (replacing African Americans in the most recent census). Many Hispanics report experiencing extensive discrimination, so we describe them as 'racialized.' But Hispanics have been divided among the race categories used by the U.S. census. Officially, many Hispanics are 'Whites,' though segregated statistically from 'non-Hispanic Whites.' Hence, for a number of reasons, we cannot compare Hispanics' experiences across all three countries. First, Australia and Canada lack comparable groups. Each has a small immigrant Latin American minority, but unlike U.S. Hispanics, they are not fragmented by race, with about half classified as 'non-White.' We might compare U.S. Hispanics with French Canadians, Canada's largest minority, but French Canadians are considered 'White,' though some francophone immigrants and refugees are non-White. U.S. Hispanics, in fact, are a unique minority, one that experiences racialization but is not officially categorized as a race. In chapter 7, therefore, we compare them over time to show how Spanish speakers have been racialized in the United States, as well as the disadvantages of being racially fragmented in a race-based system of restorative justice.

A third problem with cross-country comparisons relates to how countries differ. There are two main approaches to comparisons: one selects the 'most similar systems'; the other selects the 'most different systems.' Scholars of comparative politics usually compare regime types (democratic or authoritarian), levels of economic development (developed, developing, least developed), state architectures (federal or unitary), or institutional structures (parliamentary or congressional). With no previous cross-cultural comparisons of how states make race to guide us, we have selected countries that constructed their founding race regimes and then administered them in similar ways. All three were British colonies and still employ an English common law system; all three are economically affluent and have stable, democratic, federal governments that continue to be dominated by a White majority. But they also differ – for example, the most prominent American race regime, slavery, did not exist in Australia or Canada.

Slavery was abolished in Upper Canada in 1793 and in the British Empire in 1833. (Australia was built by mostly White convicts and settlers.) So slavery was institutionalized as a race regime only in the United States, where it was *foundational*. As noted earlier, the race categories in the first U.S. census were 'free,' 'slave,' and 'Indian.' These categories were quickly polarized into 'White' and 'Black' (still later 'non-White') (Nobles 2000). All subsequent race categories were based on this polarization, which created a race hierarchy into which new immigrant groups were fit. The United States also differs from Australia and Canada in how it became more populated and more powerful than either. It dominated first its hemisphere and then the entire world. Indeed, the United States is so exceptional that it is rarely included in multicountry comparisons.

The consequences of these differences have affected the nature of this book's comparison. First, systematic comparison is easier regarding the period before the Second World War. But in the United States, more groups have immigrated and been racialized than in Australia or Canada. This means there are fewer groups we can compare across all three countries, because the U.S. race narrative is more extensive. Also, the American experience is more extensively documented because its population is vastly larger. (Canada's population is smaller than California's.) In addition to this, far more American scholars are studying race issues. Furthermore, because U.S. economic, political, and military power vastly exceeds Australia's or Canada's, it was 'the leader of the free world' during the Cold War, a status that involved it in conflicts around the world. This leadership role had a profound effect on its 'race making' dynamics. That is, instead of race making relating largely to domestic fears and conflicts, it was increasingly a response to international conflicts, though there is some debate about the directionality of this. As chapter 7 illustrates, newer racializations such as Islamophobia were a response to international crises. For the Australian and Canadian governments, the question increasingly is whether they will follow the U.S. government's lead by imitating racializations such as Islamophobia. We will be comparing race making *within* all three countries when possible. That said, information about the United States is more abundant and easier to access, and there is more U.S. race making and unmaking to study. So if this book seems to overemphasize American race making, it reflects that country's leading role in 'making race' as well as American leadership in resisting and dismantling race regimes.

Table 1
Comparing the demographics of the United States, Canada, and Australia

Country	Category	Percentage	Count
United States (2009) **The American census** **asks about Hispanic** **origin and race.**	White alone, including White Hispanic Americans	79.6	244,298,000
	White, non-Hispanic	65.7	199,851,000
	Hispanic, all races	15.8	48,419,000
	Black or African American alone, including Hispanic Americans	12.9	39,641,000
	Black or African American alone, non-Hispanic	12.3	37,682,000
	Asian alone	4.6	14,014,000
	Two or more races	1.7	5,324,000
	American Indian or Alaska native alone	1.0	3,151,000
	Native Hawaiian or other Pacific Islander alone	0.19	578,000
	Total population	**100.0**	**307,007,000**
Canada (2006) **The Canadian census** **asks about population** **group membership.**	Non–visible-minority population	83.8	26,172,935
	Total visible-minority population	16.2	5,068,095
	South Asian	4	1,233,275
	Chinese	3.7	1,168,485
	Black	2.5	783,795
	First Nations	2.2	698,025
	Filipino	1.3	389,550
	Métis	1.3	389,785
	Latin American	1	304,245
	Arab	0.9	265,550
	Southeast Asian	0.7	231,425
	West Asian	0.5	156,700
	Korean	0.4	138,425
	Multiple visible minorities	0.3	104,215
	Japanese	0.2	60,415
	Inuit	0.2	50,480
	Total population	**100.0**	**31,241,030**

Table 1
Comparing the demographics of the United States, Canada, and Australia (*continued*)

Country	Category	Percentage	Count
Australia (2006)	Australian	37.1	7,371,824
The Australian	English	31.6	6,283,650
census asks about	Irish	9.1	1,803,741
ancestry.	Ancestry not stated		1,609,443
	Scottish	7.6	1,501,201
	Other		1,397,647
	Italian	4.3	852,418
	German	4.1	811,540
	Chinese	3.4	669,890
	Australian Aboriginal and/or Torres Strait Islander	2.3	517,200
	Greek	1.8	365,147
	Dutch	1.6	310,089
	Indian	1.2	234,722
	Lebanese	0.9	181,745
	Vietnamese	0.9	173,658
	Polish	0.8	163,802
	New Zealander	0.8	160,681
	Filipino	0.8	160,374
	Total Population	**100.0**	**25,410,601**

Sources: U.S. Census Bureau, 2010, 'Annual Estimates of the Resident Population by Sex, Race, and Hispanic Origin for the United States: April 1, 2000, to July 1, 2009' (NC-EST 2009-03); Statistics Canada, 2009, 'Ethnocultural Portrait of Canada'; Australian Census 2009, Cat. no. 2068.0 – 2006 Census Tables: Ancestry by Country of Birth for Parents by Time Series; Australian Census, 2010, Aboriginal and Torres Strait Islander Population, 1301.0 Yearbook Australia, 2008.

Figure 1   Population Shares by 'Race' Categories

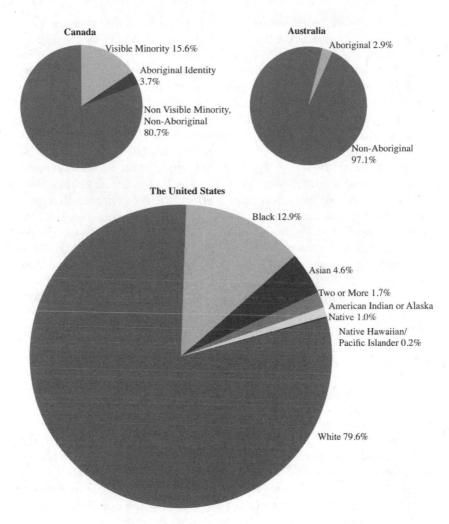

The Facts of the Matter

In this section we outline the factual situation for Indigenous peoples and other non-Whites in the three countries. Appendix A lists the sources from which we drew our statistics. We almost always use government sources. This will let you examine the data for yourself. We then discuss in some detail the ideology and practices embodied in democratic racism, which is the current dominant race regime in all three countries. This is important if we are to understand that the unjust state of affairs that resulted from centuries of racialism is not easily reversed because it is supported by majorities in democracies. That is, those Whites who espouse racialist ideas have the electoral clout to make their views stick. Many fear that their privileges will be attacked if things change. Not surprisingly, non-Whites disadvantaged by the race regimes that governments still maintain are suspicious of those governments, because they respond to 'the will of the majority' and because predecessor governments created race regimes and did little to eliminate racialism. Members of permanent minorities, who must depend on the sporadic goodwill of privileged Whites for change, may prefer some kind of self-government or may resort to violence against ongoing racial oppression. Not one of these countries has fully dismantled its race regimes. Moreover, the process of doing so is fraught with difficulties when Whites perceive non-Whites as increasing and threatening to end White supremacy in numbers – an obvious threat to the status quo.

The Facts of the Matter – Canada

In the 1996 Census, Statistics Canada reported a total Indigenous population of 799,000, or about 2.8 per cent of Canada's population. In the 2006 census, this number rose to 3.8 per cent countrywide. Though Indigenous people are a tiny minority in Canada as a whole, the history of their contact with Europeans (and European diseases) in the east means they now make up a larger proportion of the population in the four western provinces and in the three territories. So, for example, in 2006, Prince Albert, Saskatchewan, was about one-third (34.1 per cent) Indigenous people; and Winnipeg was home to nearly 64,700 people of Indigenous descent.[5] Also, in 2006, 84 per cent of the people in the new northern territory of Nunavut were Inuit.

The Report of the Royal Commission on Aboriginal People (RCAP), appointed after the bitter 1990 conflict between the Mohawks and the

Table 2
The facts of the matter – Aboriginal/all races, Canada

Measure			All races, population	Aboriginal peoples
Health and mortality	Life expectancy (2001)	Men	77 years	70.4 years[a]
		Women	82.1 years	75.5 years[a]
	Infant mortality by race of mother (2001)		5.2 per 1,000 births	7.2 per 1,000 births[b]
	Rate of diabetes (2002–3)		4.3%	14.5%[c]
Socio-economic status	Unemployment Rate (2006)		6.3%	14.8%
	Median income (2006)		$26,618	$16,796
Education	Persons who have not completed high school (2006)		15%	34%
Justice system	Imprisonment rate (2006)		0.6 per 1,000	4.2 per 1,000
Political representation	Representatives in the House of Commons		100%	1.6%
	Representatives in the Senate		100%	5.8%

[a] Data are for Registered Indians. [b] Data refer to First Nations. [c] Data are for First Nations adults living on reserve. For information on visible minorities in Canada, a good starting point is Statistics Canada's theme page on Ethnic Diversity and Immigration: http://www.statcan.gc.ca/subject-sujet/theme-theme.action?pid=30000&lang=eng&more=0
Sources: Indian and Northern Affairs Canada 2004; Statistics Canada 2006, 2008; Library of Parliament 2010, 2010a; Health Canada 2008; Public Health Agency of Canada 2007, 2009, 2009a; Policy Research Initiative 2008; Correctional Service of Canada 2009; Public Safety Canada Portfolio Corrections Statistics Committee. Please consult the Canadian statistics bibliography in the reference section and appendices.

Quebec police and Canadian military at Kanehsatake (Oka), Kahnawake, and Akwesasne (near Montreal), noted that Indigenous peoples' life circumstances and chances in Canada differed little from those of Australian Aborigines as portrayed in the *Sydney Morning Herald* (cited above). Much of the RCAP Report was ignored by politicians, academics, and journalists. Many 'ordinary' Canadians resisted its findings, despite the general goodwill expressed toward Indigenous peoples in public opinion polls. The UN ranks Canada high in the world in its quality of life, yet Canadians are shocked to learn that its Indigenous peoples are living in Third World conditions. Add to this that Indigenous communities have been severely depleted by the 'diseases of colonization.'[6]

Canadian government statistics have long shown a picture of White privilege and Indigenous disadvantage. The life expectancy for Indigenous men in 2001 was 70.4 years; all other men had a life expectancy of 77 years. Indigenous women fared better, with a life expectancy of 75.5 years; whereas all women fared better still, with a life expectancy of 82.1 years (2001 figures, Department of Indian and Northern Affairs – DIAND). Infant mortality rates appear to have improved over the past decade, but are still worse (7.2 per 1,000) than for the Canadian population generally (5.2 per 1,000) (DIAND 2005; 2001). (Data gathering problems have been reported, suggesting that we should be cautious when interpreting the data for Indigenous infant mortality.) Indigenous people are three to five times more likely to contract diabetes than the general population; 14 per cent of all reserve-based Indigenous people suffer from that disease (Health Canada 2009).

In 2005, 21 per cent of Indigenous people were below the Statistics Canada low-income cut-off; that was almost twice the 11.1 per cent for non-Indigenous people (Noel 2009). About 60 per cent of children in Indigenous families live in poverty. A major reason for Indigenous peoples' poverty is high unemployment. In 2006, the unemployment rate for all Aboriginal-identity Canadians was 14.8 per cent, considerably higher than the 6.3 per cent unemployment rate for non-Aboriginals. Unemployment was worse on reserves, where 24.7 per cent of Aboriginal people were unemployed (Statistics Canada 2006b). High unemployment on reserves is often blamed on First Nations' leaders' attempts to achieve self-government with too small a land base; but high urban unemployment suggests that additional factors are involved, including low levels of education.

High rates of incarceration of Indigenous/Aboriginal people are evident in all three countries. Indeed, race regimes are maintained partly through incarceration, which involves the police, the judiciary, and the prison system. These high levels of incarceration are legitimized by discourses about Indigenous criminality, drunkenness, and rebelliousness. Statistics for incarcerated Indigenous people in Canada actually show a small improvement between 1996 and 2006. In 1996, just 2.8 per cent of Canada's people were Indigenous, but they were 18 per cent of federal prisoners. In 2008–9, Correctional Services (2009) data showed that though the Indigenous population had increased to 3.8 per cent, it accounted for 17.3 per cent of federal prisoners. Non-White, non-Indigenous people were about 16 per cent of the Canadian population in 2002, but just 11 per cent of federally incarcerated prisoners. This challenges the myth that non-Whites generally commit more crimes than 'ordinary' (White) Canadians. Black Canadians were overrepresented as federal prisoners, at 6 per cent. But it is difficult to determine whether more non-Whites are imprisoned or whether they serve longer for offences that are more lightly treated when Whites perpetrate them.

Educational statistics show an encouraging upward trend. In 1991, 17 per cent of 'status' Indigenous people (those recognized as 'Indians' under federal regulations) had less than nine years of schooling and only half were expected to complete high school, compared to 69 per cent of all Canadians who completed high school. By 2006, just 33 per cent of Aboriginal adults aged 25 to 54 had less than a high school education, compared to 13 per cent of the non-Aboriginal population (Statistics Canada 2011). But school attendance in the past often led to cultural assimilation, menial jobs, and racism, so the key issue may be less about how long Indigenous young people attend school, than about who controls the schools they attend, and what they are taught in them. Especially encouraging is the fact that, by 2006, 44 per cent of 'status' Indigenous people were post-secondary graduates who held university degrees or college or trades program completion certificates (Policy Research Initiative 2008). Consequently, Indigenous graduates now hold management positions in their schools, in social services, in the police and judiciary, and in local governance. This has made *de facto* self-government possible as Indigenous people assume more governance and administrative roles.

It is important not to view Indigenous people as 'poor victims,' for they have a long history of resistance to colonization and attempts to achieve self-government. That said, since Confederation in 1867, only twenty-eight members of the House of Commons are known to have had Indigenous heritage. Given their small numbers and the absence of reserved seats for Indigenous people (as exist in New Zealand for the Maori), it is difficult for Indigenous people to be elected to Parliament. They should, however, be doing better with appointed offices. Yet even in the Senate, whose members are appointed by the government of the day, only fifteen Indigenous senators have been appointed since Confederation. The Library of Parliament reports that in 2010, just 5 of the 305 members of the House of Commons were of Aboriginal descent (1 Inuit, 1 First Nations, 3 Métis). This is fewer than the eight or nine MPs we would expect on a representation-by-population basis. The rates, however, are higher in the western provincial and northern territorial governments. In Nunavut, which is a public government (i.e., not restricted to Indigenous participants), a majority of members are Inuit. In 2006, 7.8 per cent of MPs were non-White and non-Indigenous, occupying 24 of 308 seats. This, though, compared poorly to the 16 per cent of the Canadian population that was non-White and non-Indigenous.

The Facts of the Matter – Australia

In 2006, there were 517,200 Aboriginal and Torres Strait Islander people constituting 2.5 per cent of the Australian population (Australian Bureau of Statistics 2007). Between 2005 and 2007 the life expectancy of Aboriginal men was 67.2 years compared to 79 years for all non-Aboriginal men. Life expectancy for Indigenous women was better (72.5 years), but White Australian women could expect to live a decade longer (82.6 years).[7] The infant mortality rate for non-Aboriginal babies was 4.2 per 1,000, while 12.7 Indigenous babies died for every 1,000 born – a rate almost three times higher.[8] In Table 3, we overview the 'facts of the matter' of lives in Australia.

Aboriginal children in Australia still are far more likely to be removed from their families and put into care than non-Aboriginal children. In New South Wales, 28.7 of every 1,000 Aboriginal children were removed to foster or institutional care in 2005–6 compared to just 3.5 of every 1,000 non-Aboriginal children – that is almost nine times as many. Government data estimate that some 50,000 Aboriginal children have been removed from their homes and communities in recent decades and placed in White homes and institutions. This resembles the policy of the forced removal of Indigenous children to residential schools in North America. The goal has been to assimilate them. More recently, North American Indigenous communities have had to struggle to prevent social service agencies from removing children 'for their own good.' Social services claim that alcoholism, sexual assault, incest, and even the dangers of house fires place Indigenous children at risk if they are left in their own communities. Now that more Indigenous communities have taken control of their own social services in the United States and Canada, the removal of children has declined.

In Australia in 2007, in a military-style 'intervention,' the federal government under John Howard took control of seventy-three Aboriginal communities in the Northern Territory (NT) on the grounds that sexual assault was rife. Interpreting this 'intervention' is difficult because the empowering legislation enabled the federal authorities to suspend the

Table 3
The facts of the matter – Indigenous / non-Indigenous Australia

	Measure	Non-Indigenous peoples	Indigenous peoples
Health and mortality	Life expectancy (2005–2007) Men	78.7 years	67.2 years
	Women	82.6 years	72.9 years
	Infant mortality by race of mother (2001–2005)	4.4[b]	12.7[b]
	Rate of diabetes (2004–5)	3.8%	6.1%
Socio-economic status	Unemployment rate (2006)	5%	15.6%
	Median weekly income (2006)	$642	$362
Education	Persons who have not completed high school (2006)	51%	77%
	Persons who have completed a non-school qualification[a] (2006)	46.8%	24.7%
Justice system	Imprisonment rate (2006)	129.2 per 100,000	2255.5 per 100,000
Political representation	House of Representatives	100%	0%
	Representatives in the Senate	100%	0%

[a] Includes vocational training, trades certificates, college diplomas, and university degrees.
[b] Data not available for all jurisdictions. Statistic calculated based on only four jurisdictions.
Sources: Australian Bureau of the Census 2006, 2008, 2008a, 2009, 2009a, 2009b;
Wang et al. 2005; National Centre in HIV Epidemiology and Clinical Research 2008;
Australian Institute of Criminology 2008.

rights of Northern Territory Indigenous communities. In particular, their right to keep White developers out of Aboriginal territories was suspended, which led some critics to argue that the 'for the good of the children' justification hid a land grab sanctioned by the federal government. (See chapter 6.)

In 2006, the unemployment rate for Australian Aboriginal people was 15.6 per cent, more than three times the rate for non-Aboriginal Australians (5.1 per cent); for Aboriginal young people, the rate was even higher. Median income was much lower for Aboriginal people: $362 per week, compared to $642 per week for non-Aboriginal people. Also, 38.7 per cent of Aboriginal households were classed as low-resource, compared to just 8 per cent of non-Aboriginal households. A large proportion of Aboriginal households are entirely dependent on government benefits, which makes them especially vulnerable to government control. In the Northern Territory 'intervention,' for example, the federal government imposed paternalistic restrictions on how government benefits could be spent.

Aboriginal Australians are arrested, judged, and incarcerated in disproportionately large numbers, mostly by White Australians. In 2006–7 the rate of Aboriginal incarceration was 2,924 per 100,000. In June 2007, 397 out of every 100,000 Aboriginal young people were in prison (Australian Institute of Criminology 2008). The Report of the Royal Commission to Investigate Black Deaths in Custody reported that 17.2 per cent of those who died in prison were Aboriginal. Between 2000 and 2009 the Aboriginal imprisonment rate actually increased from 1,248 to 1,891 per 100,000 population. (There was also a slight increase of 6 per 100,000 for non-Indigenous people.[9])

Aboriginal people play virtually no role in administering Australia's judicial or penal systems, despite high numbers of Aboriginal prisoners. In New South Wales around 2000, there were just two Aboriginal barristers (lawyers who go to court) out of 1,750; there was only one Aboriginal judge out of 146; and there was only one Aboriginal magistrate out of 129. And change will be slow coming, for only 59 out of 13,264 police officers and just 16 of the 1,202 recruits at the New South Wales police academy in 1999 were Aboriginal. By comparison, U.S. tribal courts and police forces are increasingly common now that Indian communities are assuming more responsibility for governance (see chapter 4). Also, practices such as First Nations' sentencing circles are being incorporated more and more into Canada's mainstream justice system; at the same time, the numbers of Indigenous lawyers and judges are increasing.

Australia's Aboriginal people suffer from the same diseases of colonialism as Indigenous people in Canada and the United States. Twenty-one per cent of Aboriginal men are at 'high risk' from alcohol abuse, compared to 8 per cent of non-Aboriginal men. Aboriginal women also have high rates of high-risk alcohol consumption, which results in frequent birth defects. After adjusting for age differences between the two populations, Aboriginal people 18 and over are twice as likely to be smokers as non-Aboriginal people. And in 2005, 6.1 per cent of Indigenous people had diabetes compared to 3.8 per cent of all Australians.

But, 7 per cent of Aboriginal people aged 25 to 54 in the Northern Territory and Queensland (both with large Aboriginal populations) had high blood pressure compared to 9 per cent of non-Aboriginals (Wang et al. 2006).

Aboriginal HIV infection rates declined between 1996 and 2006 (National Centre in HIV Epidemiology and Clinical Research 2008). But in 2000, cancer deaths reported for Western Australia, South Australia, and the Northern Territory were 40 per cent higher for Aboriginal people. Between 1997 and 2001, the annual incidence of cancer among Aboriginal men was 541.4 per 100,000; for Aboriginal women it was 393.3 per 100,000. Despite these epidemic rates, governments spent just 8 per cent of their health budgets on Aboriginal people's health services.

Although in Canada, improving education rates are a hopeful sign about Indigenous peoples, in Australia, by contrast, just 32 per cent of Aboriginal kids make it through twelve years of schooling compared to 73 per cent of non-Aboriginal children. Again, however, who controls the schools, who teaches, and what they teach determine whether higher levels of educational completion promote enhanced life conditions, and greater self-determination. In 2007, Aboriginal students were 5.6 per cent of all students, but only 1 per cent of teachers. Even where Aboriginal people are a majority, they rarely control their own schools or influence curricula. Unlike in the United States, where self-government is well under way, or in Canada, where a generation of university, college, and technical graduates is beginning to take over the direction of schools and social services, Whites are still firmly in control in Australia. As in the police, judicial, and prison systems, schools are White, and English is the language of teaching; the result is assimilation more than empowerment.

The Australian pattern is usefully contrasted with the bilingual policies developed in nearby New Zealand. Revival of the Maori language has increased self-determination and self-esteem. In Australia in 2006, by contrast, just 12.1 per cent of Australian Aboriginal people reported speaking in their homes any of the 250 Aboriginal languages spoken in 1788. And this figure is likely to decline, for just 10 per cent of younger Aboriginal people report fluency in an Aboriginal language (Australian Bureau of Statistics 2006).

White Australians control the schools, local governments, courts, and prisons. They also overwhelmingly control the legislatures that make the laws. Currently there are no Indigenous members in the Commonwealth (federal) House of Representatives; and previously there were only two Aboriginal members of the (elected) Senate. No Aboriginal person has ever sat in New South Wales' state parliament since its founding in 1856, and only ten Aboriginal people have ever been members in all of Australia's state parliaments combined. Only in the Northern Territory have Aboriginal people been represented in anything like their presence in the population, with 10 seats in 2008, albeit reduced to 8 in the following election. But the Northern Territory legislature lacks the full powers of a state, and its powers can be suspended unilaterally by the federal government, as happened in the recent 'intervention.' (See chapter 6.)

The Facts of the Matter – The United States

In this section we provide basic statistical profiles for Native Americans and African Americans both within the United States and compared to Australia and Canada. Does the profile for U.S. American Indian (AI) and Alaska Native (AN) peoples more resemble the Australian situation or the Canadian one?[10] (Table 4 outlines AI/AN peoples' life circumstances and life chances.) In 2009 the AI/AN population was 3,151,000, or 1 per cent of the U.S. population. This was an 18.3 per cent increase in numbers from 2000 (U.S. Bureau of the Census 2010b). Note that the data available tell us little about Native Americans living in large cities; also, some states do not report data for Native Americans. Thus, the data showing better AI/AN life expectancy in the United States than in the other two countries could reflect the absence of information on urban-dwelling Native Americans, especially the descendants of those who were forcibly removed when the federal government imposed detribalization (see chapter 4). Conversely, those data may reflect the positive consequences of self-government in the provision of services, which most Indian tribes assumed in the 1980s. Native Americans living on tribal lands seem to have better life chances than their counterparts in Australia and Canada, though collective poverty is part of the price they pay for tribal independence and self-government.

Native Americans' lack of political clout in mainstream governments also may be a price they pay for tribal self-determination and self-governance. The U.S. Senate reports that there have been only three senators of Native American heritage since 1776, and one Native Hawaiian senator. And the Federal Judicial Center reports that there have been only two AI/AN judges in the federal justice system out of 2,887 since 1789. So Native American life chances and circumstances

Table 4
The facts of the matter – United States

Measure			All races, population	White	Hispanic	Black	American Indian and Alaska Natives
Health and mortality	Life expectancy		77.7 years (2006)	78.2 years (2006)	N/A	73.2 years (2006)	74.5 years (1999–2001)
	Infant mortality by race of mother (2005; per 1,000 births)		6.7	5.7	5.53[a]	13.7	8.1
	Per cent with diabetes (2006)		7.8%	6.6%	10.4%	11.8%	16.5%
	HIV/AIDS rate per 100,000 (2007)		21.1	9.2	27.7	76.7	12.8
	Suicide rate per 100,000 (2006)	Men	18	21.4	8.8	9.4	18.3
		Women	4.5	5.6	1.8	1.4	5.1
Socio-economic status	Per cent of persons living below the poverty level (2008)		13.1%	9%	20.7%	24.7%	25.3%
	Per cent of families below the poverty level (2008)		9.5%	6%	18.5%	21.3%	21.4%
	Median household income (2008)		$52,029	$64,427	$40,566	$40,143	$37,815
Education	Per cent of persons who have not completed high school (2007)		14.3%	9.4%	39.7%	17.2%	19.7%
	Associate's degree or bachelor's degree		27.5%	29.8%	15.6%	21.8%	18.1%
	Graduate or professional degree		9.9%	11.1%	3.3%	5.7%	4.5%

Table 4
The facts of the matter – United States (continued)

Measure		All races, population	White	Hispanic	Black	American Indian and Alaska Natives
Justice system	Imprisonment rate per 100,000 (2008) Men	952	487	1200	3161	921 (both sexes)
	Women	68	50	75	149	
	Federal judges, as of 30 April 2010 Active judges	761	607	59	85	0
	Senior-status judges	507	465	12	26	2
	All judges since 1789	3194	2923	91	159	2

(a) Number is for children of Mexican mothers only.
Sources: National Center for Health Statistics 2009; U.S. Bureau of the Census 2010; Centers for Disease Control and Prevention 2009, 2009a, 2010; Snyder and Dillow 2009; Minton 2009; Sabol, West, and Cooper 2009; Federal Judicial Center 2010; Sickund, West, and Cooper 2010.

have improved in tribal territories; but when it comes to representation in political and judicial systems, their situation resembles the one faced by Native people in Canada. Also as in Canada, the Indian population in the United States is geographically concentrated, and so is more influential in a few states, notably New Mexico.

In 2001 the life expectancy of AI/AN people was 74.5 years, which compared well to the 'all races'[11] average of 76.9 years. This 2.5-year gap was the smallest among the three countries. Similarly, the infant mortality rate for babies born to Native American mothers in 2005 was 8.1 deaths per 1,000 births, which compared well to the 6.7 'all races' mortality rate – again, the smallest gap among the three countries. However, the overall infant mortality rate in the United States is much higher than in either Australia or Canada. Youth mortality rates showed a larger gap, with 3.9 per cent of AI/AN people aged 15 to 34 dying compared to 0.24 for 'all races' for the same ages. The rate of incarceration for Native Americans is 4 per cent (1 in 25), compared to less than 1 per cent for the U.S. population. Thus, increased tribal self-governance is correlated with improved longevity and better infant mortality rates. It has also given significant control of policing and the administration of justice on tribal lands to Native Americans, who experience high rates of incarceration as well as higher mortality rates among young people.

One cost of greater tribal self-determination is collective poverty. In 2008, 25 per cent of Native Americans lived below the poverty line compared to 13.1 per cent of 'all races.' This meant that in 1990, 43 per cent of AI/AN children lived in poor families, compared to 19 per cent of children of 'all races.' In 2008, the median AI/AN annual income was $37,815, compared to $52,029 for 'all race' households. This gap means that the proportion of children living in poor families is still very high. A common explanation for Native American poverty is inadequate education. In 2005–7, 19.7 per cent of the AI/AN population had not completed high school, compared to 14.3 per cent of the 'all race' population. These statistics are incomplete, however, in that they lack evidence regarding the AI/AN population in cities and in non-reporting states.

African Americans

As of 2009, the largest race minority was African Americans, who accounted for approximately 39.6 million of the U.S. population, or around 12.9 per cent. (Hispanics are a larger and poorer group, but technically – that is, as defined by the U.S. census and other government statistics

– they are not a race. See chapter 7.) There also are mixed-race people, including President Barack Obama, who self-identify as African American, and who would have been classified as such for most of U.S. history. Because of its size – it has more members than the entire populations of either Australia or Canada – this group has had the largest impact on the politics of race in the United States. Relative to Native Americans, who are a very small minority, African Americans are a large minority. Indeed, in some places they are a majority. In some southern states, over 35 per cent of the electorate is African American. Because of its size, the experiences, culture, literature, and ideas of the African American community have influenced Aboriginal Blacks in Australia as well as Blacks in Canada.

African Americans are a large minority compared to Native Americans; even so, they are underrepresented in the federal government. Since 1776, only six Blacks have sat in the U.S. Senate[12] and just 115 have been elected to the House of Representatives. Recently, though, affirmative recruitment in 'minority majority districts' has accelerated the election of African Americans; but as we discuss later, this practice has come under attack in the federal courts. Very few African Americans serve as federal court judges. The Federal Judicial Center reports that there have been only 133 African American federal judges since 1789 of a total of 2,887. Just two Black justices have served on the Supreme Court. (The first Hispanic judge was appointed in 2010.) Hence a familiar pattern emerges: African Americans are arrested and judged by Whites and are incarcerated much more often than would be suggested by their proportion of the population. (We explore this further in chapter 4.)

In 2007, 82.8 per cent of African Americans aged 25 and over had graduated from high school, compared to 90.6 per cent of non-Hispanic Whites. But progress has been made since, especially in Black-majority districts, where school curricula are now more reflective of African American experiences. In 2007, 13 per cent of African Americans had earned a BA, compared to 20.7 per cent of non-Hispanic Whites (National Center for Education Statistics 2007). African Americans are generally less well educated than their (non-Hispanic) White counterparts. African Americans are also less healthy, less employed, and less likely to be in positions of authority than Whites or other race minorities, except Native Americans, Alaska Natives, and Native Hawaiians. Note here that Hispanics, while not 'officially' a race, have some life chances and circumstances as bad or worse.

As in 2007, the incarceration rates for African American men (3,138 per 100,000) and women (150) were higher than for Hispanic men (1,259) and women (79), and also for White men (481) and women (50). As a group, Hispanics are less homogeneous than African Americans. While they have speaking Spanish in common, the U.S. census assigns them to different racial categories. But as we show in chapter 7, they are racialized as a group. Many are mestizo or mixed race; many others are European culturally. So it is difficult to determine whether the exclusion and oppression of Hispanics is produced by race or by language or by some combination of the two; or how much the unauthorized migrant status of some Hispanics plays a role. Hispanics are more likely *not* to have finished high school (40 per cent) than African Americans (17 per cent) or Whites (9 per cent). Undoubtedly, unauthorized migrant status and lack of English play a role in these education statistics.

In 2006 there was a five-year difference between African Americans' life expectancy (73 years) and the life expectancy of White Americans (78.2 years) and all Americans (77.7 years). This speaks eloquently to how race-based oppression persists over time; so does the 2005 difference in infant mortality between babies born to African American mothers (13.7 of 1,000 die) and babies born to White mothers (5.7 of 1,000). African Americans suffer poorer health, as shown by rates of diabetes, hypertension, and HIV infection. The 2007 statistics for median household income indicate a difference of more than $20,000 between African American ($40,143) and Hispanic ($40,566) families and White families ($61,355). In 2008, moreover, 18.5 per cent of Hispanic households and 21.3 per cent of Black households but only 6 per cent of White households fell below the poverty level. Race, language, and migrant status determine who is rich and who is poor, who is healthy and who is not.

Race and Life Chances: A Few Comparisons

In all three countries an impartial eye might conclude that the politics of race have resulted in poorer life chances and more negative life experiences for Blacks, Indigenous peoples, and most other non-White minorities. Table 5 compares the life conditions and chances of Indigenous people in the three countries. Life expectancy differences between Aboriginal and non-Aboriginal men range from a high of 11.5 years in Australia to a low of 2.5 years in the United States, with Canada in the middle at 7.4 years. The life expectancy gap for women is 9.5 years for Australians and 6.6 years for Canadians.

Table 5
Aboriginal/non-Aboriginal Canada, United States, and Australia, compared

	Measure		Canada		United States		Australia	
			All races pop.	Aboriginal peoples	All races pop.	AI/AN	Non-Indigenous peoples	Indigenous peoples
Health and mortality	Life expectancy	Men	77 years (2001)	70.4 years (2001)[a]	76.9 years (1999–2001)	74.5 years (1999–2001)	78.7 years (2005–7)	67.2 years (2005–7)
		Women	82.1 years (2001)	75.5 years (2001)	N/A	N/A	82.6 years (2005–7)	72.9 years (2005–7)
	Infant mortality by race of mother (per 1,000 births)		5.2 (2001)	7.2[b] (2001)	6.7 (2005)	8.1 (2005)	4.4 (2001–5)[d]	12.7 (2001–5)[d]
	Percentage with diabetes		4.3% (2002–3)	14.5%[c] (2002–3)	7.8% (2006)	16.5% (2006)	3.8% (2004–5)	6.1% (2004–5)
Socio-economic status	Unemployment rate		6.3% (2006)	14.8% (2006)	8.2% (2009)	13.6% (2009)	5% (2006)	15.6% (2006)
Education	Percentage of persons who have not completed high school		15% (2006)	34% (2006)	14.3% (2007)	19.7% (2007)	51% (2006)	77% (2006)
Justice system	Imprisonment rate		0.6 per 1,000 (2006)	4.2 per 1,000 (2006)	754 per 100,000 (2008)	921 per 100,000 (2008)	129.2 per 100,000 (2007)	2,255.5 per 100,000 (2007)
Representation	Representatives in the Lower House (March 2010)		100%	1.6%	100%	0.2%	100%	0%
	Representatives in the Upper House (March 2010)		100%	5.8%	100%	0%	100%	0%

[a] Data are for Registered Indians. [b] Data refer to First Nations. [c] Data are for First Nations. [d] Data are for First Nations adults living on reserve. [d] Data not available for all jurisdictions. Statistic calculated based on only four jurisdictions.

The U.S. infant mortality rate is 6.7 deaths per 1,000 for all races but 8.1 per 1,000 for American Indians, a difference of 1.4. per 1,000. The spread across the three countries is similar for infant mortality differentials, ranging from a high of 8.3 more deaths per 1,000 births in Australia to a low of just 1.4 more deaths in the United States, with 2 more deaths per 1,000 in Canada. The rate of non-Aboriginal people who finished high school is 26 per cent higher in Australia, compared to just 5.4 per cent in the United States, but 19 per cent in Canada. Unemployment rates follow a similar pattern, with 10.6 per cent more Aboriginal people unemployed in Australia compared to 5.4 per cent more in the United States and 8.5 per cent in Canada. The spreads in incarceration rates are quite extreme in Australia, with 963 more Aboriginal people incarcerated per 100,000 compared to 167 more in the United States. The Canadian rate is 420 per 100,000. Similar patterns are evident regarding disease rates. The better outcomes in the United States may reflect Native communities' assumption of governance responsibilities; however, worth noting in this regard is that many Native American governments are financed heavily by income from gambling casinos and tobacco sales. Australian governments have sanctioned no real self-government, and this may be one factor contributing to Australia's very negative rates. The partial U.S. data suggest caution, however, when making inferences about the link between self-government and life chances. That said, in most regards, the life chances for Indigenous people in Canada are more similar to those in Australia than to those for Native Americans and Alaskan Natives.

All three countries being discussed are democracies, so we might expect all three to promote equality for all their citizens. But it is the very fact that they *are* democracies with *White majorities* that leads to denials of racism and to dismissals of the statistics provided above. The significance of such statistics is often downplayed. In theory, the election of a president of African heritage in the United States should augur well for improvements in African Americans' lives, but it has become apparent that because he must function within a government marked by institutionalized racialism, some of his efforts are being obstructed.

Democratic Racism

In this section we explore the ideas and practices that comprise democratic racism, which is the race regime that has existed in these three countries since the Second World War. Though democracy is defined in different ways over time and place, we resist instinctively the idea that a country can be democratic and hold racialist ideas at the same time. Yet the facts suggest this is the case. So while this book's first principal theme is that 'states make race,' its second theme is that in settler democracies, White majorities maintain racialist practices that enable them to perpetuate their privileges and political dominance. This disadvantages and marginalizes non-White minorities, which find it difficult to change things *because* they are minorities and must persuade some Whites to support their cause.

Figure 2 shows the patterns of political representation in each country's federal legislature relative to the make-up of its population. In none of these countries are race minorities represented in the national legislature (lower house) at a level that reflects their numbers. In Australia, Aboriginal people are 3 per cent of the population, yet no Aboriginals sit in House of Representatives. In Canada, Indigenous people are 3.7 per cent of the population and hold 2.6 per cent of the seats in the House of Commons. Other race minorities combined ('visible minorities') constitute 16.2 per cent of Canada's population but hold only 7.8 per cent of those seats. Statistics regarding the level of representation of race minorities in the U.S. House of Representatives show that African Americans come closest to their population share, with 9.5 per cent representation (12.9 per cent population share). Hispanics do less well, with just 5.1 per cent of representatives (15.8 per cent population share). Similarly, the representation of Native Americans and Asians and Pacific Islanders lags well behind their population shares. This underrepresentation affects the patterns of life conditions and life chances we reported earlier. Without political clout or self-government, how can change occur?

The statistical profiles explored in the previous section show significant differences in the life conditions and political representation of White Australians, Canadians, and Americans, on the one hand, and race minorities on the other. The data presented in this edition indicate that there has been little significant improvement in the decade since this book's first edition. Indeed, it points to some deterioration. Indigenous/Aboriginal Australians, Canadians, and Americans, Blacks or African-Americans, and Hispanics do not live as long as their White counterparts. Their babies are more likely to die in infancy; they are less healthy, less well educated and housed, and more likely to be unemployed. In all three countries, race minorities are much more likely to be in prison, to die while incarcerated, and (in the United States) to lose

Figure 2   Population Shares Compared to Political Representation

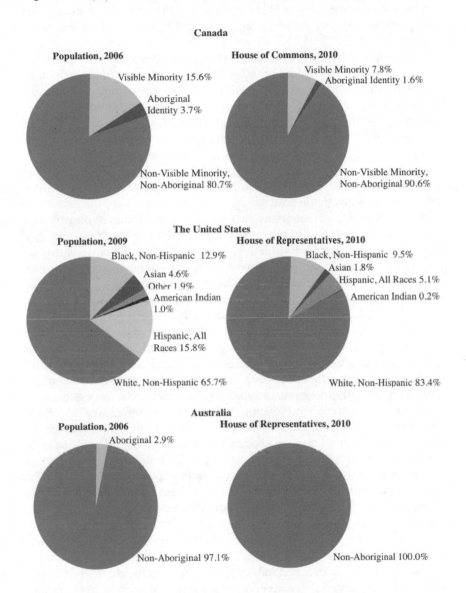

their right to vote permanently after incarceration. It is important not to overemphasize differences in these patterns. In all three countries, race minorities are greatly disadvantaged compared to dominant and more affluent Whites.

Explaining why such systematic inequality based on race exists in three of the world's wealthiest and supposedly freest and fairest democracies is our main task in this book. These race minorities could easily be better represented in legislatures and other decision-making bodies – for example, by giving them more of the political clout they need to change their lives through democratic processes, which presently favour majorities. But there are no special seats assigned to minorities in these countries' national legislatures, as exist in New Zealand for the Maori, though the United States has experimented with affirmative recruitment, as we will show.

Democracy is a way of organizing a country's decision making based on the equal treatment of citizens. But until the twentieth century, the 'right to equal treatment [was only] applied to those … of equal status … [not] to all people.' As a result, only those 'people who possessed the key aspect(s) deemed to be shared [by citizens] are allowed into the democratic decision-making club' (Catt 1999, 7–8.) Historically, democratic governments have coexisted with slavery and other forms of oppression and exclusion; and states considered 'democratic' have denied people citizenship because of their sex, religion, or ethnicity or their lack of property as well as their 'race.' President Abraham Lincoln praised 'government of the people, by the people, for the people.' But when he emancipated the southern slaves, only men gained the right to vote; former Black women slaves were excluded from 'the people,' just as White women were. Democratic decision making is about self-government through representative democracy that gives citizens the right to vote – that is, to choose and dismiss those who govern them. It can also mean the right to run for election. In early democracy, dominant White male property owners denied those who served them even the right to vote. When former male slaves had the constitutional right to citizenship, other laws demanding high literacy, as well as practices such as poll taxes, took it away. Those who insisted on exercising their rights often encountered violence, even death.[13]

As democracy developed, new groups were included, so that today it is widely assumed that universal suffrage has always been the norm. The long and often violent U.S. struggle for civil rights by African Americans and women brought large numbers into active citizenship for the first time. That struggle had global impacts, inspiring smaller struggles in Australia and Canada. But actually making all adults equal citizens has not been achieved *in practice* in settler states with White majorities. Despite international disapproval and efforts to deconstruct the complexities of state-made race regimes, high levels of racism persist, as do many legal remnants of racial exclusion. The result is *democratic racism*, a new race regime in which White Australians, Canadians, and Americans combine democracy and racialist views and practices.

Democratic racism is a race regime that includes a racialist ideology as well as norms and practices that 'permit and sustain peoples' ability to maintain two apparently conflicting sets of values' (Henry et al. 1997, 13). Recent decades have been especially complex politically in these three states because of the contradictions between democratic values of equality, justice, and fairness and various ideas associated with racialism, especially White rule and the belief that non-Whites are inferior. Racialist ideas that purported non-White inferiority had been discredited by the Second World War, but new racialist ideas emerged that stressed cultural differences between Whites and non-Whites. In this section we explore the core ideas that characterize democratic racism.

Frances Henry and her colleagues (1997) in *The Colour of Democracy* focused on how democratic racism is manifested in Canada. They identified myths that many White Canadians hold about non-Whites, myths that include the contradictory ideas of democratic racism. Those myths maintain on the one hand that people are equal and should be treated the same; and on the other that race minorities are poor, unhealthy, uneducated, incarcerated, and powerless because of something in their culture that makes them lazy or unambitious. 'Bridging ideas' enable people to avoid seeing the contradictions between believing in equality or a 'fair go'; and their racialist ideas. Some ideas involve denial: 'racism just cannot exist in a democracy.' If you deny that racism is even possible, you are also denying the reality of what non-Whites experience. In essence, you are telling them: 'you are imagining it.' Or 'you must have done something to end up in jail [or poor].' Such statements assume that Whites are better judges than non-Whites of whether racism still exists.

A second practice involves minimizing the effects of racism by equating them with Whites' experiences, such as being discriminated against for being fat, or saying that 'everyone faces discrimination sometimes.' This trivializes racialism's harms by making them seem *less* harmful or by setting them into competition, as in 'White immigrants also faced discrimination.' Of course that is true. But it assumes that non-Whites, being immigrants, must go through a hazing on entering their new country, when what they really experience is systemic racism, denial of jobs, and even violence. Moreover, many non-Whites are not immigrants to the countries studied. It also ignores that while some White immigrants become powerful and affluent, very few non-Whites ever experience such upward mobility.[14] The key idea of democratic racism is this: 'White people experienced it too, so it can't be racism.'

Victim blaming is another common response to complaints about racism. Some claim that 'minorities cause the problem by not fitting in,' or that 'we'd have no problem if they all went back to Africa or wherever they came from.' The thesis again is that non-Whites cannot be 'real' Australians, Canadians, or Americans. While most racist acts in these countries are committed by Whites against non-Whites, race-related violence is often blamed on the failure of minorities to fit into 'our society.' For some, the solution is exclusion: 'the government should keep them out.' And minorities are blamed for being too different. Many fear that tolerance of minorities will change 'our' national identity. Victim blaming is also used to reconcile democracy with racialism against Indigenous peoples and others who aren't immigrants. Indigenous/Aboriginal people in all three countries are blamed for suffering from much higher rates of diabetes than Whites: 'they are sick because they don't take care of themselves.' Also, most Whites do not try to understand how various self-abusive behaviours, such as alcoholism and child abuse, are consequences of colonialism. A more common response is to blame the victim. Moreover, such ideas are often adopted by immigrants who know little about internal colonialism in these settler societies.

Denial also takes the form of accepting that there is a problem but rejecting any kind of race-based explanation: 'race isn't the issue.' Many insist that 'everything would be okay if only they were more like us.' Race minorities are seen as having or causing cultural problems by thinking, worshipping, dressing, or cooking differently. Now that expressing overt racism has become unacceptable except among close friends, defining 'the problem' has become crucial. Though the statistical profiles show White privilege and non-White disadvantage, this contradicts the common conviction that race cannot be what causes these in a democracy. The idea of White privilege is especially hard for White majorities to swallow. Instead, non-Whites are blamed for the disadvantages they experience: 'they lack the skills and motivation to succeed.' This, in effect, is an attempt to change the problem by denying that White privilege exists in the form of having the right connections or attending 'the best schools.' It also entails ignoring that non-Whites often cannot gain access to the education or training they need in order to succeed.

The premise here is that Whites succeed on their own merits, not because of White privilege. This discourse uses democratic values to deny the possibility of racism. Claiming to be products of a meritocracy implies that people of minority races don't have sufficient merit to hold the job, to be president, to live next door, or to marry 'our' daughters. Even if White privilege did not exist today, to ignore its effects earlier would be to deny the realities of past racialism, which are fully documented. Revealing here is the astonishingly large percentage of Americans (20 per cent as of April 2010) who in opinion polls insisted that President Obama is not qualified to be president. Few give his race as the reason, but the reasons they do advance are thinly disguised racism. 'Birthers' believe that he is ineligible to be president because he was born outside the United States. Some Republican congressmen have proposed legislation that would require presidential candidates to 'prove' they were born in the United States.[15] Furthermore, many Americans insist he is a Muslim. For many White Americans, a man with an African, Muslim father who was born in the multiracial state of Hawaii, who lived in Indonesia as a child, and who has a foreign-sounding name doesn't seem like an 'ordinary American,' let alone someone qualified to be 'their' president.

Conflict between racialism and democratic values is also evident in discussions about how to resolve the problems that race minorities face. Especially in Canada, much faith is placed in government policies: 'multiculturalism is enough.' But multiculturalism as a government policy was designed to resolve the problems experienced by White immigrants, not the problems faced by race minorities. Moreover, many Whites are critical of multiculturalism. But not all race minorities are immigrants or ethnic groups. In all three countries, there is also widespread belief that education is the solution: 'racism comes from ignorance, so education is the answer.' This means that White adults need not change their behaviour or views; better to leave it to the next generation. Reliance on education also ignores that what is being taught to the next generation is tightly controlled by those with political power, who overwhelmingly are White and who usually reject race-based analyses. As long as education takes Whiteness as the norm and ignores the history of racialism, it will be more part of the problem than part of the solution.

Displacement is the solution most commonly proposed by White majorities. But displacement means expecting the victims of racialism to solve on their own the problems they experience. Examples of displacement are the idea that 'racism is *their* problem' and the taunt 'if you don't like it here, go back where you came from.' Faced with evidence that 'states make race,' many Whites then insist that governments fix the resulting problems by limiting or ending immigration, incarcerating refugees, or even deporting immigrants or refugees, authorized or not.

Another popular idea advanced is a colour-blind society in which governments 'just treat everyone the same.' This apparently democratic practice actually reinforces the status quo. If democracy operates purely as majority rule, permanent minorities can have little hope for the future, because being treated 'the same' means they will stay minorities unable to do much to advance themselves. Treating people the same does not have the same results as treating them fairly. The latter may mean treating them better now to compensate them for past oppression or discrimination; or extending to them opportunities for self-government. Defenders of racialism also often pit one democratic value against another: 'maybe racism exists, but people have the right to free speech, too.' They expect government to defend individuals' (free speech) rights to express their views, even if doing so creates a hostile environment of racism for non-Whites at work or at school. This also assumes that rights such as freedom of speech are without limits. But in all three countries, there are laws restricting or punishing some speech acts (libel, sedition, etc.), so why should racist speech have absolute protection?

States' efforts to take corrective action often face resistance, with many claiming that 'anti-racism is just racism in reverse.' Affirmative action intended to help oppressed minorities overcome racist disadvantage has been undermined by courts in the United States on the grounds that it is not colour-blind. Australian governments have replaced compensatory programs for Aboriginals with more repressive interventions. Such reactions constitute backlash.

Democratic Racism as Backlash

Democratic racism is part of the backlash against the efforts made by democratic governments to deconstruct earlier race regimes and to compensate for the effects of racialism. Alternatively, it is a reaction against improvements in the life circumstances of race minorities, such as President Obama's election. Some White citizens respond in hostile and even violent ways against efforts to ameliorate the effects of race regimes, especially when they feel threatened by attempts to end race injustice. They continue to support racialism even when it is no longer respectable to express that support overtly. In these societies with White majorities, backlash reactions draw upon democratic values – for example, by demanding that everyone be treated the same. Programs to redress the effects of earlier state regimes are rejected as anti-democratic. In this book we focus on backlash by state actors while noting that actors in society, such as the media, also play a role.

Though we use the singular term 'the state,' governments comprise many institutions – legislatures, executives, police services, courts – that may disagree with one another. Elected representatives may implement affirmative action programs; judges may then deem those programs unconstitutional. All three states discussed in this book are federations, and the governments at different levels may disagree on such issues. In some U.S. states, for example, citizens who disagree with affirmative action have used direct democracy mechanisms such as ballot initiatives to try to stop it.

Again, a common problem with combating backlash is that many Whites cannot relate their privilege to the disadvantages that race minorities face. A common belief in Australia, for example, is that Aboriginal people receive large amounts of 'taxpayers' money' in welfare. Many White Australians perceive efforts to improve the lives of Aboriginal people as unfair, in the belief that democracy requires everyone to be treated the same. There is a great deal of wilful ignorance about how Aboriginal people live; yet even when their life circumstances are made known, they are blamed and may even be punished for the impact of centuries of racialism. In a later chapter we discuss a recent military-style 'intervention' by the Howard government, which denied forty Aboriginal communities in the Northern Territory any autonomy. Indeed, it has become *easier* to blame the victims of centuries of racialism for the effects of that discrimination, for many Whites believe that Aboriginal people are no longer subject to discriminatory laws and practices. It is harder to prove that racialized minorities lack opportunities for education or decent employment when there are no overt laws that keep them out of jobs, schools, or housing. So the backlash analysis concludes that if they are poor and unemployed, then 'they don't want to work' or 'it's their culture to live like that.' These racist views, especially when held by state actors, are now more easily disguised.

Backlash involves resistance to change, especially change in response to visibility and successes by anti-racist, equality-seeking movements. Many members of the dominant White majority, and even those of more privileged minorities, attack equality seekers' struggles for justice. They even see Whites and privileged minorities as the *victims* if they lose some of their privileges. It is probable that those who already enjoy relative power and/or privilege will always react against programs that force them to share their power and privilege. Moreover, Whites who are relatively disadvantaged because of poverty or lack of education may react especially strongly because they perceive a threat to their opportunities to 'move up,' and because they feel that no one is supporting programs to redress White poverty.

The following are some tactics of backlash:

- *Silencing and isolation.* These include ignoring, marginalizing, discrediting, and threatening those who seek equality and redress. For example, when African Americans explain the effects of slavery, they are ignored or told 'that's all in the past – get over it.'
- *Denying that change is needed.* This includes derailing efforts to achieve change: Examples: 'Oppression doesn't happen any more'; 'Affirmative action is so passé'; 'The market always chooses the right person if left alone'; 'There are jobs if the unemployed want to work.' Denying the need for change is a common government response.
- *Inaction and sabotage.* This involves adopting policies or passing laws, and then not implementing or enforcing them. Sabotage pits oppressed groups (women, race minorities, people with disabilities, gays and lesbians) against one another and forces them to compete over who is the most oppressed and most 'worthy' of affirmative action.
- *Reverse onus.* This involves blurring who the victim is – for example, by constructing Whites as 'victims' of 'reverse discrimination.' Groups whose members are oppressed or marginalized on objective measures such as we described in the last section are displaced; and 'victim status' is awarded to those whose privileges are being threatened by redress measures. When Whites dominate and control state institutions, as well as important societal institutions such as

the media, schools, and universities, this inhibits people's ability to perceive oppression, discrimination, and marginalization.

- *Dividing equality seekers.* Some equality seekers have internalized ideas that justify their oppression. As a result, they half-believe what racists say about them, may accept oppressive practices for other non-Whites, and turn against other equality seekers with their own backlash ideas and practices. This weakens the power that equality seekers could have if they formed alliances and worked together. A key idea we advance in this book is that oppressing one race minority makes it easier to oppress others. The persistence of earlier race regimes reinforces democratic racism and makes change especially hard to achieve.

Outline of the Book

This book is organized to help readers to (a) develop an understanding of how racialism originated in settler states and (b) perceive the mechanisms that have been used to construct and maintain the race regimes that administer systems of privilege, domination, oppression, exploitation, and marginalization.

Our approach to the history of race politics is comparative, institutionalist, and historical. We compare how the three settler states have 'made race' across time. Broadly speaking, all three did so by applying government powers to construct race categories, which in turn gave meaning to racialist terms and denied to those who had been racialized such things as citizenship, a political voice, the rights to entry and mobility, and access to societal resources. Their life chances were diminished as a consequence. But the politics of race also involve actions by those who have been racialized, who struggle against state institutions to contest the categories that have been imposed on them. Race regimes have both material and ideological dimensions. They are embedded in the political institutions that we will be exploring, including electoral systems, party systems, courts, bureaucracies (such as census bureaux), and the federalist system itself, which does so much to construct and maintain race regimes. Other social institutions have played key roles in constructing meanings about race – especially churches, schools, universities, museums, and the media. But our main focus in this book is on the institutions of the three states, including political institutions, such as political parties, which are integrated into systems of governance.

The plan for the book is as follows. In chapter 1, we explore the reasons for focusing on the role of democratic states in our comparison of the politics of race in Australia, Canada, and the United States. We then explore two foundational race regimes: internal colonialism, which existed in all three societies; and slavery, which only existed in the United States. We show how settler states were implicated in racialism and made their race regimes part of the institutions of governance through state-sanctioned racialism. We also show how the growth of democratic ideas and practices developed earlier and more quickly in these colonies of settlement than in European states or in colonies of exploitation. Indeed, we theorize a symbiotic relationship between Whites-only democratization and state-enforced racialism. This is evident in how racialism was embedded in state institutions as normalized and systemic rather than as incidental. This is why race remains so powerful in settler-society politics despite extensive efforts to deconstruct race regimes. Racialism was so central to the founding of these old settler states that it became virtually invisible.

In chapters 2 and 3, we explore the post-foundation race regimes that have been constructed in the three countries, showing how each new race regime rests on the foundational regimes in terms of practices and ideas. The regimes considered are these: segregation, Whites-only nationalisms, and exclusionary regimes such as 'White Australia.' Chapter 3 also explores multiculturalism, which seems on the surface to depart from racialism and Whites-only race regimes. In practice, however, multiculturalism often resembles democratic racism because its commitment to racial equality is quite superficial.

The three governments used Whites-only nationalism to create solidarity among White citizens who had been divided – for example, after civil war. As a consequence, the politics of race has been deeply embedded in these political systems, making racialism a crucial element in many political issues. In chapter 4, we highlight the importance of *federalism* as a means of organizing governance to permit segregation by state or provincial governments – in this way, federalism perpetuates racialism overtly in some states even while the central government seems to be supporting race-blind equality. First-past-the-post majoritarian electoral systems in all three countries foster local control of candidate selection and local rules for elections, and this enables racialism to survive in some parts of the country long after federal authorities have officially ended it. Federalism long allowed such practices as

Whites-only primaries, which exclude non-Whites from candidate selection processes where they are majorities or large minorities.

In chapters 5 and 6, we outline different approaches to deconstructing race regimes, showing how recent and how incomplete these efforts have been. We compare the relative merits of bottom-up and top-down approaches to change and of different strategies. We conclude that the ideology and mechanics of representative democracy pose formidable obstacles to making governments responsive to race minorities when the majority of citizens are White. In assessing the prospects for change, we stress that what White majorities consider solutions may not be sufficient or effective, nor may they be acceptable to those who experience racialism and who foresee a future as permanent minorities while Whites continue to hold most of the political power. In such cases, small minorities may view self-government in autonomous political units as a better solution. But for large minorities – such as African Americans in the United States, especially since the election of 'one of their own' as president – more head-on confrontations with the White majority may be in the cards. The forming of alliances among large minorities is another possible feature of the politics of race. Certainly, high turnout by both African American and Hispanic voters was a significant factor in the election of President Obama.

Chapter 7 explores the concept of racialization, which theorists use to explain how diverse groups of immigrants have been integrated into the race hierarchy of the United States. Not all such groups have been non-White. Some, such as the Catholic Irish, resisted racialization, using their White skins to avoid classification as non-Whites. The chapter explores how different Hispanic communities have been racialized over the centuries. Mexican Americans were absorbed when the U.S. government incorporated northern Mexico after a brief and bloody war. Subsequent groups of Hispanics were also racialized as they entered the United States as colonial subjects, immigrants, or refugees. Hence Hispanics have been racialized even though they are not 'officially' a race. Middle Easterners, who were categorized as White on entry, also have been racialized, especially after the 9/11 attacks, as a result of the government's resort to Islamophobia, which we will describe. Finally, the chapter considers the racialization of 'Asians.' In all three cases, we focus first on how the power the United States increasingly wields internationally has affected the dynamics of race politics in these countries. As the United States came to dominate first the Americas and then the world, U.S. government actions abroad affected race dynamics at home. The chapter shows how the Australian and Canadian governments either imitated or resisted how Middle Easterners were being racialized in the United States.

Finally, in chapter 8, we present the conceptual basis for our analyses of the politics of race. Definitions for the key concepts, which appear in bold italics, are in alphabetical order. Dip into this chapter as you read the other chapters, especially if the meaning of a term is unclear.

Appendix A contains references for 'The Facts of the Matter,' and Appendix B lists websites to help readers investigate further. We often used government websites. This is not because we believe that governments are more trustworthy on issues of race; we do not. Government data almost always are 'conservative' and present the least damaging case. But government data also illustrate conditions that even governments cannot deny. This does not mean that each government will agree with all of our interpretations of 'the facts.' But we often drew our explanations from government inquiries, such as Royal Commissions.

Discussion Questions

1 Define race regimes and explain why we are studying them.
2 Explain what Anthony Marx means by 'states make race.' Give examples from each of these three White settler states.
3 Is 'race' a modern idea?
4 Why don't the authors consider education the solution to race discrimination?
5 Explain democratic racism in your own words.

1 Foundational Race Regimes

In English-speaking countries, political science has had little to say about race. When discussed, race is treated as a policy issue or as a problem for the courts or the police. Race relations receive more attention as a problem in Australia and the United States, where race riots occur; whereas in Canada, race tends to be seen mostly as a problem that exists somewhere else. Canadian governments enacted sanctions against South Africa, prohibiting trade, thereby pathologizing *apartheid*, that country's official system of oppression, racism, and White supremacy. That is, most Canadians and probably also most Australians and Americans considered it abnormal for a government to privilege some citizens because they are White, while disadvantaging others because they are non-White. Australia, Canada, and the United States viewed apartheid-era South Africa as a rogue state, even while their White citizens viewed their own states as 'normal' democracies.

In this chapter we show that Canada, Australia, and the United States are racialist states because, like apartheid-era South Africa, their governance systems have also, from their very foundation, been based on *race regimes*. We also argue that the governments in these *supplanting* (Day 1996) or *settler societies* (Stasiulis and Yuval-Davis 1995), established through British colonialism, created race regimes as part of the founding, consolidation, and administration of their institutions. These countries remain so deeply marked by their race-based histories that government efforts to deconstruct race regimes, which began in the 1960s in response to international disapproval and internal activism and protests, have had limited success. Far from fading away as many expected, race issues actually are now more prominent in contemporary politics; and new race formations are being formed, often in response to international conflicts. The concept of race has been discredited as lacking scientific validity, yet the experience of being racialized still matters profoundly in the politics of these democracies. Though we consider racism to be socially constructed, its effects continue to underpin political systems of privilege and disadvantage because the race categories that state elites created in their making of race persist.

Repealing laws is insufficient for eliminating race regimes institutionalized in many state structures, norms, and discourses. Unless we understand governments' roles in constructing race regimes, we cannot grasp the dynamics of the present-day politics of race. To end racism, we must understand how race-based systems of oppression and privilege have been institutionalized in government processes in the three countries. But this process of understanding encounters deep resistance. For example, few Canadians know that South Africa's pernicious apartheid system was based partly on the system of passes, reservations, and restricted mobility that Canadian governments used to control Indigenous peoples and exploit their lands and resources. South Africans learned horrifying details about how apartheid actually worked through a Truth and Reconciliation Commission (Krog 1998). Similarly, reconciliation committees of White and Aboriginal Australians briefly explored the details of race-based rule. But such well-meaning grassroots efforts were no match for governments determined that the past wasn't their business. In the United States, some descendants of slaves are demanding reparations, and some slave owners' descendants are exploring where their wealth originated. But in Canada, ' racism ... [is] a taboo topic [because] Canadians have long prided themselves on being non-racist, and tend to resist any discussion of even the most obviously racist aspects of our history' (Christiansen 1996, 142–3). Only sanitized myths are admissible in Canadian history classes, and this has kept multiracial or multicultural content out of Canadian schools until recently. Christiansen claims that White Canadians are in a state of denial about 'even the most obviously racist aspects of ... [their] history.' Non-White Canadians agree that it is hard to fight the polite silence produced by such denial.

The invisibility of race in political science has deep roots and reflects the fact that the theories on which the field has been built are the products of Europe at the height of its project of *colonialism*. A key concept – the *nation-state* – assumes that the norm for a polity is homogeneity. In Europe and in settler societies, elites believed that all *citizens* in a nation-state should share a common ancestry, language, religion, culture, *and* race. Those who did not 'fit' or who could not be assimilated could be denied citizenship or access. This was substantiated by the doctrine of *nationalism* – the claim that people within a state's territory should be the same and that a 'historic' *nation* had the right to be self-governing within its own state.[1] In settler societies, race doctrines were used to justify why Europeans had the legal right to supplant the original owners of the lands they invaded. In addition, race doctrines were used to legitimize the treatment of those supplanted, enslaved, or excluded. Most Europeans at that time viewed 'race' as a natural phenomenon – as an 'essence' of the human species. It is now understood that 'race' is a 'historically grounded social construction' with a 'dynamic and shifting' meaning (Cowlishaw and Morris 1997, 3) that changes over time and place. What race means depends on when and where the concept was created; on who created it and who is using it; and on why.

In this chapter we focus on how each settler government constructed its founding regime based on racialism (belief in White race superiority), which legitimized systems of privilege, oppression, dispossession, and exploitation. Not all Whites were privileged. Australia, for example, was built by (mostly) White convicts exiled usually forever from Britain. Indentured White servants, whose labour was owned by their masters for a fixed period, helped build the United States. In Canada, French-speaking populations incorporated under British rule experienced discrimination. In all three countries, White non-British immigrants helped build the country but also experienced discrimination. Some of these immigrants were racialized (see chapter 7). Race regimes were not necessarily motivated by race fear or hatred. Other motives were economic gain and grandiose visions of the political domination of vast continents. What *did* characterize race regimes was racialism embedded in official, state-promoted *ideologies* and laws that were central to each system of privilege and disadvantage. And these were not casual, accidental, or local arrangements: race regimes were created by governments, were expressed in constitutions and laws as well as in informal practices, and were part of the main institutions of each state – its legislatures, executives, police, courts, and bureaucracies, and in the military as well. Other institutions – including schools, newspapers, churches, and popular culture – were used to inculcate racist values and assumptions. That said, state institutions were central to constructing and maintaining race-based systems of privilege and disadvantage.

Why a State-Focused Approach?

Comparative studies of the politics of race take different forms. In this section we explain why we have chosen a state-focused approach rather than one that examines race issues from the vantage point of individuals or social movements. As Hanchard and Chung (2004, 319–20) have observed, most of the debate over the politics of race has so far revolved around definitions, not on how the politics of race functions across several countries. Broadly speaking, the debate over definitions is between *essentialists*, who conceptualize 'race' as a primordial feature of the human species, and *constructivists*, who view 'race' as a social construction. Hanchard and Chung argue that scholars of comparative politics generally should be more interested in the politics of race than in defining the concept of race. There are many more debates about what social factors produce the disadvantages that 'having race' entails. If not biology, what 'causes' race to fall on one group rather than another? Social constructivists debate the causes of race-based power dynamics – generally referred to as the 'race relations' approach. Hanchard and Chung reject this approach and call for analyses of race to shift their focus to the 'patterns and occurrences in which race is meaningful in [the] dynamics of power and politics' (322). But shifting to a comparative study of the politics of race still requires a focus within that framework. Hanchard and Chung (324) identify four main comparative approaches, each with a specific methodology: the comparative political economy of race; comparative analyses of culture, symbols, and ideas focused on race; comparative studies of social movements focused on race; and state-centred approaches.

In this book, our work is primarily state-centred and emphasizes the role of a particular kind of state in creating and maintaining race categories and the rules under which race regimes operate; in transmitting and enforcing inequality; and in sustaining or deconstructing race categories and regimes. In contrast to the liberal idea that states are neutral mechanisms, state-centred approaches to the politics of race assume that race has been and still is a central principle of states. Anthony Marx claims that 'states make race' (1998); Omni and Winant (cited in Hanchard and Chung 2004, 329) insist that in the United States 'the state *is* inherently racial.' In this book we do not make universal claims (i.e., that all states create race); nor do we accept American exceptionalism. Instead we argue that states make race in settler societies. Also, in our theorizing about how states do this, we limit our comparison to three democratic, settler federations with large White majorities. Our limited comparison allows us to focus on the extent to which the politics of race still dominates. By treating 'race' as a political phenomenon, we can examine how it is deployed in elections, administration, public policy debates, legislating, judicial decision making, and the prison system.

'States Make Race'

Throughout this book we explore different race regimes constructed by governments in these three settler societies over four centuries. These race regimes include internal colonialism, slavery, segregation, White nationalism, and democratic racism. More recent race formations considered include Islamophobia. We also compare the regimes that governed Asians in the late nineteenth century and in recent decades. In this chapter we explore the race regime that was foundational to all three societies – internal colonialism – as well as slavery, which was also foundational in the United States. Our goal is to demonstrate how race regimes work, how settler states used them, and how this resulted in states that are different from European states.

One defining feature of *democratic racism*, which is the current race regime in Australia, Canada, and the United States, is denial that race matters or that racialism still exists in a systematic form. Another is denial that our democratic governments are implicated in any surviving forms of racism. In current thought, racialism is firmly located elsewhere or in the past. It is also considered a product of abnormal psychology or a sign of backwardness that can be eliminated only by education. In all three countries until recently, it was acceptable to voice racism overtly. Statements such as 'Australia is owned and run by White people not Black. We took it and have fought several wars to keep it and our freedom' (*Wimmera Mail-Times*, cited in Cowlishaw and Morris 1997, 20) are now seen as something many people want to forget or as the sentiments of extremists. Yet they still seem perfectly acceptable in some venues. Race consciousness and the labelling of people by race are increasingly seen as problems to be eliminated through education. But extreme social and economic inequality between Whites and non-Whites still exists in all three countries. So even though discrimination based on race is considered abhorrent by many citizens, and even though our governments now guarantee citizenship and legal equality regardless of a person's ancestry, race conflicts continue to infect politics in all three countries, with racist views rarely far below the surface of polite conversation, especially in some periods. But why does race, now condemned as an erroneous concept, remain so potent? Why do racialist ideas still hold so much power?

As we argued above, political science tells us little about race or racialism mainly because it sees both as *incidental* to the character and functioning of states. So police discrimination and violence against non-Whites is attributed to a few 'bad apples' in police forces, not as a consequence of state actions. Ignored is the fact that Indigenous and Black people are imprisoned in numbers that far exceed their proportion in each country's population. Ahistorical explanations attribute racism to (bad) individuals or to rogue states. Just as good people are expected to reject racist ideas, 'normal' states are expected to reject racialism. Yet as we have seen, democratic ideas and racist ideas can and do coexist. In each of the three countries we are studying, states have used race to privilege Whites and to benefit those of (White) European ancestry. Yet most political scientists assume a neutral state with no history of race oppression.

Ahistorical explanations often assume that racism is part of human nature – something that exists everywhere and at all times. While the building blocks from which racialism can be constructed (fear of strangers and a tendency to blame others when things go wrong) are present in many societies, it is well documented that the concept of race on which modern racialism is built was invented fairly recently by Europeans to make sense of their experiences of conquering, enslaving, and oppressing others different from them in terms of their faith, culture, and/or skin colour (Markus 1994). To understand the potency of racial oppression, therefore, we must understand the history of how our states have used race ideas to justify supplanting, enslaving, and oppressing others.

The persistence of political theories based solely on European experiences has hidden the fact that race and racialism have not been incidental to the founding and politics of settler states. The states that White Europeans built in the colonial spaces of the British Empire have ruled through race regimes that have legitimized killing, dispossessing, enslaving, deporting, excluding, oppressing, and exploiting Indigenous peoples, Africans, Asians, and Pacific Islanders. To understand the potency of race and racialism in politics today, therefore, we must study the specific histories of foundational race regimes and White racial thought and how both are linked to colonialism. In particular, it is important to expose the role that governments have played in order to

understand how each state 'made race' and has altered or added to its
race regimes over time.

Comparing from a State-Centred Approach

European states engaged in *colonialism* for close to five hundred years
and throughout that process generated race doctrines to legitimize their
actions in colonial projects. However, systematic race regimes administered by governments and state institutions are characteristic only of
settler societies. Settler colonialism established new societies that dispossessed and supplanted Indigenous nations. Colonial settlers and
subsequent immigrants then settled and exploited Indigenous peoples'
lands for the benefit of the 'mother' country and, despite often having
overcome many hardships, for the benefit of later arrivals and their
descendants.

Colonial settler states had to treat members of the supplanting society
differently from Indigenous people because they had sanctioned forced
dispossession. Having done so, they sought to control land distribution
on behalf of the Crown. The *rule of law* established first by colonial
governments, and then by the settler states, involved at least two distinct regimes, both of which allocated privilege and disadvantage on the
basis of criteria that quickly morphed into race categories as doctrines
were developed to justify supplanting Indigenous peoples. Far from
being neutral administrators of a single legal code and standard of justice, these states were always instruments for supplanting pre-existing
Indigenous societies. They did so by managing two (sometimes more)
legal and administrative regimes: one for settlers, the other for Indigenous people. In this, states in supplanting societies were different from
most European states[2] – or at least, different from the norm embedded
in Western liberal thought about 'the' state.

One example of the essentially race-based nature of settler states is
the American colony of Carolina, founded in 1670, almost two hundred
years after Christopher Columbus in 1492 opened the way for Spain's
dominance. Carolina was not the first British colony in the Americas; it
is of interest here because John Locke, theorist of the liberal state and a
founder of modern political science, wrote its *Fundamental Constitution*
while employed by Lord Ashley Cooper, a Lord Proprietor (investor) in
the colony. In 1670, slavery and the slave trade were still legal in the
British Empire; and among the constitution's 120 provisions were carefully written terms for establishing and administering slavery. Locke's

guide for the settlement of the colony discouraged the enslavement of Indigenous peoples on pragmatic grounds. In his *Second Treatise of Government*, he explained that to enslave a man is to put yourself in 'a state of war' with him, however lawful your conquest and his captivity (1924 [1690], 127–8). Enslaved 'Indians,' knowing the country, could easily escape, and the settlers would be endangered by retaliation from their relatives. Provision 110, however, granted to every freeman 'absolute power and authority over Negro slaves' (Ball 1998, 30). The government of the Carolina colony, therefore, had *categories* of people under its control, one of which was in Locke's own words at war with the other. The labour system established in the British North American colonies had three tiers: slaves (Blacks and some Indigenous peoples), indentured servants (Whites, usually poor English or Irish), and free citizens, very few of whom were not White. For a brief period, convicts were transported to some American colonies, but they were not central to North America's development, as they were in Australia.

The legal system for the emerging colonial state and its principles concerning citizenship were complex. Some enslaved Indigenous people were exported to Caribbean plantations, where they could not escape easily; at the same time, African slaves were imported from across the Atlantic. The Indigenous nations were at first willing to share their lands with the Europeans. But by 1715, assaults, rapes, enslavement, and murders committed by Whites – as recorded by the colonial Carolina state – led fifteen nations to form an alliance to defend themselves and their lands by repelling the British settlers. In the resulting Yamasee War, the coalition was defeated by the fledgling Carolina state with survivors forced west or dispersed. Carolina's Commission on Indian Affairs was dismantled in 1716 in the belief that Carolina's 'Indian problem' had been solved. But its last act was to ban the enslavement of Indigenous men over fourteen.

Where Indigenous communities survived war, enslavement, exportation, and disease, they became *internal colonies* within colonial states. Colonial states such as Carolina, then, initially managed two race regimes – internal colonialism and slavery. What 'the colonial state' was at that point is historically complex. 'Colonial' has several meanings: first, it referred to relationships between an imperial power – Britain – and its White settler colonies. It was clear to Locke, though not always to those born in Carolina (for example), that the purpose of colonization was to enrich Britain. Throughout the empire, actions in the interests of Britain were administered by British officials and enforced by the British military. But the colonies were far away, and over time, significant self-rule developed in the colonies, especially as more and more colonists were not born in Britain. So a second important usage of the term describes the internal colonial relationship formed between colonial/ settler governments and the Indigenous nations that survived efforts to supplant them.

The settler states inherited military and bureaucratic structures and practices, as well as legal doctrines and ideologies. Through all of these, they administered race regimes initiated by Britain. Ultimately, there were conflicts of interest between the settler governments and Britain; in the case of the thirteen colonies, these led to a revolutionary war and the Declaration of Independence by the new United States. When the British government abolished slavery throughout its empire in 1833, the Canadian and Australian colonies, which had been settled later than the U.S. colonies, followed suit, for British colonial authority was sustained mainly by the colonists' need for British military protection. Both Canada and Australia inherited ways of dealing with Indigenous peoples developed by British authorities. But it was the emerging settler states that developed the race regime of internal colonialism.

In his comparison of race relations in the United States, South Africa, and Brazil, Anthony Marx argues that the state's involvement in creating foundational race regimes has much to do with the potency of race in modern politics. European societies practised discrimination based on race, the meaning of which changed over time. In Germany, for example, the Nazi state killed, imprisoned, deported, and enslaved millions of people based on Hitler's race theories. But such actions were not considered proper uses of state power, and as a consequence, Germany (like South Africa) was viewed as a rogue (bad) state. In Australia, Canada, and the United States, however, such actions were considered proper – indeed, they were seen as central to the state's basic rationale. That is, a central role of settler states was to supplant the Indigenous nations whose land the new settler states had seized and settled and now held. As long as there was competition among European colonial powers in North America, each needed to cooperate with some Indigenous peoples; in addition, the fur trade fostered economic cooperation. But once Britain had 'won,' except in the now independent United States, cooperation was no longer needed, and the oppression involved in internal colonialism became fully expressed. As the settler states advanced across their continents, their previous Indigenous allies resisted being supplanted.

At first, the colonial powers often followed rules set out in European law, in some cases even signing treaties with Indigenous leaders. But as soon as White settlers required the dispossession and removal of Indigenous inhabitants, force was used. As with slavery, internal colonialism succeeded because the settler states undertook acts of war against some inhabitants of their territories. Initially, these acts were justified by religious differences (i.e., those enslaved or removed were not Christians), which imitated the reasons Europeans used for colonial conquest elsewhere. Quickly, though, race doctrines were developed that asserted the inferiority of the victims. States incorporated these doctrines into laws, policies, administrative practices, and educational materials. Colonial and settler states did not just incidentally 'make race'; 'making race' was among their central purposes. We can understand, then, why racialism is so deeply rooted in our politics by exploring how states operated in their race making. The settler states on which we focus also had to develop rules about citizenship as well as nationalist sentiments in order to create solidarity among those granted citizenship. But they also had within them groups of people with whom the state, to quote Locke, was at war. Furthermore, each settler state could hold the huge, continent-wide territory claimed only by settling the land with immigrants, and those selected usually shared the same race identity as the founding settlers.

What Are Race Regimes?

A state-centred approach assumes that racialism is not simply something developed by bad people or fringe elements without government action and support. Rather, it is a consequence of deliberate state action. A state-centred approach assumes that the state is acting deliberately and officially to establish and maintain a race-based system of privilege and disadvantage. We are not arguing that all who run state institutions *currently* support racialism. We are saying that their predecessors in those institutions did and that some elements of race regimes are still embedded in settler state institutions and laws.

Race regimes are political systems of privilege and oppression established and maintained by states. 'States are compulsory and continuous associations claiming control of society within a territory' (Marx 1999, 4). From the first, colonial and settler states set out to supplant Indigenous rulers and to establish colonial rule over Indigenous territories. At the time, there were no single societies[3] within the territories over which those settler states ruled. Like states in Europe, these colonial, settler states claimed a monopoly on the legitimate use of force. In this regard, they acted through the imported institutions of government: legislatures; police, prisons, and courts; bureaucracies and civil servants; and the military. Each of these structures initiated or maintained the practices, ideas, and relationships that constituted race regimes.

Race regimes are political systems made up of ideas, structures (institutions), practices, and relationships through which states establish, maintain, and change official systems of racial domination. It is important, therefore, to learn how each institution has contributed to the creation, maintenance, and transformation of race regimes. States have either created or adopted and sanctioned the 'race categories' around which regimes of inclusion and exclusion, privilege and oppression, have been institutionalized. Categories such as 'Indian,' Black, and White still exist in popular culture, having achieved their potency through the power of the state and the law. They were established by states and so continue to have power, though states now disavow them.

In this section, we outline each element of race regimes separately, though the elements function together. Also, more than one race regime has characterized most colonial/settler states most of the time. Race regimes, then, are political systems composed of the following:

- *Structures,* including legislatures, laws, courts, police, and the civil service, through which the dominant elites of supplanting societies administer relations between race-defined groups so as to establish and maintain dominance.
- *Practices,* including habits of deference and subordination, such as the distinctive clothing worn by slaves in colonial Carolina to distinguish them from non-slaves, or the practice in segregated societies of non-Whites having to step off the sidewalk to let Whites pass, or restrictions relating to professional employment, education, and literacy.
- *Ideas,* including *ideologies*[4] such as race doctrines, that serve as frameworks for organizing, justifying, and maintaining relations of dominance and subordination. One example of racial doctrine is *social Darwinism*, which distorted Darwin's theory of evolution to justify racialism with the erroneous idea that Europeans were superior people, who ought to rule because they were more 'civilized' (evolved) than less-developed ('primitive') people, whom they *racialized.*

- *Relationships*, which structured the arrangements of power,[5] dominance, and subordination between those people (Whites) whom race regimes classified as superior and those (non-Whites) categorized as inferior because of their race as constructed and sanctioned by the regimes' ideas.

A race regime exists, therefore, when the government and other state institutions treat one or several groups of people already in the country, or wishing to enter it, differently in terms of status, rights, and benefits because of their race, which we understand as a category assigned to them either because of physical characteristics (such as skin colour) or because of a legal status such as 'slave' or 'Indian.' This definition applies to the race regimes of the supplanting states that emerged as a consequence of Britain's colonial expansion between the sixteenth century and the mid-twentieth. We use the term *colonialism* to refer to *the process whereby European powers took control of and exploited an already occupied territory, appropriating land and resources, extracting wealth, and benefiting from cheap labour.*

Race regimes are intrinsic to settler states because state action was needed to supplant Indigenous peoples and hold their lands. Hence, we conceptualize the founding race regime to be *internal colonialism* – the only race regime present in Australia, Canada, and the United States to administer relationships between each supplanting state and the Indigenous peoples and leaders supplanted. It was also intrinsic to the society that each settler state developed within the territories appropriated. But the regime was not static – it changed significantly over time, especially where it coexisted with other race regimes such as slavery. In colonial Carolina, for example, internal colonialism and slavery were instituted at the same time; and some Indigenous peoples were also enslaved.

Prior to Britain's defeat of French colonialism in 1759, some four thousand African and Indian slaves, most of them held by bishops and priests in domestic servitude, coexisted in French Canada with some autonomous Indigenous nations that were treated as allies, while others were treated as internal colonies. Indeed, until Britain abolished the slave trade (1807) and slavery (1833) in its empire, slavery and internal colonialism coexisted throughout British North America. However, slavery was never the basis of economic production in what became Canada, as it was in the U.S. South and the Caribbean. This is because a cold climate and poor soil made untenable plantation methods for growing cotton, sugar, rice, and other plantation crops. With this in mind, we separately examine each race regime, emphasizing common elements in all three countries.

In adopting a state-centred approach, we are not suggesting that racialism is to be blamed solely on the officials who administered the regimes or on those who governed the settler states. Race regimes were also maintained through structures and practices in non-governmental institutions such as churches, schools, and charities. In some cases, those institutions did the bidding of governments – for example, churches ran most of the residential schools where generations of Indigenous children were incarcerated to be 'civilized' (i.e., to be stripped of their culture, religion, and language). Similarly, newspapers, theatres, universities, museums, and art galleries promoted the race doctrines that sustained the regimes. Official military and police violence was applied; but some of the violence used to establish and sustain race regimes was unsanctioned. Moreover, most citizens of each state supported – and even demanded – government-administered race-based oppression and exploitation. Indeed, citizens used their increasing democratic power to promote racial prejudice. Nor should we view 'the state' as monolithic: the elites who controlled different state institutions or different branches of government did not always agree about race regimes. This is evident in the conflict between the northern and southern elites that led to the American Civil War. We must also note that state institutions could disagree among themselves about aspects of race regimes. An example is the disagreement between President Andrew Jackson and the U.S. Supreme Court in the 1830s about the status and rights of Indigenous nations, such as the Cherokee nation, which had survived colonial invasion and supplantation.[6]

Each of the three settler societies discussed in this chapter established a federal rather than a unitary state. As we discuss in chapter 4, *federalism* is a way of organizing a state with two levels of government sharing sovereign decision-making power, each government interacting directly with citizens and each having final authority in some fields or jurisdictions. The federal state structure meant that governmental power was divided between the central/federal government and the state/provincial ones. The much larger size of these three settler countries relative to European countries also made federalism important. Moreover, it allowed the central government to exert its authority in some matters over a vast (indeed, empire-sized) territory. Federalism also allowed for significant local control and variation in race regimes. In both the United States and Australia, the pre-existing colonies that came together to create the new federations retained the race regimes developed earlier. In the United States, slavery and internal colonialism coexisted with a Bill of Rights: federalism disguised the contradictions.

Internal Colonialism

The founding race regime in Australia, Canada, and the United States was internal colonialism. This regime changed over time, however, mainly because initial contact occurred at different dates and different stages in Britain's imperial history both in each country and in different regions of each country. Each settler state, as it expanded its rule over new territory, encountered new Indigenous peoples in different contexts. We use the term internal colonialism to refer to *a political system under which supplantation, settler control, and domination over Indigenous communities and their lands were established, maintained, and regulated.* In the regimes thereby established, the colonized Indigenous peoples, including Mexican Americans (see chapter 7), were forced to live within but also apart from a new White society not of their making, one in which they were denied most rights to political and social involvement. Police, military, and bureaucratic structures regulated their movements; the cultural bases of their communities were undermined; and their aspirations were blighted by the imposition of European culture by the settler state. Their legal systems were supplanted, and they were forced to either accept domination by the settler state or violently resist. Changes in these regimes in the twentieth century reduced somewhat the oppression this entailed, but elements of the internal colonial regime persist to this day, and its effects are evident in the troubling data relating to Indigenous people's health, housing, education, employment, and mortality.

How Indigenous peoples were treated at any point in time varied significantly, because the communities and nations being supplanted varied in their capacity for armed resistance, their potential value as allies of the settlers, and their relative immunity (or lack thereof) to the diseases that Europeans brought with them. Competition among European colonizers in North America made some groups valuable as military allies or as trading partners. So it would be incorrect to understand internal colonialism as a regime that always constructed all Indigenous peoples as victims; or as something they were always unable to resist. Some Indigenous peoples resisted successfully, or they moved to where the settlers were not (yet), or they played one European power off against another to preserve their independence – often for decades. Ultimately, colonial rule was established throughout the territories now occupied by these three (physically) large, federal states.

This was different from the outcome in New Zealand, where the military strength and prowess of the more homogeneous Maori peoples prevented the full establishment of internal colonialism. Maori men and women gained political clout in the settler state while most Indigenous peoples in Australia, Canada, and the United States experienced massacres, wars, denial of rights, confinement to reservations and missions, loss of their lands, the banning of their spiritual, cultural, and political practices, and forced 'civilizing' in residential schools. So while we should not underestimate Indigenous people's agency in resisting and negotiating with settler states, in Australia, Canada, and the United States, few Indigenous nations escaped significant negative effects – disease, death, dispossession, and social disintegration – from internal colonialism.

The seemingly easy domination and dispossession of many Indigenous peoples in North America led European imperialists and settlers alike to believe that European Whites must be a superior race and to accept race as a justification for different treatment. It seemed natural that the life chances of individuals should be determined by the race categories to which internal colonialism had assigned them. Instead of seeing the conditions of Indigenous peoples as consequences of their loss of land and of their communities being supplanted, it came to be seen as their own fault, or even as their choice in that they were 'savages' who could not or would not live a 'civilized' (i.e., European) way of life. Racism often interprets culture as determined by biology; thus many colonizers saw the poverty, high death rates, and otherwise depleted lives of captured and incarcerated Indigenous peoples as the result of their culture. In seventeenth-century British North America,[7] colonists interpreted their easy victories over disease-weakened 'Indians' as a function of their being heathens (i.e., not Christians). This religious bigotry, which also made Europeans despise Jews and Muslims, morphed easily into racism. Indigenous culture and faith came to be seen as inherited by peoples who were more primitive (less developed) than Europeans. Though a few Europeans saw value in the simplicity of Indigenous societies, describing their inhabitants as 'noble savages,' most colonizers and settlers despised those whom their invasion had harmed and feared them long after there was any danger of retaliation.

The common view of political theorists was that all non-Whites – anyone they assigned to a subordinate race category – could legitimately be treated in ways that those within the dominant group would not tolerate. Scottish political philosopher David Hume, another founder of modern political science, wrote in 1754: 'I am apt to suspect the negros, and in general all the other species of men … to be naturally inferior to the Whites. There never was a civilized nation of any other complexion than White, nor even any individual eminent either in action or specula-tion' (cited in Markus 1994, 9). Thus Hume dismissed the civilizations, high cultures, and great peoples around the world, including in the Americas, according to the characteristic racist thinking that was then emerging out of European's brutal and exploitive contacts with darker-skinned peoples. Markus argues that racist thought was not necessary for European settlers to establish colonial rule. Their motives were mainly economic, and in each country, invasion initially or ultimately triggered warfare. Extermination, enslavement, rape, the incarceration and indoctrination of prisoners, and theft of children were all part of the warfare against Indigenous peoples. Out of these experiences, and out of slavery, race doctrines emerged that colonizers then used to legiti-mize the undeclared and still unacknowledged wars. Eventually, as-pects of these wars of usurpation as well as ideas about them were institutionalized in the race regimes of internal colonialism; they were embedded in laws, practices, and cultural values that justified a system of institutionalized oppression.

As a race regime, therefore, internal colonialism emerged once colo-nial power shifted from being based on force and physical destruction, to being a governmental regime that operated through ordinary modes of state administration. In *The Way We Civilize* (1997), Rosalind Kidd uses these concepts to demonstrate that in Australia the state of war on the frontier lasted well into the twentieth century in the north and that the administration of the state of Queensland perpetuated a brutal form of internal colonialism up until the end of the twentieth century. The concept of the frontier is useful in understanding a place and time in which normal governmental authority has yet to be established. Before such authority is established ('sovereign authority'), the supplanting group's interests are advanced openly using force and the physical de-struction of Indigenous peoples by official state agents (military and police) and volunteers (settlers, pastoralists) without penalties. Under a governmental regime, by contrast, the interests of the supplanting, settler society are achieved through ordinary state laws and regulations, administration (bureaucratic regulation), courts, and legislation, as has been the case with the Canadian and U.S. Indian Acts. The ultimate goal of internal colonialism was the removal of Indigenous peoples from their lands so that settlers could possess and settle on them, or sell them to others. A frontier existed wherever and whenever there was a war of dispossession. Over the vast territories each of the settler states now controls, there have been many different frontiers, and the frontier phenomenon of naked sovereign dominance has occurred over a long period of time. The ideological justifications, and the portrayals of Indigenous peoples as vicious enemies, were deeply embedded in the settler states' popular cultures, just as formal rationales were planted deep in their laws and religious, academic, and artistic texts.

The 'rules' that settler societies applied to justify European occupancy also varied over time and place. In North America, as long as there was competition from other European powers, Britain proceeded according to basic international law (European in origin) because Indigenous nations were valuable allies, first during the British conflict with the French and then later, after 1776, with the United States. Royal proclamations claimed sovereign rights over Indigenous people's lands for the British Crown, and also established rules for their sale and that promised protection from illegal usurpation. Britain and later Canada signed treaties with some Indigenous nations, which often were not honoured. After the War of 1812,[8] there were few incentives for even this limited restraint. U.S. settler governments made and broke many treaties, promising safety if eastern nations moved to 'Indian country' west of the Mississippi, but then failing to protect the displaced nations against further invasions by land-hungry settlers. Greatly strengthened by the Civil War, the U.S. army fought a long war against Indigenous peoples in the west. It imprisoned Indian leaders and incarcerated survivors on reservations so that their lands could be cleared for farming, ranching, mining, oil exploitation, roads, and railways. On the reservations, the survivors starved as their traditional food source – buffalo – was deliberately slaughtered. This made them dependent on the government for meagre rations.

Though more orderly, the history of dispossession in Canada after 1812 was as devastating as in the United States. Still fearful of peoples they had harmed, especially where Indigenous peoples had resisted, the Canadian and U.S. governments closely regulated the survivors' movements; for example, they established reservations, instituted passes, banned spiritual ceremonies, and set out to obliterate all signs of Indigenous nations through 'civilization.' In Australia and in late-settled British Columbia, frontier colonialism was conducted under somewhat different rules. The legal principle and political myth of *terra nullius* governed the process. According to European laws about colonization, supplanting was legitimate provided that three main conditions were met: first, no other European power owned or occupied the land; second, the original inhabitants ceded rights through treaties or by accepting (token) payments; and third, the supplanters occupied the land through efficient dispossession, which usually meant that they fenced and farmed it (the presumption was that it had been 'empty'). These 'rules,' however, were mainly proof against claims to the lands by other European colonizers. By declaring the land 'empty,' Britain could establish penal colonies and free settlements in Australia without troubling to negotiate treaties or buy land. Since there were no serious European competitors, British colonizers did not need to form alliances with Indigenous communities in order to gain control of the continent. Violent usurpation took place after 1788 in East and South Australia and continued into the late 1930s in isolated Western Australia, Queensland, and the Northern Territory. In the process, 'Europeans dispossessed indigenes to the extent that they were able to and needed to' (Markus 1994, 18), without feeling any need to sign treaties with, or even acknowledge the existence of, Indigenous communities.

The Persistence of Internal Colonialism

Aspects of internal colonialism as a governmental regime persist to this day in Australia, Canada, and the United States. Though the histories of usurpation and colonial settlement differ across the three countries because of the time and context of initial contact with Indigenous peoples, the mechanisms through which internal colonialism regimes have been administered are strikingly similar. This is not surprising, given that the three settler states had their origins in British[9] colonialism and settlement. These three federal states with common law systems borrowed freely from British colonial policy and one another. The elements of governmental regimes of internal colonialism as established and administered by the three settler governments included the following:

- *Incarceration.* Passes and mobility restrictions kept Indigenous peoples concentrated on reservations, at mission stations, and in schools and training institutions. Leaders who challenged internal colonial rule were imprisoned.

- *Segregation.* The legal separation of Indigenous peoples[10] justified early the idea of 'fatal contact' – that 'primitive' peoples were destroyed by contact with 'civilization.' Survivors of usurpation were then kept out of sight and unable to join forces to resist.
- *Dispossession.* The removal of Indigenous communities from their lands by legal means (legislation, regulation, court decisions, military removals) was legitimized by the false thesis – argued by Locke – that they did not own their land because they had failed to use it 'properly' (i.e., fence it, farm it, and build permanent buildings) or because they were nomadic.[11]
- *Regulation and repression of reproduction.* On the Australian missions where Aboriginal survivors were incarcerated, they could not marry without the agent's consent, which was often denied. Rates of reproduction among Indigenous peoples declined everywhere, though there was a rise in the numbers of mixed-race people born of marriage with settlers, cohabitation, or rape (Métis, 'half-breeds').
- *Denial of civil rights.* Rights to freedom of movement, to marry freely, to assemble, to freedom of association, property rights, and so on, were all denied.
- *Denial or limitation of legal rights.* Australian Aboriginal peoples had no right to testify in court even on their own behalf. In Canada, they had no right to employ lawyers to regain their lands. Their right to enter into contracts was denied or limited because their legal status was as wards (legal children) of the federal state.
- *Denial of political rights.* Internal colonialism denied Indigenous people rights to participate in the settler state (e.g., by voting or running for office). It also forced termination of traditional governments, which in North America caused their replacement by controlled and co-opted 'band' officials or 'medal chiefs.'
- *Denial of social benefits enjoyed by citizens.* The Mothers' Allowance in Australia was denied to Aboriginal women; so were other benefits granted to citizens in all three countries.
- *Repression of spiritual practices and cultures.* North American settler governments saw such practices as the basis of possible resistance by Indigenous nations to settler occupation. They also saw them as 'savage' and eliminating them as essential to saving 'heathen' souls.
- *Forced removal of children.* Boyco (1995) describes this as cultural genocide, because children were removed from their families to be forcibly 'civilized,' often in brutal institutions designed to eliminate Indigenous languages and cultures ('kill the Indian in the child')

while training Indigenous peoples to fill menial jobs in settler societies, into which they were expected to assimilate but from which they were rejected by prejudice. Thus they were marginalized, exploited, and oppressed because of their race.

- *Forced assimilation.* Light-skinned children were removed from their homes for adoption in the expectation that they would be absorbed ('bred out to White').
- *Inculcation of legitimizing ideologies.* Whites and Indigenous peoples alike were exposed to ideas that justified White superiority on the grounds that 'savages' were inferior. This concept, spread by popular culture as well as academic and 'high' culture, naturalized the regime's ideas and power arrangements so that neither the oppressors nor those oppressed questioned them.

The Current Impact of Internal Colonialism

It is common to distance the current governments of Canada, Australia, and the United States from these previous state actions of usurpation and repression. If considered at all, usurpation is viewed as something that Britain did as a colonial power, or as ancient history. Most citizens of these countries consider colonial incursion to have been 'inevitable,' or they see it as 'water under the bridge.' Some even claim it was beneficial for Indigenous peoples. Ignorance of what happened and its consequences is common and, some argue, wilful. Denial is possible because after the frontier periods, internal colonialism was administered mainly by bureaucracies through departments such as Indian Affairs,[12] which were responsible for 'the Indian problem' or 'the Aboriginal problem,' or through arm's-length institutions, including the churches, which ran missions in Australia as well as residential schools in Canada and the United States.

Because Indigenous peoples were locked away on reservations, where they were denied political and civil rights, knowledge about the state activities through which internal colonialism was administered was largely invisible to citizens. This fostered denial and wilful ignorance. Many ancestors of today's Australian citizens were convicts forcibly transported to Australia; many ancestors of North Americans today had fled to the New World from famine, poverty, or religious oppression in the Old; or they had been imported as indentured servants or orphan workers. Many free settlers, motivated by the desire for a better life for their children, endured great hardships in settling the land. So the important thing is not who was to blame, but learning what happened and acknowledging that all non-Indigenous citizens have benefited from the usurpation of lands under internal colonialism even if their ancestors were not directly involved in that process.

Australian historian Ann McGrath warns her countrymen and women: 'Irrespective of where their ancestors were born, all Australians enjoy the spoils and suffer the consequences of the British invasion[s]' (1995, xxiv). The same is true of Canadians and Americans. Understanding this will help us understand why it has proved so difficult to dismantle race regimes and to redress their effects. Internal colonialism was institutionalized for more than a century; settler states had to administer two distinct political and legal regimes – one for White settlers and one for Indigenous subjects. Citizenship as a legal status that accords rights, especially the right to participate in electing governments, was expanded rapidly – first to all White men and then to White women. But most non-Whites were excluded; and Indigenous people were encapsulated within White democracies while enjoying few rights or benefits from them.

An important debate in all three countries is whether internal colonialism still exists. Though Indigenous peoples in each country now have the legal rights of citizenship, McGrath believes that Australian Aboriginal peoples remain partly colonized because their communities are not self-governing and because their lands have not been returned to them. Recent government actions, moreover, indicate that Australian governments still basically represent the interests of the majority of White Australians.[13] The dismantling of internal colonialism is more advanced in the United States than in Australia and Canada. But some elements of internal colonialism remain in all three countries. Indigenous peoples are such small minorities of the population that they cannot deflect governments from pursuing the interests of the White majority. This is justified by democratic theory that holds that the majority should rule.

The main elements of colonial dispossession and oppression have been institutionalized; that is, built into each state's laws, political practices, and institutions. Internal colonialism and oppressive practices based on race and administered by the settler states have been integral parts of those states. In each case, 'government policies and racial theories were intertwined' (McGrath 1995, 15). In each, the political system has been shaped and deformed by its involvement in maintaining the foundational race regime. In each country, administrative, legislative, and judicial practices and race doctrines have also made it easier for states to develop additional race regimes. McGrath concludes that 'Australian colonialism made Aborigines foreigners in their own land' (1995, 1). Having been instituted as an official policy, government exclusion or oppression based on race became the way to deal with those who are different. A similar situation has prevailed in Canada and the United States. Whites' denial of Indigenous rights, especially regarding land, reflects deep fears about this collective history.

Slavery

As in Carolina, in some colonies in North America the regimes of internal colonialism and slavery were established more or less simultaneously. Slavery increasingly involved the systematic kidnapping of people from Africa and was supported by a belief that people with Black skin[14] and 'negroid' body types were 'naturally inferior' and so could legitimately be enslaved. British wealth, like the wealth of some other European countries, rested on the slave trade – that is, on the buying, transporting, and selling of kidnapped Africans and their descendants. These countries also gained from the profits of forced labour on plantations producing staple crops such as cotton, rice, and sugar. 'Free' (i.e., usurped) land worked by the labour of slaves, who received no pay, generated huge profits. Slavery was not new as an economic system; it had existed in ancient times. Here, we study it as a race regime, one that denied citizenship and civil rights to Blacks both in the United States and, indirectly, in Canada and Australia. Our focus in this book will be on why slavery negatively affected the legal, political, and civil status of African Americans long after abolition.

As a race regime, slavery is a set of ideas, practices, and relationships organized and administered through the institutions of a state in which people are made into and used as slaves. Slaves are legally the property of another person and can be bought and sold as property.[15] Whether or not slaves had rights depended on the form of slavery in a particular state. In the United States, slaves had no rights, and this had a significant impact on their lives even after slavery was abolished. As slaves, they were denied legal, civil, and political rights and could be killed, bought or sold as property, and separated from blood kin or spouses and children. Of the three settler states discussed in this book, slavery existed as a race regime only in the United States. It was incorporated in slaveholding states when the confederal union was created in 1776. Slavery existed in the British North American colonies and New France before the British ended the legal slave trade in 1807. Slaves were freed in British territories by 1833. Technically, then, slavery never existed in the Canada formed in 1867. Indentured servants replaced slaves as domestic servants. In Australia, legal slavery never existed. Though Aboriginal workers and indentured workers (mostly Hawaiians and Melanesians) were harshly treated as 'virtual slaves,' people were not bought and sold. Convicts who had been exported to Australia to reduce overcrowding in British prisons were used as forced labour, but they were freed when their sentences ended, if they had survived the harsh treatment and environment.

What made slavery a race regime in the United States instead of simply an economic system was the involvement of states in its defence and maintenance. In South Carolina, for example, prior to 1776, the colonial state passed legislation about how slaves could be punished for the offences of slow work or refusing to work. The Duke of Saxe-Weimar visited the Work House in Charleston in 1769. He reported that it contained machines in which slaves were punished through torture at the request of their masters or by order of the police (Ball 1999, 305–6). Colonial governments also maintained police forces and raised militias to hunt runaways, prevent slave revolts, and punish or execute escapees.

It is useful to distinguish between *societies with slaves* and *slave societies*. Ira Berlin argues that in societies with slaves, 'slaves were marginal to the central productive processes; slavery was just one form of labor among many' (1998, 8). In slave societies, by contrast, slavery was the very basis of economic production. More important, Berlin asserts, in slave societies, 'the master–slave relationship provided the model for all social relations' and the slave-owning elite was the ruling class that controlled the institutions of the state (Ball 1999, 305–6). In the colonies that became the United States there were both societies with slaves *and* slave societies.

The War of Independence fought by the thirteen American colonies against Britain had a strong albeit complex impact on slavery. First, the British manipulated the issue of slavery in their struggle against the American colonies, promising slaves their freedom if they joined the British and thereby undercutting the colonists' production of rice and other staples. Second, however, the powerful ideas unleashed by American patriots and their supporters began an 'Age of Revolution' that led to the end of the old regimes based on ascribed status (i.e., assigned at birth), unearned privilege, and rigid hierarchies. Ultimately, these ideas – and the revolutions of which they were part – resulted in the establishment of political democracy, free labour, social mobility based on merit or achievement, and legal equality (Ball 1999, 358–9). In the northern U.S. states, which were 'societies with slaves,' the power of these values eventually eroded the basis of slavery – though not of racism, which actually grew stronger as Whites and Blacks competed for work on the free labour market. In the southern states, which were 'slave states,' slave owners used their ability to dominate state governments to pass or revive laws that established slavery as the dominant political regime. The construction of a federal political system in the United States permitted the North/South differences to persist; and the ability of slave owners and their supporters to dominate the central institutions of the federal state prevented those who opposed slavery from using the power of the federal government to interfere with race regimes that used state power to protect slaves as property. Until the 1850s, the slave states dominated the federal government, thereby blocking efforts to develop federal power against 'states' rights.' The doctrine that the states, as the original polities that had joined together to create the republic, had the fundamental right to support slavery developed in this period as well.

Resistance against slavery existed almost from the beginning of settlement. In 1740, for example, the South Carolina Assembly reported to King George II that slave insurrections had resulted in deaths in and around Charles Town (Charleston) (McKissack and McKissack 1996, 2). After 1776, however, the revolutions in America and France 'set before the world the revolutionary concept that liberty and equality were the rights of all men' (ibid., 5). The slave revolution led by Toussaint L'Ouverture (1791–1803) in the French colony of Saint-Dominique, however, had especially profound consequences. Ultimately successful, it resulted in the abolition of slavery there and in the founding of Haiti as the first Black nation in the Western Hemisphere. Refugees who fled to the United States helped spread fear of similar consequences, especially where slaves outnumbered Whites.

In 1800, increased repression using state power resulted in Gabriel's Rebellion (Gabriel Prosser, Henrico County, Virginia), as well as the New Orleans Revolt in 1811 and Denmark Vesey's rebellion (Charleston, South Carolina) in 1822. The slave states responded. After a Virginia slave, Nat Turner, staged an uprising with seventy comrades in 1831, South Carolina's lawmakers passed a bill (1834) that banned literacy among African Americans to stop them from reading abolitionist newspapers or anti-slavery tracts. By 1850, every southern state had a law forbidding the teaching of slaves to read or write. Those who risked their lives, moreover, weren't always slaves like Nat Turner. Gabriel Prosser was a free African American, a tavern keeper, and literate (McKissack and McKissack, 1996, 61). Denmark Vesey also was literate and bought his freedom, although his wife and children were still enslaved (ibid., 72–3). Whites who taught slaves to read and write also were punished. In 1831, Georgia posted a reward of $5,000 for the capture and arrest of the *Liberator*'s founder, anti-slave activist William Garrison, so that he could be convicted on a charge of sedition under Georgia law.

By the time Britain declared an end to the legal slave trade in 1807,[16] slavery in the United States, which was 'infamously brutal' (Marx 1998, 56), was also being affected by the fact that the slave population was increasingly made up of U.S.-born slaves. With the slave trade ended, possibilities for manumission were steadily foreclosed; thus, South Carolina made it impossible by law to free a slave after 1841. Not only did states' actions become more restrictive. By 1850, the southern states were using the states' rights doctrine and threats of secession to demand and get a federal statute – the Fugitive Slave Act – that compelled authorities in non-slave states to capture fugitive slaves and return them to their owners. Previously, if they reached 'free' soil, they had been freed.

Slavery was a race regime, one that employed federal and state institutions – legislatures, courts, bureaucracies, the police, and ultimately the military as the United States moved toward civil war. But many institutions of civil society, including schools, churches, and newspapers, were also involved in inculcating the ideological components of the regime. The defence and justification of slavery required the demonization of African Americans as 'primitive' or 'subhuman' that they were outside the bounds of society and its protections. This encouraged the development of images of African American distinctiveness and inferiority, which in turn provided the racist foundations on which a caste-like system of segregation was built after the Civil War resulted in the legal emancipation of slaves. In 1863, during the Civil War, Abraham Lincoln promulgated the Emancipation Proclamation, which ended legal slavery for most African Americans. But in the aftermath of this, a new regime of radical segregation was established according to which Blackness became a mark of permanent inferiority. Black nationalist W.E.B. Du Bois explained: 'Slaves were not considered men. They had no right of petition. They were divisible like any other chattel. They could own nothing; they could make no contracts ... hold no property ... they could not control their children; they could not appeal from their masters; they could be punished at will' (cited Marx 1997, 58).

Though slavery ended as a legal status in 1863, the race regimes built around slavery remained more or less in place with brief interruptions for another century. In part, this was because the Civil War was not primarily a crusade to grant justice and rights to African Americans. Certainly, African Americans who fought in the war or who supported the anti-slavery movement had that goal. Many White anti-slavery activists, however, had quite different values. Many were proponents of free labour and saw slavery as unfair competition. In the northern states, this first became evident in the decades after 1776. African Americans were excluded by unions, by competition from immigrants, and by the custom of segregating them from decent work, housing, or public spaces. Berlin concludes: 'Free Black men and women sank to the base of northern society, marginalized, impoverished, and despised' (1998, 359). State lawmakers, in the north as well as the south, passed laws that denied Blacks the right to travel freely, and African American men were denied the basic rights of citizenship – to vote, to sit on juries, to testify in court, to serve in the militia, even to deliver the mail. Many anti-slavers sought to protect the north from 'Black pestilence' or to keep Blacks out of the west (Richards 2000, 3). Many who had once opposed slavery now disavowed their earlier support for equality. White Methodists and Baptists, for example, denied African Americans their place in congregations that had previously been biracial (Berlin 1998, 361). Consequently, in the north, where slavery had been replaced by free labour well before the Civil War, African Americans still were a despised minority; while not enslaved, they were oppressed. In the southern states a similar pattern developed after the Civil War despite a decade of 'reconstruction' during which northerners punished White southerners by denying them rights briefly given to African Americans. The important point was that very few Whites, even dedicated anti-slavers or the deeply religious, believed in the equality of Blacks and Whites. This allowed the deeply oppressive race regime of segregation based on skin colour to persist for another century or more.

Conclusion

In the case of both internal colonialism and slavery, White settlers gained enormously from usurped, free, or cheap land and from forced labour. Those in Britain who ran the land companies, the slave trade, the convict trade, and the immigration companies also benefited. In the settler states, relatively poor White immigrants also gained economic status and political rights from the settler states that administered these foundational race regimes. As we will show in the next chapter, the end in legal terms of these regimes did not mean that ex-slaves and Indigenous peoples were incorporated as citizens with equal rights and the same life chances as Whites. The stigma of being Black or being an 'Indian' marginalized and excluded them from nations that were increasingly democratic – if you were White. Non-British immigrants, including Greeks and Italians, were also racialized. In addition, non-Whites were excluded from immigration, especially in Australia, or they were exploited as menial workers. Colour bans and segregation systems against Blacks, Asians, or 'Indians' were maintained by the laws, courts, police, and other institutions of state and civil society for too long for the stigma that race entailed to be eliminated. Race doctrines to justify the usurpation, enslavement, and destruction of cultures were too deeply embedded in laws, practices, and culture to be easily reversed. Hence caste-like systems of segregation, oppression, and exploitation continued for many years afterwards, so that they formed the underlying basis of the current politics of race.

Discussion Questions

1 Which characteristics of the Australian, Canadian, and U.S. settler states produced the inequalities that race minorities experience?
2 What roles did colonialism play in creating the race regimes discussed in this chapter?
3 What are the advantages of a comparative, state-focused approach to studying race-based discrimination? Are there disadvantages?
4 Define an ideology in your own words. Give examples of how ideology is embedded in settler states' discourses or practices.
5 What circumstances unified Whites in these settler states?

2 Subsequent Race Regimes – Segregation and Whites-Only Nationalism

In chapter 1, we explored how three settler states – Australia, Canada, and the United States – dispossessed Indigenous peoples. We also showed how those states' institutions created and administered the foundational race regimes of internal colonialism and slavery. In this chapter we explore two subsequent race regimes that those three settler states created. The first is *segregation,* a system of White supremacy and privilege in which non-Whites are denied access to land, employment, housing, schooling, and public facilities – things that Whites have reserved for themselves. The term 'segregation' means to keep the races apart; in some cases, though, as in the United States, those who have been 'segregated' are often kept close at hand, even living in Whites' houses to work as domestic servants, when this does not threaten White supremacy. The second race regime explored in this chapter is *Whites-only nationalism,* such as the White Australia policy that the fledgling Commonwealth government created to keep Australia a 'White man's country.' Whites-only nationalist regimes were constructed through state controls on who could immigrate, work, and become citizens. While each country's national ideal varied somewhat in specifics, the mechanisms used to keep the nation White were similar, with governments excluding and even deporting those who did not embody the White ideal.

In this chapter we explore how British imperialism shaped these two subsequent race regimes. Britain was the European power that created the colonies out of which these settler countries developed. But it was not the only European power planting colonies on lands occupied by Indigenous peoples. Britain's racialist policies differed from those of Spain and France, with which Britain was in competition. British colonialism in North America and Australia developed several centuries after Spain planted its colonies in the 'New World' and almost as long after France launched its colonial ventures. Spanish and French colonial policies were the product of absolutist monarchies and were influenced by the Catholic Church. British colonialism was undertaken by private companies, albeit with royal support and military protection. Because British colonialism was a later venture, especially in Australia and Canada, it was shaped by two main modernizing forces – the Reformation and early capitalism. King Henry VIII declared himself (and later monarchs) head of the Church of England, replacing the Pope. Consequently, British[1] colonialism was Protestant, not Catholic; thus it did not heed papal rules about imperial expansion, which had split the non-European world between the Spanish and the Portuguese. Britain instead developed its own rules.

Britain itself was a product of conquest and internal colonialism. The English monarchy had created Britain by conquering Scotland and Ireland and by absorbing Wales. Indeed, Ireland was England's first colony, having been settled by English overlords and transported Scots, who took and occupied indigenous lands using military force.[2] Throughout Britain, practices similar to those of colonization were used to enclose common lands; to convert such lands into private property, landowners claimed absolute ownership and drove away the peasants whose ancestors had worked those lands for centuries. Some of the people displaced in this way drifted to the towns, where some found work in the new factories; others stayed on the enclosed lands to work in the mines. Still others were pressed into the army or navy; or were transported to the colonies as criminals, often for theft; or emigrated to the colonies if they could raise the fare. Each of these fates was a result of economic changes brought on by the Industrial Revolution and emerging English capitalism. Spanish and French colonialisms had been part of the old, Catholic, absolutist Europe; British colonialism, by contrast, was part of the modernizing social, economic, and political changes that were buffeting Europe. Britain's settler colonies eventually became nation-states in their own right with majority White populations. The United States achieved its independence much earlier than Australia and Canada, which were part of Britain's second empire.

The new settler societies presented a paradox regarding the politics of race. One result of the timing and nature of British colonialism was that pressure developed for the government to institute education systems and to grant civil and political rights to free British settlers. On the one hand, then, the timing and nature of Britain's colonial projects resulted in increased democratization for White settlers and their descendants; while on the other, state institutions enforced race regimes that denied land, liberty, and the proceeds of their labour to Indigenous peoples and Blacks who had been enslaved. Political rights for Whites went in tandem with a systematic denial of rights for Indigenous peoples and Black slaves. Moreover, all three settler states denied entry to other non-Whites in order to keep the new nations White, and denied rights to those few Asians and other non-Whites who had managed to get in. Democratic ideas, which were more influential in Australia and the United States, were based on *equality among citizens*. But few non-Whites were citizens, and rarely were questions raised about their exclusion from citizenship or from entry into the country.

The paradox that settler democracies increased political rights for (male) Whites at an early point, while at the same time administering race regimes that excluded, dispossessed, oppressed, segregated, and assimilated non-Whites categorized as 'others,' is the central theme of this chapter. Australian Roberta James (cited in Cowlishaw and Morris 1997) theorizes that liberal democracy and racism are historically entangled, not the polar opposites they are assumed to be. She suggests that racialism was so deeply entrenched in the founding of settler states that most White settlers could not conceive of the non-Whites they encountered as ever being equal to them. In fact, the more democratic these White settler states became, the more rigidly and totally they excluded non-Whites. Physical characteristics such as skin pigmentation, as well as associated cultural practices considered 'primitive' and 'uncivilized,' were judged to disqualify these people from ever being included in the new (White) nations.

Most theorists of liberal democracy conceptualize *citizenship* in terms of inclusion in the nation. That is, citizens enjoy the status of equals *among equals* in a culturally homogenized nation. Equals are 'civilized'; whereas racialist doctrines and settlers' experiences cast non-White 'others' – especially Aboriginal or Indigenous people – as 'savage' or 'primitive.' This mindset made it impossible for non-Whites ever to be incorporated as citizens in the White nation, even when they had been granted the right to vote. In Britain as in most of Europe, White (male) workers were denied political rights until the late nineteenth century (with women and non-Christians waiting until well into the twentieth century). By contrast, White democratization proceeded much earlier in the settler societies, which based their national solidarity on race exclusion. In the United States, White manhood suffrage existed by the 1830s. In both Canada and the United States, immigration was opened early on to all White Europeans; whereas in Australia, immigrants were required to be of British origin, and when non-British Europeans were later admitted, they encountered discrimination.

There are other important differences regarding the settler states' policies and experiences. The United States was a slave state[3] and fought a bitter civil war, partly over slavery. The United States was formed as a consequence of rebellion against Britain in the eighteenth century, whereas Canada and Australia were part of Britain's second empire and gained their independence slowly, without armed struggle. Neither experienced a civil war or its aftermath. Well into the nineteenth century, Australia was deeply affected by its existence as a collection of convict colonies (South Australia excepted) and by its isolation to the south of Asia, far from Europe. Canada was shaped by its founding by the United Empire Loyalists, who had rejected the American Revolution, and by French Canadians, who constituted a large minority, struggled for cultural survival and just treatment. The Loyalists included communities of former slaves who had been promised land to settle. The land assigned to those former slaves was poor, and they faced many of the same social experiences of segregation in their communities in Ontario and Nova Scotia as their counterparts did in the northern U.S. states.

Segregation and White Supremacy

Australia, Canada, and the United States now all have majority-White populations of European origins, who settled on lands taken from Indigenous peoples. The affluence enjoyed by most White citizens in these countries has its origins in the exploitation and sale of free land, the forced labour of slaves, and later the cheap labour of former slaves and despised groups of immigrants. In each country, disease, the violence of conquest and settler occupation, and systematic exclusion and mistreatment has reduced the Indigenous populations to less than 3 per cent.

The pattern of White majorities has done much to distinguish settler societies of British origin from South Africa and Latin America, in that Whites are usually minorities in the latter. In the former Spanish colonies of Latin America, for example, larger Indigenous populations survived than in the British settler societies. Furthermore, Indigenous people were less often integrated by marriage into White settler societies.

Instead, the surviving Indigenous peoples as well as Blacks and their descendants (after slavery was abolished) were pushed onto unproductive lands, isolated on missions or reservations, or segregated in marginalized urban communities. Violence and segregation made them easily exploited. In Spanish and Portuguese America, larger surviving Indigenous communities and the scarcity of White women resulted in majority mixed-race (mestizo) populations, which after emancipation were integrated into the settler societies at their base. By contrast, forced miscegenation (rape) occurred in Britain's settler societies, but skin colour inhibited integration.

The supposed paradox of increasingly democratic political systems for Whites, combined with oppressive race regimes justified by racialism, is therefore not a paradox at all. The end of slavery, or its absence, did not mean that race-based oppression ended or failed to develop. Rather, it signalled the need to *intensify race consciousness* if Whites were to maintain their economic, political, and cultural power. Democratic principles served to justify that domination as long as Whites were a majority. But without slavery, or after slavery ended, 'miscegenation' (marriage or sex across race categories) would occur to weaken those claims unless laws and practices were put in place to keep the 'races' separate. Moreover, where race minorities were of any size – as in the United States with African Americans – White dominance depended on finding ways to deny such minorities any political power. So states passed laws to prevent intermarriage and to sanction such things as literacy tests and poll taxes to preserve White rule. Racialism and segregation were part of the process of building White democracies in these three settler states; they also permeated their nationalisms and distorted their sense of justice.

'Jim Crow'[4] Segregation in the United States

From the time the United States was founded, slavery and race prejudice were in conflict with the stated values of the new republic. When the founders wrote of the self-evident truth that 'all men are created equal,' their values did not include men who were 'Indians' or African Americans any more than they included women or Asians. As we shall see in chapter 4, federalism obscured this conflict, since it was mainly state governments that constructed the 'Jim Crow' race regimes on which we focus in this section.

Slavery in the United States was concentrated in the south, which depended on it economically. Many northern states with economies based on free labour had passed legislation ending it. But this rarely reflected a belief that African Americans were equal to White citizens – which almost no one believed even if they considered slavery unjust. The abolitionist movements that arose in Britain and the northern states actually promoted racist beliefs and doctrines. Faced with abolitionist arguments that slavery was unjust, supporters of slavery developed and supported race doctrines that justified it because of the supposed inferiority or 'primitiveness' of African Americans. This accorded with Aristotle's thesis that some people were 'slaves by nature,' which could justify the institution. These doctrines were used to legitimize segregation and the continued White domination of African Americans after slavery ended.[5] During slavery, legal and other mechanisms for maintaining social distance and control had been less necessary than after emancipation. And segregation became the principal mechanism for those purposes after emancipation. As Anthony Marx (1998, 69) concludes: 'Only when abolition undermined slavery as a basis for social distinctions was a biracial order fully elaborated.' In the United States, which is the focus of this section, segregation was a race regime constructed and enforced by southern state governments. These regimes segregated African Americans from Whites at many levels, denying them the citizenship rights that the federal government had conferred on (male) Black former slaves through a constitutional amendment. Segregation regimes also denied African Americans the right to participate in White society, though this did not exclude them from being exploited in poorly paid, menial, and unsafe labour, and in domestic work in Whites' houses, where they raised the household's White children.

In the United States, 'one drop of [non-White] blood' was considered sufficient to exclude people from White society, citizenship rights, and participation in the nation. After the Civil War, the federal government imposed several decades of Reconstruction (1867–90), during which the victorious northern states deprived southern Whites of political rights while agents of the federal government provided education, land, and political and civil rights to the former slaves. During this period, Black men were majorities in some districts. Hence Blacks sat in Congress and in the state legislatures – something that southern Whites determined they never again would allow once they had the power to end it. Reconstruction was betrayed by northern Republicans, who withdrew the military, so that by 1896, White southerners had regained power over their state legislatures. They put in place the new race regime of *segregation*. During Reconstruction, they had developed vigilante organizations such as the KKK[6] to keep Blacks 'in their place'; now they used state police, courts, and prisons to re-establish White rule.

In 1896, in *Plessy v. Ferguson*, the Supreme Court legitimized extreme – 'Jim Crow' – segregation and agreed that it could be applied to anyone with any Black blood, including persons who were seven-eighths White. *Plessy v. Ferguson* makes it clear that even federal state power could be used to uphold segregation. The federal Supreme Court upheld the view that separate (segregated) facilities in education, housing, transportation, and other public facilities were not unconstitutional provided that they were 'equal.' So despite the federal government's postwar constitutional guarantees of full citizenship rights to the former (male) slaves, such rights in essence now depended on where Blacks lived. The case also showed that the strategy for maintaining White dominance after the Civil War included curtailing race mixing except in work situations dominated by Whites. As late as 1967, sixteen states had laws against miscegenation (Marx 1998, 70).

Because most Americans accepted the racist belief that race differences were inherited along with associated cultural differences, strict separation was seen as the only way to protect the White race from being contaminated by intermarriage or 'breeding' across race lines. This strategy reflected the large size of the ex-slave African American population. By contrast, strategies in Australia started with isolation and segregation. Then, when it became clear that Aboriginal peoples were not a 'dying race' as had been thought, the goal switched to physical and cultural assimilation – 'breeding out to White.' This strategy, which reflected the small size of the Aboriginal population, divided Aboriginal communities internally (see below), whereas U.S. segregation policies fostered internal cohesion and solidarity.

In Canada, segregation existed as a community custom supported largely by local laws. But it never existed as a race regime administered by federal or provincial governments. In periods characterized by military and commercial alliances, traditions of intermarriage existed such that a White man would gain the support of his Indian wife's family or clan when exploring or developing the wilderness. This resulted in mixed-race Canadians, who were often voluntarily educated in residential schools and who would play important roles in later settlement and economic development – for example, as employees of the Hudson's

Bay Company. Another product of this tradition were the Métis, a community of mixed-blood francophone Indigenous people with a settled land base in what is now Manitoba. After 1812, however – and especially after the 'rebellions' in the latter part of the nineteenth century – the approach changed. The Indian Act was intended to reduce the numbers of Indigenous people for which the federal government was responsible and to give Whites access to communal lands, which happened when Indigenous women 'married out.'

Jim Crow Segregation as a Race Regime

Unlike Indians, who were kept apart from White society on reservations, African American ex-slaves and their descendants were wanted as a permanent underclass whose labour could be exploited. Some Whites, including President Abraham Lincoln, favoured returning the former slaves to Africa – as did some African Americans. The affluence that Whites enjoyed and on which U.S. democracy was based depended on free or cheap land as well as cheap labour. Few Whites, though, seriously challenged the assumption made by the U.S. Supreme Court in its *Dred Scott* decision (1857) that African Americans – who were 'separated from the White by indelible marks' – were ever intended to be granted 'full citizenship' (Marx 1998, 121). Even Lincoln admitted: 'I am not nor ever have been in favor of bringing about ... the social and political equality of the White and Black races' (Marx 1998, 121). If even the great emancipator of the slaves believed that 'Blacks must remain inferior,' how could masses of largely uneducated Blacks be incorporated into an emerging democracy made possible by relative equality among Whites; or be part of the Whites-only nation being reconstituted after the bitterness of the Civil War?

The federal architecture of the United States permitted the coexistence of slave and free states. It now permitted two different approaches to the presence of African American ex-slaves and their descendants. In the south, full citizenship for Black men was maintained by force during Reconstruction. Southern nationalism glorified the Confederacy as the political vehicle for White supremacy based on a slave regime. To 'bind up the [White] nation's wounds,' the central nation-state sold out the ex-slaves in the southern states by basing reunification on a Whites-only nationalism. After a decade of being politically powerless, former Confederates were required only to swear allegiance to the Union to resume citizenship, which they used to create rigid, state-enforced segregation regimes in southern states and to remove through local laws the rights promised to African American men by the constitution. Lincoln's successor, Andrew Johnson of Tennessee, 'ignored the moral imperative of ... meeting Blacks' expectations and instead pursued ... the pragmatic need for immediate reconciliation with the South. Johnson ... assist[ed] the defeated and economically devastated South ... minimize[d] federal intervention, granting ... states' rights lost in the war' (Marx 1998, 127).

After Reconstruction, during which the federal government used its power to improve the lives and protect the rights of ex-slaves, southerners used their reclaimed control of state and local governments, threats and use of violence, and legal manoeuvres to impose 'Jim Crow' or strict segregation regimes. African Americans who had been enfranchised were now declared 'unfit to rule,' and intense propaganda regarding the threats of 'negro domination' produced widespread support for the new race regime. Exclusion or segregation seemed the only possible path once deportation was abandoned as impractical. Integration was viewed as unthinkable and Black citizenship as intolerable. Things had to go more or less back to the way they were before the war. The main elements of segregation as a race regime in the United States were as follows:

- State and local laws segregated education facilities, housing, transportation, recreation facilities, and employment.
- Sharecropping and menial, dangerous, and domestic work were made African Americans' lot.
- Citizenship rights to vote and run for office were removed by state and local laws requiring property[7] and literacy tests, which were administered to exclude African Americans. This was backed up by intimidation and violence against those who dared to register to vote.
- Poll taxes (i.e., taxes for the right to vote) effectively denied the vote to African Americans who otherwise managed to qualify.
- African Americans were excluded from juries, most public education, and the professions.
- African Americans were denied most civil rights; moreover, the police and courts were used to enforce segregation.
- State agencies disseminated propaganda to justify segregation and its promotion in education and the media. This naturalized the regime.

In the north, where fewer African Americans lived, employers gained from the presence of low-paid Black workers, for it meant they were able to keep the wages of White immigrants low. Ideology as well as customary and institutional rules (e.g., regarding mortgages and insurance) maintained occupational, educational, and residential segregation, thereby excluding African Americans from most public institutions. In the south, hoodlum power and lynchings backed up legal aspects of the regime; and judges, police, and officials turned a blind eye to the abuses of those who had voted them into office and who could vote them back out. In the north, African Americans were no more accepted as equals than they were in the south. Nonetheless, some northerners called for reforms, and all efforts were resisted to repeal the Fifteenth Amendment, which had granted formal citizenship to African American men. Ultimately, it was the federal organization of the U.S. states that permitted African Americans to be legally citizens with rights established under the Constitution, even while being denied substantive civil, political, or social rights by local and/or state laws. Marx argues: 'America's great invention of federalism was an offspring – or at least a stepchild – of America's great tragedy of slavery' (1998, 60). Federalism fostered segregation.

Segregation was created as a race regime to control and exploit African American ex-slaves and their descendants. Its exclusion of Blacks made possible the new Whites-only American nationalism, which after the Civil War re-created solidarity between northern and southern Whites. It also affected those controlled by other race regimes, thereby increasing state oppression of Native Americans and restricting immigration of racial minorities. For example, Asian immigration was restricted rigorously, but Whites from Europe were encouraged to immigrate. Expansion westward on the North American mainland, in the Caribbean, and in the Pacific was also legitimized by race doctrines. Americans – understood to be White – claimed a 'manifest destiny' to rule 'inferior' non-White peoples. The federal government's concessions to states' rights left one part of 'the race problem' to be worked out by the states. But immigration was deemed to require a strong federal hand; and on the western frontier, Native Americans not restrained on reservations became targets of a war of extermination. The military, which was under federal control, remained segregated until the Second World War. But segregated Black units – the Buffalo Soldiers – joined the war against 'Indians.'

Despite attempts by generations of African American leaders to end the legal segregation regimes, it was not until 1954 that the U.S. Supreme Court in *Brown v. Board of Education* overturned *Plessy v. Ferguson*. In doing so, it repudiated the 'separate but equal' doctrine and mandated school desegregation. In its decision to overturn *Plessy v. Ferguson*, the

Court concluded that segregated education was not compatible with the U.S. Constitution's guarantees of equal rights. *Segregation had been the will of the majority,* certainly in the southern states and likely elsewhere as well; many White citizens believed it was necessary and most wanted it to continue. Nonetheless, from its inception, the legality and morality of segregation had been challenged. This points again to the paradox raised at the beginning of this chapter: *racialism and democracy grew together,* and race regimes such as Jim Crow segregation were supported by White majorities.

During Andrew Jackson's presidency (1825–33), egalitarian democracy with majority rule as its key principle became a dominant theme in U.S. political life. To allow for full expression of majority rule, restrictions on White, male suffrage were removed, property qualifications for office were abolished, and appointed positions were reduced and/or replaced with elected ones with term limits. Democracy largely was associated with majority rule. In Jackson's time, this resulted in the forced removal of 'Indian' nations like the Cherokee from their lands in Georgia, despite the Supreme Court's ruling against removal. The majority sentiment was anti-Indian, and Jackson believed that the majority favoured removal.

Alexis de Tocqueville in *Democracy in America* (1835) wrote that egalitarianism and majority rule were mixed blessings, even for White men, because they could allow 'the tyranny of the majority to prevail.' With democracy understood as majority rule, and a culture that found Black/White equality virtually inconceivable, segregation expressed the democratic will of the White majority. Even in the southern states where most Blacks lived, Whites were the majority. And where African Americans had voting rights, districts were carefully shaped (gerrymandered) to dilute Blacks' votes, and Blacks were intimidated or legally excluded from voting or running for office. Thus, segregation expressed the will of the majority in many parts of the United States, whose federal structure allowed segregation to persist in law in the southern states into the 1960s – and, in practice, into the present in some areas. Segregation benefited Whites, leaving Blacks available for cheap labour as sharecroppers (who worked White land for a small share in any profits) or as domestics. All the while, they were denied their political and civil rights as citizens.

Segregation in Canada

Many Canadians believe that their country is distinguished from the United States by a history of fairer treatment of Indigenous peoples,

Blacks, and other 'visible minorities.'[8] But we can sustain this belief only by denying our factual history, for careful examination of federal, provincial, and local laws and policies reveals many contrary cases. Roger Nichols in *Indians in the United States and Canada* (1998, xvii) writes that there were strong similarities between U.S. and Canadian policies: 'the Indian–White story in Canada resembles that in the United States closely.' Moreover, where the stories differed, it was not always Canadian policy that was more just. Native Americans gained citizenship much earlier in the United States and achieved self-government more easily.

Though slavery never existed in Canada on a large scale – or at all after Confederation (1867) – all Blacks were stigmatized to some extent by it. Blacks in Canada were affected by local segregation regimes devised to maintain social control and distance. Since slavery had been abolished in the British Empire before Confederation, Blacks were descendants of slaves, Loyalists, or ex-slaves freed by the British during the revolution or the War of 1812; or they were escaped slaves who had sought freedom by leaving the United States via the Underground Railway. Ironically, Mohawk leader Thayendanega (Joseph Brant) came to Canada as a Loyalist with thirty Black slaves, who built his house near present-day Burlington (Boyco 1995, 150). Most Blacks in Canada faced segregated schools, housing, and employment, as well as discriminatory laws and racist practices. Blacks were considered unfit for citizenship in Canada, just as they were in the United States.

Blacks in Canada differed, though, in how they dealt with the racism and discrimination they faced. Some worked to build strong, self-sufficient communities in which they could prosper and support one another. Others believed they should go to Africa or the northern U.S. states, which many did rather than endure Canadian racism. A third group, represented by Mary Ann Shadd, who edited the *Provincial Freeman* in Windsor, argued that Blacks should struggle for equality and integration into White Canadian communities. Conflict over the alternatives often split Black communities. The small number of Blacks in most provinces meant that the laws on segregation were local and that racist practices were uneven. Upper Canada (later Ontario) in 1849 and Nova Scotia in 1865 passed legislation providing for segregated schools for Black children. British scholar J.F.W. Johnson on his 1850 tour of North America, however, reported that a Black man served on a jury in Halifax (Greer and Radforth 1992, 300). Few Blacks in Nova Scotia enjoyed the right to vote; the Halifax juror must have been a property owner to be a juror. Later we will describe how only in 1910, with the federal Immigration Act, did race emerge as a legal category that kept potential immigrants out. The Indian Act regulated Indigenous peoples' lives under one federal act and department; in contrast to this, segregation governing Blacks was a patchwork of local laws and practices.

At the beginning of the twentieth century, the federal government launched a campaign to recruit immigrants to fill the Canadian West and hold its huge land mass against the covetous Americans. African American communities from Oklahoma, including educated and self-sufficient business people and experienced farmers, sought to immigrate to Manitoba and Alberta. The results of this reveal that Canadians' racism was as deep as that of Americans. The common Canadian view was that Americans had race problems *because* they had African Americans. A *Globe and Mail* editorial (27 April 1911) warned: 'If we freely admit Black people from that country we shall soon have the race troubles that are the blot on the civilizations of our neighbours' (reported in Boyco 1995, 155). The widely expressed view was that Black immigration should be stopped and that Blacks already in Canada should be strictly segregated or deported. Also in 1911, the Edmonton City Council passed a resolution banning Blacks from the city.

After 1899, the federal government favoured a ban on the immigration of Blacks. Covert bureaucratic action (scrutiny of prospective immigrants, ironically by an inspector named White) was favoured over overt (and potentially embarrassing) legislation. Then on 31 May 1911, the Laurier cabinet passed an Order in Council banning all Black immigration. Laurier feared that his hoped-for free trade deal with the United States might be scuttled if U.S. officials became angry about this. So he quashed the order and instead adopted rigorous medical exams, propaganda in U.S. newspapers about anti-Black sentiment in Canada, and other covert means to keep Blacks out. Railway companies cooperated by enforcing an unofficial ban on Black immigrants. Nonetheless, MPs rose in the House of Commons to demand stricter measures such as a total ban to 'preserve Canada for the White race' (Boyco 1995, 158). Nor were Blacks the only non-Whites affected. When Asians were admitted, they were restricted to urban Chinatowns. While federal immigration laws restricted entry, it was mainly local acts that maintained segregation.

In Canada, segregation survived many attempts to end it. Mobilizing opposition was always difficult because of the small numbers of Blacks in most communities. The military was segregated through two world wars, and the Red Cross carefully maintained separate Black and White blood banks. Boyco (1995, 164) notes that 'there was a long history of

Canadian courts upholding segregation laws.' This included a 1946 Supreme Court decision upholding segregation in the *Viola Desmond* case, which involved a segregated movie theatre in Halifax. In 2010 the government honoured the deceased Desmond as 'Canada's Rosa Parks'; yet the Supreme Court decision was never overturned. Provincial anti-discrimination laws (Ontario in 1944; Saskatchewan in 1947) began to turn the tide, but such laws were generally implemented as a response to international pressure and shaming. Meanwhile, segregation persisted in clubs, sports facilities, education, and employment. Moreover, residential segregation continued for some years after the embarrassing laws were repealed. Once race was removed as a legally sanctioned basis for exclusion in Canada's Immigration Act (1967), the complexion of Canada's large cities changed rapidly and a new era began in the politics of race in Canada.

Until the 1960s, segregation was the principal race regime in Canada in terms of its impact on the lives of Blacks and Asians. Largely local, and patchwork in nature, its legality was upheld on a number of occasions by the Supreme Court. It coexisted with a covert 'White Canada' regime that prevented the immigration of Blacks and Asians. Indeed, between 1899 and 1960, such immigration was effectively banned, albeit through covert measures. The small numbers of Blacks relative to the United States, and the segregation of Blacks and Asians in their own communities, allowed most Whites to deny that Canada had a race problem. In Canada, as in the United States, many Whites supported segregation, which thus probably enjoyed majority endorsement.

Segregation in Australia

In Australia, segregation did not exist as a race regime apart from internal colonialism because Australia's Indigenous people are Blacks. They were never slaves legally and were not imported from Africa. Segregation was just one strategy that the settler government used to maintain internal colonialism. The main goal of segregation was to confine Aboriginal people to missions away from towns – indeed, away from any White settlements.

The goal in this was not to prevent miscegenation. In 1828, for example, George Arthur,[9] the governor of Tasmania, issued a Proclamation of Demarcation that ordered a 'temporary separation of the colonial from the British population of this territory' (McGrath 1995, 319). The Aboriginals were expelled – that is, captured and removed by force. A similar policy developed in the other colonies. Aboriginal people had to carry passports to travel in their own country, having been declared enemy aliens in the seized and settled districts.

Segregation policies, purportedly for the 'protection' of Aboriginal peoples, were part of British colonial policy. But each British colony in Australia developed its own strategies and practices. Initially, segregation applied only to the dispossessed Aboriginal peoples, not to all Blacks, who included a small proportion of convicts transported to Australia. Markus (1994, 55) estimates there were about 900, 300 of whom had been transported from South Africa. In the first half of the nineteenth century, skin colour was less important than legal status. So neither the Black convicts nor their descendants were segregated. The scarcity of White women also shaped the policy, so segregation was a strategy applied to most Aboriginal people but not to all Blacks. Thus until the mid-twentieth century, when all-out assimilation policies were adopted, most colonies had two policies: they segregated 'full-blood,' 'tribal' Aboriginals on missions, but also tried to assimilate the 'half-breeds' who had resulted from mix-race sex. Indeed, 'breeding out to White' was encouraged. These policies created cruel separations within Aboriginal families and communities. Given the frequency of rape by White men at a time when there were very few White women, most Aboriginal women had 'half-breed' children, who if they were light-skinned were removed from their mothers to be adopted, taught to be domestics, or assimilated as prostitutes to service White men.[10]

What, then, did segregation policies and practices entail in Australia? Such policies varied from state to state both before and after federation, so we will not trace the history of policy changes in each. Instead we will outline the general approaches and assumptions common to all states, with some concrete examples. Policies also varied and changed within the general framework. Moreover, demography played a significant role in how segregation worked. Where few Aboriginal peoples survived diseases and frontier wars, 'protection' of the survivors was a more sincere goal than where larger Aboriginal communities survived on land the settlers coveted. The former situation applied in urban areas in South Australia, Victoria, and New South Wales; the latter in Queensland, Western Australia, the Northern Territory, and rural parts of the settled colonies. In Tasmania, Whites believed until recently that all Indigenous Tasmanians had perished, whereas in fact significant numbers of sexual partners of White men survived.

Segregation policies and practices were implemented after the cessation of frontier wars against Aboriginal peoples. Forced removals of Aboriginals by Whites in frontier zones continued in Australia for more than 150 years. By 1888, there were only about 60,000 Aboriginal people left on the continent (Day 1996, 130). Some were targets of segregation policies and practices. Ideology and wishful thinking held that Aboriginal people were a 'dying race.' They were thought to be 'primitive,' and it was assumed they would perish if they were not separated and protected from the 'stronger' Whites. But the segregation regimes weakened and reduced Aboriginal communities by separating light-skinned people and assimilating them, and also by keeping 'tribal' peoples out of sight and taking their lands, resources, and children from them.

Within the legal system, segregation began as a separate system of 'justice' applied to Aboriginal peoples whether or not they lived on missions. McGrath (1995, 30) concludes: 'Segregation policies therefore meant not only separate living places but special sets of regulations and an insular, subjective judicial system.' Under the influence of race theory, trivial behaviours such as untidiness were criminalized when 'committed' by Aboriginal peoples. 'Immoral conduct' (unauthorized sexual relations) was punishable by incarceration. Children were taken from their mothers by police or detained in delinquents' homes solely because of their skin colour. For much of the history of Australian segregation, Aboriginal people were denied standing in the courts because as 'primitives' and 'heathens,' they could not swear on the Bible. Even so, they were subject to the authority of the courts. The frequent procedural exclusion of Aboriginal people from the courts, even in cases affecting their lives, and the creation of segregated legal systems subsequently, were as fundamental to the blighting of their lives as the rigorously enforced ban on their living near White settlements.

At the core of the local systems of segregation was the determination of White Australian workers to exclude Aboriginals from all but the most menial employment. Segregation literally kept them out of the paid workforce so that White workers would have no competition in the 'working man's paradise.' In the United States, segregation regimes were designed to exploit African American labour; but in most situations in Australia, segregation worked to protect the jobs of White men from competition from exploitable Aboriginals or Asians. There were several exceptions to this. In remote outback areas where the pastoral industry prevailed on sheep and cattle stations, Aboriginal men worked as drovers and women as domestics. Though technically they earned wages for their work, they rarely received them because employers deducted costs of housing, food, clothes, and supplies. Those who worked on missions also received notional wages, which were mostly withheld, reflecting White views of Aboriginals' inability to handle money. The goal in the 'White man's paradise' was an exclusively European workforce with no non-Whites to drive wages down. Segregation contributed to the realization of that goal, as did the White Australia policy, which (see below) kept most other non-Whites out of Australia or deported them.

In 1893, ex-parliamentarian Archibald Meston, reporting on how Aboriginal peoples were treated, insisted that 'segregation ... was the best option to save the Aboriginal race from plummeting to extinction and to secure the White race from "contamination" through mixed-race births and disease' (Kidd 1997, 45). Queensland's colonial Home Secretary, linking Meston's ideas to rhetoric about reform, persuaded the Queensland Assembly to legislate a program of 'compulsory rescue' and retraining. Kidd documents Queensland's complex and repressive bureaucratic program over the next century to segregate 'Aboriginals.' The new laws did not apply to Aboriginals as a 'racial' group but to a specific *social* category. 'Half-castes' over sixteen who were not living with or as 'tribal' Aborigines were not covered by the laws and were instead to be assimilated – 'bred out to White.' Those who were covered by the segregation regime were subject to strict monitoring on missions, which were closed to the public. This division of the Aboriginal population served the state government's purposes. To segregate all Aborigines in missions or camps would have involved a heavy financial cost to the taxpayers. Because camps and missions were on poor land, there were few traditional Aboriginal foodstuffs available to those who resided in them, making those who had been segregated dependent on government-provided 'rations.' Those not covered by the regimes were also segregated, however, since local councils forbade them to live near Whites, denied them medical care, and denied their children access to public schools.

As late as the 1980s, the Queensland Aboriginal Department operated as a secretive agency of government. The life conditions it produced for Aboriginal people were marked by oppression and poverty: derelict housing, lack of education, minimal employment, alcoholism, domestic violence, low self-esteem, community disruption, and individual despair. To this day, many Australians view such diseases and behaviours as the result of flaws in the Aboriginal character. The recent 'intervention' in the Northern Territory by John Howard's federal government was framed in terms of Aboriginal men committing child sexual abuse as a result of drinking to excess, using pornography, and spending welfare money on those things rather than on essentials. Kidd argues that in fact, these so-called character flaws were fostered by the state-administered policies of segregation and assimilation under a regime of internal colonialism.

Again, it is important to realize that segregation was supported by the democratic majority. Premier B.D. Moorehead expressed the majority perspective: 'The Black fellows had to go ... The aboriginal race was [not] worth preserving. If there were no aboriginals it would be a very good thing' (Markus 1994, 37). Early approaches included 'clearing' territories, military-style, of their Indigenous occupants, as in Tasmania. Adopted later were 'out of sight, out of mind' policies of segregation and assimilation. Some White actors, in their well-meaning efforts to save and protect Aboriginal survivors, only victimized them further. Most White Australians, though, excluded them from humanity as a 'primitive' or 'subhuman' out-group. To 'save' them, 'half-breed' children were removed from their mothers as babies to be adopted if their skins were light; or incarcerated in institutions until they were old enough to become farmhands or domestics. Those domestics quickly ended up as prostitutes. To assimilate 'half-breeds' into White society, they were prohibited from living on missions and forced to sever their links with kin, culture, and language.

Overt policies of segregation and denial of rights became untenable after the Second World War because of international pressure. The high cost of supporting segregated Aborigines led to the adoption of forced-assimilation policies for all. In most states, Aboriginal survivors could gain freedom of movement, as well as civil and political rights – including the right to drink – provided that they 'acted White' and disassociated themselves from kin who maintained Aboriginal culture. Yet segregation persisted in housing, health, schooling, social clubs, employment, and so on. In country towns, for example, Aboriginal people are still often unwelcome in assisted housing and live together on the margins of the White community. Large cities still have Aboriginal districts dating back to the times when 'well-behaved' Aboriginal people could live near Whites as long as they 'acted White.'

Profound racism and egalitarian democracy grew in tandem in Australia to a greater extent than in North America. White democrats demanded the rule of law and a 'fair go.' Until a decade ago, fair wages were established through central arbitration tribunals. Aborigines were denied any such benefits by policies administered by democratically elected governments and supported by White majorities. When the Australian federation was formed, Aboriginal people were excluded from the jurisdiction of the Commonwealth government. They were not counted in the census, and the Commonwealth government could not legislate on their behalf. Even after the 1968 referendum changed the constitution, Commonwealth government programs to improve Aborigines' lives imposed assimilation. While no longer forcibly incarcerated, Aboriginal people are still victims of the values of the White majority – values that have made racialism integral to Australia's democracy, just as in Canada and the United States.

State-administered segregation reinforced racialist beliefs in Aboriginal inferiority. Their new status of legal equality did not disrupt the racist character of populist egalitarianism. In fact, Barry Morris argues that racism now thrives on the 'we are all equal' assertion. He writes that with the end of legal inequality and official segregation, most White Australians now blame Aborigines' negative life conditions on the Aboriginal people themselves. Critical Whites assume that since they are legally equal, Aboriginal people are poor, badly educated, unemployed, drunk, in ill health, and so on as a result of 'bad character,' bad living, or deviance. This practice of blaming the victims of racism is endemic in the thinking of all three countries and is fundamental to democratic racism.

Whites-Only Nations, Nationalism, and Nation Building

A core experience that Australia, Canada, and the United States share is that each society has been dominated by White descendants of British colonizers. In each, moreover, Whites are dominant in terms of economic, political, and cultural power and enjoy a large numerical majority. The democratic values of the new nations supported the idea that Whites had the right to segregate, exclude, or discriminate against non-Whites because they were a majority with the right to get 'their' government to rule in their own interests. This is, of course, a populist, majoritarian interpretation of democracy, one that ignores the importance of protecting minority rights. But this interpretation resonates strongly in these settler societies, each of which is handicapped by the fact that, since they had been formed by highly diverse immigrant 'stock,' the governments promoted a common sense of collective identity through race-based nationalism.

The circumstance of large White majorities holding increasingly democratic sentiments and moved by endemic racism produced two major outcomes. First, it resulted in popular nationalisms based on White solidarity, which in turn sanctioned the segregation, oppression, or attempted assimilation of non-White minorities. Second, it resulted in immigration policies based to varying degrees on race exclusion (see chapter 3). In theory, restricting in-migration worked against each country's goal of developing a continent and holding it against competition. Each settler state's primary need was to populate its land with people who could provide productive and reproductive labour. Yet to varying degrees, each country also tried to *limit* immigration by excluding non-Whites or at least keeping them from becoming citizens.

In each case, the experience of dispossessing Indigenous peoples shaped the country's subsequent responses to other race minorities. In the United States, the experiences of slavery shaped profoundly how other non-Whites were categorized and treated. There was no single model of how to deal with those categorized as racial inferiors. Indeed, there were differences in how specific race minorities were treated across the three countries and sometimes within them. In Australia, for example, Aboriginal peoples were placed outside the legal system, but the Chinese who had entered as miners or merchants before the White Australia policy was established were located within it and thus had some civil but no political rights. Yet some U.S. states categorized the Chinese with Blacks, Indians, and Mulattoes. For example, California in 1850 passed a law prohibiting Chinese from testifying in court against 'Whites,' who were defined as having less than one-eight part Negro blood (Markus 1994, 62). Across the three countries there are both similarities and differences regarding how particular non-White groups were treated and which level of government did the classifying.

We also find both similarities and differences in how race regimes were constructed and administered. In each case, however, the increasingly democratic states acted to satisfy the demands of the majority of citizens, who were White. Each government established and maintained a hierarchy of race categories through which to administer racialist practices of exclusion, as a means to legitimize the exploitation and oppression of non-White minorities. These subsequent race regimes, which were layered on top of the regimes of slavery and internal colonialism, kept the best land, White women, employment, education, medical care,

housing, social benefits, and political rights and positions for White settlers and their descendants. In the newer countries, such as Australia,
the government acted to benefit British settlers and their descendants.
Thus the socio-economic basis of White democracy was built up by denying good land, education, jobs, social benefits, and so on to non-
Whites in varying ways and degrees according to their place in this
state-maintained race hierarchy.

When exploring these issues, it is important not to conceptualize
White settlers and their descendants as all-powerful; nor should we
view all non-Whites as powerless victims. Among the White populations were convicts, indentured servants, poor Irish Catholics escaping
famine, marginal farmers, and those fleeing religious oppression. There
were also conquered French Canadians and Hispanics who had been
abandoned by their home countries when wars transferred populations
from one nationality to another. The White majorities also included poor
workers and women, who populated the land and laboured without
rights and who lived brief, hard lives while doing so. Nonetheless, settler governments were influenced increasingly by the enfranchised
White majority, even if governments generally ruled in the interests of
the more affluent White settlers.

White Nationalisms

In all three countries, governments used race prejudice to maintain
solidarity among the well-established White settlers and their depen-
dants. They did this by developing nationalism, through which White
solidarity maintained discipline among the 'in-groups,' who supported their government's nation-building projects. The content of Whites-
only nationalism varied among the three societies, but how such
nationalism was applied in nation-building was basically the same. In
each case, Whites-only nationalism was rooted in the racist idea that
the settler nation was a 'White man's paradise.' This created solidarity
– a sense of 'we-ness' – among otherwise disparate people in societies
undergoing high rates of immigration and constant internal migration.
But it also muted class conflict, especially in North America, in that
the sensibilities of those on the inside, whatever their class, were pitted against those who had been excluded or marginalized because of
their race.

This use of Whites-only nationalism to create national solidarity was
most evident in the United States, which faced the task of overcoming

the divisions created by the Civil War. In Canada, which faced French/ English conflict, British settlers struggled to assimilate waves of non-British European immigrants. Canadian nation builders, then, faced a similar problem, though they addressed it with a more covert Whites-only nationalism strategy. Likewise, in Australia, south of Asia and far from Britain, the governing elites demanded a solid commitment from newcomers to its traditional values and White Australia policies.

To understand why the leaders in these settler societies used race categories and doctrines to create cohesive nation-states, we must first understand the nature of European-style nationalisms, the diverse forms that nationalisms take, and how nationalisms functioned in settler states, in which there often were minority communities that also saw themselves as nations. First, we will explore what *nation* and *nationalism* actually mean. Perhaps no other concepts are as controversial in political science. Various theories exist regarding what a community must have to be considered a nation. The factors often discussed include a common language; a shared culture and traditions; a shared religion; a common attachment to a territory; and a common history and mythology.

To many, these theories hold that members of a nation feel they are different from non-members and from members of other nations; and that members of a nation are bound together by a 'deep, horizontal comradeship.' Those who view nations in this way believe that nations have rights – in particular, the right *to exclude those they consider foreigners;* and the right *to be autonomous or self-governing* (i.e., free from the political control of other nations). Some theories posit that nationalism is a political ideology that upholds a nation's claim to independence, self-determination, and/or autonomy. But not all nationalists seek political independence in the sense of having their own sovereign state. Some seek *cultural* autonomy – the right to control decisions about the community's cultural issues, such as language rights and religious freedoms. Many communities do demand their own state, however, and seek to separate or cast off foreign rule.

In most European countries, the development of centralized states generated pressure to homogenize culture within a nation-state's borders in order to create a society in which all citizens would speak the same language, worship in the same way, and share an identity. In settler societies, nation building also – perhaps predominantly – involved asserting dominance over the prior, dispossessed owners of the territory and creating a sense of solidarity among diverse immigrant groups against those prior owners.

Many scholars reject the idea that nations are natural entities. Instead, they claim that nations, like races, are socially constructed by nationalisms. This view is common among those who study settler societies. Raymond Breton (1986, 85) claims:

> Nationalism is an ideology, a system of ideas that orients the social construction process and legitimizes its outcome ... [It contains] principles of inclusion and exclusion. Who is an insider and an outsider? Who has the 'right stuff' to be considered a member and not an alien? Who can rightfully claim access to the resources controlled by the collectivity? Whose language and culture is to be embodied in the public institutions of the society?

In settler societies, these were burning questions as nation-building proceeded.

Similarly, Benedict Anderson conceptualizes a nation as 'an imagined political community ... imagined as both inherently limited and sovereign' (1983, 6). He believes that people imagine nations in which they would feel at home. He conceptualizes the nation as sovereign and nationalism as the product of a particular historic moment – the European Enlightenment – and thus as marked by an abstract individualism that ignores sex and class because the nation by definition is supposed to be comprised of homogeneous individuals. But especially in settler societies, European concepts often failed to square with reality. By their nature, settler societies were not homogeneous – at best they could be 'civic' nations, with solidarity revolving around shared institutions. But this was insufficient for constructing the degree of solidarity required to hold settler societies together, and hence race became the fulcrum of that solidarity.

Indigenous scholars challenge European theories of nationalism. Mohawk political scientist Gerald Alfred in *Heeding the Voices of Our Ancestors: Khanawake Mohawk Politics and the Rise of Native Nationalism* (1995) claims that Indigenous nations existed prior to European colonial powers' invasions and that Indigenous nationalism was based on values different from those deployed by European nations. He insists that though the new settler states became dominant, Indigenous communities were and are nations – a view upheld in the nineteenth century by the U.S. Supreme Court, which declared Indian tribes *domestic dependent nations*. This establishment of legal nationhood did not prevent the U.S. government from oppressing Indigenous peoples. But their

legal standing as signatories to treaties with colonial and settler governments challenges the European theorists' belief that there can only be
one nation associated with each state. This belief underlies a basic concept of Western political science: that the proper political form is a nation-
state in which one homogeneous nation is joined to one state and rules
over a territory.

Most European theorists assume that a successful polity requires
cultural, linguistic, ethnic, and racial homogeneity. In *Nations and
Nationalism* (1983), for example, Gellner asserts that homogeneity
('monogamy') is required between the dominant culture and its political
incarnation. If not, the dominant culture will use the state to create
homogeneity by repressing or eliminating other cultures, faiths, and
languages within its territory, be it 'peacefully' through assimilation or
forcibly through conquest, war, or ethnic cleansing. Settler societies
present a special circumstance, since they first must create a population
that gains the territory claimed by prior owners; then gain control by
enslaving or exploiting non-Whites; then expand its population and
control through selective immigration and assimilation. Creating a common sense of nationhood raises problems. In all three settler societies,
racialism was the tool used to foster solidarity among the White majority in order to generate a nationalism to bind together people of diverse
origins and conflicting values.

'Binding Up the Nation's Wounds' –
Nationalism after the U.S. Civil War

Anthony Marx in *Making Race and Nation* (1998, 23) argues that 'race was
not chosen randomly as a bulwark for [U.S.] nationalism.' State-building
elites in the United States used race to consolidate their support and to
create cohesiveness among northern and southern Whites who had been
bitterly divided by the Civil War. Race became the main marker of inclusion in the nation, which like citizenship was for White Americans only.
Racial discrimination had not been an explicit part of nationalism during the revolutionary era, though it existed in practice. The Declaration
of Independence, the U.S. Constitution, and the Bill of Rights reflected
universal beliefs and values that *could* apply to men and women, White
and Black, though in fact they did not. After the Civil War, the consolidation of postwar segregation race regimes made it apparent that, indeed,
the words and values of these documents were not intended to apply to
all. Confederate nationalism had built an identity around the justness

of slavery and the social system that it enabled privileged Whites to enjoy. The assassination of President Lincoln by a Confederate sympathizer and ten years of Black citizenship during Reconstruction (imposed coercively to punish southern Whites) extended the war's bitterness. To bind up the wounds and create a cohesive nation that was a precondition to economic development, northern leaders joined southerners in a common value – racial superiority. Marx concludes that 'nationhood was institutionalized on the basis of race; the political production of race and the political production of nationhood were linked' (25). As well, the flood of White European immigrants, mainly into the north and to open up the west, demanded a strong notion of race-based solidarity capable of muting emerging expressions of class consciousness.

What did institutionalizing nationhood on the basis of race involve? Recall that the Civil War did not result largely from pressures for racial equality. So while northern leaders were willing to use federal power to end slavery through war and force the states that had seceded back into the union, they had not rejected racist ideas any more than southerners had. During Reconstruction, 'Blacks jumped at the opportunity for inclusion and participation … expected as reward for their war efforts' (129). But the election of Black legislators and the Freeman Bureau's program of education and social services for southern Blacks so threatened and appalled southerners that the prospect of living in a reunited nation-state seemed to them impossible. The Black (male) franchise also reinflamed north/south conflict, thus 'undermining the prospect of unified White loyalty to the nation-state' (131). Ultimately, northern leaders would use the shared belief in White superiority to construct a postwar race-based Whites-only nationalism. African Americans were returned to a life not very different from the one they had lived under slavery, except that they could move north, which many did.

But Blacks' exclusion again from citizenship, and their *de facto* restriction to menial jobs and poor education, justified White belief in African Americans' inferiority. Hence they were excluded from the new emerging nation, a project based on extension of the economic progress in the northern states, progress that in turn was based on free labour. Also excluded were Native Americans, whose dispossession permitted American expansion westward; and by the cheap labour provided by Asians, Hispanics, and other non-Whites.

Between the 1890s and the 1960s, the U.S. federal government became increasingly active in military and economic affairs, but it did not

interfere with state-legislated and locally administered regimes of segregation and oppression. Instead it promoted nation-state consolidation
based on White solidarity and privilege. The 'American dream' was for
'White folks,' and American prosperity was for 'White folks.' The United
States, like the other two settler societies discussed in this book, fought
wars to defend democracy with segregated militaries. Basing the consolidation of the U.S. nation-state on race domination, exclusion, and
White privilege had other significant consequences besides these. It generated strong African American resistance as cohesive identities and
powerful traditions of protest developed; ultimately, these would enable Blacks to challenge the White American nation. Federal and state
governments and institutions were implicated in maintaining race hierarchy in ways that affected many other policies, especially justice and
immigration policies. Nationalism based on Whites-only solidarity
meant that challenges to segregation were considered unpatriotic, even
communist. In the remainder of this chapter, we will explore these dimensions of the politics of race in relation to the White nationalisms of
Australia and Canada.

The 'White Australia' Policy and Australian Nationalism

The semi-autonomous colonies that came together to form the Australian
federation all had White Australia policies from the 1890s. The same continued as a Commonwealth policy until it was repealed in 1972. Markus
(1994) identifies three characteristics of the policy that were common to
it in all periods. First, it restricted or denied entry into Australia, and it
enforced the deportation or relocation of some residents because of their
race, according to categories assigned by the state(s) and by state agents
such as immigration officers. Second, it involved policies aimed at exter
minating some groups (Aboriginals) or limiting their reproduction – for
example, by excluding Chinese women – in order to keep Australia's
population 'White.' Third, it denied citizenship rights to those who had
been admitted to do useful labour, while segregating those labourers
from the mainstream society and excluding them from the nation. Moreover, those to whom the policies applied included some Europeans (Italians, Greeks, and others from Mediterranean or Slavic populations),
whom inspectors racialized according to skin colour. The policy was applied to Asians, Pacific Islanders, and people from the Middle East.

Australia is a clear example of how Whites-only nationalism shaped
the character and behaviour of a settler society, even when it cost money

to preserve the nationalist ideal of a White working man's paradise. Restricting or denying entrance to Asian and Pacific Island workers, for example, resulted in lost profits for plantation owners, who wanted them to work on the plantations in the northern tropics. Chinese were also targets for exclusion because they competed with Whites in the gold fields. By 1888, all of the colonies that made up Australia had passed laws vigorously restricting the entrance of non-White labour. Consequently, the Asian population in Australia declined sharply between the 1890s and 1901. Indeed, 'the entry of any non-European to Australia was a cause for concern by the 1890s. Racism continued to gain strength, fueled by ... the growing tide of [White] nationalist sentiment' (Markus 1994, 113).

Australia took the path of excluding non-European labour rather than admitting and then exploiting non-Whites. Some scholars contend that the desire to 'keep Australia White' more effectively is what led the colonies to federate. After federation, legislation excluding non-Whites was 'a forcible manifestation of the growing sense of [White] Australian nationalism' (Jayasuriya 1997, 40). The goal was the 'preservation of British Australian nationality' as implied by the slogan 'a nation for a continent; a continent for a nation.' Jayasuriya concludes: 'Henceforth, what was generally known as the White Australia policy became the symbol of Australian nationalism ... The requirement of racial homogeneity and monoculturalism was considered to be a necessary condition of nationhood' (40).

The decision to exclude non-White *and non-British* potential immigrants, and to deport or restrict the reproduction and/or mobility of non-Whites already in the country, flowed from decisions already made in constructing Australia's founding race regimes. It also reflected White Australians' sense of being a small population spread thinly along the coasts of a large island on the edge of densely populated Asia. The determination to exclude rather than to exploit non-British labour, despite the high cost,[11] also reflected the strong egalitarianism that marked Australian Whites-only nationalism. The hallmark of this was 'mateship' among Australian soldiers (diggers) and workers. White Australian women won the vote in some states very early and could vote in Commonwealth elections from 1901. But they were excluded from this ethos of mateship, although they were needed to reproduce White Australia and so were treated as part of the nation in that regard.

White Australians agreed that the immigration of non-British people should not be allowed but their political leaders often differed on how this goal should be achieved. Some favoured a direct approach, as had been followed in the New South Wales Coloured Races Restriction Bill of 1896. But the British government feared reaction from its Japanese allies and from the empire's non-White citizens. So, as in Canada, various wide-ranging indirect measures were adopted. But measures of the sort taken by the southern U.S. states to get around constitutional guarantees of citizenship for Black men also were copied in Australia, and the White Australia legislation of 1901 provided for the exclusion of any immigrant 'who when asked to do so by an officer fails to write out at dictation … a passage of fifty words in any European language directed by the officer' (Markus 1994, 115). (An aspiring immigrant from Italy could be examined in Swedish, for example, leaving the immigration officer to determine whether s/he was 'White.') In 1905, 'any European language' was changed to 'any prescribed language' to reduce offence to Britain's Japanese allies. Moreover, this test was not just administered on entry; up until 1932 it could be administered within a year of entry, and after 1932 within five years. After 1909, no one seems ever to have passed the test, which suggests that the skills of the bureaucrats who administered it had increased.

Australia's national identity was so tied to the White Australia policy that it undertook many changes in approach to secure the core goal of Australia as a White democracy in which all who laboured were equal. First, those whom racism dictated could not be part of the nation were excluded, including dark-skinned Europeans until 1945.[12] From 1945 to 1965, however, a new approach admitted Europeans generally but vigorously imposed a policy of Anglo-conformism or *assimilation*. Entrance now was possible provided that NES (non–English-speaking) immigrants abandoned their ethnic ways and became 'true' Australians. Australian nationalism was incompatible with non–Anglo-Celtic language, names, customs, or foods. (NES sports fans who cheered for visiting foreign teams were berated by the press as recently as 1997.)

Pushed by international disapproval of the 'White Australia' policy after the race-driven horrors of the Second World War, Australia grudgingly admitted non-British Europeans and then some Middle Eastern and Latin American immigrants. Markus suggests that another major change reflected the new belief that Aboriginal people could be assimilated ('bred out to White'). This also in turn opened the doors to some 'mixed race' Asians 'if they could convince officials that they were predominantly "White"' (Markus 1994, 157). Notwithstanding these changes in the application of the policy, ideology changed little, and prejudice and discrimination persisted.

Not until 1972, under Gough Whitlam's Labor government, did Australia officially reverse its White Australia policy and begin to deconstruct or restructure these race regimes. As we discuss in chapter 3, Australian nationalism shifted to incorporate limited support for multiculturalism, though strong elements of democratic racism persist.

'White Canada' Policies

Canada's principal nation-building crisis has been the conflict between French and English. As Lord Durham reported after the 1837 rebellions, the founding problem was the conflict between two (White) nations within a single state. Indeed, until recently, political science in Canada focused almost entirely on this conflict. Nonetheless, race was an element in the construction of both founding nationalisms; and pan-Canadian nationalism and early federal immigration policy specified that Canadian citizens would be White. Moreover, the existence of a founding race regime has shaped Canada's response to non-White immigrants. The first wave of White nationalism after Confederation occurred between 1880 and 1920. In this section, we focus on the race hierarchy that made the exclusion and exploitation of non-Whites part of Canadian Whites-only nationalism.

Canadian leaders always conceived of Canada, in the words of the first prime minister, as 'a White man's country' (*Hansard*, 19 June 1869, 887, cited in Calliste and Dei 2000, 57). In competition with the United States, the Canadian state thrust itself westward, seeking sea-to-sea domination for the White settler nation. With a sparse White population, one-third of which was francophone, Canada's leaders sought to populate the vast northwestern territories with immigrants of British origins or with White Europeans who could be assimilated into a new and predominantly British nation.

From 1880 to 1900, a form of colonial nationalism developed among British Canadians whereby they asserted local interests and their desire for autonomy, but within a framework of continuing ties to the British Empire and its glories. The Imperial Federation movement expressed this mix of sentiments: Canadians would express their own interests, but Canada would be an autonomous unit within a federated empire. Eddy and Schreuder (1988) conclude that this British Canadian colonial nationalism benefited from race solidarity and privilege as it focused on creating a White Canada. Indeed, it racialized French Canadians and other non-British Whites, placing them in a hierarchy of 'races'[13] or nations in a position subordinate to the British and British Canadians. The strength and longevity of this colonial nationalism was largely a consequence of 'its capacity to incorporate into itself members of other ethnic communities' (Senese 2000, 121). As British Canadian colonial nationalism morphed into (English) Canadian nationalism, it assimilated millions of White, non-British Europeans.

In the first two decades of the twentieth century, Canada admitted almost three million immigrants, almost all of them White. To understand Canada's Whites-only nationalism in this context, we must consider immigration policy, education policy, and the administration of justice. Immigration and education policies were assimilationist for groups that could be assimilated; they excluded or 'fenced out' those deemed not assimilable. Canada, like other White settler societies, needed more inhabitants. To hold the lands taken from Indigenous peoples and against White competitors, multiple waves of immigrants were needed. Canada's covert 'Whites only' policy differed from Australia's primarily in its approach to White, non-British immigrants, which Canada absorbed early and in large numbers. Canada sought 'suitable' immigrants who could assimilate to the English language and to English Canadian culture, thereby also weakening the numerical strength of French Canada. Some potential immigrants were excluded; others were encouraged to settle. Potential immigrants were assigned to ranked categories. *Preferred* immigrants were from Great Britain, the United States, and France, followed by northern and western Europe. When these categories did not produce enough applicants, then *non-preferred* immigrants (Ukrainians, Italians, Poles, etc.) were admitted. English Canadians worked energetically in schools and settlement agencies to assimilate those in the non-preferred categories, with the goal of turning them into Canadians who would speak English and adopt Canadian ways. Whatever stigma the non-preferred White immigrants faced, they could eventually be included, and their children surely would be.

Recruitment of those in the *undesirable* category also occurred from time to time; for example, Chinese were recruited as temporary workers to build the Canadian Pacific Railway across Canada. Once the railway was built, however, White labour demanded the removal and exclusion of Asian workers. Lisa Marie Jakubowski in *Immigration and the*

Legalization of Racism (1997) demonstrates that, as in Australia, Canadian governments used indirect, bureaucratic methods to exclude potential 'undesirable' immigrants and to deny those already in Canada the status of citizens.

Canada's first Immigration Act, passed in 1910, did not use the term 'race' as a legal category to exclude or restrict immigration (13). But it did use indirect approaches, several of which Jakubowski describes. First, the 1885 Chinese Immigration Act imposed a head tax on Chinese men and blocked the entry of Chinese women and children. The head tax rose from $50 in 1885 to $100 in 1900 and to $500 by 1903. Since Chinese immigration increased despite the head tax, the Canadian government banned Chinese immigration via the Chinese Exclusion Act (1923), which was repealed only in 1947. As in Australia, the case of Japanese immigrants was more complicated because of Japan's status as Britain's ally. Here, the federal government in 1907 negotiated a 'gentleman's agreement' with Japan in which Canada would not pass exclusionary laws against Japanese but 'the Japanese government was to voluntarily restrict the number of people permitted to emigrate to Canada' (Jakubowski 1997, 13).

Regarding residents of India, Canada passed the Continuous Journey Stipulation in 1908, which forbade immigration 'otherwise than by continuous journey from countries of which they were native or citizens.' As with prospective Black immigrants, the CPR cooperated with this stipulation by not selling through-tickets to Canada from India. In 1914, the *Komagata Maru* with 376 mostly Sikh passengers attempted to land in Vancouver, having stopped along the way from India, and was denied entry by a naval vessel. This revealed the fundamental racism of Canada's nationalism. Jakubowski quotes from an immigration pamphlet that provides 'reasons' for the exclusion: 'Canada is situated in the North Temperate Zone ... The climate is particularly suited to the White race. It is the ... new homeland of the British people ... [who] soon find themselves at home in Canada' (15). The Immigration Act of 1910 explicitly used the term 'race.' The 1919 version, which was amended to add 'nationality,' denied entry to 'any nationality or race of immigrants ... deemed *unsuitable* ... or *undesirable*' (16). The test of whether a group was unsuitable or undesirable was explicitly linked to racial ideas and Anglo-conformism. The goal was 'to ... keep out ... those belonging to [races and] nationalities unlikely to assimilate and who consequently prevent the building up of a united nation of people of similar custom and ideals' (16).

We can see theories of nationalism and race interacting here as in Australia and the United States. But a central characteristic of Whites-only nationalism in both Canada and the United States was that they assimilated non-British Europeans quite effectively: in Canada, to create White English Canada; and in the United States, to create White America. Some aspects of these White immigration policies would persist. In Canada in 1967, a new Immigration Act was passed based on a 'points system' that ended much of the long-standing overt and bureaucratic exclusion, although critics argue that elements of racism persist in how points are assigned.

Conclusion

In the next chapter we explore the politics of race in all three countries through the prism of immigration and refugee policies and through an exploration of multiculturalism. A key point from this chapter to carry forward into the next is the importance of institutions in transmitting the practices and ideas associated with race regimes to subsequent generations long after legislation has been repealed and long after new legislation repudiating race-based policies has been enacted. The title of a famous British book says it all: *There Ain't No Black in the Union Jack* (Gilroy 1987). In Britain, as in the settler states we have been studying, Whites-only nationalism projects an image of who is British, Australian, or Canadian, and the odds are that many people would still exclude non-Whites from their image of these nationalities. The United States is more complex. It has the reputation of being a 'melting pot' where 'the first new nation' was created. But it, too, is a White nation to many, even now that it has a non-White president. In the next two chapters, we explore how recent generations have struggled to implement change and how racialist ideas and practices remain embedded within institutions.

Discussion Questions

1 What role has nationalism played in Australia's treatment of its Aboriginal people?
2 How did the United Kingdom's history as an empire affect the race regimes constructed in Australia, Canada, and the United States?
3 What are the fundamental differences between the United States as a 'slave state' and Canada as a 'country with slaves'?

4 Explain the basis of the 'Jim Crow' image in U.S. society and how it still affects African Americans today.
5 Was Canada exempt from segregation in its policies and practices?

3 Immigration Policy and Multiculturalism

Until recently, Australian, Canadian, and U.S. political elites explicitly treated their countries as White men's. But since governments in all three sought continent-wide domination, they had to import immigrants, both free and coerced, to build the nations they dominated. Other settler societies – in Latin America, for example – were more densely populated when the Europeans arrived, and more Indigenous people survived the conflicts and the diseases the Europeans brought with them. Hence the governments of these three settler societies discussed in this book faced serious labour shortages because Indigenous people were fewer to start with and had been reduced even further by the violence of colonial contact and by disease. These settler societies faced the basic question of how to recruit large numbers of voluntary and involuntary migrants over long periods of time. The British settler elites established self-sustaining colonies that quickly became independent of Britain except for defence, and those colonies ultimately formed federations. The Whites-only nationalisms that drove Canadian and American westward expansion had the capacity – which 'White Australia' did not – to assimilate large numbers of non-British immigrants. In the early twentieth century the Canadian government absorbed nearly three million immigrants, settling them on land taken from Indigenous people, in a successful effort to hold the West against the United States. With so many White immigrants assimilated, British North America gradually became English Canada, French Canada's strength in numbers having declined somewhat. Notwithstanding the myth of the 'Canadian mosaic,' Canada was a melting pot like the United States, and its governments pursued a policy of Anglo-conformism, not multiculturalism.

In this chapter we explore the comparative politics of race as manifested in the more recent immigration and diversity management policies of these settler societies. Though we discuss all three countries, this chapter focuses most on Australia, which has encountered a greater number of conflicts and debates about immigration.[1] We explore recent policies regarding authorized and unauthorized immigration, but contextualize them by recognizing that colonization involved initial migrations of White settlers who took over the countries they entered. We also explore the multicultural policies in each of the three societies, describing how they are part of diversity management strategies in Canada and Australia, whereas they are part of 'bottom-up' anti-racism coalition building in the United States.

In the 1960s all three governments abolished their explicitly racist immigration policies, in Australia and Canada largely because of pressure from the United Nations. Despite their new and apparently nonracist immigration policies, the White descendants of European settlers (and of British settlers in Australia) remained politically dominant and in control of immigration policy. By now, however, more authorized immigrants were coming from countries in the global South, who had darker skins, and non-Christian religions; and as a consequence, immigration became a political lightning rod to some extent in the politics of race in all three countries. Canada and the United States are both quite heterogeneous societies; Australia is more monocultural. Canada and Australia have recently experienced high levels of authorized immigration; the rate of immigration is lower today in the United States, though it experienced very high rates in the previous century. However, the United States experiences high rates of *unauthorized* migration, especially along its southern border. Immigration reform, amnesty, the rights of unauthorized immigrants to state services, and the fence being built along the Mexican border are all hot-button political issues in the present day. Both Canada and Australia face boatloads of unauthorized immigrants trying to land on their shores. Australia repels these ships before they land and incarcerates any refugee claimants who do land. The case of the *Tampa* (see below) was a flashpoint issue in the previous Commonwealth election and likely contributed to the defeat of John Howard's government. It is only since the federal Conservatives led by Stephen Harper won a majority after years of minority parliaments that similar strategies have been announced in Canada.

Immigration in Settler Societies

Historically, colonization and immigration have been overlapping processes in these settler societies. In each, the story of nation building by the dominant White population is simultaneously a story of recruiting suitable immigrants and settling them on lands from which Indigenous peoples have been dispossessed,[2] while other European settler groups are being assimilated. The United States acquired territory by conquest, misrepresentation, or purchase, in the process incorporating large mixed-race and Indigenous groups. When international disapproval brought an end to overtly racist policies in Australia and Canada, immigration control became especially important because neither policies of assimilation nor policies of exclusion had been wholly successful in those countries (Stasiulis and Yuval-Davis 1995, 23). Their general strategy has been to recruit those who can be assimilated while incorporating at least some authorized immigrants who are different but seem most assimilable. As we explore below, many observers contend that multicultural policies were originally developed to address this problem. International pressure has had limited impact on the United States because of its postwar status as a superpower. In any event, its long experiences with slavery, segregation, and persistent state racism protected by federalism have made the situation more fraught.

In all three countries, both political polarization and conflict over immigration control tend to map onto economic recessions. These are wealthy countries with White majorities that tend to enjoy high living standards, so especially in periods of economic shrinkage, White citizens defend their privilege from 'aliens' – a category whose construction draws upon historical notions of racial and ethnic inferiority (Stasiulis and Yuval-Davis 1995, 24). Who is constructed as an 'alien' changes with changes in global politics. So while in the 1960s and 1970s, Australian gatekeepers admitted light-skinned people from the Middle East (e.g., from Lebanon), assuming that they could be assimilated, post-9/11 attitudes have created conflicts that are visible in overt expressions of hostility, including riots.

In this chapter, first we explore the politics of race in relation to immigration in Canada. Then we consider the partisan conflicts over immigration policies in the United States. Finally, we consider the issues raised by immigration policies in Australia. In the section for each country, we also consider how multiculturalism has been developed and deployed as state policy.

Immigration and Multicultural Policy in Canada

Canada's Immigration Act of 1967 introduced a points system that ended much of the overt and covert bureaucratic exclusion of those who in the past had been considered undesirable. Though the numbers of non-White immigrants increased significantly after the 1967 act was passed, creating a more multiracial population, some bias has remained. This is evidenced by the fact that of the eighty visa offices outside Canada in 2010, eleven were in Europe and six in the United States, compared to just eighteen for all of Asia and the Pacific region and just seventeen for Latin America and the Caribbean.[3] Subsequent legislative reforms have tried to respond to some criticisms made by pro-migrant groups.

In both Canada and the United States, overtly racist immigration policies were removed in the mid-1960s. Since then, immigrants have increasingly come from countries outside Europe (Abu Laban and Garber 2005, 525). The Immigration and Refugee Act of 2002 created three categories: those admitted for economic reasons, by far the largest; those admitted for humanitarian reasons; and those admitted to enable family reunification. Recent Conservative government's statements on immigration have emphasized Canada's labour needs. But immigration policy is somewhat more complex than this: it is a shared federal/ provincial responsibility, and Quebec is concerned about the possible immigration of English-speakers – or those likely to assimilate to English – at levels that would swamp the 'French fact' in Canada. So while the federal government hunts for affluent immigrants who can bring capital and generate jobs, Quebec strives to increase francophone migration. This makes immigration and associated language training programs part of the competing nation-building projects and potential conflicts between the two. This further complicates the race dimension of immigration in Canada.

In the 1990s, as the numbers of White immigrants to Canada declined, the proportion of immigrants who are non-White increased to 73 per cent – a percentage that continues to climb (Esses et al. 2007, 115). While the overt racism of the past has lessened, more subtle forms of discrimination have emerged. With Canada's historic need for labour and the decline in European immigrants (Hawthorne 2007, 4), the latest data show that the country has come to depend heavily on Asia as the primary source countries of economic applicants. In 2004, for example, China contributed 18 per cent of immigrants to Canada, India 11 per cent, and the Philippines (7 per cent) (Hawthorne, citing Hiebert 2006, 4). Markedly different groups make the transition to professional employment in the first five years after migration. Employers favour immigrants with English- or French-speaking backgrounds or from Western countries whose training systems are comparable to Canadian ones. So about 60 per cent of professionals from South Africa, Australia, and New Zealand have found work in their own profession or a related one within five years of arriving in Canada, as have about 50 per cent for those from Britain, Ireland, northwestern Europe, and the United States (Hawthorne, citing Hiebert 2006, 4). Those from non–English-speaking, non-Western countries, Hawthorne suggests, experience deskilling or skill discounting.

Esses and colleagues (2007, 114–17) have found that foreign credentials are an asset only for those who are *not* members of a visible or religious minority. Thus, when it comes to physicians licensed to practise in Canada, foreign training and experience produce higher evaluations for White applicants than for Chinese or East Indian ones, even when their qualifications are identical. Non-White economic immigrants in particular find that their skills, even when they have been valued highly during the application process, are devalued or not recognized when they actually seek employment. The immigrants who are most likely to be deskilled in this way are members of (or look like members of) Canada's race minorities – that is, they were among those 73 per cent of (non-White) immigrants in the 1990s. This suggests that despite revamped immigration laws, deeply entrenched racialism may come into play when non-White immigrants seek employment. And employment is the key to gaining the full privileges and benefits of Canadian citizenship.

It needs to be asked why those who act on the basis of racist attitudes are not stopped or punished. First, effective remedies require institutions that immigrants can approach for redress. But government institutions offer limited redress because of policy legacies holding that education is the most valuable tool to apply against racism. Canada's liberal valorization of re-education, however, inhibits effective sanctioning of those who harm specific individuals because of their skin colour or other attributes of racialization. Citizens can resort to the Charter of Rights and Freedoms to protect themselves from race-based acts or bias by governments, provided they can and will go to court. But the Charter provides no protection when those acts are carried out by non-government institutions or individuals. In such cases, those who experience racist acts must make their claims in front of a federal or provincial human rights tribunal. (Human rights protection is under provincial jurisdiction unless the institution is under federal jurisdiction.) This limits legal redress, because Canada's human rights laws and tribunals emphasize education and reconciliation. Access to the courts under human rights law is possible only after the griever has sought remedy from a human rights tribunal, which can take a long time.

The federal government adopted official multiculturalism in 1971. Constitutional recognition of Canada's multicultural heritage was entrenched in the Charter of Rights and Freedoms in 1982. In theory, this should foster diversity and compensate for the current effects of past racist policies – policy legacies – by acknowledging that people from many cultures have contributed to building Canada. Indeed, multiculturalism policy and discourses have led many race minority immigrants to expect that they will have the same life opportunities as White Canadians. Most immigrants, though, perceive multiculturalism as largely symbolic and as not very effective at equalizing access to critical resources and job opportunities. Freda Hawkins (1991, 215) writes that on the one hand, 'multiculturalism was a highly political phenomenon, involving ... [a] special relationship between government and ethnic communities, but that the relationship was difficult to handle politically in a liberal democratic society which has already established values and traditions relating to citizenship, justice, equality, political participation and human rights.'

Multiculturalism has focused largely on public celebrations (such as Black and Asian history months), on public funding for academic research, and on media coverage of the successful settlement of high-profile refugees, mainly from Africa and Asia. Mainly symbolic, it has fostered the appointment of Indigenous people and immigrant race minorities as Governors General and Lieutenant Governors of the provinces and territories (Isaac 2008), but the proportion of elected politicians who are 'visible' minorities is less than those groups' percentages in the population, as noted earlier. There is some evidence that in the future, constitutional multiculturalism may positively affect legal cases brought by race minorities. But the extent to which minorities will be required to adapt to Canadian laws remains untested. Cases involving polygamy, which currently are working their way through the courts, will provide a better indication of the appropriate balance between equality rights – in this case, women's – and the rights of religious minorities, both of which are protected by the Charter.

But the overall perception of White Canadians is that multiculturalism is largely the concern of minorities, many of whom are non-White. They perceive Canada as defined by its anglophone or francophone character. Ironically, multicultural policy was developed originally by a Liberal federal government to placate *White* ethnic minorities (Ukrainians,

Italians, Poles, etc.) – that is, it was a legacy of Prime Minister Pierre Trudeau, who introduced bilingualism policies, most notably the affirmative action hiring of francophones, whom the Royal Commission on Bilingualism and Biculturalism found were underrepresented in the federal civil service. When other White ethnic groups protested against the entrenchment of the 'two founding nations' narrative of (White) Canada's development, Trudeau declared that having two official languages would not mean having an official culture. Whatever Trudeau's motives, successive Liberal and Conservative governments have used multiculturalism to create a bureaucracy – the Department of Canadian Heritage – to politically target segments of ethnocultural communities, to promote international trade, and to serve as a flagship for global discourses on multiculturalism (Abu-Laban and Gabriel 2002).

Relative to our study, it is also important to highlight some provincial debates and criticisms of this federal policy. Quebec governments, for example, tend to view multiculturalism as a federal policy designed to undercut their claims by conflating them with those of immigrant ethnic groups. Many Indigenous people also reject multiculturalism on similar grounds, arguing that it tends to frame their differences as racial and equate them with the claims of immigrant race minorities. Describing themselves as First Nations, they assert their claims within a framework of internal colonialism, in which they are the only Indigenous people, with everyone else being immigrants or descendants of immigrants.

The Québécois also resist multiculturalism's focus on culture rather than language. Quebec governments have developed a competing policy of *interculturalism,* which stresses that immigrants must accept Quebec's core values, defined as including women's equality and secularism, and adopt French as their public language and as the language of their children's education. Interculturalism is intended to undercut the federal government's policy of multiculturalism, given that Quebec shares constitutional responsibility for immigration with the federal government. Other provinces have adapted, reformed, or repealed the federal Multicultural Act by advancing their own statutes. But as Garcea (2006) notes, their citizens are more aware of federal multiculturalism policy, especially since 1982, when the Charter entrenched respect for Canada's multicultural heritage as a constitutionally protected value. (Article 27 states: 'This Charter shall be interpreted in a manner consistent with the preservation and enhancement of the multicultural heritage of Canadians.') Intercultural policy reflects Quebec nationalism and aspirations for autonomy or even sovereignty; this nationalist project has strongly affected its governments' approaches to cultural diversity regardless of party. From the perspective of non-White immigrants, however, the functions of multicultural and intercultural policies are similar – to incorporate them into the dominant (White) francophone and anglophone cultural frameworks.

Many anti-racism scholars and activists argue that, whatever the origins of Canada's official multiculturalism policy, it has become part of the federal state's strategy for managing diversity, notably regarding race. Bannerji (2000, 9) sees it resulting from 'the juxtaposition of a rapid influx of Third World (mostly not-White) immigrants ... as well as ... a moment of growing intensity of the old English-French rivalry, and as a diffusing or muting device for francophone nationalist aspirations ... as a way of coping with the non-European immigrants arrival ... [and of sidelining] the claims of Canada's aboriginal population.' By reducing the demands of all of these groups into cultural claims, the state can manage them within the existing framework of Canadian nationhood. Multiculturalism forms part of the (federal) state's constitution and its administrative apparatus only in Canada, which suggests that Ottawa is aware of the intractability of such diverse demands when they are expressed in terms of race or class conflict. Official multiculturalism constructs categories such as visible minorities and people of colour in an effort to incorporate their various multicultures into an overarching (White) Canadian culture. Bannerji (37) believes that this administrative language protects ideologies and practices that are already in place and that it is postulated on the pluralist premises of a liberal democratic state, premises such as legal equality. This helps us understand why, for example, human rights tribunals treat cases of individuals rather than groups; why they lack proper enforcement powers and must rely on education and reconciliation; and why they often constitute roadblocks to groups wishing to pursue court action.

Immigration and Multicultural Politics in the United States

In all three settler states, the desire for free or cheap labour has been a key factor in terms of *which* groups states have recruited for the labour pool and *how* that recruitment has been carried out. In the United States, the enslavement of Indigenous people and Africans was a key recruitment tool, but convict labour and indentured (White) labour also played a role. So did the unpaid labour of White and non-White women and the exploitation of poor, non-unionized workers. Replacing this labour pool later on were the occupants of appropriated or purchased territories in Mexico and immigrants from Asia and, more recently still, from other parts of Latin America, the Caribbean, and South Asia. Most analyses of U.S. immigration history ignore or discount the displacement of Indigenous peoples and focus largely on race and population issues through the lens of slavery, the Civil War, and the Civil Rights movement. They view the conflict as a dynamic one between the White majority and African Americans. In this book, we also consider immigration and race issues with regard to other populations, notably Hispanics/Latinos.

The politics of race and immigration displayed similar trends in all three settler states until after the Second World War, when the United States became a superpower. Until the 1960s, each state had its own system of immigration quotas, which favoured (most) European migrants; and each had its own exclusionary system aimed at non-White groups. All three countries legislated to exclude Chinese immigrants, requiring payment of ever-higher head taxes by those men allowed to enter. Women were more rigorously excluded. The United States replaced its European-focused quota system in the 1960s with a global quota system and a multicategory visa structure. Successful applicants obtained a green card – the official document that opened access to jobs and services and eventually to full citizenship. Unlike in Australia and Canada, however, demand for authorized immigration to the United States from Whites remains strong.

Immigration policies, laws, and management approaches are at the core of nation building, sovereignty, and identity. This makes immigration control one of the most contentious issues that politicians face in all three White-majority settler states. Immigration control is probably the single most contentious issue in American domestic politics today, though its salience has varied over time. Immigration control involves both federal and state institutions, including the U.S. Supreme Court, which interprets immigration law; congressional committees, which make that law; and the Justice and Homeland Security departments, which administer laws and rulings and through their regulations now make *and* enforce policy (Rosenblum 2009, 29). Unauthorized immigrants and their supporters organize huge rallies to politicize their plight; for example, in 2006, they held a 'day without immigrants,' which was intended to bring the economy to a crawl and to show their economic importance (Swain 2007, 7). In 2010, large demonstrations in

Washington protested against President Obama's neglect of immigration issues. Also in 2010, thousands marched across U.S. cities against a controversial new immigration law enacted in Arizona (CBC 2010).[4]

Next we highlight some aspects of the politics of race in relation to immigration in the United States, including unauthorized migration, amnesty, the California legislation that denied unauthorized immigrants state services, the fence along the Mexican border, and current pressures surrounding reform. We focus mainly on issues affecting unauthorized, race-minority migrants, but their issues and the political and socio-economic conditions of authorized immigrants often coincide when the latter are poor and of minority race. Hence all non-White immigrants can be easy targets for racist stereotyping by the public, the media, state and federal legislators, judges, and other government officials.

The Civil Rights movement promoted changes in the Immigration Acts in 1965 – specifically, the removal of overtly racist provisions. The resulting new acts allowed a massive influx of *authorized* immigrants from Latin America, Asia, Africa, and the Caribbean (Walton and Smith 2003, 94). Meanwhile, economic globalization and refugee situations worldwide have placed great pressure on the United States. (See chapter 7 for an analysis that links U.S. activities as a hemispheric and then global superpower with these pressures.) It has been estimated that unauthorized immigrants (whom opponents describe as illegal and 'alien') are less than 2 per cent of the U.S. population – 12 million people in a population of over 300 million. Nonetheless, that proportion has generated a major political ruckus at times, because these immigrants are densely concentrated in a few states along the Mexican border. (Yet in earlier decades, Mexican immigrants were actually *solicited* after laws limiting Asian immigration were passed.) In 1990, California had over 45 per cent of the country's undocumented residents. By 2010 that had dropped to 24 per cent as a result of repressive policies (see below). Most other undocumented residents live in North Carolina, Georgia, Tennessee, and Arizona (Pickus and Skerry 2007, 98), and most are Hispanics from Mexico and Central America. (See chapter 7 for a detailed description of the multiple origins of the Hispanic population, now the largest minority in the United States.)

In recent decades, the demand for cheap labour in the formal and underground economies has fuelled a great deal of unauthorized immigration. The United States is seen everywhere as a land of opportunity; thus it is a magnet for immigrants seeking better lives. Australia and Canada currently have higher rates of authorized immigration than the United States; but the latter has a (proportionately) larger problem with unauthorized entries. Over the past fifty years, the pull of the United States has been globalized by the Americanization of cultural media dominated by Hollywood, Disney, and telecommunications, all of which have spread the American Dream worldwide. For unauthorized immigrants, the risks of criminal conviction and deportation, perhaps even a life without an identity, are not a deterrent. Not all unauthorized immigrants are from racialized populations, but many are. We focus on racialized populations in our analysis, but we are not unaware of the negative situations facing White unauthorized immigrants, many of whom are women from countries of the former Soviet Union and its satellites, who have been coerced into sexual slavery from former USSR countries and in Eastern Europe.

How the issue of unauthorized, race-minority migrants is framed depends on who does the framing. Media reports, including television news, radio talk shows, newspapers, and online blogs, portray unauthorized immigrants, especially those of Hispanic/Latino background, as enemies to poor African Americans, with whom they compete for jobs, housing, and political clout. Areas with high concentrations of poor African Americans, Asians, and Hispanics experience racial tension, crime, and gang warfare, which media outlets attribute to unauthorized immigration. Such claims are often drawn from census data showing that Latinos now equal or exceed African Americans in terms of population proportion. This is seen as a source of tension within these communities; it is also feared by the dominant White majority. This is of no small significance, for immigrants, regardless of their status, tilt the relative proportion of the competing minority populations, and this greatly affects political representation in state and federal bureaucracies and institutions.

The Center for Immigration Studies reports in its 2010 survey that most members of Hispanic, African American, and Asian minorities prefer that unauthorized immigrants be removed from the country and consider the current level of *authorized* immigration too high (Camarota 2010, 2). But Wingfield and Feagin (2010) see the portrayal of conflict between African Americans and Hispanics as an example of the 'hard' version of the White framing of such phenomena – a framing that is often openly racist and that public commentators resort to when rationalizing racial hierarchies, which they do in part by describing non-Whites as in conflict with one another. Wingfield and Feagin (167) contend that conventional White framing has portrayed both Latino and

African Americans as prone to criminal behaviour and poverty. The dominant White majority often uses this sort of racial framing to pit these two broad groups against each other. In the 2008 presidential primaries, some news media claimed that Hispanics would not vote for Barack Obama if he won the Democratic presidential nomination, because they preferred (White) Hillary Clinton. Some even predicted that Hispanics would vote for John McCain. Yet as it turned out, 67 per cent of Hispanics in exit polls reported voting for Obama (174). Moreover, Hispanics and African Americans support each other in state and local elections, in civil rights activism, and in other political activities such as those aimed at improving social benefits and welfare. That said, coalitions between African Americans and Hispanics are not always smooth. For example, in 1975, the Leadership Conference on Civil Rights (LCCR)[5] did not support action to end discrimination against language minorities. Hispanic groups had to fight on their own to have language rights covered by the Voting Rights Acts. At the time, this soured their relations with African American members (Walton and Smith 2003, 122).

Divisions are inevitable when race minority groups are pitted against one another by White politicians and media in the contest for scarce employment and life resources. Conservative White elites experience coalitions among race minorities and increases in their numbers as especially threatening because of the political power that such coalitions can wield. Indeed, often as not, the intense debate around unauthorized migration is portrayed as a conflict between race minorities, who support open migration, and the White majority, which does not. Yet many members of racialized minorities oppose increased immigration levels, whereas business groups dominated by White elites have much to gain from high levels of immigration – especially of unauthorized immigrants, who are easy to exploit. Not surprisingly, while federal Republicans (Bush and McCain) supported reforms that would have left the system more or less intact, Republicans at the state level favour crackdowns. What emerges from this picture is that hostility in the United States to immigrants – authorized or not – unquestionably relates to race, as well as to commentators' perceptions of their own economic situations.

Amnesty policies involve either pardoning immigrants for their unauthorized entry or providing some path to full citizenship for those already in the country. Such proposals usually reflect the fact that the federal government, which is responsible for enforcing immigration policies, has been administratively overwhelmed by the present numbers of unauthorized immigrants. To understand why amnesty policies are being demanded from some quarters, we next examine the development of immigration legislation since 1965. With passage of the Immigration and Nationality Act (1965), which ended the bias favouring Europeans, the number of people wanting to immigrate to the United States began to vastly outstrip the quotas of visas allocated to countries around the world. That 1965 act, which was changed repeatedly, precipitated major increases in unauthorized entry (Wroe 2008, 20). Those who could not enter took advantage of visitor's visas, staying after they had expired, putting down roots, working in the underground economy, establishing families, buying homes, and so on. This was facilitated by the absence of documentation at the federal level – for example, birth certificates in most states are issued by local authorities, making it fairly easy to adopt the identity of someone who was born in the United States but has since died. At the same time, more migrant workers admitted from Mexico to work in agriculture stayed after their seasonal contracts had expired. Over the decades, hundreds of thousands more risked arrest by crossing the porous international border.

In 1986, faced with an obvious immigration crisis, the U.S. Congress passed the Immigration Reform and Control Act (IRCA), which focused almost exclusively on illegal immigration. It offered amnesty to undocumented residents who could prove that they had arrived prior to 1 January 1982, and this provided a path toward temporary residence status, then permanent legal status, and then – five years later – citizenship (Wroe 2008, 20). There have been several subsequent amnesties, and until recently, undocumented immigrants who had U.S.-born children could obtain a green card. Every year, 50,000 undocumented residents win a green card in Homeland Security's Diversity Lottery (Pickus and Skerry 2007, 101).

Congress has passed numerous laws regarding unauthorized immigration, such as the Illegal Immigration Reform and Immigrant Responsibility Act (IIRIRA). Passed under President Bill Clinton in 1996, it created the category of unlawfully present persons and imposed temporary or permanent bars on re-entry into the United States for those convicted. Up until that time, immediate deportation could have occurred only after conviction for an offence that could lead to five or more years in prison. Now, a conviction for a minor offence could make an individual eligible for deportation. Initially, the law applied retroactively to all non-citizens convicted of deportable offences; however, in 2001 the Supreme Court ruled that individuals who pleaded guilty to a deportable offence before the law's enactment could not be deported unless they had also pleaded guilty to a deportable offence *before* the law was passed. This law also doubled the number of Border Patrol agents to ten thousand over five years, and it called for fences to be built along parts of the U.S.–Mexico border. It also authorized state and local law enforcement personnel to enforce immigration law if there was a mass influx of aliens. And it made it possible for the Attorney General to delegate immigration law enforcement to state and local police after training and a formal agreement with the Justice Department. This part of the law has been implemented by California, Florida, Arizona, and North Carolina as of 2006 (National Immigration Forum 2007).

Following the IIRIRA's passage, Operation Hold-the-Line in Texas, Operation Safeguard in Arizona, and Operation Gatekeeper in California all built fences at strategic points along the border with Mexico. Fences also have been built in New Mexico. The fences have been criticized for their cost, for being ineffective, for increasing the physical risks of crossing the border illegally, and for destroying habitats. In addition, the tribal lands of the O'odham, Cocopah, and Kickapoo nations have been split by the fences, and some municipalities and landowners object to the building of fences on their lands. Attempts to legislate comprehensive immigration reform having failed, the Secure Fence Act was passed in 2006, authorizing and partly funding the construction of seven hundred miles of barriers along the border. Then in 2010, President Obama signed the Recovery and Reinvestment Act, which provided over more than $400 million in funds to strengthen security and infrastructure at southwestern entry points on the Southwest border.[6] Clearly, that amnesty has not stemmed the tide of undocumented immigrants; moreover, although the punishments have greatly affected Mexicans and other Latin Americans crossing the border, other immigrants, too, have also experienced arrest, imprisonment, and deportation. For example, some of the unprecedented criminal activity in Caribbean countries is carried out by deported U.S. residents, many of whom left their island of birth when very young and learned their criminal behaviour in the United States.

The 9/11 attacks were a watershed in U.S. immigration politics. They especially affected Hispanic people, as well as Arab/Middle Eastern populations, who mistakenly were all thought to be Muslim. (See chapter 7 for a discussion of Islamophobia.) U.S. immigration policy is now inextricably linked to 'security' policy and counterterrorism practices. And immigrant communities (authorized and unauthorized) are experiencing the negative consequences the most. Measures the federal government has taken include criminalizing immigrants who fail to conform to new change-of-address requirements and transferring to state and local authorities the responsibility for enforcing federal immigration law. In both cases, Hispanics have experienced the most negative effects, despite there being no evidence of their involvement in terrorism. (The consequences of the fact that some look like stereotypical Arab terrorists are discussed in chapter 7.) For example, driver's licences are needed to participate in daily life in the United States beyond driving: such ID is needed for banking, renting an apartment, and receiving utilities. Since 2001, many states have enacted restrictions on immigrants' access to driver's licences, with great disruption resulting. Many legal immigrants have lost their jobs because of the intensified emphasis on workplace enforcement against hiring undocumented immigrants. The Aviation and Transportation Security Act (2002) requires that all baggage screeners be U.S. citizens, and this has linked citizenship to national security, again resulting in the loss of jobs for thousands of *authorized* immigrants. Many undocumented immigrants who worked in any way on military bases – and even in public transportation or garbage removal – have also lost their jobs.[7] The evidence suggests that the 2001 attacks have made life difficult for *all* race-minority migrants, authorized or not.

Twenty-four states allow ballot initiatives (to generate policy/laws); a further (overlapping) twenty-four states allow for popular referendums; some states allow for both (National Conference of State Legislatures 2006). In the 2006 general election, more than 230 ballot initiatives that would have affected minority-race immigrants were proposed, though few actually made it onto the ballot, and only a few of these addressed immigration issues. But seven of the twenty-five states that have declared English their official language did so using a ballot measure (Ballot Initiative Strategy Center 2010). The first immigration-related ballot initiative, in 1994, was California's Proposition 187, which proposed that unauthorized immigrants be denied access to many federal and state-funded public services. In 1995, eleven lawsuits were filed against the resulting law, so the courts barred it from taking effect. In 1998, courts ruled that those provisions involving federal powers (1, 4–9) were unenforceable but that provisions 2 and 3, dealing with counterfeit citizenship documents, could stand. In 2004, Arizona's Proposition 200 passed, requiring proof of citizenship to register to vote, photo ID to vote on Election Day, that all applicants for public benefits demonstrate

U.S. citizenship, and that government officials who failed to report suspected immigration violations be subject to a fine. A week after it passed, the U.S. Attorney General announced that the initiative would not affect any benefits under federal law; nor would it affect access to public housing, health care, or post-secondary education, all of which involve federal funding. Nonetheless, legal challenges are pending, including one against the AG's interpretation of the initiative. The U.S. Congress's repeated failures to pass comprehensive immigration reform measures in 2006 prompted still more initiatives, with immigration-related measures passed in three states: Arizona, Colorado, and New Mexico (see the National Conference of State Legislatures for details). In 2008, however, few initiatives made it onto the ballot, and two of those which did, failed.

In thirty-one states there are 'sanctuary cities' that have enacted policies to protect unauthorized immigrants by refusing to let their resources or employees be used to enforce the oppressive provisions of federal immigration laws. This usually involves prohibiting city employees, including the police, from determining an individual's immigration status. This dates back to 1979, when Los Angeles enacted Special Order 40 prohibiting police officers from inquiring after a person's status or arresting people for immigration law violations. Sanctuary cities include Washington, New York City, Dallas, Austin, Jersey City, San Francisco, Miami, and Phoenix. In 2007 the U.S. House of Representatives tried to apply fiscal pressure to end sanctuary practices, passing legislation making such practices a felony. Neither effort passed the Senate. Georgia and Tennessee, however, have successfully legislated to prohibit and/or punish sanctuary practices.

Multiculturalism in the United States

In Canada, multiculturalism was a top-down policy developed by the federal state to help it manage diversity, partly by creating a discourse of a peaceful coexistence. In the United States, it is an aspect of government policy only regarding such things as government funding for museums to support exhibits about diversity. Historically, nation building in the United States involved the 'melting pot' metaphor, with many ethnic groups combining to form a new American identity, albeit with English as the common language and with British-based legal and electoral systems. Because both federal and state government institutions historically maintained rigid legal categories of White and non-White to administer slavery, laws forbidding mixed-race marriage, segregation, and so on, differences understood as racial could not be melted and mixed-race (White/non-White) individuals were categorized as non-White. (See chapter 1 for a discussion of Census Bureau categories.) Because the historical legacies of these race regimes persist – not least in government statistical categories – they shape American life and politics and make a multicultural vision potentially radical. For example, inter-racial marital/sexual relations are now largely tolerated in cities outside the south, but many people remember a time when they were illegal and could result in the lynching of African American and other non-White men. But the rapidly growing racial diversity of the U.S. population resulting from immigration and intermarriage has created both inter-racial conflict and political cooperation across state-made racial catego-ries. Without such cooperation, Barack Obama could never have been elected president, especially given the profound determination of many Whites that 'no Black man will ever run *my* country.'[8] It is in this context that multiculturalism becomes an ideological tool for bottom-up alli-ance building. But such alliances are complex, because they combine native-born people with immigrants whose experiences of racism differ. Whether or not they are immigrants, African Americans are racially cat-egorized, though if they are immigrants, they also experience ethnic differences. Hispanics, meanwhile, are categorized as an ethnic com-munity but are internally divided by race. Can multiculturalism help bridge all of this diversity?

Commenting on official and White uses of multiculturalism, radical African American activist Angela Davis in 1996 offered a metaphor many now use instead of the melting pot; she likened the multicultural society of the United States to a salad made up of many colourful and beautiful ingredients (cited in Bannerji 2000, 15). Against the United States' powerful nationalism bent on assimilation and characterized by a general drive to 'Americanize' all diverse cultures within its boundar-ies, the salad image doesn't seem very radical. In the 1980s, most anti-racist activists and scholars in the United States rejected multiculturalism because they thought it replaced race and racism with an emphasis on *cultural* diversity, thus ignoring race minorities' inferior political and economic power, which made it hard for them to use their cultural diversity creatively.[9] It was their development of the concept of cultural *hybridity* – which some consider basic to multiculturalism – that gave multiculturalism a populist and more radical face.

In *Revolutionary Multiculturalisms* (1997), Peter McLaren claimed that in contrast to the hard-edged borders created by state race categories that make cross-category political relations so difficult, multiculturalism provides a freeing sense of indeterminacy as well as overlapping cultural identifications and social practices (cited in Bannerji 2000, 190). Others stress multiculturalism's discursive potential for creating more fluid identities without the hard borders of state-made race categories. One example relates to U.S. feminists, who tried to construct a political category of women of colour to unite African American and Hispanic feminists around their shared experiences and identities. In this effort, multiculturalism's re-conceptualization of identities as shared and relational (women of colour) rather than foundational (Chicana, Black) is valuable. Hence multiculturalism from below can be a strategy involving the forging of an oppositional/coalitional identity in which women *become* and are not *born* women of colour (Bannerji 2000, 25). Ruth Frankenberg (1993) extended this radical potential to White feminists in her controversial analysis of the social construction of Whiteness. Ultimately, multiracial approaches and critical anti-racism have been more effective bottom-up strategies for contesting the current race hierarchies and undermining democratic racism in the United States. Meanwhile, though, multiculturalism has been adopted by corporations eager to manage diversity among their employees and to sell merchandise and services to racially diverse consumers.

Immigration and Multicultural Politics in Australia

Earlier, we explored the White Australia policy rescinded in 1972. In this section we examine the race aspects of Australia's immigration policy after 1972. Our analysis considers immigration policies first from 1945 to 1990, and then up until the defeat of the Howard government. We discuss multiculturalism in these sections on immigration and then the problems facing Australia's refugee policies in recent decades, especially the treatment of asylum seekers, which scandalized many in the international community. Australia's multicultural policy was a political lightning rod in a way unmatched in the United States or Canada. So this chapter ends with an assessment of Australia's treatment of non-White and/or non-Christian refugees and asylum seekers. Ironically, while the White Australia policy ended with little domestic controversy, party political manipulation of its racist residues and xenophobic attitudes resulted in widespread international condemnation of the federal state's policies and practices.

Conflicts over immigration involve three main issues: the *size* of the intake; its *composition;* and whether the settlement of immigrants should focus on *assimilation* or take a multicultural approach, which helps new-comers retain some aspects of their natal culture. Regarding size, governments respond to the economic and popular climate of their time. Conservative critics tend to claim that the intake is too large. In Australia, there were two main issues regarding composition – the acceptability of Asian and other non-White/non-Christian immigrants, and the extent to which admission should be based on family reunification rather than how prospective migrants fit with the country's economic needs. The more those arriving were non-British – and later, non-European – the more resistance there was to multicultural settlement policies and practices, and the more emphasis was placed on strict assimilation to the language and values of the dominant, White, Anglo-Celtic majority.

Policy changes in the 1970s and 1980s opened entry for the first time to some highly educated Asian migrants, but the numbers were small and the policy produced only small increases in non-White immigration overall. Indeed, though we discuss immigration and refugee intakes separately in this section, we note here that it was largely through the admission of refugees over the next four decades that non-White in-migration increased. International agencies and the country's allies pressured Australian governments to take their share of refugees from conflicts zones in Asia and the Middle East, and this resulted in the entry of two sizeable groups of refugees: Vietnamese ('boat people') and Lebanese. After the Second World War and into the 1950s, non-British but White migrants had been required to work for some years outside the large cities, but most eventually settled in the larger urban areas. Once established, southern European immigrants organized themselves to demand more opportunities to sponsor their family members. They succeeded, and this increased the size and visibility of these communities, against which a conservative reaction developed against immigration and especially against multiculturalism.

Immigration policy in Australia after 1945 was as planned and regulated as it had been under the White Australia policy. State-assisted passages continued to bring many British immigrants, as did an open-door policy for New Zealanders. When pressed to meet its international obligations regarding refugees, Australia accepted many White displaced persons (DPs), choosing especially those from the Baltic and other northern European countries. Through the 1950s and 1960s, however, it also accepted refugees from Lebanon and Turkey. (See chapter 7 for a discussion of why the census authorities categorized such people from the Middle East as White.) Much later, some refugees from Southeast Asia and Latin America were accepted as well. Since 1986, though, increasing racism led to a downturn in the intake of non-White refugees.[10]

By 1972, immigration from the United Kingdom was declining and demands were increasing to admit refugees from around the world; faced with this, Gough Whitlam's Labor government rescinded the 1901 Immigration Restriction Act (a.k.a. the White Australia policy) and re-oriented immigration policy. At first, this generated remarkably little fuss and disruption. Jayasuriya (1997, 61) has described the new policy as a well-planned exercise in social engineering, one that was based on two main government strategies: dispersal and non-confrontation. Dispersal was intended to discourage ethnic enclaves, which many British-origin Australians greatly opposed, and to encourage integration. But xenophobia and racism, and most immigrants' desire to live near those with whom they shared a common heritage in the more cosmopolitan big cities, resulted in the failure of the dispersal strategy. To promote integration, governments supported Good Neighbour Councils, language training, and assisted housing. But these programs rarely produced the desired assimilation. Of the three countries examined in this book, it is Australia that has the weakest record for incorporating immigrants into its political system – including non-British European migrants. Virtually no race-minority politicians were elected in that country before the defeat of the Howard government. Consequently, immigrant and refugee groups have clung to multiculturalism, which seems to offer policies that would enhance their life chances and conditions and permit them to bring family members to Australia and reunite their families.

The new immigration policy, which enjoyed multiparty support, increased significantly the number of migrants settled. Between 1945 and 1985, Australia's population doubled, with immigrants, refugees and their offspring accounting for 50 per cent of the growth and 60 per cent of workforce growth. This increased the ethnic diversity of the population as the proportion of people of British ancestry dropped by nearly 10 per cent over four decades, making Australia a more multiethnic society. In recruiting non-White immigrants, federal governments carefully selected mixed-race professionals and academics, many of whom were already in the country or with family there. Indeed, the practice developed of marketing university education to Asian students and then recruiting them as immigrants. One study found that this first cohort was more similar to native-born Australians than earlier White immigrants from southern and eastern Europe. But a bureaucracy schooled for decades in administering the White Australia policy implemented the new policy so conservatively that progressive media contended that it was subverting the new policy. Indeed, except for Vietnamese refugees, there were far more university graduates among Asian immigrants in the 1970s and 1980s (almost all) than among White Australians.

It was the inept handling of South Asian boat people – refugees whom the Australian government admitted only reluctantly, under strong international pressure – that likely triggered a reaction against migration, and especially against non-White refugees and the family-reunification policies that increased their numbers. By contrast to small numbers of well-educated Asian immigrants, between 1978 and 1985, about 150,000 refugees arrived from Vietnam, Laos, and Cambodia, most of them at the lower end of the occupational spectrum. They 'experience discrimination and disadvantage disproportionately compared to other … refugees in the past, and even in the present' (Jayasuriya 1997, 63). These refugees faced low wages, poor housing, poor health, unemployment and underemployment, and difficulty accessing unilingual English-language social services. Women were especially disadvantaged, though ultimately some states developed multilingual services for non–English-speaking (NES) women.

There is extensive evidence that the labour market segmentation resulting from immigrant and refugee settlement in this period was immensely beneficial to Australian industry – and capital. But it also led to poverty and disadvantage for minority-race refugees while creating a labour aristocracy of the (White) Australian working class (Jayasuriya 1997, 64). The resulting inequalities were compounded by difficulties that race-minority children experienced in schools. For minority-race refugees, assimilation simply did not work as an effective settlement strategy. Initially, concepts of integration and cultural pluralism were used to sketch less hard-line alternatives. Ultimately, the concept of multiculturalism was borrowed from Canada. Australians, though, developed a distinctly culturalist version of multiculturalism as settlement policy lacking the structural or instrumental aspects of multiculturalism, which focus on claims for equal life chances. The adapted policy focused on the social benefits of helping immigrants retain some aspects of their ethnicity, at least early on. It funded some language instruction and minority-language media; ultimately, however, it involved mainly state-level services to manage diversity. Many of those who reacted against these multicultural practices favoured assimilation on the assumption that social cohesion and stability require a homogeneous society. Conservatives reacted bitterly to this cultural dimension of multiculturalism, perceiving any support for immigrants to retain their heritage languages, customs, and traditions as a threat to Australia's national identity. At the same time, multiculturalism did not help minority immigrants, who experienced race-based discrimination and disadvantage.

Jayasuriya (1997, 71) reports that a stable hierarchy developed according to which White immigrants were preferred over 'coloured' refugees by (White) Australians. However, 'there … [was] neither overwhelming acceptance of immigrants … nor outright rejection of immigration.' He shows how right-wing historians, politicians, and media commentators fomented anti-Asian racism, a key feature of which was denunciations of multiculturalism. It was right-wing rants that dominated the discourse with ethnic organizations, religious groups, and progressive activists, who for their part were campaigning against monoculturalism and Anglo-conformity. In this way, multiculturalism came to symbolize what many Australians of British heritage perceived to be the undercutting of their traditional values. Though conservatives were divided over whether immigration produced positive or negative economic effects, they all agreed that a multicultural approach to settlement was unacceptable.

Papers presented at a conference named 'Cultural Diversity in Australian Society,' held in 1989 in Melbourne, and sponsored by the State of Victoria Office of Multicultural Affairs and its Advisory Council, suggest the range of views about immigration and against multiculturalism. Dr Eve Fesl presented 'A Koorie View,' which revealed that Aboriginal people were hostile to multiculturalism (in much the same way that First Nations were in Canada). More original were arguments by some presenters that the Australian government should stop immigration for environmental reasons, or because it was yielding no economic benefit. Sociologist Dr Katharine Betts (1991, 156)[11] claimed that over-dependence on welfare-state services by immigrants was threatening Australia's already minimal programs, though she also acknowledged that this purported overuse was a myth except as it related to those race-minority refugees for whom racism resulted in unemployment. Betts also noted darkly that 'some of the resistance of White taxpayers in the United States to paying more for social welfare reflects their perceptions that "their" taxes are being spent on the needs of a population that is disproportionately Black.' According to Betts, the presence of *some* immigrant or refugee communities that used more services on average than native-born Australians would soon produce a similar race-based backlash in Australia. Her target in all this was family reunification, which she claimed was being resorted to too heavily by race minorities, especially Vietnamese and Lebanese. Betts (1991, 168) blamed federal multicultural policies for creating the family reunion category, as demanded by immigrants' organizations. In her view, such policies were feeding Australians' widespread and growing opposition to immigration.

The turning point in Australia's immigration policy happened when bipartisan support ended for it and conservatives began to exploit the issue for partisan political advantage. In 1988, John Howard, then leader of the Liberal opposition, who would later become prime minister, broke the previous consensus on non-White immigration and multiculturalism by expressing strident opposition to both. (Australia's Liberal Party is a conservative party.) In Canada, legislation establishing multicultural policies had been passed with unanimous consent; by contrast, because of growing partisan polarization, governments in Australia never established a national statutory basis for multiculturalism. Jupp (2002) believes that Howard (temporarily) lost his leadership because of public opposition to Asian immigration, which left him in the party-political wilderness for decades. In 1989, however, instead of legislation, Labor Prime Minister Bob Hawke announced a National Agenda for Multiculturalism, which set strict limits on how much support immigrants could expect for preserving their diversity. Howard had also rejected any multicultural practices and supported Anglo-Celtic conformism. He denied that racism informed his views, yet he blamed racist demonstrations on overly high levels of immigration and on unreasonable generosity to non-White/non-Christian refugees.[12]

By 1990, conservative opponents had killed multiculturalism as a potential alternative legislative framework for determining how Commonwealth governments should treat culturally different and non-White immigrants. Multiculturalism became little more than a culturalist discourse about service delivery mainly in states with Labor governments. That discourse offered little guidance for navigating the legal and moral dilemmas that Australian governments faced after the 9/11 attacks, especially when security issues began intersecting with issues surrounding the treatment of asylum seekers. With no real discursive alternative to assimilation, and with popular fears of non-White diversity being fomented, how refugees and especially asylum seekers should be treated became a highly controversial issue in Australia, and the country's practices provoked criticism at home and in the international community. Conservative critics portrayed multiculturalism as sanctioning the swamping of true Australians and as devaluing the pioneer work and spirit of the old Australia. This resembled conservatives' opposition to any official acknowledgment that present-day White Australians are responsible for or benefit in any way from the awful conditions of Aboriginal people, conditions that have been documented by many official inquiries and commissions. Howard and his conservative academic supporters declared that past actions, while regrettable, had been well intentioned and in any case were irrelevant in the present. Victims of racism, be they Aboriginals or refugees, were blamed for their own life conditions – for example, waves of anti-Asian violence were blamed on the high number of Asians who had been admitted.[13] In other words, neither the racism of ordinary Australians nor conservative promotion of the old White, British Australia were to blame.

Comparing the Treatment of Refugees and Asylum Seekers

Since 2001, the three White-majority settler states under discussion here have faced conflicts relating to how they treat unauthorized immigrants and refugees. As noted earlier, in 1996, during the Clinton administration, the U.S. Congress passed the IIRIRA, which created the category of an 'unlawfully present' person and sanctioned temporary or permanent bars on re-entry to the United States as well as incarceration pending deportation. There have been challenges to this law, and in *Zadvydas v. Davis* (2001) the U.S. Supreme Court limited the federal government's right to hold potential deportees indefinitely. But challenges to mandatory detention provisions have not succeeded.

Canada detains some immigrants indefinitely, though not as aggressively as the United States, and not as proactively as Australia. Under the 2001 Immigration and Refugee Protection Act (IRPA), the Canadian Border Services Agency can arrest non-citizens who may have breached the act if there is reason to think they pose a danger to the public, if their identity is in question, or if there is reason to believe they won't appear for immigration/deportation proceedings. Officers can also detain people at a port of entry if they have reasonable grounds to believe that the person is inadmissible for security reasons or has committed human rights violations. Immigrants and refugees, however, are protected by the Charter of Rights, which requires that the reasons for an arrest be disclosed to them, that their home government be notified, and that legal representation be provided to them (CBSA 2011). When citizens or immigrants have been incarcerated apparently indefinitely without reason or trial on suspicion of being security threats, the courts have held this to be a breach of the Charter. In 2008 the federal government amended the IRPA to revise the security certificate scheme that the courts had criticized. That amendment introduced special advocates who could review a summary of the evidence of the alleged security threat but could not share that evidence with the accused. Citizens cannot be held under this revised law – only permanent residents and foreign nationals. In the aftermath of 9/11, Canada also introduced an Anti-Terrorism Act, which allowed police to arrest suspects and detain them without a warrant.[14] However, the bill expired in 2007 when its renewal was opposed in the House of Commons.[15]

Both the United States and Canada have human rights regimes that limit how governments can treat immigrants and refugees, but concerns about security since 9/11 have weakened those regimes. Notwithstanding claims to the contrary by former President George W. Bush, even those who have been incarcerated as enemy combatants have some legal rights, though U.S. conservatives challenge this, as was evident in conservative commentary on the Nigerian Christmas bomber. Australia lacks a bill or charter of rights, so limits on how the executive may act are imposed more often by the Senate than by the High Court. In the absence of a successful Senate veto, the mandatory detention of unauthorized refugees arriving by boat (hereafter asylum seekers) resulted in a large incarcerated population, including children. This has been highly controversial. The first detention centre outside urban areas was established in 1991 at Port Hedland, when mandatory detention was imposed on all asylum seekers arriving by boat. At the time, most of these people were refugee families fleeing a brutal regime in Cambodia. This form of detention was not imposed on asylum seekers arriving by plane, on the grounds that since they required visas in order to fly, they must already have been vetted by Australian immigration officers overseas. In this way a *de facto* race-based system was created, given that those who arrive by plane with a visitor's visa and then seek asylum on landing are largely White and from Europe, whereas most boat people are Asians or Middle Easterners fleeing threats to life.

Currently Australia has five immigrant detention centres. Stated government policy is that children not be held in detention centres: families and their children are supposed to be held in alternative low-security facilities (Department of Immigration and Citizenship 2010). But families with children *were* held in isolated detention centres under the Howard government, which generated international criticism. In 2007–2008, the government reported 4,514 people in mandatory detention. A 2010 census reported that number nearly halved. But with just 229 exceptions, the 2,505 people in mandatory detention were all non-White asylum seekers from Afghanistan (922), Sri Lanka (671), and Iraq (214), with smaller groups from China, Indonesia, Iran, Burma, Vietnam, Palestine, and Nigeria. Why did the Australian government endure international censure for its policies, when the problem on its face is an apparently small one?

Ozolins (1993) suggests that under Prime Minister Hawke, Australia's Labor government had already backed off from the diversity promotion potential of multicultural legislation in favour of a wishy-washy agenda with no legislative sanction. Moreover, in 1991 the immigration program was reduced (the high-water mark was 1989), with immigration from Asia cut, mandatory detention introduced for asylum seekers arriving by sea, and the Port Hedland detention centre opened to house 'boat people,' then mainly from Cambodia. While a special assistance category was introduced in 1992, mainly for (White) Yugoslavians fleeing state collapse and civil war, temporary protection visas were routinely used for authorized Asian refugees, with few gaining permanent residence. (Most exceptions have been Chinese graduates of Australian universities.)

When bipartisan support for multiculturalism ended in the 1980s, both the Labor government and the (conservative) Liberal/National party coalition supported ratcheting down Asian immigration and restricting family reunification. Neither government strongly opposed increasingly harsh measures against non-White asylum seekers. The main cause was the economic rationalism policies adopted by both governments. Bett's critique of the family unification category, outlined above, reveals one dimension of such policies: migration must benefit the nation's economy, which means admitting only those with capital to invest and/or education and skills that will generate economic development. The conservative and Labor economic rationalists both demanded that 'family' be defined in strict, nuclear terms, which would keep out economically unproductive grannies and young kiddies. They were divided about the economic benefits of cultural diversity, however, with some emphasizing the costs of maintaining social cohesion in a heterogeneous workforce, others that in a more and more globalized economy, a diverse workforce with multiple language skills could be a positive advantage.

More than half the immigrant intake was economically beneficial once a new points system was introduced in 1999. Those not bringing skills or capital were denied access to social benefits for the first two years. The main thing that economic rationalists agreed on was the economic drag of having to receive many uneducated refugees and asylum seekers, who would likely cost Australian taxpayers at least initially. Ironically, the costs incurred because of the extreme measures the government undertook to keep boat people from landing on Australian territory have far exceeded the cost of settling them to the point at which they would become taxpayers. After abolishing the remains of the Commonwealth's multicultural apparatus immediately on winning government in 1996, Howard reduced the humanitarian intake to 12,000, where it stayed for more than six years. The Howard government claimed that refugees only needed safe haven until things returned to normal, at which point they would return home. This denied most refugees the opportunity for permanent settlement. Permanent residence status became a concession granted to a lucky few.

New detention centres were established, such as Woomera in the desert in 1999. Under a blanket order to incarcerate asylum seekers arriving by boat, they filled up with those waiting for deportation, whom Australia could not lawfully send home to war zones or oppressive circumstances. Facing uncertainty and the possibility of lifelong incarceration without having committed a crime, desperate detainees – most of them Iraqis and Afghans – protested with violence against their jailers, one another, and themselves. Despite the isolation of the detention 'warehouses,' the news of this violence eventually escaped. Then in 2001, the government's actions against the Norwegian ship *Tampa* revolted the international community, and many Australians.

Between 1975 and 1989, only two thousand asylum seekers arrived in Australia directly by boat. Their numbers rose between 1990 and 1995, when nearly two thousand more landed. Mandatory detention for anyone without a visa until all procedures, including appeals, were completed, did not deter these people. Jupp (2001, 189) identifies two changes in 1997 that likely contributed to the *Tampa* incident. First, control of the detention system was transferred to a private U.S. prison administration company to reduce costs. Jupp claims that this resulted in a punitive approach to detainees, some of whom were children. Second, government policy changed from granting permanent visas for those arrivals eventually deemed to be refugees, to granting only temporary safe haven. The UN convention forbids discrimination against undocumented asylum seekers, because it is so difficult for them to obtain documents during civil disturbances or from hostile, authoritarian governments, especially in countries with weak record keeping. Despite being a signatory to that convention, the Howard government interned those who landed seeking asylum without a visa. Most of these people were Asian and non-White. But it did *not* intern those (mainly White) who sought asylum after arriving with a temporary visa.

When the *Tampa* picked up 433 asylum seekers from a sinking boat, the Australian authorities refused to allow it to disembark or even stand off from Australian territory at Christmas Island; instead it used military force to remove them and drive them out of Australian waters. Jupp (2001, 193–6) points to the fact that most of the asylum seekers were Muslim, and both the government and the populace claimed that there was a link between adherence to Islam and terrorism. Border Protection laws were adjusted retroactively so that the asylum seekers rescued by the *Tampa* were deemed not to have landed and so that Christmas Island was excluded from Australia's 'migration zone.' At considerable expense, the government paid Papua New Guinea and Nauru to house the *Tampa* boat people until they could be processed, although none were given residence.

Some scholars and opposition politicians describe what happened in the 1990s regarding asylum seekers as policy blunders. Jupp sees them as part of a deliberate election strategy – indeed, a successful one for the Howard government against electoral threats from the far right. In 1997, Queenslander Pauline Hanson formed the One Nation party, which in its platform opposed Asian immigration, refugee programs, and Aboriginal rights (among other things). Having demonstrated that Australia had never faced waves of asylum seekers landing in anything like the numbers experienced by the United States, Jupp (199) asks: 'How did Australia get into a situation where its international reputation and credibility [were] … thrown away for the sake of stemming such a small flow?' His answer lies in the one million votes that Hanson's One Nation party attracted in 1998, many of them from Howard's coalition partner, the National Party. He demonstrates how each change that the Howard government introduced regarding immigration, refugees, and asylum seekers – including removing Christmas Island from Australia's migration zone – either had appeared on the One Nation platform or had been proposed by Hanson herself. Jupp (2001, 199) also conceded that the *Tampa* episode and other apparent policy blunders were outcomes of 'a process begun by … Howard in 1988 of playing on popular fears of immigration and multiculturalism. It marked the revival of racist and xenophobic popular attitudes, encouraged by the breakdown of bipartisan consensus and by the … pursuit of … American[-style] … "wedge politics."'

Howard had manipulated race-based immigration and refugee issues for party-political gain. Besides this, some have pointed to highly troubling legal features of Australia's refugee regime. Howard used *retroactive legislation* in dealing with the *Tampa* problem, a solution considered unacceptable under a rule-of-law system. Katharine Gelber (2004)[16] describes how detainees facing indefinite incarceration were unable to get relief from the High Court on civil rights grounds although Australia is a signatory (1980) to the International Covenant of Civil and Political Rights, which forbids arbitrary detention, and to other international rights protections. Bearing that in mind, cases involving the Australian government's actions toward (non-White) asylum seekers are especially troubling because they reveal that legal mechanisms are lacking in Australia to constrain executive actions. Albeit over minority views, the High Court has ruled that indefinite detention of non-citizens at the will of the executive is neither punitive nor unconstitutional. This grants the executive virtually untrammelled power over aliens, despite the many international rights documents to which it is a signatory. This demonstrates the problem that arises when a parliamentary government has a majority and when the practice of judicial review, which limits executive acts, doesn't exist. The separation of powers limits U.S. executive dominance, as does the Charter combined with opposition from provincial premiers in Canada, albeit to a lesser degree. But in Australia, the High Court cannot always protect the rights of the most vulnerable. While it ruled positively on Aboriginal rights in the *Mabo* and *Wik* cases, the Court's judgments were overruled by the virtually untrammelled power of a majority government.

Conclusion

In previous chapters we explored how three White-majority settler states structured and restructured race regimes as part of their nation building. Each state created the laws, discourses, and practices on which White privilege and the oppression of non-Whites were based. These states also constructed categories that assigned people to conditions of privilege or oppression. (See chapter 7 for a discussion of census categories.) Subsequent race-based policies and practices governing immigration and regarding multiculturalism were based on their predecessors. Immigration serves as a prism through which to observe how racialism is sustained. Immigration is largely a federal power, so federal bureaucracies have heavy responsibilities for administering categories in relation to immigrant and refugee status. But the judicial system also can play an important role. Political conflict over immigration became increasingly polarized to some degree in all three countries. The Canadian and especially the U.S. federal governments tend to devolve responsibilities to state and local governments, which have seized that responsibility, especially where nationalism or anti-immigrant bias makes immigration a hot-button issue with the electorate. In Australia, the Commonwealth government has a stranglehold over powers relating to immigration and refugee status. Indeed, it can be argued that along with regulating the economy and controlling citizens, control over immigration is its *strongest* power.

There is much to admire in these settler societies as liberal democracies. But beneath the democratic veneer are discourses and practices that deny race-minority migrants rights and benefits that the White majority enjoy. Some non-White asylum seekers are even denied their liberty. While their national discourses and postwar immigration laws reflect democratic ideas, the promise of equal treatment or a fair go made by these states remains unfulfilled in practice for race-minority migrants, especially unapproved asylum seekers and those seeking to unify their families. The multicultural policies of these states differ. But in terms of top-down approaches, their failure to promote race equality is a frequent theme, which we pursue further in chapter 6. So while Australia no longer officially administers a Whites-only immigration regime, it incarcerates non-White asylum seekers, who overwhelmingly come from poor, war-torn countries of the global South. Canada has a history of similar albeit sporadic reactions against 'boat people.' Similarly in the United States, those who look like Hispanics are often treated as illegal immigrants, even though most Hispanics are legal immigrants and many of their families are indigenous to the southern United States. Hence, while many of the laws, discourses, and practices that sustained race regimes were rescinded officially after the Second World War, race-minority migrants may still experience incarceration, stigma, and unequal treatment from the state.

Discussion Questions

1 What are the core ideas of multiculturalism, and is it the solution to the race minorities' disadvantages in the three White settler societies?
2 Is Quebec's policy of interculturalism different from multiculturalism? If so, how? If not, why not?
3 Compare the White Australia policy with the Canadian and U.S. immigration policies regarding race.
4 How did the events of 9 September 2001 affect multicultural discourses and practices in Canada?
5 Under the Howard government, Australia's multicultural policies and practices largely were discontinued. How did this affect the treatment of race minorities other than Aboriginal peoples?

4 Federalism and Electoral Systems: Mechanisms of the Politics of Race

In the preceding chapters we examined the foundational and subsequent race regimes and the role they played in the historical evolution of White majority rule in Australia, Canada, and the United States. We also showed how the contradictory mix of egalitarian and racialist values that we characterize as democratic racism currently permeates all three countries. In this chapter we explore the political institutions that have maintained White rule – specifically, *federalism* and electoral systems. In federal systems, sovereignty – the power to make binding decisions for a society – is divided vertically between a central and state/provincial governments, both of which relate to citizens directly. Federal and state/provincial governments cannot abolish each other without ceasing to be a federation.

Each of the three federations discussed in this book began as groups of British settler colonies and each has a common law legal system, albeit with French civil codes in Quebec in Canada and Louisiana in the United States. Each also has a single-member electoral system but in Australia the system is not 'first-past-the-post' and elections to the Senate are proportional. Also, each country began as a 'supplanting society' that dispossessed Indigenous peoples, albeit incompletely, by force, purchase, or treaty. In each case, the process imposed a White-majority settler society and state on its territory and dominated peoples. Each federation was founded before an industrialized economy was developed and when government involved less regulation. Each also has a hard-to-amend written constitution, so that many changes occur through judicial decisions and interpretations and intergovernmental negotiations. In this chapter we also explore the proposition that the federal state architectures and federal political dynamics that characterize these three White settler societies have helped maintain race regimes and White rule.

The Founding of White Settler Federations

When the Founding Fathers created a *republican federation* in the United States at the end of the eighteenth century, their goal was a central government just strong enough to defend against external threats and internal disorder. They decided to limit its power by dividing government powers *vertically* through federalism and *horizontally* by separating the legislature, the executive, and judiciary into competing institutions. They also adopted *bicameralism,* which divided legislative power between two competing institutions, as well as a Bill of Rights to limit what government can do still further. Thus, the formula for limiting central state power was *federalism* plus *bicameralism* plus the *separation of powers* plus a *Bill of Rights,* all of which were intended to fragment state power and thereby protect the liberty of citizens – that is, White men with property, which at the time included slaves.

The founders' theory of limited government posited that dividing government into multiple, competing sites would protect citizens from the tyranny of concentrated, centralized government power. They assigned to the states most of the (then) important governance activities, such as policing, because they considered state-level institutions, being 'closer to home,' easier for citizens – White men of property – to control. Moreover, with many governance sites there would be many elective offices for citizens to hold, including (elected) judicial offices. Given that many of the Founding Fathers were slave owners, these institutional arrangements were designed partly to protect slavery from federal interference.

Seven decades later, founders in the British North American colonies created a *parliamentary* form of federalism that also divided power vertically between federal and provincial governments; but which they combined with a parliamentary governance system that fused the executive and legislative powers horizontally in a cabinet at each level; all of this was capped with a constitutional monarch represented in Canada by a Governor General. British Canadian founders had at first favoured a unitary state; however, Quebec francophones and leaders of the Maritime colonies demanded a federal union. The civil war then raging in the United States led the founders to oppose a decentralized federation, for which they blamed states' rights. Hence, the original version of Canada's parliamentary federalism featured a strong central government, with Lieutenant Governors in each province, appointed by the federal executive, who could set aside (*reserve*) provincial laws that the federal government could *disallow*. Indeed, the first prime minister, John A. Macdonald, hoped that the provinces would fade away except as administrative units. He also hoped that a strong federal government would assimilate French Canadians and Indigenous peoples.

In Canada, only White men could be citizens, but by 1867 slavery had long been abolished in British territories. Non-White populations were very small, partly because of racist immigration policies. The faith, language, and civil law of Quebec's French majority were constitutionally guaranteed, however, and clerical and anti-modern nationalist elites would soon turn that province into a fortress to defend against modernization and assimilation. That fortress would stay intact until the 'Quiet Revolution' after the Second World War, when Quebec quickly modernized on the basis of language.

In 1901, the founders in the Australian colonies created a parliamentary federation combined with a constitutional monarchy. But being admirers of American federalism, they also adopted an elected senate with equal representation for the states. Living as they did in a continent-spanning, sparsely populated country on the edge of Asia, Australians' preoccupation with race was as intense as that of Americans. So the division of powers they adopted imitated that of the United States: they assigned to the states all powers over relations with Aboriginal peoples. Relations between White settlers and Indigenous peoples in North America involved treaties and military and trade alliances in addition to violence. In Australia, by contrast, the British settlers while establishing their rule declared their continent *terra nullius* – that is, an empty land with no settled governments. The Aboriginal peoples, Australia's sole inhabitants for more than 40,000 years, actually did have institutions of governance, but they also differed in appearance from Indigenous peoples in North America. Their Black skins and nomadic lives made settlers unwilling to acknowledge there had been either settled governments or landownership. The colonies were determined to retain control over Aboriginal peoples, their lands, and their mixed-race progeny. In the Northern Territory, the Commonwealth government controlled policies governing Aboriginal peoples. The federal constitution gave the Commonwealth government power over all issues involving other non-Whites – notably over immigration policy, which it used to establish the 'White Australia' race regime.

The elites who developed these federations resorted to various philosophical, religious, moral, legal, and scientific ideas to legitimize White rule. How they maintained White rule varied over time. Each colony, throughout its long pre-federation history, had developed its own way of dominating Indigenous peoples, depending on their numbers and whether Whites needed them mainly in economic roles or as military allies. In Australia, for example, mixed-race children were removed from Aboriginal communities and taught 'civilized' (i.e., European) ways with the goal of incorporating them into White societies, albeit on the bottom rung. In the United States, where there also were many mixed-race people, 'one drop' of Black blood made people legally and socially 'Black.'

Understanding Institutions

The historical legacies sketched above shaped the federal institutions, practices, and discourses (hereafter federal arrangements) and often remain embedded in them, helping maintain White rule. 'Making race' also involved processes from below, but in this chapter our focus is on state and political institutions, such as party systems, that support White rule directly. We consider the fate of these arrangements as each federation became increasingly democratic. Because the citizens in these federations were White,[1] democratic majorities supported White rule. Moreover, even when non-Whites gained citizenship, these federations continued to be dominated by White majorities, except in some parts of the south. Generally speaking, White majorities must be persuaded to deconstruct mechanisms of White rule and to adopt affirmative action mechanisms to reverse its effects. Hence this chapter's broader purpose is to explore the relations among federalism, White rule, and democracy over time.

We have adopted a *historical institutionalist* (HI) framework to compare the ways in which federal arrangements in each country have sustained White rule. HI assumes that each political system is made up of institutions – legislatures, tax departments, courts, political parties – that are more durable than the individuals who participate in them. Institutions are stable patterns of behaviour that participants experience as larger than themselves. Each institution has rules of appropriate behaviour that shape how individuals act within them, as well as ideas or norms that legitimize that behaviour. So we can predict how members of the U.S. Congress will behave as legislators, for example, compared to

Canadian or Australian members of Parliament (MPs). While we experience institutions such as elections as constraining our behaviour through their rules, institutions were created by groups such as the founders we just discussed.

Groups of individuals can change institutions, but usually they do not, because of *inertia*, that is, the inability to imagine alternatives; or because of the high energy costs involved. HI calls this *path dependence,* in that once institutions are established they normally proceed along the paths established for them, for it takes more energy for participants to effect change than to let matters proceed along their path. That said, crises and shocks (critical junctures), or unintended consequences of founders' designs, can disrupt an institution's path, resulting in restructuring, the setting of a new course, a change in purpose, or a dismantling.

An HI framework lets us compare how federal arrangements have facilitated or maintained White rule. Among the rules that constitute political institutions are those specifying who may participate; hence we can compare legal and *de facto* access as it relates to non-Whites. HI also lets us see how each federation's historical legacies have been embedded in institutional rules that often facilitate White rule. An HI approach also helps us understand how the balance of power between levels of government, and among institutions at each level, has been recalibrated as the polity responds to a critical juncture. For example, after the American Civil War, victorious northern politicians established political rights for 'Freedmen' (emancipated male slaves) in the defeated southern states – rights that federal troops defended during the Reconstruction period. But when the troops were withdrawn, and Whites regained control of their states, in part through lynching and other violent acts by groups like the Ku Klux Klan, Whites restructured political institutions by legislating 'Black Codes' and 'Jim Crow' segregation regimes.

Federalism – Theories and Practice

Hueglin and Fenna (2006, ch. 3) identify three traditions[2] of modern federal thought. *Consociational* theories of federalism emerged after the Reformation, when Protestants in Catholic states demanded the right to live in separate self-governing communities, which Althusius (1557–1638) called *consociations.* Althusias theorized a multilevel governance system, with sovereignty shared and negotiated among governance councils at different levels, each composed of representatives from lower consociations. Republican federalism in the United States was the first modern form of federalism put into practice. The thirteen colonies that successfully revolted against Britain first experimented with a *confederation*, in which each new state retained its sovereignty and delegated limited power to a weak central government for common defence. Confederation's failure led to a republican federal constitution with a (still resisted) stronger central government.

Because the federal government would have elected institutions, albeit based on a limited franchise, the founders feared that majority rule would threaten property rights, especially those of slave owners. So they designed new federal institutions in such a way that citizens would directly elect only the House of Representatives. Also, senators were selected by state legislatures until 1913. Presidents to this day are chosen indirectly by an Electoral College and the candidate with the highest popular vote may lose in the Electoral College. These institutions would compete with one another, further limiting their power. The 'gridlock' in Washington today, with fewer than 10 per cent of bills introduced becoming law, was deliberately created to limit central government power. A Bill of Rights – the first ten amendments to the U.S. Constitution – was intended to protect citizens from arbitrary government actions. Since only propertied White men could be citizens, the Bill of Rights 'tended to support the authority of male heads of households ... [over] their dependents' (Ritter 2009, 61). Indeed, the federal governance system was designed to protect White male citizens' authority over slaves, servants, wives, and children against 'interference.'

The ideas that shaped U.S. federalism and the theory of limited government, with its radical commitment to individualism, have their roots in classical liberalism. Canada's parliamentary federalism, by contrast, acknowledges some collectivist influences, similar to those illuminated by European consociational theory. The British Canadian founders and their conservative francophone allies in Quebec rejected most features of U.S. republican federalism, including its anti-statist philosophy of limited government. They added to federalism's vertical division of powers the philosophy of responsible parliamentary government in which legislative and executive power is fused in the powerful cabinet, which governs. The main power the elected legislators (MPs) exercise is over the public purse. To avoid conflicts with the elected House of Commons, which the cabinet dominates, the founders adopted an *appointed* Senate that lacked the legitimacy of election. Instead, the government appointed senators to represent regions and the governing party. Charged with providing a 'sober second thought,' senators can delay and amend legislation; however, they lack fiscal power.

Republican Federalism and White Rule in the United States

In this section we explore the compromises relating to slavery that the U.S. founders accepted in order to achieve union. Those compromises shaped republican federalism's institutional forms, many of which are to this day embedded in the U.S. system. The founders and citizens in all three federations discussed in this book considered White rule natural. But U.S. republican federalism adopted structural properties that facilitated the continuance of slavery and supported White supremacy and segregation, especially in the southern states. Even abolitionists assumed that White rule would continue after slavery ended because virtually all Whites assumed they were inherently superior, which justified White rule. Slavery, then, was one aspect of a system of White rule for which federalism provided a framework.

William Riker (1964, 5) theorized that federalism was 'the main alternative to empire as a technique of aggregating large areas under one government.' The U.S. founders accepted federalism in order to gain a central government that would be strong enough to defend against external military threats and internal civil discord, without requiring southerners to give up slavery. The British promoted federal union in both Canada and Australia because they were eager to lighten the costs of colonial defence. In all three cases, only federal union could facilitate the expansion of the new countries to the point that each stretched across a continent. To that end, these three White, settler unions needed to dispossess the land's Indigenous owners. Riker claims that federalism enabled them to achieve territorial expansion through agreement, which is less expensive and less difficult than through conquest. But he is incorrect when he conflates the constitutional agreements that the White founders negotiated among themselves with the subsequent dispossession of Indigenous peoples. Dispossession happened both before and after federal union, and in some cases federal governments signed treaties with Indigenous owners *before* dispossessing them. Where Indigenous peoples retained some land, *internal colonies* were created; these, however, often were reduced to 'reserves' of worthless land that were too small for the survivors to support themselves in traditional ways. This in turn made them dependent on federal governments for survival. Indigenous survivors, like former slaves, were dominated subjects who were denied most rights.

How did federalism facilitate White rule? And how was White rule linked to republican federalism's limited government theory? The leading nineteenth-century liberal theorist, Lord Acton (1907), valued U.S. federalism because of its ability to restrain democratic majorities and to protect the rights of the propertied class from them. He posited that the limited government established by U.S. federalism worked by dividing power between the federal and state governments; and by creating federal and state majorities that often conflicted with each other, thereby cancelling each other out and preventing the formation of an absolute majority. This in turn prevented both the positive and negative effects of the sort generated by unobstructed majorities in unitary states. Moreover, members of the various U.S. institutions were chosen by different electorates; they competed and came into conflict, which again prevented the formation of a single democratic majority.

Acton believed that the structural properties of U.S. federalism created a conservative bias by making it difficult to change the status quo. Even those who favoured limited government acknowledged that it facilitated the status quo of White rule. This entangled limited government with federalism's 'race dimension' in that it largely prevented the central government for over a century from making reforms that might have addressed race oppression, except briefly during Reconstruction.

Riker valued republican federalism's ability to limit 'big government.' But he also pointed out that 'if in the United States one disapproves of racism, one should disapprove of federalism' (1964, 155). By weakening the central government, federalism allowed 'racisms' to persist. Riker later claimed (1975, 155–6), however, that 'federalism was never the culprit in American racism'; rather, 'the real cause of racist behavior' was 'the preferences of Whites.' He concluded that 'all ... federalism ever did was to facilitate the expression of racist beliefs and the perpetuation of racist acts.' It did not make people racists. However, he also believed (1987, xiii) that 'the racial dimension of judgment' was removed when the federal government passed civil rights laws in the late 1960s, which the Supreme Court did not strike down as it had a century earlier, in effect signalling the defeat of Reconstruction. And the federal government used its military and legal powers to enforce civil rights laws in the 1960s and 1970s, as it had during Reconstruction. So 'for the first time in American history,' it was 'possible to value federalism ... as a deterrent to statism' with no qualms about 'the racial dimension.'

But did the racial dimension of U.S. federalism end when legal sanctions against race discrimination were introduced and enforced, as Riker claims? Were the 'racial dimensions' of republican federalism in the United States removed by legislation and enforcement? Or do they remain embedded in federal constitutional arrangements? Our argument, based on the HI understanding of institutions, is that such dimensions *cannot* be removed without restructuring the institutions in which they are embedded. Riker contends that individuals' preferences produce 'racism' and that when those preferences are changed, racism disappears. Employing rational choice theory, he conceptualizes institutions as the sum of people's *current* preferences. He assumes that the preferences of a majority of (White) citizens were changed by the new civil rights laws and/or because of the troops enforcing them. This would have eliminated any racial dimension in federal institutions. Riker dismisses the idea that institutions have long-term historical legacies (which is our argument), claiming that any able politician can effect change by manipulating institutional rules. That is, he believes that any rules that previously mandated White rule are eliminated when most people's preferences change.

The different conceptions of institutions employed by rational choice and HI theorists make understanding the nature of institutions key to theorizing about the effects of federal arrangements that sustain White rule. Were the historic legacies of slavery associated with U.S. federal arrangements eliminated as easily as Riker claims? Marx (1998, 60) describes federalism as 'America's great invention' but also as 'an offspring ... of [its] ... great tragedy of slavery.' Can the institutional compromises that were associated with slavery and segregation be eliminated as easily as Riker's theory claims? The federal arrangements implicated in maintaining White rule were these: the constitutional division of powers; the selection rather than election of senators until 1913; a 'high bar' for amending the constitution; state control of the federal franchise; and the Electoral College and indirect s/election of presidents. Below we explore how these institutional arrangements supported White rule.

The founders also valued those federal arrangements that inhibited democratic majorities, and Riker suggests that we can separate this purpose from their compromises relating to slavery. Most limits on central government power, though, arguably originated in both objectives. Mulcare (2008, cited in the abstract) contends that many southerners were so fearful that a unified northern majority 'could hinder slavery's expansion or ... existence' that they 'worked successfully to curtail federal power even in areas seemingly unconnected to slavery.'

Thus southern politicians opposed federal involvement in road improvement, believing it would help unify (centralize) the North and thereby threaten slavery. Moreover, during the 'first 150 years of the American Republic, the Supreme Court interpreted the Constitution as requiring strict limits on the national government's authority to regulate markets and promote public welfare' (Ferejohn and Weingast 1997, vii).

The Impact of Slavery on Institutions –
Example of the Electoral College

A U.S. president is not elected by popular vote, but rather by winning a majority of delegates in the Electoral College, which is made up of fifty state colleges plus one for the District of Columbia. Each state has as many Electoral College votes as members of Congress, and except in Maine and Nebraska, Electoral College votes are assigned to candidates on a 'winner takes all' basis. So the presidential candidate winning a plurality of votes in a state gets all of its Electoral College votes. Thus in 2000, George W. Bush won a majority of Electoral College votes, even though Al Gore won a majority of the *popular* vote. This undemocratic system was one of a series of compromises that the founders accepted in order to accommodate the interests of the slave states. They ruled out direct election of the president by the people partly because they feared 'the people,' but also because the slave states claimed it would favour the north because slaves could not vote. Election by Congress was ruled out because it would violate the separation of powers. And election by the states was rejected because it violated the federal government's independence from the states. The Electoral College compromise favoured the slave states because each slave was counted as three-fifths of a citizen in determining the number of House of Representatives districts, a number duplicated when the numbers of Electoral College delegates were calculated. This bias is clear when we note that four out of five presidents over the first three decades were Virginia slave owners.

The original purposes and rules of institutions can be changed over time, as they are taken over and put to different uses by new classes or social interests. Since the American Civil War, when the southern states' population advantage ended, a number of states have restructured their rules about how their Electoral College contingents are s/elected and how they are to behave. Party elites continue to be suspicious of direct majority election of the president, though the original racial impact of this mechanism is no longer evident. Moreover, African Americans' distribution across the states has changed over the centuries, many having moved north after Reconstruction failed. Whether this marginally restructured Electoral College would disadvantage an African American presidential candidate was not definitively determined until 2008, when the strategy of Senator Obama's campaign exploited the strong concentrations of African American voters in the large Northeastern and Midwestern states to win a majority of Electoral College votes[3] and a popular majority.

Federalism and Race – The Electoral and Party Systems

Southern Whites benefited from the slavery compromises on which federal union was based. Except during Reconstruction, they gained from being able to exploit the labour of former slaves as sanctioned by the many laws associated with legal segregation. The constitution gave the states control of the federal franchise, and southern states denied African American men the vote, even though the 14th and 15th amendments guaranteed it to them. Women and other non-Whites also were denied citizenship rights, making it easier to exploit and oppress them – to deny them property rights, educational opportunities, and even the right to marry whom they chose. But after emancipation, federalism also meant that African American men could 'vote with their feet' by moving north, where they could find better economic opportunities and avoid *de facto* disenfranchisement and 'Jim Crow' laws and practices. Wherever they went, however, African Americans experienced *de facto* segregation and discrimination. White rule was sustained by the constitution, which gave 'autonomy to local majorities' (Riker 1964, 155), which in turn inhibited the development of universal rights and freedoms. As a result, African American political elites came to favour 'uniformity in national policies, as opposed to multiple state policies,' believing them 'more likely to result in universal rights and freedoms' (Walton and Smith 2010, 27). 'States rights' favoured Whites' interests, not theirs.

Federalism established a system of competing elites operating in national versus state and local political arenas. While in Canada different party systems operate at each level of government, in the United States and Australia the same two-party systems operate at both state and federal levels as well as in most local governments. Unlike the centrally organized, top-down party organizations common in unitary states, the two main U.S. parties are each composed of many state and local parties, each controlled by a corresponding state or local elite and run according to its own electoral rules. (In Canada, the federal government controls its own electoral processes with a common set of rules administered by an independent electoral agency.) Historically, the party out of power in Washington defends 'federalism,' state government, and small government, while fighting against an 'intrusive' central government. After Reconstruction, Democrats claimed to be defending White homes and families by demanding strict limits on central government power. But after the New Deal era of President Roosevelt's state-interventionist policies in the 1930s and early 1940s, this became associated with the Republican Party.

U.S. party politics historically involved race-based attacks by those out of federal power – attacks that portrayed those holding federal authority as exposing vulnerable White women to danger from Black men. TV attack ads launched by George H.W. Bush's presidential campaign showed menacing pictures of Willie Horton, a 'dangerous Black criminal' who purportedly attacked a 'vulnerable' White woman while on temporary furlough from prison. This incident was blamed on Bush's opponent, a Democratic governor from the northeast. Both Republicans and Democrats have historically invoked 'fears about the loss of male power ... linked to race, class and regional identities.' Central government authority has been seen as threatening 'White men's superiority over Black men' (Edwards 1997, 168) unless controlled by 'our party.' Moreover, though it is no longer acceptable to use explicit racism in American federal politics, the linkage between federal government power and loss of White men's power, which stirs 'deeply-rooted values in American politics' (168–9), persists as a subtext.

Frymer (1999) claims that the U.S. two-party system has been a form of institutionalized racism designed originally to 'marginalize Black interests by keeping ... slavery off the national political agenda' (cited in Walton and Smith 2010, 131). For nearly two centuries, the party system did basically nothing to serve African Americans, because no party represented their interests by opposing White rule. The constitution gives states the right to determine who can vote federally. This legitimized various exclusionary mechanisms, including bogus literacy tests, poll taxes, and all-White primaries. Between 1840 and 1860, those African Americans who could vote often supported the anti-slavery Free Soil and Liberty parties. But then as now, third parties rarely could elect their candidates. Third parties often offer what African Americans want, but the electoral system prevents third-party candidates from succeeding.

The single-member, winner-take-all (or first-past-the-post) electoral system, based on local control of candidate selection and electoral rules, was designed to create artificial majorities and preserve two-party competition. Primaries in some states have expanded the groups from which candidates are selected but remain essentially local processes that are easily manipulated. This electoral system, which originated in the British parliamentary system and facilitated slavery compromises, persists because local communities want to choose their representatives and because party elites won't surrender control of their turf. Supporters of White rule have used this electoral system against African Americans' political interests, from the end of Reconstruction to Florida in 2000, when local election officials kept voters waiting many hours to vote in race-minority districts. Without oversight from a neutral, independent agency, White supremacist legacies mar U.S. democracy; the result is that free and fair elections are not guaranteed to all citizens everywhere. In a later section we explore the consequences of unfair election rules for African Americans.

The Republican Party gave freed African Americans a choice for the first time during Reconstruction (1868–77), when it opposed the Democratic Party, which at the time stood for racism and White supremacy, especially in southern states. As a result, about 80 per cent of African Americans who could vote supported the Republicans until 1936, despite betrayals, such as 'the compromise of 1877,' when the Republicans in power withdrew troops from the South in order to gain the White House. This ended Reconstruction, though the process of southern Whites regaining citizenship and state power, and redrafting state constitutions to effectively deny all African Americans the right to vote and hold office, would take until about 1900 to complete. By abandoning them to state control, federal Republicans consigned African Americans to Jim Crow segregation and numerous forms of *neo-slavery*. Gurin, Hatchett, and Jackson state that 'the history of the Black electorate' is 'characterized by ... continual commitment to the electoral system and repeated rejection by one party or another' (cited in Walton and Smith 2010, 133).

In 1936 a majority of those African Americans who could vote, for the first time supported the Democrats despite the party's racism and its exclusion of African Americans from the party organization in the South. In the depths of the Great Depression, which struck non-Whites harder than Whites, Roosevelt promised material gains – jobs, housing, electrification, and social security. Nonetheless, a significant minority stayed Republican. But from 1936 to 1964, African American voters enjoyed the benefits of a two-party system, with both parties responding to African American concerns to win their votes, especially in the Northeast and Midwest. African Americans helped elect Truman in 1948 and Kennedy in 1960. But the New Deal coalition began collapsing in 1948, partly because of Truman's integration of the armed forces and the federal government's efforts to end chain gang neo-slavery. Supported by White southern Democrats, a 'Dixicrat' presidential candidate won the Electoral College seats of four Deep South states.

The 1950s Supreme Court rulings against segregation, and Congress's passage of civil rights laws in the late 1960s, which the federal government enforced with troops, resulted in most African Americans supporting the Democratic Party. But by the 1990s, Democrats were taking African American voters for granted, realizing that they found the Republicans a worse option. Once again, many African Americans withdrew from politics outside their own communities, or they supported third parties. African Americans played an important role in democratizing the Democratic Party in the 1960s, when the Mississippi Freedom Democratic party, excluded by the all-White 'regular' Democrats, demanded to be seated at the national convention. As a result, the Democratic Party began opening itself to African Americans, women, and various non-White and sexual minorities.

After the 1990 elections a trend toward *deracialization* developed, which perhaps explains why African American candidates won in some White-majority districts. It has been suggested that these candidates avoided race-specific issues and transcended traditional group-power assumptions. The thesis is that they were elected by running deracialized campaigns that avoided polarization by supporting tax cuts and education reform rather than affirmative-action, or anti-poverty policies. As Senator, Obama presented himself as someone whose background let him *transcend* racial divisions. Moreover, some of his policy commitments were closer to those of independents, such as his insistence that affirmative action be class based; he argued, for example, that his daughters should not be eligible for affirmative action university admission (Walton and Smith 2010, 143). But the U.S. party system has been organized around race conflict for so long that Obama was unable to transcend it throughout the campaign. Though his opponent, Senator John McCain, avoided overt racist attacks, his running mate Sarah Palin did not. The underlying racist script of many opponents of federal government power is evident in the discourses of southern 'Tea Party' activists and in the revival of 'states rights' claims and the whitewashing of slavery and neo-slavery during southern Confederacy pilgrimages. In the next chapter we discuss President Obama's campaign attempts to transcend race in more detail.

White Rule, the Courts, and the Division of Powers

Each of the three federations discussed in this book has a *written constitution* that outlines the pacts its founders made regarding institutional structures and the division of powers; and each has a High or Supreme Court to resolve conflicts and interpret the pact. The U.S. Constitution divides power between federal and state governments, with specific powers assigned to the federal government; those powers not explicitly assigned to the federal government are reserved for the states, or for the people. The 10th Amendment reinforces 'states rights,' but its Article VI, the 'supremacy clause,' states that the national constitution and federal laws are supreme. Moreover, the 14th Amendment specifies that 'the national government must ensure that state actions do not deny citizens due process, privileges and immunities and rights to equal protection of the laws' (Schram 2002, 347). While the 15th Amendment explicitly protects the right of freed African American men to vote, from 1878 to the late 1960s, federal power was not used to protect African Americans' rights so specified. In this section we show how the federal features of the judiciary facilitated more than a century of White rule.

The contradictions among various provisions of the American Constitution regarding federal and state powers made the Supreme Court as powerful an institution as the presidency. Its interpretations determined whether pro- or anti-slavery forces, and later pro- or anti-segregation forces (and more recently, Bush or Gore), would prevail as they fought to dominate the republic's institutions. The Supreme Court was intended to be an independent body, but at first it was not very powerful. Over time, though, it made its own power by developing the practice of *judicial review*, whereby it interposed itself between the states and the federal government. Through its jurisprudence, it could substantially alter the division of powers as written in order to increase the authority of one level of government or one institution over another. Over time, it favoured slavery, the states, and White rule.

Walton and Smith (2010, 226) argue that, except between 1940 and 1980, 'the Supreme Court has been a racist institution, refusing to support universal freedom for African Americans ... For much of its 200 years the Court ... [took] the position that the rights of African

Americans ... existed only as Whites might choose to grant them.' The Supreme Court is a political institution that decides national policy and is as influenced by public opinion as other political bodies. FDR nominated the first African American appointed to any federal court, and there have been only three non-White judges among the Supreme Court's 110 justices. Moreover, presidents and senators 'tend to select judges from their party, who share their ideology' (Walton and Smith 2010, 227). So Democratic presidents Carter and Clinton appointed 14 and 19.5 per cent African American judges respectively to the federal courts. Republican presidents Reagan and George W. Bush named 2.1 and 0.7 per cent respectively.

The Supreme Court declared unconstitutional few laws – state or federal – until the 1910 to 1940 period, when conservative judges overturned progressive reforms relating to property and industrial relations. Since 1950 there have been two further periods of activism: first, when liberal Courts promoted civil rights, liberties, and freedoms; and second, more recently, when the Court sometimes again leaned toward a conservative states' rights agenda. The most famous race-focused cases have dealt with slavery and segregation. In *Plessy v. Ferguson* (1896), the Court declared segregation constitutional as long as the separate facilities provided were equal. Then in 1954, in *Brown v. the Board of Education*, Chief Justice Earl Warren declared separate facilities in education 'inherently unequal.' *Brown*, though, did not declare that states must integrate their schools. That took another fifteen years and enforcement by federal troops to achieve. Liberal courts supported and conservative courts rejected mechanisms to desegregate universities and schools, such as affirmative action and busing. Regarding the latter, 'White flight' to the suburbs and residential segregation meant that U.S. public education could be integrated only by busing students from poorer inner-city schools to affluent suburban ones. But this required busing across school district boundaries, which the Supreme Court would not mandate. So '50 years after *Brown*, most African American children remain in schools which are separate and unequal' (Walton and Smith 2010, 235).

The Supreme Court's decisions on voting rights had better outcomes. The Court interpreted the Voting Rights Act (1965) as requiring conditions for casting an 'effective vote' – that is, that African Americans had the right to choose 'one of their own.' Thus the Court sanctioned redistricting so that African Americans and other race minorities would be majorities in some districts. For a century, southern state officials had gerrymandered[4] districts to create White majorities. Now the Court supported using the same technique to create *minority-majority districts*. In 2009 this helped elect 8,000 African American office holders (out of 82,000 nationwide), including 42 congressmen and congresswomen, as well as the president. But in *Shaw v. Reno* (1993), the Court ruled minority-majority districts unconstitutional because they involved 'impermissible racial stereotyping.' In *Easley v. Crowmartie* (2001), however, the Court tried to specify when race can be used for redistricting. Minority-majority districts remain a contested issue.

Effects of Judicial Federalism – Neo-Slavery and Disenfranchisement

The U.S. federation has a two-tier judicial system in which federal courts interpret the federal constitution and laws and state courts interpret state constitutions and laws. This *judicial federalism* differs from the more integrated judicial system in the Canadian federation. Independent, state-level judicial systems were tools of White rule in southern states and were directly implicated in re-enslaving hundreds of thousands of African Americans between 1878 and 1945. The constitutional division of powers assigns responsibility for criminal law and policing powers to the states. Reconstruction failed when federal troops were withdrawn, and the re-enslaving of African Americans began through forced labour systems including sharecropping, debt slavery, and convict leasing. Latinos were subject to a system of peonage in New Mexico.

Hundreds of forced-labour camps throughout the South were 'operated by state and county governments, large corporations, small-time entrepreneurs and ... farmers' (Blackmon 2009, 7). The system of 'leasing convicts' involved criminalizing African Americans for trivial offences such as vagrancy (not being able to show you are employed), littering, drinking, leaving their place of employment without their employer's permission, 'talking loud' to White women, or adultery. White state legislators passed laws that criminalized such behaviour. While such 'offences' carried only short sentences, the practice of charging 'convicts' the costs of the judicial system, which few could pay, greatly increased their length. Convict brokers paid these costs and 'leased' these 'convicts' to the highest bidder. State and local government agencies would lease out convicts directly. This system made it appear that many ex-slaves were criminals, or that African Americans' poverty resulted in theft and other crimes.

Neo-slavery also disciplined African Americans outside its grasp. Sharecropping – families working Whites' land, which was often owned by their former slave masters – was another form of neo-slavery. Many sharecropped their whole lives under near starvation conditions because they knew that if they were caught trying to leave, their men and boys would be condemned to forced labour under conditions in which disease and brutal violence killed many. Moreover, women and children were either thrown off the land or forced to try to continue without their menfolk's work. Blackmon (2009, 7) concludes: 'the South's judicial system had been wholly reconfigured to make one of its primary purposes the coercion of African Americans to comply with the social customs and labor demands of Whites.' Elected sheriffs and state judges gained from criminalizing large segments of the African American community, in terms of their own remuneration and also by eliminating potential leaders and 'trouble makers.' In this way they maintained the advantages of White rule. Because those involved purportedly were 'criminals,' northerners' outrage was muted and federal authorities' determination to act was thereby weakened. When federal officials did try to take action in federal courts, they found that no laws existed against holding slaves.

Entire southern communities were advantaged by this system of criminalizing African Americans to force them into quasi-slavery. One among many benefits of 'convict farming' was low taxes, in that chain-ganged 'convicts' performed work on roads and other public projects. Blackmon documents that many major national corporations profited from forced labour in a system protected by judicial federalism. Federal intervention was mustered to end forced labour only during the Second World War, to put an end to Japanese and German propaganda decrying its existence.

This history of neo-slavery enabled by federalism, which persisted into the 1940s, helps explain why 'so many African Americans [have a] fundamental mistrust of our judicial processes' (Blackmon 2009, 402). And as we saw in the Introduction, the criminalization of large numbers of African Americans and other race minorities on the flimsiest of grounds persists today, with serious effects. African Americans are still imprisoned at much higher rates than White Americans and other race minorities, reflecting biases in the laws – for example, penalties for using cocaine, Whites' 'drug of choice,' are lower than for using crack, African Americans' drug of choice.

Since many states deprive convicted felons of the right to vote, there are political consequences for race-related criminalization. In Mississippi, where African Americans are 37 per cent of the population, for example, they are three times as likely as Whites to have lost the right to vote after a criminal conviction. Mississippi also makes it harder to regain the right to vote than to impeach the president. In the 2004 elections, nearly five million people were denied the right to vote because of a criminal conviction (Walton and Smith 2010, Box 2.2). In the 1996 election, more than 200,000 African American men were denied the right vote under Florida law, which also makes regaining the vote very difficult. Had their votes been restored in 2000, Vice-President Gore would have won the presidential race if only half of them had voted for him.[5]

The corruption of southern state judicial systems for over a century has had permanent consequences. Hundreds of thousands of African Americans were sentenced to forced-labour camps or chain gangs at any given time between the end of Reconstruction and the Second World War. In a practice inherited from the British and unchanged since colonial days, the incomes of judicial officials were paid out of the proceeds of these systems; so were court expenses, witnesses' fees, and even the cost of the food eaten by jurors, officials, and prisoners – all were paid for by the forced labour of those the system had convicted. This kept tax rates in southern states low, as did the provision and repair of infrastructure by chain gangs. The judicial system's integrity was another casualty. African Americans who fell afoul of the law for any reason found themselves swept into a system designed to deliver them up as forced labour. Many southern communities still depend on penal institutions, filled disproportionately with African Americans, for employment and income from government grants. Though much attention legitimately focuses on issues such as the bias against appointing African Americans to state and federal courts, the long-term effects of judicial federalism and the effects of corrupt historical practices embedded in southern judicial systems also require exploration and reform.

Federalism and Indian Tribes in the United States

The original balance of power in the U.S. constitution was 'calibrated to the ongoing dispute about slavery' (Marx 1998, 60). 'Indian tribes' were subject mainly to federal powers, notably those over commerce, war, and treaty making. In this section we explore the relations of those tribes to U.S. federalism in the founding era, as well as two subsequent key moments.

Indian tribes' relationship with the U.S. federal government began with the American Revolution, which ended their relations with the British Crown. In Canada, by contrast, relations between Native peoples and the Crown persisted after Confederation (see below). During the revolution, various Indian tribes allied themselves to one side or the other. After the revolution, those that had sided with the revolutionary army struggled to establish nation-to-nation relations with the new federal government. They did not join the federation as constituent states; nor was a government-to-government relationship established by the founders in the constitution.

But some tribes did try to fit in, becoming 'civilized' and even slave owners. When the federal government sought to remove them from their lands, however, they aggressively pursued self-determination and recognition of their sovereignty. In the 1820s and 1830s a series of Supreme Court cases resulted in their characterization as 'domestic, dependent nations.' Though their international status had been superseded, the Court determined that they retained internal sovereignty. Their status did not help them when White settlers' land lust focused on their lands; and Court rulings about their rights did not prevent presidents starting with Andrew Jackson from having them forcibly removed to territories west of the Mississippi. Nor did it protect them after the Civil War, when the army at Congress's behest waged a war of extermination to free up 'Indian' lands in the West.

The treatment of the tribes that survived dispossession, removal, and extermination was affected by the Court's characterization of the tribes as 'domestic, dependent nations.' The U.S. federal state treated all tribes the same in legal terms instead of dividing them from one another, as was done by the Canadian federal government and Australian state governments. Once their populations began to rebound, American tribes began to develop internal governance capacity again, with relatively little interference. This reflected their legal status more than different views about 'Indians.' 'Indians' in the United States, as in Canada and Australia, were demonized for resisting dispossession and were viewed as obstacles to 'civilization' and economic development. Their children were removed to residential schools for assimilation. But in relation to the federal system, they had legal standing as nations. Until 1871 the federal government signed treaties with tribes whose lands they planned to take. Treaty making ended in the United States in 1871, but until 1978, when the Indian Claims Commission (ICC) was closed, tribes could sue the U.S. government for treaty violations. Between 1871 and 1946, tribes had to petition Congress to pass a special jurisdiction act permitting them to sue. After 1946 and until 1978, that right was automatic. In Canada, treaties were signed in some areas but not in others; but hiring lawyers to press land claims was illegal under the Indian Act until 1951. No treaties were ever signed in Australia.

The judicial standing that tribes attained in the United States in the 1830s was of some value eventually. Starting in 1887, the federal government began to force the break-up of tribal reserves under the General Allotment Act (the 'Dawes Act'). Designed to detribalize and assimilate Indians, it allowed individual Indians to purchase tribal land and eventually to sell such land to non-members (Steinman 2005, 106). Though this ended in 1934, detribalization was exacerbated by federal 'relocation' of many Indians to cities. Consequently, half of tribal lands in many cases are now occupied by non-members, which affects the kind of self-government tribes can develop.

Steinman (2005) identifies three possible types of Indigenous government: a *land-based government* accountable to a tribe or nation, which is possible only if most residents of a territory are tribe members; a *public government*, which is possible if Indigenous people are a majority within a unit of the federal system, as is the case in Nunavut in Canada; or a *community-of-interest government*, which represents the interests of people who share group membership with no claim over territory, and which is the only option possible for urban Indians or where most people who own traditional tribal land are not tribal members. Claims to tribal sovereignty over territory are vulnerable where tribal members are a demographic minority. Since the 1980s, instead of seeking status as a third level of government in the federal system, many tribes have started to increase their governance capacities, establishing tribal self-government on a piecemeal, *ad hoc* basis. But where there are a majority of Whites within reserve boundaries, tribal police, courts, and so on only govern tribal members who choose to be governed.

Promoting his 'new federalism' initiative, President Ronald Reagan acknowledged Indian tribes' government-to-government relations with the federal government. Reagan's goal was to promote diminished federal responsibility and justify reduced funding, which could be achieved if local tribal governments assumed more governance responsibility. Reagan also promoted tribal economic development; and many tribes now fund their governance activities through revenues from casinos or tobacco sales. In 1984 the federal Environmental Protection Agency (EPA) issued a policy statement that also recognized a tribe's rights to government-to-government relations. Since then, the EPA has included Indian tribes in environmental laws as independent governments rather than as subordinates or subdivisions of the states (Steinman 2005, 110).

This practice has spread to other executive departments, accelerated by scandals in 1987 in the Bureau of Indian Affairs. Congress has passed legislation giving tribal governments that request it more flexibility in administering federal funding, first under the Tribal Self-Government Demonstration Project, and then on a permanent basis. The government-to-government approach has quickly spread throughout government.

Tribal governments are not legally recognized as a third order of government in the U.S. federal system. They are not public governments, and attempts to enforce tribal laws on White citizens likely would result in the federal government extinguishing their powers, as happened in Hawaii when Whites agitated to overthrow the monarchy. Moreover, recent Supreme Court decisions have retreated from the nineteenth-century 'domestic dependent nation' decisions, ruling that tribes are membership organizations only able to control their members, if they are willing. Greater autonomy has resulted from Reagan's decision to shrink the federal government and cut taxes. The U.S. federal system has been flexible enough for the tribes to restore some of their governance powers.

Federalism and White Rule in Canada

At Confederation, slavery had not existed in Canada for decades. Even when it had, the numbers of slaves had been small because Canada's climate was inhospitable for plantation agriculture. The Fathers of Confederation agreed that policy making and administration for 'Status Indians'[6] should be a federal responsibility, as in the United States. Prior to the 1837 rebellions, the focus of federal laws had been on voluntary education as well as 'gradual civilization' – for example, by enfranchising 'Indians' on condition that they become 'civilized' by giving up performance of Indigenous cultural practices. Between 1869–70 and 1960 a series of Indian Acts were passed that compelled assimilation, banned Indian spiritual practices (potlatch, sun dance), criminalized the hiring of lawyers for land claims, and incarcerated Indian children in residential schools to assimilate them.

How did being a federal responsibility affect Indigenous people and other minority race groups? Every decade, the federal government conducted a census in which each person was carefully categorized by their skin colour. As of the 1901 census, 96.2 per cent of Canada's population was White, 'reds' were 2.4 per cent, 'yellows' were 0.41, and Blacks were 0.32 (Backhouse 1999, 4). Census categories were a means for the federal government to control non-White populations. This was done in part through discriminatory immigration policy, which kept out most Asian and Black aspiring immigrants, and in part through rigid control of 'status Indians.' Asians and Blacks experienced segregation in education and housing, as well as intimidation by the Ku Klux Klan, as was evident in a case in Oakville, Ontario (see Backhouse 1999, 173–225). These categorizations had profound consequences, for they divided Indigenous people into those with 'status' and those without. The former were under federal control, the latter were ignored by the government or lived in the country's vast hinterlands, and therefore neither counted.

In 1939 the Supreme Court ruled that 'Eskimos' were 'Indians' within the Canadian constitutional framework and so were covered by the Indian Act (Backhouse 1999, 18–55). This demonstrates the power of bureaucratic categories when it comes to maintaining White rule within the framework of a federal system. To social scientists, categorizing 'Eskimos' as 'Indians' was nonsense;[7] even so, the ruling made them a federal rather than a provincial responsibility. The case arose after several years of widespread starvation in the North resulting from the demise of the caribou and marine creatures the Inuit depended on. The federal government demanded that Quebec share the costs of providing them with relief. Already burdened with welfare costs during the Great Depression, the Quebec government insisted that the Inuit were 'Indians' and thus the responsibility of the federal government under Section 91(24) of the British North America Act (1867). Accepting as evidence mistaken conflations of two Indigenous communities by early White cartographers, historians, and clerics, the Court agreed with Quebec. Legally, 'Eskimos' were 'Indians,' which meant that the federal government had to pay.

Federalism's territorial focus makes it ill-equipped to protect or advance the interests of non-territorial race minorities like the Black communities in Nova Scotia and Ontario. In part because their territorial claims were recognized in treaties, Status Indians were entitled to economic support from the federal state, albeit at minimal levels. But being categorized as Status Indians also subjected them to harsh restrictions relating to their occupations, geographic mobility, spiritual and cultural practices, and even whom they could marry. One outcome of this categorization, which divided Indigenous peoples into Status and Non-Status, was that the provinces were not responsible for providing education, health, welfare, or other social services to those categorized as Status Indians. Non-Status Indigenous peoples as well as Métis escaped the legal restrictions imposed by the Indian Acts but not the stigma of being 'Indians.' In any case, discrimination affected all categories, and the provinces rarely provided services to Non-Status or Métis communities.

In the United States, the revolutionary break with Britain had forced Indian tribes to develop a new relationship with the U.S. federal system. In Canada, by contrast, relations between Indigenous nations and the Crown persisted after Confederation, now mediated, however, by the federal government. New treaties – 'numbered' treaties – were negotiated with nations across the West, though not in British Columbia and Quebec, where no treaties had been negotiated previously. The lives of Indigenous peoples in Canada have been greatly affected by the bureaucratic categories that divide them. Constitutionally, the federal government is responsible for Status Indians, while the provinces are responsible for providing education, health care, welfare, and other social services to Non-Status Indians and Métis. But historically, the provinces have delivered services in a way that fosters assimilation, by providing them to individual citizens, not to Indigenous communities.

Indigenous communities often suffer from falling through the cracks, with neither the federal nor a provincial government accepting responsibility for providing services to them. In addition, there has been a history of conflict arising from the fact that the provinces have *default jurisdiction* over Status Indians on reserves in fields that are legislated by the federal government but administered by the provincial ones, such as policing, resource management, and child welfare. Depending on their ideological orientation, provincial governments often do not accept the right of First Nations communities to govern themselves. This problem is illustrated by struggles between Euro-Canadian and Indigenous principles and interests regarding Indigenous children.

Provincial welfare authorities and family courts claim to be acting for the benefit of the individual child when they legitimize non-Indigenous families raising Indigenous children. Yet First Nations communities consider a child's relations with the community and its culture as a whole. U.S. law recognizes the right of 'Indian tribes' to have their culture respected in such contexts; Canadian governments do not.

Divisions generated by the mismatch between the federal legislative power and the provinces' administrative responsibilities, and the categories of Indigenous people constructed by both levels of government, have produced negative effects. Depending on how it is categorized, each Indigenous community has a complex and ambiguous status *vis-à-vis* the federal system. Add to this that governments ignore such categories when doing so suits their purposes. Thus, provincial administrative practices have legitimized 'scoops' during which welfare departments have removed Status Indian children from reserves, and family courts have let White families adopt those children 'for the good of the child.' But when it comes to provincial governments providing infrastructure to reserves – such as roads, electrification, or public housing – they are 'not our responsibility.' The services the federal government grudgingly provides to reserves are often substandard, resulting in poor health and education along with high unemployment on reserves. The many Status Indians – often half of them – who move to the cities in search of better living conditions and opportunities may receive no federal services and as individuals are eligible only for provincial services.

The development of governance capacity on reserves has been inhibited by the linking of Indigenous self-government claims to the interminable process of settling land claims. Because there is no allotment process in Canada, reserve land remains collectively owned; and most people living on reserves are members of the nation. But under the discriminatory provisions of the old Indian Acts, women who married men of other Indigenous communities (or categories) or who married White men were denied 'status' and the right to live on the reserve, and so were their children. With the new constitutional sex equality clause (s. 28) of the Charter of Rights (1982), the federal government repudiated these parts of the Indian Acts and restored the legal status of those excluded from the government list. But the (largely male) leaders of some communities refused to readmit these women and children, arguing that only the nation could determine who its citizens were. Some community leaders prevented these people with reinstated federal status from moving back onto the reserves where they were born, often justifying this by pointing to a housing shortage. This conflict has further divided many reserve communities along sex lines; and organizations of Indigenous women, especially those seeking the restoration of their rights, have opposed expanding the powers of reserve governments and/or demanded that the Charter of Rights be applied to First Nations governments.

Political Clout and Developing Autonomous Governance Capacities

The federal division of powers makes Status Indians a federal responsibility but denies federal services to their Non-Status counterparts. This disadvantages those in both categories, for Canada's provinces have extensive resources and powers relating to social welfare and infrastructure provision. Without agreements with provincial governments, reserve communities are shut out of provincial economies. Because of their communal status, Status Indians cannot sell reserve land or own their houses. Hence they cannot arrange mortgages or loans to start businesses. Where no treaties have been signed – in Quebec, for example – government-to-government agreements have been reached, and this has had important consequences, albeit largely for communities willing to work within Quebec's nation-building framework. Quebec's determination to develop its hydroelectric power as a basis for its own national project forced it to negotiate with Indigenous communities that claimed the lands to be flooded. Hence Quebec governments have been willing to work on a nation-to-nation basis with many Indigenous groups. But there have also been many conflicts between conflicting, sovereignty-claiming groups over fishing rights (Restigouche), land use (the Oka standoff), and policing.

Some provincial governments refuse to provide infrastructure for which they are responsible to 'federal Indians'; and federally provided social services often are well below the standards of provincial services. Consequently, people on some reserves live in poor conditions.[8] After many decades of repression, during which they were forbidden even to hire lawyers to pursue their land claims, Indigenous peoples' political clout is limited, given that they are only about 3 per cent of the population in a democracy with a White majority. First Nations' organizations such as the Assembly of First Nations (AFN) have some influence with the federal government. Indigenous groups' dealings with provincial governments are affected by their numerical clout in specific constituencies or in the governing party. That clout is often weakened by the federal/provincial division of powers, by the categories the federal system has created, and more recently by sex-based divisions.

In the United States, cohesive support for Indian sovereignty exists; in Canada, by contrast, that support is undercut by divisive government categories, the greater power and resources of the provinces, and the refusal of most governments to relate to First Nations on a government-to-government basis. Comprehensive land-claim settlements have started to produce various forms of self-government, however, including local governments with Indigenous majorities, and membership-based governments accountable to Indigenous communities. Another emerging trend is *treaty federalism,* in which newly negotiated or restructured treaties specify how specific Indigenous governments will fit into the federal system. Though the new Canadian Constitution (1982) recognizes 'Aboriginal rights,' several decades later it remains unclear what those rights actually are. In British Columbia and Quebec, where no treaties previously existed, however, province-wide negotiating frameworks have resulted in some comprehensive land-claim settlements that include governance rights. The federal government is involved in case-by-case negotiations. One major outcome of this process was the establishment of Nunavut, Canada's third territory, in 1999.

Nunavut is the first unit of the federal system with an Indigenous (Inuit) majority that can dominate the territory's public government (unless many more Whites move to the Far North).[9] Having been created by dividing the Northwest Territories (NWT) into two jurisdictions, Nunavut provides the Inuit with a form of self-government; its autonomy is limited, however, because it is fiscally dependent on the federal government. The establishing agreement permits future resource exploitation from which Inuit will benefit but over which they will have limited control. In northern Quebec, a semi-autonomous region with an Indigenous majority is also developing governance capacity and some autonomy. Similar arrangements are being developed in other provinces. However, the Supreme Court's ruling in *Vander Peet* (1996), which constitutionally protected Aboriginal rights exercised at the time of first contact with the British, suggests that the Crown's sovereignty will prevail over Aboriginal rights claims based on abstract principles of self-determination. It remains to be seen whether Aboriginal rights will be solely cultural or include collective economic and political rights as well.

Federalism and White Rule in Australia

When the Australian federal system was formed, the constitution left Aboriginal peoples under the control of the states. Each state retained its constitution, judiciary, and public service; and the founders assumed that the states would legislate and administer in most of the same areas of activity as had been delineated before federation. This locked into place laws and pre-federation practices. Smallacombe (2000, 157) contends that 'dominant colonial ideologies are inherent in Australian institutions.' Aboriginal people were mentioned in just two clauses in the constitution: Section 51(xxiv) assigned the Commonwealth government responsibility for governing over races except the 'Aboriginal race'; and Section 127 stipulated that 'in reckoning the numbers of people of the Commonwealth ... aboriginal natives shall not be counted.' A constitutional referendum eliminated these clauses in 1967, giving the states exclusive responsibility for Aboriginal affairs, except in the Northern Territory. The 'territories power' (s. 122) allows the Commonwealth government to act on NT Aboriginal issues without constraint.

Between 1901 and 1967, each of the states treated Aboriginal people differently. Where few Aboriginal people lived, 'half-castes' performed menial roles for White society, and some could vote. Where more Aboriginal people had survived, states restricted them to church-run 'missions,' where they had few rights; or they exploited their work as domestics or in the pastoral industry. Only in remote places did they escape government control.

Founding elites assumed that the new Commonwealth government would have a limited role, principally in defence, trade, and control of immigration. But two world wars expanded its mandate – for example, they led to the development of invalids', soldiers', and old age pensions. Aboriginal people, including those who had fought in Australia's wars, were denied these benefits. Indeed, they were explicitly or covertly denied almost all benefits that Australia's expanding welfare state provided to White inhabitants. The Commonwealth Franchise Act (1902) had disenfranchised all Aboriginal people, including those whom the states had given the franchise (Chesterman and Galligan 1997). In theory, the 1948 Nationality and Citizenship Act conferred citizenship, but it was window dressing, since legislation and administrative practices routinely excluded Aboriginal people from legal and material benefits conferred on White citizens by the increasingly active Commonwealth government. Aboriginal peoples also lacked political representation. Just two Aboriginal Australians have ever sat in the Commonwealth parliament – Senators Bonner and Ridgeway. Only in the Northern Territory have Aboriginal representatives been elected in even modest numbers.

The legal fiction that Australia was *terra nullius* with no Aboriginal governments before White contact was used to legitimize Aboriginal people's exclusion from Commonwealth administration and politics. And laws passed before 1967 by the Commonwealth government for the NT were similar to those passed in the states; so had Aboriginal people in the states been subject to Commonwealth laws, there likely would have been little difference in outcome. Australians at first believed that Aboriginal people were 'a dying race.' They later favoured assimilation, and as a consequence, light-skinned children were forcibly removed and taught European ways. Between 1902 and 1967, Aboriginal people were like African Americans: subject to unquestioned White rule within what was essentially a unitary state. After the Second World War, international disapproval of racism and colonialism forced superficial changes. But absent Commonwealth oversight or constitutional rights protection, there was little meaningful change.

For nearly seven decades, state governments were able to treat Aboriginal peoples however they chose, and the Commonwealth government truthfully could say 'not our department.' Australia was a Whites-only democracy with a majority that supported White Australia immigration policies, and the Commonwealth government was as motivated by racism as the state governments, so it could hardly have been expected to act much differently. Aboriginal people again were divided between government 'half-caste' and 'full-blood' categories; by multiple federal governance levels; and by their own languages and community loyalties. Governments historically saw Aboriginal people's presence as 'a problem' to be solved, and adopted various bureaucratic theories and practices to do so, including confinement, exclusion, exploitation, and forced assimilation, practices still in use.

After the 1967 referendum, the Commonwealth tended to defer to state governments regarding Aboriginal affairs. But in the NT, land rights were the responsibility of the Commonwealth government. After a 1966 strike by the Gurundji people at Wave Hill Cattle Station for fair wages and land rights, the new Whitlam Labor government established a Royal Commission chaired by Justice Woodward to determine an NT land rights policy. Before Woodward's recommendations were implemented, the Governor General dismissed the Whitlam government, leaving its successor to implement them.[10] The Fraser government passed the Aboriginal Land Rights (Northern Territory) Act (1976), which established Central and Northern Land Councils. As a result, some communities have the power to limit access to their lands.[11] The modern land claims movement in the states also began in the late 1970s, when the Noonkanbah community in the remote Kimberly region tried to stop multinational mining companies' intrusions onto their land and sacred sites. The Western Australia government responded 'with a military-style invasion' of their community (Beresford and Beresford 2006, 69). Despite such actions, the power of the states has declined, and this has weakened their capacity to restrain federal government powers. Both state and Commonwealth governments have used military-style invasions against Aboriginal people.

The Decline of State Power and the Struggle over Native Title

Although Australia's founders intended the federation to be decentralized, state power has been weakened by constitutional amendments, High Court decisions, and a vertical fiscal imbalance.[12] During the 1940s the High Court confirmed the Commonwealth's fiscal dominance over major sources of revenue, notably income and excise taxes. Two of the eight successful constitutional amendments since founding have affected the division of powers. In particular, the 1946 amendment had strong consequences, for it gave the Commonwealth the authority to legislate social services – an important shift in powers toward the Commonwealth. Also far-reaching were the 1967 amendments, which established concurrent state and Commonwealth powers over Aboriginal peoples. A series of High Court decisions permitted the federal government to act in fields previously considered to involve states' 'implied immunity.' Finally, unlike the Canadian federal government, which cannot legislate in provincial jurisdictions to implement international treaties, the Australian High Court has conferred a 'treaty power' on the Commonwealth.

State power has also declined because the Labor Party, which formed Commonwealth governments for key decades, promoted centralized policy making. The Australian Labor Party historically has been hostile to federalism, contending that the states have obstructed progress. With the states weakened, national policy decisions increasingly have occurred in closed intergovernmental arenas, with little parliamentary consultation federally or within the states. The Council of Australian Governments (COAG), established in 1992, develops, initiates, and monitors implementation of policy reforms of national significance. COAG, which includes the prime minister, the premiers, the territorial chief minister, and the local government association president, is closed to lobbying. Neither COAG nor the ministerial council provides any access for representatives of Aboriginal peoples, who have been constructed as 'problems' to be solved.

In 1983 a prospective legislative framework for Aboriginal rights was presented to the Commonwealth parliament and the UN. The framework included land rights, the authority to protect sacred sites, control of mining companies' access to Aboriginal lands, and compensation for lost lands. Beresford and Beresford (2006, 69) report that this comprehensive Aboriginal rights policy framework was scuttled after a 'brazenly self-interested campaign by multinational mining companies ... [which] ran one of the most infamous political advertising campaigns in the nation's history.' That scare campaign undercut an approach to empowering Aboriginal peoples that would have given them land, resources, and some degree of self-determination. The Commonwealth Labor government backed down from the proposed framework, fearing a backlash from 'middle Australians,' who had been made to fear that the granting of land rights would transfer power to Aboriginal peoples, making non-elite Whites subject to 'Black power.' Only when the High Court ruled in 1992 that some native title had survived under common law did the government pass a scaled-down version, the Native Title Act (1993).

The Role of the Courts

With little progress on land rights, some Aboriginal groups went to court. About 42 per cent of Australia is covered by Crown leases to the pastoral industry for land on which vast sheep and cattle stations have been developed. In *Mabo* (1993) and *Wik* (1996), the High Court ruled that under common law, native title was extinguished only when there had been a law or a government action that showed a clear intent to do so. The Court also ruled that granting pastoral leases did not necessarily extinguish all aspects of native title and that some aspects could coexist with leaseholders' use rights. In *Wik*, the Court also ruled, however, that in a conflict between the exercise of native title and leaseholders' rights, the latter would prevail. But establishing even limited native title under common law was unacceptable to the Howard coalition government and to the pastoral and mining interests that supported it. Howard introduced a '10 point plan' to 'bring greater certainty to land ownership.' The resulting Native Title Amendment Act (1998) removed rights won in the 1993 legislation. The UN Committee on the Elimination of Racial Discrimination concluded that 'while the original 1993 Native Title Act was delicately balanced between the rights of indigenous and non-indigenous title-holders, the amended act appears to create legal certainty for governments and third parties at the expense of aboriginal title' (cited in Beresford and Beresford 2006, 70).

The Howard government removed NT Aboriginal rights in another military-style 'intervention,' discussed in more detail in the next chapter. In *Ward* (2002), the Western Australia Court upheld the state government's claim that whether native title rights had been extinguished could be determined by comparing native title rights with the rights granted in leases. That is, the High Court wasn't the final, definitive arbitrator of native title issues. In effect, the Commonwealth government had undone the High Court's rulings. Clearly, that Court lacks the power in the federal system to adjudicate relations between Indigenous and settler populations – a power that its Canadian and especially U.S. counterparts have long had. Since Australia lacks a bill or charter of rights, it lacks a tradition of defending citizens' rights against Commonwealth or state government abuses, and this has limited its scope. Under the Native Title Amendment Act (2009) the High Court is to determine whether specific claims should be mediated by the National Native Title Tribunal, heard by the Court, or dealt with by some other body. The goal is a comprehensive system for mediating agreements, a process the Court will manage for government.

The Aboriginal and Torres Strait Islander Commission (ATSIC)

In 1990 the Hawke Labor government established the Aboriginal and Torres Strait Islander Commission (ATSIC), which gave Aboriginal communities an independent national voice for the first time. Though ATSIC was never responsible for program delivery, it was blamed for the lack of progress, in that Aboriginal people's lives improved very little during the fifteen years of its existence. ATSIC was plagued with problems from the beginning. Some representatives were charged with corruption; few had any experience of governance. Nonetheless, for the first time Aboriginal people had elected representatives who spoke to the Commonwealth government on their behalf. Because everyone 'in charge' in Aboriginal communities is White – police, teachers, nurses, administrators, and judges – what most Aboriginal people basically want is some 'local control over their own affairs within the states in which they live' (Maddison 2009, 32). Despite its flaws, ATSIC provided some self-government, albeit limited.

When the conservative Howard coalition was elected in 1996, it was determined to reverse Labor's Aboriginal policies, especially as they related to native title. This brought it into conflict with ATSIC leaders, making Howard determined to shut them down. Howard believed that Aboriginal peoples did not need separate representation. ATSIC leaders were demanding a modern treaty and an apology.[13] Howard insisted that 'an undivided nation does not make a treaty with itself'; and he claimed that his generation could not be expected to apologize for (usually well-intentioned) acts of earlier generations. This neglected the fact that many acts for which Royal Commissions called for apology and recompense – for example, regarding 'the stolen generations' and 'deaths in custody' – had been acts of his generation. Then Labor opposition leader Latham gave Howard the political cover he needed to abolish ATSIC when he said that, if elected, Labor would abolish it. Howard did so in 2005.

Howard's determination to eliminate ATSIC undoubtedly reflected his frustration that it opposed development. When legislation to terminate ATSIC was debated, Labor agreed that ATSIC had failed, and in the 2004 election it campaigned for an alternative that would retain the regional and local structures that were part of ATSIC. In the event, ATSIC's roles were assigned to the Office of Indigenous Policy Coordination and buried in the Department of Families, Community Services, and Indigenous Affairs. The National Indigenous Council appointed to replace ATSIC is not elected and does not represent the views of Aboriginal communities. Without a national representative body, Aboriginal communities have had to struggle hard against the loss of autonomy entailed by the Shared Responsibility Agreements, which the Howard government imposed. Funding for those communities is tied directly to intrusive, paternalistic conditions. The Rudd government that followed Howard's tentatively introduced some new regional structures, but it did not restore ATSIC, nor did it create a new representative, national Aboriginal body.

Conclusion

When we compare how minority-race communities have related to governments within the three federal systems, Australia has the highest failure rate in a policy field marked by many failures. In Aboriginal policy making, all three governments – but especially the Commonwealth government – hold all the cards and provide little space for Aboriginal people to participate in policy making. In Australia, ideological polarization regarding Aboriginal rights, especially over land, means that policy reversals are frequent, with few opportunities for community development. By contrast, Indian tribes in the United States are developing significant governance capacities and have found a place within the federal system.

Does the federal system contribute to these failures and successes? Does federalism provide potential solutions? The original division of powers in Australia created a dysfunctional situation regarding

Aboriginal policy making because the two levels of government did not have to cooperate, nor have they had to learn to do so since. In Australia after 1967, the federal system fragmented policy making for Aboriginal people. There was no oversight on states' actions until 1976; and the Commonwealth government still acts without oversight in the NT. This parallels the disadvantages that African Americans experienced because of the U.S. federal system until the Second World War.

The opportunities that federalism provides powerful or larger interest groups – such as 'forum shopping,' that is, moving their focus from one government level to the another – have never been available to Indigenous communities, with their small populations. Indeed, in general terms federalism makes it harder for smaller, disadvantaged peoples to influence policy making. Yet the federal system does provide forum shopping for opponents of Indigenous peoples' rights – opponents such as the powerful mining and pastoral interests, which in Australia profit from exploiting Aboriginal peoples and their lands.

In addition, the relative strength or weakness of a country's court system plays a role. For example, the weakness of the Australian High Court has largely closed the judicial route to change. Conversely, a strong, independent-minded court can be an ally in terms of providing legal recognition of rights. In Australia state governments have not been allies for race minorities, small or large. In any case, the current weakness of the Australian state governments limits the opportunities they can provide to Aboriginal communities for contesting the actions of a domineering Commonwealth government. Because the states were dominant in Australia until 1967, however, the likelihood of the states and Aboriginal peoples ever becoming allies is small. In short, Aboriginal peoples in Australia have experienced all of the disadvantages but none of the advantages of federalism. Maddison (2009, 24) suggests that Australian Aboriginal peoples 'experienced less ... formal political autonomy than [in] any comparable settler society.' And the role of the High Court is now as manager of native title cases for the Commonwealth, not as a mediator between Aboriginal claims and the federal state.

Does federalism disadvantage race-minority communities that have been marginalized by White rule and racism? Riker initially claimed that if you oppose racism in the United States, you must oppose federalism. But after civil rights legislation was passed and was being enforced, he claimed that federalism just 'facilitate[d] the expression of racist beliefs and the perpetuation of racist acts.' In both the United States and Canada, federal institutions were designed to facilitate union, in the first case by letting southerners protect slavery and in the second by providing French Canadians some self-government in Quebec. But Canadian federalism categorized, divided, and oppressed Indigenous communities, especially between the 1870s and the 1980s. In Australia, the division of powers was explicitly designed to exclude Aboriginal peoples from federal politics, which it did for seven decades. Institutions specifically designed to maintain White rule are especially hard to change. Riker's claim that passing laws, and even getting a majority of people to obey them, will transform institutions and dislodge White rule clearly isn't supportable. Institutional transformation is very difficult to achieve. Moreover, in each of these three countries, federal governments have used military force against race minorities claiming their rights, as well as against those who oppose White rule. All three of these federations are also democracies in which majorities have supported White rule. In the next chapter we explore different ways they have tried to end White rule and transform institutions; and the successes and more often failures they have encountered.

Discussion Questions

1 Compare how federalism affects the administration of race regimes in these three settler states.
2 Distinguish between federalism's effects on race minorities that are territorially organized and have their own provincial or state government, and its effects on race minorities that aren't and don't.
3 How does a historical institutionalist approach reveal how federal arrangements maintain White rule in these three countries?
4 How do the single-member, first-past-the-post electoral systems common to these three societies affect the politics of race?
5 How does power sharing among levels of government obstruct or facilitate the process of ending race-based oppression?

5 The Politics of Race: Contexts and Bottom-Up Approaches to Change

In the next two chapters we explore how those privileged by racialism *resist* change and how those oppressed by race regimes *promote* change. Top-down approaches are state-driven; bottom-up approaches can involve political parties, interest groups, and/or social movements. Both also involve discourses that either legitimize the status quo or justify change. Some laws embodying race regimes have been rescinded – for example, the United States has abolished slavery and legal segregation; all three governments have made Indigenous people citizens; the 'White Australia' and comparable laws have been revoked; and all three governments have ended Asian exclusion laws. But such acts have rarely also eliminated the state practices involved or fully discredited discourses that legitimized them. In these chapters, therefore, we also focus on practices and discourses that facilitate or obstruct change.

It seems a simple matter to dismantle race regimes: a legislature passes a law; a court strikes down a law or a president issues a proclamation. But race regimes and especially covert practices and racialist discourses are deeply embedded in governance institutions, constitutions, and political organizations. Moreover, rescinding race regimes in some cases has negative outcomes for those who are supposed to benefit. An example is Canada's Indian Act, which supposedly was 'reformed.' Yet some of its repressive elements remain in place because Status Indian activists have resisted the government's efforts to repeal it entirely, fearing that their rights as 'Indians' will be abolished and that assimilation will result.

Some approaches to dismantling race regimes seem motivated more by governments' desire for political gain than for the sake of undoing the consequences of those regimes. For example, in 2006 the Harper

Conservative government in Canada apologized and offered $20,000 in restitution to each Chinese Canadian forced to pay the discriminatory head tax to enter Canada under the Head Tax and Exclusion Act. Many suspected that Harper's apology was motivated by his government's desire to win electoral support in Chinese communities. But his government's subsequent efforts to compensate Indigenous people who were harmed by their experiences in residential schools because of previous governments' official policies of assimilation and of abuse by school employees and administrators show that motives usually are mixed and that we should concentrate on governments' actions.

In contrast to top-down approaches, bottom-up efforts such as the reparations movement in the United States to obtain compensation for the descendants of slaves have made little headway, despite plenty of evidence that present-day corporations and family businesses prospered greatly from their slave holdings, which are the basis of current wealth. One approach that began as bottom-up is the reconciliation movement, in which many 'ordinary Australians,' shamed by what they had learned about past governments' racialist policies and practices, said 'Sorry' and tried to develop a better understanding by interacting with local Aboriginal people. Independent inquiries revealed harmful government practices – some recent – that removed light-skinned Aboriginal children (the 'stolen generations') from their families and had them adopted or sent them to training schools to be assimilated. But party-political polarization developed around this issue, and despite the outcry these revelations triggered, conservative Prime Minister John Howard refused to apologize, claiming that his generation wasn't responsible for previous governments' acts. The Labor party prime minister who followed Howard, Kevin Rudd, did apologize to the 'stolen generations' – an indication of how bottom-up approaches get drawn into party-political competition, which can undercut their value.

Rescinding race regimes faces two main problems. First, as we've shown, race regimes and racialism were integral to establishing governance institutions in these settler states, which makes undoing them somewhat like trying to unscramble the eggs in an omelet, especially since amending their constitutions is very difficult, particularly in Australia and the United States. Moreover, the courts' sometimes quixotic interpretations make the outcomes of race-related reforms through judicial review uncertain. Nonetheless, when constitutional systems undergo restructuring, for whatever reason, opportunities may arise to bring about changes in race regimes. The process of claiming control over amendments to the Canadian Constitution (which after Confederation remained with the British parliament) created such opportunities in 1982 when the Trudeau Liberal government proposed to embed a Charter of Rights and Freedoms. The government's proposed Charter contained equality rights provisions that various equality-seeking movements considered flawed. Consequently, they joined forces and achieved more powerful equality rights guarantees (Section 15), which included a provision (s. 15b) permitting affirmative action. The new clauses provided important levers for equality seekers to effect change. The same process inserted new discourses recognizing governments' commitment to Indigenous rights and multiculturalism, which weakened the legitimacy of long-embedded racialist assumptions in constitutional and other political discourses. The coalition to create the Charter's final form combined top-down, government-initiated efforts with bottom-up initiatives by equality seekers.

The second major barrier to dismantling race regimes is that these federations have democratic political systems with White majorities who expect 'their' governments to act in their interests. For example, transferring fishing or logging quotas to Indigenous peoples to rectify past exclusions, or affirmative action provisions to recruit race minorities for jobs or university places, go against the grain of democratic thinking, which valorizes majority rule and treating everyone the same. One of the key issues we will examine, then, is the extent to which such democracies will ever be made responsive to non-White minorities. We theorize that the answer depends on whether the minorities are large (e.g., African Americans and Hispanics in the United States) or small (e.g., Indigenous peoples in all three political systems). There is evidence, discussed in chapter 6, that in some circumstances, large minorities can make governments respond to their needs and demands. Moreover, coalitions among minorities or between minorities and sympathetic Whites can enhance the political clout even of small minorities, as reflected in the joint efforts of equality seekers to change Canada's constitutional equality provisions. Remember, though, that large White majorities are not likely to surrender their power easily.

White majorities have retained their political dominance by excluding non-White minorities from positions of power or by restricting access to those positions, especially in powerful institutions and in the major political parties (i.e., the ones that have the potential to form the government). Historically, the major parties have agreed with one another when it comes to maintaining White rule and to excluding or limiting non-Whites in positions of power in governing parties, executive and judicial positions. Recently, this is an issue around which the major parties in each political system have become polarized, especially where large race minorities have penetrated the party or institution(s) most open to them. As we discussed in chapter 4, opponents of change manipulate the federal system, using the veto points each system provides to obstruct federal governments' efforts to rescind or redress the consequences of racialist policies. In the United States, counter-movements use state governments to get reactionary laws passed, such as the recent anti-migrant laws in California and Arizona. When courts strike down repressive state laws, (White) democratic majorities sometimes resort to ballot initiatives, which enable voters to embed repressive rules in state constitutions and/or overturn judicial decisions. In a few cases, however, one or several meso-level governments may be more progressive and begin a process of reform.

In this chapter we mainly explore bottom-up approaches to dismantling race regimes and redressing their effects. We also show how discourses about democracy – especially regarding majority rule – can be appropriated by powerful movements that oppose reform and that pressure federal governments to water down attempts to rescind race regimes and ameliorate racialism's effects. In chapter 6 we examine top-down approaches, though our narrative will show that this distinction often is artificial.

Attempts to rescind race regimes resulted in the development of democratic racism, the race regime discussed in this book's Introduction. Even with good intentions, many of those working to dismantle race regimes and to erase the influence of racialist discourses are still part of institutions that developed symbiotically with those same race regimes and that had racialism as their central value, albeit less overtly in recent years. Not surprisingly, people educated when racialism was still acceptable could not dismantle race regimes fully, so these early attempts produced the hybrid values of democratic racism. How each country combined the competing values of democratic equality and racialism differed, however, because the two processes – eliminating racialism and working to preserve (White) majority rule – took different paths.

In this chapter, we theorize *contexts that affect institutional change,* consider different strategies and approaches, and provide some examples of successes and failures. (This discussion also frames the cases considered in chapter 6.) We theorize about factors that facilitate or obstruct changes, which include international pressure and globalization, as well as mobilization by race minorities (within the polity) and by international bodies (outside the polity). We also consider how social movements create political and discursive spaces within which change can occur; and we assess how discursive change promotes or obstructs changes in the politics of race. Throughout, we examine how it is difficult in democratic settler states with large White majorities to eliminate the racism embedded in their democratic structures and discourses.

The Contexts of Change

Over the five hundred years since Europeans crossed the oceans in search of adventure, converts, new lands, and riches, many different kinds of relationships – both voluntary and forced – developed between Indigenous inhabitants and invaders and settlers. Distinctive patterns emerged that shaped today's politics of race. Indigenous peoples responded to the Europeans' arrival in many different ways depending on their circumstances, expectations, traditions, and opportunities, but especially on how and when first contact took place. Where Indigenous peoples were the overwhelming majority, some used their power to repel the newcomers; others saw them as possible trading partners or allies against enemies, and welcomed them. Another factor was how various groups of Europeans behaved. On Hispaniola,[1] Columbus and the Spaniards he led used their superior weapons to enslave and exploit; other Europeans, seeking trading partners and guides into the hinterland, formed alliances with Native communities and married into them. Indigenous peoples' responses to the European arrival included active and passive resistance, accommodation and collaboration, negotiation and alliance, and avoidance. How they responded to the harms they suffered in European hands depended on the strength of their communities; but their responses also included aggressive resistance and retaliation, the taking of hostages, and war. This examination of the myriad ways that Europeans and Indigenous peoples responded to one another points to factors that shaped the politics of race then and now. The factors that shaped and changed the structural and discursive race dimensions of governance then and now are demography, geography, the legal context, international environment, and technology.

Demography

A key factor in the politics of race is *demography* – the relative population sizes and sex distributions of Indigenous peoples, Europeans, enslaved Africans, and other non-Whites; and today between White democratic majorities and non-White minorities. At first, Indigenous peoples far outnumbered Europeans; very soon, though, the diseases that Europeans transmitted killed large numbers of Indigenous inhabitants.[2] Treatment by British officials and by settlers and their governments also shrank Indigenous populations. As a consequence, the modern politics of race in the three countries discussed in this book involves Indigenous minorities who do not exceed 5 per cent of the total population. By contrast, the settler societies in Latin America and South Africa have large non-White majorities that have the right to self-government according to democratic theory.

The size of a minority affects how it can behave toward the dominant White majority and other non-White communities. In the three settler societies we are exploring, Indigenous peoples are small minorities, in contrast to New Zealand, for example, where the Maori have more political clout in part because they are a large minority (more than 10 per cent of the population). African Americans in the United States also constitute a large minority and thus have more political clout than Canada's Black population, which for most of its history was smaller than the Indigenous population. Hispanics, too, are a large minority in the United States. So, given the importance that democratic thought ascribes to numbers, a minority's size is key to how political change is shaped in relation to race. The size of race minorities also affects their behaviour when it comes to forming coalitions. Small minorities can increase their political clout in the political system by participating in coalitions with other small minorities and/or with larger minorities. Often, however, they choose to 'go it alone' by seeking self-government in an isolated polity. Both large and small minorities may need to recruit support from within the White majority.

Geography

A second major contextual factor in the federal countries we are discussing is *where* race minorities are located. For example, many African Americans migrated after the Civil War from the southern states where they were concentrated during slavery to the northern cities; this was in an effort to free themselves from Jim Crow segregation, lack of economic opportunity, poverty, and violence. In this way the 'race problem' was diffused throughout the United States, albeit mainly east of the Mississippi. Among other consequences, this produced 'Bronzeville' – Black Chicago – the inward-looking African American political scene where Barack Obama honed his politics. Diane Pinderhughes (2009) observes that *where* African Americans were located *within* Chicago shaped their politics in the era of *de facto* segregation, which persisted after the Civil Rights movement's success. 'Bronzeville,' Pinderhughes (2009, 7) explains, 'was characterized by intense residential segregation, homogeneous, concentrated political districts, consistent representation of Blacks by Blacks, with barriers to their representation in … large contests or heterogeneous areas in the city or state' (7).[3] This geographic concentration constructed differences between the values and goals of the internal, enclosed, African American political domain, which valued the collective effort that race minorities must make to effect change; and the values of individualism and egalitarianism (same treatment), which characterize the external domain of the White-dominated political system.

Pinderhughes (2009, 7) also points to geography to explain why Americans treat Hispanics as recent arrivals. Until recently, their isolation in the southwest placed them far from the centre of eastern-dominated national politics. Far from being immigrants, however, 'the US migrated to them.' But it also 'failed to honor [its] agreement … [to] recogniz[e] citizenship for the grassroots Native American, Spanish and mixed Black and White populations [in what would become Arizona, New Mexico, and California] when it signed the Treaty of Guadalupe Hidalgo in 1848.'

Where race minorities are located, therefore, and – especially in relation to federalism – whether they are concentrated in a handful of states or spread thinly across the country, affects their opportunities to make change. For a number of reasons, most non-White immigrant groups in all three countries became concentrated in a few large metropolitan areas. This has resulted in a geographic divide between large, increasingly diverse urban areas and vast rural and small-town areas where the citizens are largely unfamiliar with immigrants as neighbours. Geographic concentration and isolation may be chosen (Indigenous communities seeking self-governance) or imposed. Also, it can provide valuable opportunities as well as disadvantages. For example, it is only in Australia's Northern Territory that Aboriginal representatives have been elected in any significant numbers, because of population concentrations. But concentrations like these can also facilitate government neglect. A last point, which we will discuss in more detail later, is that the size of a non-White minority in a given political unit (i.e., a city or a state) affects how Whites in that unit perceive that minority. Whites' attitudes toward Indigenous peoples tend to be more progressive where there are fewer Indigenous people living among them. We will return to this point when we discuss the significance of Barack Obama's election as president.

Legal Context

A third factor is the *legal context* in which groups seeking change and redress make their claims. Where Indigenous peoples can point to treaties in support of their claims to land rights, for example, they may gain support more easily from the courts, international agencies, or White public opinion. While few White citizens in these settler societies have confronted the realities of colonial dispossession or the present-day consequences of slavery, courts' recognition of treaty rights, constitutional rights, and common law protections can provide minorities with legal handles around which to mobilize. So while small minorities lack 'the numbers' that democratic thought sanctions, they can use treaties, international legal regimes, and other legal rights such as the common law to make their case. In New Zealand, for example, the Treaty of Waitangi between the British and the Maori has helped the latter gain recognition of their rights. The existence of even recent constitutional rights such as Canada's Charter of Rights and Freedoms may stimulate some White Canadians' feelings of guilt and shame about how Indigenous people and other race minorities were and are treated. And when the Australian High Court ruled that the common law had protected some Aboriginal land rights, those in the ***reconciliation movement*** experienced guilt and shame because White politicians had passed laws to deny them those rights.

The International Environment

Another important contextual factor is the *international environment*, which may affect the relative openness of White-majority settler countries to change. While European powers dominated the globe, establishing colonies and trade zones, racialist ideologies such as 'the White man's burden' and discourses about 'civilization' were used to claim that Whites were naturally superior and to justify White rule. Racialism permeated domestic and international law and thinking. Thus, efforts by non-White leaders in these settler societies to mobilize peoples to achieve change faced intense discursive as well as material opposition. As minorities, they could not play the democratic 'numbers game,' and even where segregation made non-Whites a (local) majority, White public opinion ignored that fact because racist ideology classified non-Whites as inferior or 'primitive' rather than as part of 'the people.' Ideas like these permeated literature, law, science, and even religion. This racialism, which was endemic in Western civilization, began to unravel only after the horrors of racialist regimes and ideas in Germany and Japan during the Second World War were revealed. This in turn began to change the international environment in ways that affected the politics of race in settler societies, though as a superpower, the United States has been less open to such influences.

Race permeated the laws, institutions , discourses, governance, judicial, and bureaucratic practices in settler societies. Factors in the international environment after the Second World War pushed governments to begin to dismantle race regimes. International disapproval was one such factor; another was changes in other countries that influenced how oppressed minorities and/or privileged majorities perceived race regimes and racialism. In the United States, for example, African Americans had rebelled, resisted, and mobilized to seek change for more than a century after the end of Reconstruction, until the Civil Rights movement and a more radical, Black Nationalist movement emerged in the 1960s. There had been disagreement within the African American community over goals and how to achieve them. What brought the struggle against segregation into focus for some in the White majority was the international disapprobation. The United States had fought against Germany's racist Nazi regime – with segregated armed forces. It had also struggled during the Cold War with the Soviet Union to attract Third World countries in Asia, Africa, and Latin America into its democratic camp. Many of these countries, though, were engaged in their own struggles against colonial domination by White European powers and so, not surprisingly, were suspicious of the United States, which continued to deny meaningful citizenship rights to many non-Whites within its borders. These international factors began to crack the apparently seamless racism that had long upheld segregation.

Similar factors led Canadian governments to end *overt* racism in their immigration policies. As we have seen, in 1972 a new Australian Labor government rescinded the legal aspects of the White Australia immigration policy in part to avoid international sanctions. In this regard, Aboriginal peoples' campaigns for Australian citizenship were heavily influenced by the Civil Rights movement in the United States, as were anti-segregation struggles in Canada. Similarly, after Indigenous peoples had struggled against internal colonialism in the United States and Canada for centuries, the high-profile *Red Power movement* was forced into the consciousness of the White majorities as a result of global decolonization struggles against European powers. The newly liberated Third World states entered the international arena and its agencies (such as the UN), thereby triggering an international human rights movement. In each of the three settler nation-states this book discusses, international human rights discourse and the revulsion against Nazi racialism forced a reassessment of racialist practices and discourses.

The Impact of Technology

A fifth contextual factor that shaped political struggles was *technology*. The European colonial powers had gained control over entire Indigenous populations in large part because of their superior technologies of killing. Then after the Second World War, television spread around the world as a tool of mass instruction and entertainment, much as the Internet has done more recently. The power of TV was vital to the U.S. Civil Rights movement's success in ending segregation as a race regime in governments and judicial sanctions; and for establishing meaningful citizenship for African Americans. Through TV, the 'eyes of the world' focused on the U.S. Congress and courts, and on the behaviour of that country's police, military, governors, and president as African Americans struggled to be treated as citizens, and as equal human beings. The new technology made mass movements for change and their ideas contagious; it enabled discourses of equality and human rights to spread like wildfire far beyond their origins. Other technological changes, including rapid and relatively cheap travel, as well as the Internet and its social media, have also had a major impact on how people now struggle to achieve change and on how governments and counter-movements resist those who seek change.

In summary, the main contextual elements driving change in these settler societies have been as follows:

- Those who are oppressed by race regimes are minorities, which vary in size and clout, and most of whom likely will remain minorities in national politics for some time.[4]
- Whites privileged by the consequences of the race regimes are likely to remain majorities for some time in democratic political systems in which majority rule is valorized. The one exception is the

possibility – albeit unlikely – that minorities in the United States could form a coalition that would constitute an electoral majority.

- No one is leaving – that is, both White majorities and non-White minorities will continue to occupy the three states' territories and political systems together; hence their problems won't be solved by anyone's removal or elimination, though White majorities already are working to stay majorities by preventing further non-White migration.
- Given their democratic character, the theoretical assumption is that these settler states will act peacefully in dealing with those struggling to achieve change; but there is considerable evidence that state actors such as police may use violence.
- While Australia and Canada are vulnerable to domestic and international public opinion, as a superpower, the United States is relatively immune to international pressure. In all three countries security issues since 9/11 have made it easier to hide and to justify measures taken against non-White, non-Christian migrants and activists.

Top-Down versus Bottom-Up Approaches to Political Change

Systems of oppression and privilege based on race have proved extremely difficult to dismantle. Even when the legal aspects of race regimes are dismantled, their effects are long lasting and go on being reflected in the poor life chances and living conditions of peoples whose skin colours and other physical characteristics are perceived to differ from those of 'Whites.' Moreover, race regimes were so entangled in colonial expansion, migration, and settlement, and in the imperialist exploitation of resources, that they are hard to reverse. Current Europeans whose countries had colonies have little sense that their affluent and elegant civilizations were fed by the lands, labours, and resources of their former colonies. The descendants of Europeans in settler societies are much closer to the facts, though myths also avoid acknowledging the extent to which their relative affluence, comforts, and rights are consequences of settler societies' exploitation of the lands, labours, and resources of Indigenous peoples and the labours of non-White workers. Those who are part of the privileged majority have a different take on what should be changed and on how change should occur than those who belong to still disadvantaged minorities. Those who are privileged by racialism continue to deny that their advantage is based on race in any way.

Whose perspective should we take when we consider approaches to change in the politics of race? Many White Canadians believe that, unlike the United States, Canada does not have a race problem. White Australians and Americans believe that their race problems are in the past. For example, Australia's former Prime Minister Howard repudiated analyses of race politics as 'the Black armband theory' of how his continent-nation was settled, claiming that Australians should be proud of what happened despite 'a few regrettable incidents.' But are Whites, who rarely are victims of racist practices, the best authorities on whether change is needed? Are they good judges of how to deconstruct race regimes? Surely, Indigenous peoples, African Americans, and other non-Whites are better judges of whether the race regimes designed to exclude or oppress them still have negative consequences. Yet the perspectives of those who are oppressed or who are experiencing the negative consequences of race regimes are rarely included in analyses of change. Lise Noël (1994, 7) observes that when the victims of oppression do finally challenge its postulates, 'they ... are accused of "radicalism."' Whereas, those in government or who are classified as experts on 'the problem' – when it is admitted there is a problem – belong almost exclusively to the dominant group. Not surprisingly, therefore, the changes they propose rarely would disrupt the established order ('our way of life'), since their goal is to achieve change with as little disruption to Whites as possible. Often, fear that change will 'provoke' backlash is used to weaken or delay the implementation of measures. Backlash is a kind of blackmail – 'if you rock the boat by demanding change, we'll throw you out of the boat.' Often, change is hampered because the projected costs in terms of disruption are more from threatened backlash than from activism demanding change or Whites' losses in the change itself.

A frequent discursive approach used to avoid change involves *blaming the victim*. Albert Memmi believes that a racist 'does not punish his victim because he deserves punishment, but declares him guilty because he is *already* punished' (cited in Noël 1994, 129). Noël concludes that the dynamics of racial domination makes the dominators seek the cause of the victim's exclusion or oppression *in the victim*. That is, when hardcore, racist beliefs in biological superiority, for example, come under attack, Whites find it psychologically necessary to blame the victim in order to continue living with their privileges, including their political privileges, even when their racism conflicts with their long-held democratic values. Race oppression has always been legitimized by the notion that those oppressed *are guilty of their own inferiority* – because they were, after all, 'primitives' who led 'savage' lives. The consequences of systemic, state-administered race oppression – poverty, disease, slum housing, high levels of imprisonment, low levels of power – also are blamed on non-Whites' inferior character traits; for example, they are imagined to be lazy, drunken, and stupid and more recently are suspected of being agitators or even terrorists. While often not overt, victim-blaming habits of mind are also entrenched in the discourses and practices of governments and political parties; otherwise they would have to attribute Whites' resistance to change, which some leaders but few followers accept, to self-interest.

Bottom-Up Approaches to Change

Governments and experts rarely ask those actually oppressed by race regimes and their aftermaths what would improve their life circumstances. Nor do they ask the political leaders of equality-seeking movements or those few non-White 'experts' consulted by powerful (White) leaders of the dominant society.[5] And when the views of race minorities are expressed to governments, their analyses rarely prevail against the views of White experts, bureaucrats, and politicians. In the United States in the 1960s, for example, many African American leaders contended that their high levels of unemployment resulted from discrimination by unions and employers. Some anti-discrimination legislation was passed, but it was a report to the Department of Labor by a White sociologist, Daniel Moynihan (later a U.S. senator), that became 'the explanation.' Moynihan blamed male African American unemployment – and other problems – on family instability, which supposedly was caused by overpowering African American women who 'emasculated' African American men.[6] This practice of White 'expert' explanations trumping the self-knowledge and expertise of non-Whites is a common one.

What does bottom-up change require? People who are oppressed by race regimes, and disadvantaged by their consequences, rarely share a single common perspective about what needs to be changed; or about how change should be achieved. This is especially true regarding large, disparate minorities such as 'African Americans' and 'Hispanics.' One example will illuminate this point. Because TV conveyed the U.S. Civil Rights movement's activism night after night, many assumed that all African Americans shared the goal of *integration* into the United States nation as equal, individual citizens. This was indeed the goal of many, but it was just one of several approaches. Some African Americans reject integration, and the strategies it entails. Both after the end of slavery and after the Second World War, African American communities were divided over the goals to be pursued and how to achieve them, as were Black communities in Canada.

Slavery and later segregation were central to the formation of the U.S. nation-state and federation. Consequently, African Americans were dominated in ways that made it unlikely that they could later be integrated into a society organized around Whites-only nationalism and Whites-only citizenship. Other approaches to improve their circumstances were popular just after slavery was abolished: return to Africa, which Lincoln advocated and some African Americans accepted; and the development of separate, self-sufficient communities. After the Civil War, the federal government's policy of providing land, political rights (to men), employment, and education fostered a series of top-down policies called Reconstruction. African Americans who had fought in the federal armies during the Civil War expected enfranchisement and the delivery of other promised goods. Ultimately, Reconstruction failed after northern, federal republicans withdrew their support for military protection, effectively abandoning it. The federal government's imposition of political rights for African American men, which White republicans meant as a punishment of rebellious southern Whites, fostered a *backlash* after Reconstruction when state governments reverted to White control. White southerners used their regained political and social power to impose Jim Crow segregation laws and policies.

Building Self-Sufficient Communities

The bottom-up approach to change adopted by most African American communities and leaders involved developing self-sufficient institutions, especially churches and schools, which they used to improve their lives by promoting solidarity, literacy, education, vocational training, and employment opportunities. While some ex-slaves chose to return to Africa, most stayed to develop African American communities, with strong institutions for protection and advancement. Those who try to achieve bottom-up change have agency and can choose among goals and strategies. But their choices are limited by what is possible at any given time. Hence the goal of integration – even when chosen – faced huge barriers after Reconstruction failed; indeed, those barriers remained in place until the Civil Rights movement emerged in the 1960s. In the interim, the main barriers were the racism embodied in Whites-only nation building and Whites' control of the federal and state governments. White nation building and solidarity required that segregation be applied to anyone of African ancestry (the 'one drop of blood' rule).[7] Ironically, this strengthened the solidarity of African American communities. Though many African Americans moved north to escape the vicious segregationist regimes in the south, White and African American institutions and communities were separate everywhere. African American institutions – for example, schools and colleges – were poor, but they fostered improvement, advancement, employment, and especially solidarity. While African Americans jumped at the chance for inclusion and at the benefits of Reconstruction, leaders like Booker T. Washington looked to these separate institutions to develop self-reliance in former slaves, especially in the south; and to educate them for equal citizenship. This strategy produced generations of African American professionals, especially ministers and teachers, who held communities together and provided support and succour to those experiencing racialist oppression.

Not all African American leaders promoted separate communities. Some, like W.E.B. Du Bois, developed a nationalist strategy that promoted race pride and viewed segregation as a means to developing African American culture. This strategy included *consciousness-raising*. Du Bois rejected the assumption – implicit in the goal of integration – that African Americans and their culture were inferior to Whites and their culture. He had started out as an integrationist who assumed that talented African Americans should agitate for integration. In this context, he founded the National Association for the Advancement of Colored People (NAACP). But over time, he changed his views. Thus he accepted segregated officer training during the First World War as a temporary measure, assuming that African Americans' contributions to the war effort would win them recognition, integration, and expanded rights. But (southern-born) President Woodrow Wilson's struggle 'to make the world safe for democracy' still left African Americans at home unrewarded for their contributions. Like Wilson, White Americans saw democracy as a Whites-only project. Du Bois concluded that African Americans must abandon the demeaning goal of seeking integration. Instead he became 'a staunch advocate of Black nationalism, using the terms race and nation interchangeably as identities based on common blood and shared experience' (Marx 1998, 220). Du Bois used the 'one drop of blood' rule to bind those of mixed blood to African American nationalist causes.

The institutions developed by Booker T. Washington and Du Bois reflected their bottom-up strategies as well as their assessments of what changes were possible in their time. Washington founded the Tuskegee

Institute to train teachers and others to serve African American communities. He recruited George Washington Carver, an ex-slave, who with other African American scientists at Tuskegee developed products such as peanut butter, and improved Black farmers' agricultural practices as well as African Americans' nutrition. Du Bois' NAACP, which grew out of his Niagara movement, focused on the small African American middle class, from which he expected leaders to emerge (Marx 1998, 221). The NAACP focused mainly on gaining redress and rights through the courts. Whites supported both institutions and their associated movements.[8]

Before the twentieth-century Civil Rights movement Black nationalism was the only bottom-up approach that had generated a major mass movement. Its leader, Marcus Garvey, promoted race purity, self-reliance, and nationalism. Focusing on poor urban Blacks, he maintained that American Whites could not be persuaded to give African Americans rights or employment. Blacks, then, had to rely on themselves and one another. By 1923, his Universal Negro Improvement Association had nearly a million members. The focus on self-help and self-empowerment was evident as well in the unionization of railway porters, who held what often was the only job open to African American men. Led by A. Philip Randolph, the union grew strong enough that in 1941, his threat of a Black march on Washington persuaded President Roosevelt to create a Committee on Fair Employment Practices to end race-based job discrimination in war industries.

These bottom-up approaches to change were copied – albeit on a smaller scale – in Canada, where the diverse Black community was very small. The differences between those seeking integration and equal citizenship, and those favouring separation, race pride, self-help, and nationalism, were evident in both countries and persist into the present day. The massive Civil Rights movement in the United States also had international effects. As TV shrank the world, the movement's example promoted change as far away as Australia.

*Bottom-Up Approaches – Grassroots Activism
in the U.S. Civil Rights Movement*

In the U.S. Civil Rights movement, *grassroots* strategies existed at the local level, though academic analyses tend to focus on what the courts, the police, federal and state legislators, governors, and the president did. That is, they focus on state actors. Even when African American actors are considered, most academics focus on national organizations and a handful of charismatic national leaders, notably the Reverend Martin Luther King Junior. Historian Charles Payne argues, however, that 'the movement' that ultimately dislodged the mountain of racism and oppression was made up of many small groups and activists whose individual acts of courage in the face of oppression and violence made legal and political changes possible, not least by changing many African Americans' (and some Whites') minds that change could and should occur. Perhaps the best-known example is Rosa Parks, whose refusal to give up her seat on a bus sparked the Montgomery bus boycott in Alabama that started a movement to end segregation in public facilities. Parks was not the tired maid acting spontaneously, as she often is portrayed. She had joined the NAACP in 1943, had become secretary of its Montgomery Branch, and had worked in voter registration campaigns (Lawson and Payne 1998, 111ff). She ran the local NAACP Youth Council and was Secretary of the State Conference of NAACP Branches – a lifelong activist.

When we look behind famous grassroots activists like Rosa Parks, we find many networks of people, often women, who provided the contexts in which minds were changed and the skills of organizing, risk-taking, and leadership were learned. Many key local activists and organizers attended the Highlander Folk School in Tennessee. Founded during the Great Depression to teach activism to poor Whites in Appalachia, it was dedicated to interracial, egalitarian living (Lawson and Payne 1998, 102). Rather than focusing on a few charismatic leaders, Highlander emphasized participatory democracy and empowerment in the citizenship schools it ran in segregated localities, hidden from White authorities. At these schools, adults learned to read and write and how to register to vote, which usually involved interpreting part of the state constitution to the (grudging) satisfaction of a hostile registrar. During the 1950s and 1960s nearly ten thousand people learned to teach such skills, with two hundred citizenship schools operating at any time. Their basic purpose was to identify local community leaders, assist in their education and empowerment, and help them develop networks for actions.

Ella Baker was a key grassroots activist for more than three decades in North Carolina. Since 1941 she had worked for the NAACP organizing and advising branches across the south. But by 1946 she despaired of democratizing the top-down NAACP and became the first full-time organizer for the Southern Christian Leadership Conference (SCLC), which many Americans associate with Reverend Martin Luther King, who was its spokesman. Baker's philosophy of change did not revolve around a few big leaders, however; it entailed mobilizing the masses. She believed that people 'had to learn to lead themselves.' Her approach involved empowering community leaders and individuals to become self-reliant and brave when faced with oppression and violence, insisting that 'they ... are the only protection they have against violence or injustice ...' (Lawson and Payne 1998, 102).

Others, like Parks and Baker, lived lives dedicated to activism, often taking risks to stand up to violence. Their approach involved *direct action* – read-ins, eat-ins, sit-ins, pickets, protests, pray-ins, and swim-ins – which challenged segregation directly and to which local authorities and White citizens often reacted with violence. Attempts by young African Americans to attend all-White schools were one form of direct action that eventually forced the president to guard those schools with federal troops. Reverend King believed that such direct actions should occur within a strategy of *non-violence*, similar to the one developed by Gandhi, who had led India to independence by morally shaming Britain when it used violence against ***non-violent non-cooperation***, or ***civil disobedience***. But not all in the U.S. movement were committed to non-violence under all circumstances. Indeed, many grassroots activists preached self-defence when faced with violence from local and state police and White vigilantes and, rarely protected by the federal government, taught self-defence despite King's disapproval and that of the NAACP. In 1957, Robert Williams led North Carolina NAACP members in a shoot-out with Ku Klux Klan members who were attacking his community, insisting that, while he taught non-violence, he 'also believe[d] that a man cannot have human dignity if he allows himself to be abused; to be kicked and beaten to the ground; to allow his wife and children to be attacked' (Lawson and Payne 1998, 116).

Moral appeals and philosophical declarations of non-violence, therefore, mobilized fewer grassroots African American activists than did community building, direct action, and self-defence. Local leaders were disproportionately women and were rarely viewed as charismatic; nor were they prone to violence. But as one SCLC leader, Andrew Young, concluded: 'It was women going door to door, speaking with their neighbours, meeting in voter-registration classes together, organizing through their churches that gave the vital momentum and energy to the movement, that made it a mass movement' (cited in Lawson and Payne 1998, 124). When they were struck with clubs, were beaten in jail, were shot, and had their houses firebombed, Ella Baker and others helped them organize in opposition. But because their organizations displayed neither charismatic leadership nor advocated philosophical non-violence, they largely were ignored. Those local organizations, based on mutual aid and self-defence, nonetheless were the movement's backbone. This sort of community development in Chicago was President Obama's work before he entered electoral politics.

To make sense of these patterns of bottom-up activism, it is useful to recall the contextual factors outlined earlier in this chapter. Bottom-up approaches to change are sensitive to demographic factors. In the United States, African Americans are a large minority, and in some localities a majority, and can bring together mass movements of thousands of people. (There is no equivalent large race minority in either Australia or Canada.) In the 1960s and 1970s, when the new technology of on-the-spot TV coverage was being developed, a mass movement could attract widespread national and international attention. Public violence by White state officials embarrassed the federal government, especially after the courts rescinded the segregation regime and the movement became mixed-race so that TV showed White protesters being beaten and demanding federal protection. The most profound changes, however, happened in Americans' consciousness as non-Whites and some Whites decided that violent oppression by state officers and second-class citizenship could not be tolerated.

During the Civil Rights struggle, nightly TV revealed the failures of America, which persuaded some White Americans to join African Americans in marching for race justice, thereby placing themselves at risk from state violence and White vigilantes defending segregation. In 1963, for example, during the Mississippi Summer Project, White activists went south providing protection for African Americans' education and voter registration efforts in highly racist communities. But as Charles Payne (in Lawson and Payne 1998, 126) observes: 'It was a deal with the devil, premised on the idea that White lives matter and Black lives do not. The movement was betting that when middle-class White lives were placed in jeopardy, Washington would ... find some way to protect them, which would benefit Black activists as well.' By using ugly images of the nation's racism against itself, the movement provoked the federal government into using its power, and the defenders of White supremacy eventually lost their capacity to apply violence openly to maintain segregation, or to use state governments to legally sanction segregation and denial of political rights. Making the movement biracial to tap White moral feelings about racism was a strategy that the movement's leaders *chose*; but to manage biracial demonstrations required firm *elite* control, and many grassroots activists resented the energies it drained away from organizing African American communities.

The goal of *integration* eventually was achieved in public facilities by a combination of top-down changes and bottom-up mobilization. But the cost was high. While more money was now spent on the education of African American children, thousands of African American teachers lost their jobs; and the separate schools that communities had built were eliminated along with the attention to African American culture that they provided. Nor did 'integration' mean the end of White supremacy or segregation, though many of the laws that had established segregation were repealed. Residential segregation, for example, persists to this day in part because of the racialist practices of banks and the real estate and insurance industries. While the laws were changed, real equality remained elusive, and the movement fractured over how to challenge the White privilege that persisted and how to reverse the aftermath of many decades of legal segregation. Some Whites, and the federal government, acted against racist violence and state laws that denied African Americans citizenship. But they would not support the more radical and costly changes needed to end race-based poverty and stigmatization.

Winning the right to ride buses, read, pray, and swim alongside Whites – integration – did not end African American poverty or marginalization. Indeed, the economic disadvantage, poorer health, inferior housing, and lower-status jobs we profiled in the Introduction continue as the aftermaths of slavery and segregation. Some African Americans overcame them, but for many they persisted. Consequently, in the 1960s, many joined more radical movements such as the Black Panthers, or they followed leaders who, like Malcolm X, channelled their frustration that White privilege and Black poverty remained. Moreover, the elimination of legally sanctioned racism resulted in a changed discourse among Whites, and even among some African Americans who had 'made it.' With no legal restraints, they now saw African American poverty, poor health, substandard housing, limited education, and unemployment as caused by poor African Americans' character flaws. This would become a key tenet of *democratic racism*, which developed after segregation ended.

Is President Obama a Game Changer?

In 2009, what may be in a new chapter in the history of African Americans' struggle for equality was ushered in with the election of

Barack Obama to the presidency – somewhere in between a bottom-up and a top-down approach. The election of an African American of mixed White and African ancestry was unprecedented and in many ways unexpected. PBS journalist Gwen Ifill, in *The Breakthrough: Politics and Race in the Age of Obama* (2009, 1), writes: 'It is true that he accomplished what no Black man had before, but it went further. Simply as an exercise in efficient politics, Obama '08 … was historical and … transformed how race and politics intersect in our society.' What does this election tell us about the most effective approaches to change? Obama was not the first non-White candidate for president, so why did he win? Does his success signal that the same political process of running for election that has sustained Whites in power can help disadvantaged groups elect 'one of their own'? Is this, then, the best strategy for achieving change? Is having a non-White president a 'game changer'? Will the statistics showing race-based disadvantage outlined in the Introduction change in the near future? While we can't answer these very difficult questions with any certainty in this short section, we can suggest ways of thinking about them that you can explore.

Barack Obama's meteoric rise is now a familiar narrative. A Harvard-educated lawyer, he cut his political teeth as a community organizer on the South Side of Chicago. He was a state senator in Illinois and subsequently ran for the U.S. Senate in 2000 and won. In this and in his bid for the presidency, he had the support of a sophisticated team of (largely White) political operatives. He gained attention at the 2004 Democratic National Convention with a speech in which he described America not in multicultural or multiracial terms but as a whole nation unmarked by race. He declared: 'The United States of America … is not a Black America and White America and Latino America and Asian America – [it] is the United States of America' (Ifill 2009, 64). What accounted for Obama's success if, as Sinclair-Chapman and Price claim, 'a year before the start of the 2008 primary season, Black voters outside of Illinois barely knew Obama' (2008, 740)?

African Americans have run for high office since 1872, when former slave Frederick Douglass ran as vice-president. In 1972, Shirley Chisholm was the first African American woman to run a national campaign for the Democratic party's presidential nomination, followed by the Reverend Jesse Jackson in 1984 (Sinclair-Chapman and Price 2008, 739). Many other African Americans have run for president or vice-president on third-party tickets. But because of the electoral system, third-party bids are usually symbolic, though such candidates can be 'spoilers,' drawing enough votes to defeat one of the two-party candidates (usually the Democrat). Moreover, all of the candidates previously had run as African Americans. Obama's approach was different. He was an outsider in the sense that he hadn't been involved in core political African American organizations. His approach was to try to transcend race by appealing to a cross-section of Americans, and in that way – so he hoped – 'unify a diverse coalition of Americans around a progressive agenda' (West, cited in Sinclair-Chapman and Price 2008, 740).

Did Obama achieve this? Some observers believe he did, for his campaign gave equal discursive weight to African American and Hispanic demands for full citizenship and to White resentment of those same demands. That is to say, his claim of unity – 'We are all Americans' – affirms 'broad consensus on national values' while at the same time ignoring 'structural inequalities that maintain Black exclusion and subordination' (Sinclair-Chapman and Price 2008, 740). Harvey Wingfield and Joe R. Feagin (2010) have theorized that Obama's campaign discourses used 'soft racial framing,'[9] or colour-blind discourses, as a way of reflecting his racially-mixed heritage so that he would relate to both Whites and non-Whites. He did not cast himself as the first African American to win the Democratic nomination; nor did he specifically place civil rights as a key goal in his election platform. By taking this soft approach, he was able to appeal to a multiracial electorate.

Below, we consider whether Obama succeeded in transcending the race divide in his campaign. Initially, his apparently colour-blind campaign was problematic for many older African American intellectuals. Gwen Ifill (2009, 37–8) contends that a generational divide characterized Obama's campaign: 'the elders sprang up from a civil rights movement that helped create … majority-Black districts. Once inside … [those] elected … acquired a power of incumbency that virtually guaranteed re-election, year after year.' Ifill notes that while some in the White Congressional power structure may have been happy with this 'separate but equal approach,' others challenged majority-minority districts before the Supreme Court, just as they challenged other forms of affirmative action. The main beneficiaries of affirmative action racial districting were assertive young female politicians, not the 'old lions' of the Civil Rights movement, whom Ifill suggests Whites in Congress were willing to tolerate.

Barack Obama's historic rise to power in the United States places the discussion of politics and race on a different footing than for small minorities in either Australia or Canada, where there are no large national race minorities. Some analysts contend that far from leading people into a 'post-racial' America, the Obama campaign has actually accentuated the painful legacies of slavery and segregation in the United States. In chapter 6, we will consider President Obama's top-down policies and examine whether his election has made U.S. democracy more responsive to African Americans, or not. In this section we examine the empirical evidence about who elected Obama president. If the campaign strategy's post-racial discourse succeeded, we would expect an increase in the proportion of Whites voting for the Democratic party. In fact, the proportion of Whites voting Democrat declined from 2004.

Who Voted for Barack Obama, and Why

Some analysts argue that, though objective conditions existed for a landslide victory by the 'out party' presidential candidate, Barack Obama was denied a landslide, winning with 52.9 per cent of the popular vote. Moreover, though he outspent McCain (by $7.36 compared to $5.78 per vote won), the proportion of Whites who voted for him was just 43 per cent, to McCain's 55 – less than the proportion won by Senator Kerry, the unsuccessful Democratic candidate in 2004.[10]

Data from previous presidential election campaigns define a landside victory as a heavy majority won with over 55 per cent of the popular vote, such as won by Reagan over Carter. The factors usually associated with landslide victories are a serious economic crisis and an unpopular president or no incumbent president or vice-president in the race. Regarding 2008, analysts posit that 'with ... conditions so favorable to the Democrats, Obama should have been trouncing McCain ... but he was not' (Lewis-Beck, Tien, and Nadeau 2010, 71). President George W. Bush's popularity was very low, but McCain was considered ill-informed on economics and a Wall Street meltdown was under way. Even so, Obama did not win by a landslide. To explain this, Lewis-Back and colleagues (2010) disentangle the relative effects of economic voting, which would have predisposed voters to support the (out-party) Democratic candidate; and of race, which could have either a positive or a negative effect.

An NBC/Wall Street Journal poll (run 17–20 Oct. 2008) found that among regular voters, 4 per cent reported that Obama's race made it less likely that they would vote for him, whereas only 2 per cent reported that his race made it more likely. Two per cent were unsure, and 92 per cent claimed that it would have no strong effect. Among regular voters, then, Obama's race turned more voters away than it attracted. Obama won the election mainly because of high turnouts among those who do not usually vote – young, first time, and race-minority voters. Without them, McCain likely would have won.

When we consult election-day exit poll reports, we see the picture more clearly. Whatever some African Americans thought of Obama's campaign, they supported him once it became apparent he might win. On Election Day, 95 per cent of African Americans (13 per cent of voters) reported voting for him. So too did 67 per cent of Hispanics (9 per cent), 62 per cent of Asians (2 per cent), and 66 per cent of other/mixed race (3 per cent). So of the 27 per cent of the U.S. electorate made up of large and small race minorities, about 80 per cent voted for Obama, compared to 43 per cent of White voters (74 per cent of all voters). Lewis-Back and colleagues (2010, 75) conclude that 'racial esteem does not cancel out racial prejudice.' Whites who feared that Obama would act to advantage African Americans would not vote for him even if they saw him as the best candidate to deal with the economic crisis. And more than half of all respondents (56 per cent) believed that Obama *would* favour African Americans; this probably cost him many White votes, since Whites who thought that were significantly less likely to vote for him.

So despite campaign rhetoric, and the emphasis on reconciliation after his speech on race, many White voters perceived a zero sum game: they believed that while electing Obama might benefit them by 'fixing' the economy, it would also hurt them because he would favour African Americans and end their White privilege. These predictions will not be confirmed or refuted until voters face the decision of whether or not to re-elect President Obama; but at that point, other factors, including incumbency and (potentially) security issues may be in play. 'Ballot box racism,' which includes racial resentment as well as fear of such resentment, is clearly a factor when race minorities try to use the ordinary political process to make racial democracies more responsive to them.

Discussion Questions

1 Describe three 'bottom up' approaches to change in the politics of race in these three settler societies; and assess their potential for lessening White privilege.
2 Some say that the election of President Obama as the first U.S. president of African American heritage was unexpected. Can studying political science help us understand why the election

of a race-minority person in a White-majority polity should be expected rather than a surprise?

3 From this chapter, assemble the key factors in the politics of race, and discuss how they may influence each government's policies toward race minorities in the future.

4 What makes the system of White race privilege so hard to dislodge in these three countries?

5 In the past, Indigenous/Aboriginal peoples and race minorities have resisted White domination in these societies in specific ways. Do these groups use contemporary forms of resistance? If so, how effective are they? If they are not, why not?

6 Top-Down Approaches and Democratic Responsiveness

In this chapter we explore top-down, state-directed approaches to change. Our focus is on whether the settler democracies discussed in this book, each characterized by a large White majority (up to 75 per cent), are responsive to the demands and needs of the race minorities in their territories. We theorize that democratic responsiveness varies with the size of the group that is making claims through the electoral/legislative process; and that larger race minorities are more likely than their smaller counterparts to succeed in generating responsiveness, though a minority can magnify its clout by joining coalitions. Since there are large minorities only in the United States, our analysis focuses on whether Barack Obama's presidency is likely to produce responsiveness and better outcomes for African Americans. While our focus will be on federal governments, we also consider the potential responsiveness of state and provincial governments. Because race minorities that are small nationally may be large, or even majorities, in one or several states or provinces, this level of governance may actually be as important as the federal level.

We do not claim that responsiveness can occur only where there are large majorities, but this is likely to be the case in legislatures where representatives respond within an electoral logic. But in other arenas – such as lobbying, the executive – responsiveness to race minorities may involve different logics. Moreover, constitutional restructuring may provide circumstances where a coalition of equality seekers that includes race minorities can achieve change, as happened in Canada in 1982. But in most instances, when top-down strategies relate to small minorities, they usually reflect a government initiative. One example is *self-government* in relation to Indigenous minorities. We also briefly consider *affirmative action* and *multiculturalism*. That said, demands for self-government may sometimes suit the government in power, as happened when President Reagan and Republican administrators encouraged Native American tribes to assume more governance responsibility. In this chapter, we first illustrate failed top-down initiatives relating to Aboriginal peoples in two periods in Australia. We then explore collaborative approaches that involve top-down government initiatives as well as bottom-up mobilization. We then assess the top-down policy of multiculturalism from an anti-racist perspective. Finally, we consider how democratic theory that sanctions majority rule can be adapted in these White-majority, settler nation-states to make governments more responsive and accommodating. We conclude that democratic racism poses the highest barriers to both aspirations.

Top-Down Approaches

Top-down strategies toward change, when applied to race regimes, have consequences that pose problems because many in the majority will resist any action that reduces the privileges they enjoy because of their skin colour. Regardless of size, minorities are subject to the 'numbers game' that is fundamental to majority rule in democracies. Moreover, most minorities are destined to *remain* minorities, at least for some time. Hence the question is how to persuade governments, which are responsive mainly to the White majority, that it is in their interests to promote or accept change. When a significant part of the White majority resists or mobilizes against progressive change, politicians draw back. Of course, there are different interests *within* the majority, and a democratic electoral system operates through ideologically organized[1] party systems that mobilize both White and non-White voters. But even when governments genuinely seek change, they find it hard to dismantle the legal aspects of race regimes. Because many in the majority enjoy White privilege, there is both overt and unconscious resistance to change.

Also, political institutions' path dependence can obstruct change even when political actors want to achieve it. Indeed, we might well wonder whether institutions that have been the main tools of racialism can become instruments of positive change for race minorities. Some contend that they cannot and that new state structures may be needed. But changing institutions or creating new ones also requires support from the majority. However, institutional shocks, such as result from exposing notorious cases or international shaming, can bring about changes in institutional norms. So can other 'game changers.' Another way of achieving institutional change involves exploiting opportunities created in a period of general institutional restructuring. For example, when the Canadian federal government repatriated its constitution – that is, took over responsibility from the United Kingdom for amending it – it added a Charter of Rights and Freedoms. This enabled a coalition of equality-seeking movements to insert effective equality rights into the Charter. Aboriginal rights and multicultural principles also were embedded. Australia's movement to become a republic, while currently stalled, could provide a similar opportunity for embedding Aboriginal rights and a Bill of Rights in a revised constitution. However, strong political pressure would be required to seize these opportunities.

Top-Down Change and Large Minorities

Is the U.S. political system responsive to non-White minority voters? This discussion focuses on African Americans, who are a large minority. It also considers the extent to which the election of a president identified with the African American community can be expected to increase the system's responsiveness to race minority voters. In *Minority Report: Evaluating Political Equality in America* (2008), John D. Griffin and Brian Newman explore the first question in an empirical account of who the winners and losers have been in U.S. democracy. They devise numerous tests of 'responsiveness' in order to determine how decision makers respond to White and non-White voters in federal politics, especially in Congress. They begin by documenting how policy preferences differ across race groups, especially regarding welfare, health care, and 'crime,' in order to assess the extent to which government policies and spending decisions accord with the preferences of Whites compared to those of African Americans and Hispanics.

Do race minority voters get the same 'bang for their buck' from those they elect as White voters do? A key part of this analysis involves correlating the voting records of congressmen and congresswomen with the ideologies and preferences of White voters versus African American and Hispanic voters. Griffin and Newman (ch. 5) report that congressional representatives as a group are about twice as responsive to Whites' ideological and policy preferences than they are to those of non-White voters. Their research covers a period of conservative Republican dominance, however, and their findings could differ for those periods when progressive Democrats dominated Congress and held the presidency. That said, the ability of minority Republicans to obstruct the

Democrats' policy agenda suggests that responsiveness involves more than who won a majority in Congress.

These findings about the *relative* responsiveness of congressional representatives to White and non-White voters raise questions. Individual representatives may not respond more readily to White voters. Griffin and Newman found non-White representatives, for example, more responsive to non-White voters, which shows how important it is to increase the numbers of non-White representatives. They also report that the *intensity* of each group in expressing its preferences affects whom representatives support in congressional votes. So if race minorities care more about an issue than White voters, they probably can make their representatives respond to their preferences. But when White voters care intensely about an issue, they too have great power to make congressional actors heed them, as we saw during the 2011 health care reform debate.

The logic of representative democracy in the United States seems to assume that the responsiveness of elected legislatures *should* be roughly proportional to each group's size. This would reproduce the status quo, however, meaning that change would require a different logic, or different actors, or both. As noted earlier, the U.S. electoral system is based on territory, not proportionality. But historically, the (partisan) redistricting process has *gerrymandered* federal districts to prevent African Americans or Hispanics from being majorities in any district. Thus until 1994, only six African Americans had ever been elected to Congress in all-White or Anglo-majority districts. Supreme Court interpretations of the Voting Rights Act, however, permitted *minority-majority districts*, which resulted in the election of thirty-six African Americans and seventeen Hispanics in 1994 (two Republican African Americans were also elected that year in White-majority districts). In *Democracy in Practice*, Helena Catt (1999, 87–8) classifies the underlying theory that the Court applied as 'the doctrine of an equal vote' – the principle that 'a group must have a realistic opportunity to choose their own representative, [and if] geographically compact and politically cohesive ... it should not be stopped from choosing its own representative.' A later (conservative) Court ruled that race cannot be the primary factor in redistricting, but that the previous practice of gerrymandering to deny minorities a majority in a district – what the Court called *vote dilution* – must be avoided. The idea that a race minority group would choose 'one of its own' to represent it assumes that minority voters believe that a representative who shares their experiences of race is also likely to share their policy preferences and concerns, and hence will act on their behalf and in their interests. This raises the question of whether any *elected* White-majority institution can be responsive to race-minority voters.[2]

Griffin and Newman's analysis of government responsiveness is incomplete because it does not consider other elected actors, notably the president; unelected actors, including the courts (especially the Supreme Court) and the administration, which the president controls; or state and local governments, whose responsiveness is especially important in localities where there are more African Americans and Hispanics.

Affirmative Action

This involves policies and/or laws aimed at reversing the effects of historic patterns experienced by groups that have been disadvantaged because of race, ethnicity, sex, or disability. As developed in the United States, the logic of *affirmative action* is that, because of historic experiences – including slavery, segregation, and exclusion from citizenship – members of disadvantaged groups should be given an advantage (a 'leg up' or 'set aside') until the effects have been erased. How affirmative action works differs from place to place. Even within a particular country, different states/provinces may have policies that work differently; and some may have none. What they usually have in common is that they involve going beyond establishing a 'level playing field' of equal opportunity in which everyone is treated the same. 'Level field' approaches – also described as 'colour-blind' – make current discrimination illegal, whereas affirmative action policies or practices attack the effects of past discrimination/oppression by extending preferential benefits or access to members of groups shown previously to have been oppressed.

The most common areas in which governments have enacted affirmative action policies are education, wages, and employment. (The latter two policies, in Canada, are referred to as pay equity and employment equity.) Since the 1960s, U.S. federal law has provided for 'positive measures of equal opportunity for all qualified persons' to redress the effects of structural factors that had produced systemic discrimination and obstructed true equality of *opportunity*. Note that the goal has always been to provide *individuals* with equal access or equality of opportunity; it has not been to provide equal results, or to benefit groups. In the United States, affirmative action laws and policies have come to be seen as unfair by many Whites, largely because they seem to disadvantage 'innocent' Whites – that is, White aspirants to university places, jobs, and so on who are 'not guilty' of the historic acts that created slavery, segregation, and other race regimes. However, some judges accept the idea that Whites may enjoy privileged access and benefits resulting from these historic or structural systems. A second criticism in the United States is that affirmative action policies and programs perpetuate a role for race in politics. These critics argue that 'race-blind' individualism should be the goal so that race will no longer matter; and that slavery and segregation are 'ancient history' with few present-day effects. Some race minority members reject any race classification as morally odious; but many perceive affirmative action as having succeeded reasonably well in ameliorating the consequences of centuries of legal oppression.

Affirmative action in employment, education, and wages has also been implemented in some Canadian jurisdictions. Section 15(b) of the Charter of Rights and Freedoms states that affirmative action programs that address group disadvantages do not constitute discrimination. Canadian legislation, because it targets multiple groups, thus giving more people vested interests in the programs, has not been as controversial as similar laws in the United States. In Australia, affirmative action is little used in relation to race, though it has been used to some degree to fight discrimination against women and to incorporate NES (non-English-speaking) immigrants. There is Commonwealth legislation that bans racial discrimination, but as noted earlier, the federal government suspended it for its 'initiative' in the Northern Territory because it was clear that its actions were going to break that law. In the absence of a constitutional bill or charter of rights, powerful parliamentary executives can overrule even High Court judgments, leaving small minorities like Aboriginal peoples with almost no recourse.

Affirmative action, then, remains controversial as a top-down government policy. While many who benefit from such policies support them as an effective means of redressing race-based discrimination, others contend that affirmative action usually benefits most those least disadvantaged. This is because affirmative action is considered most likely to provide jobs, better pay, or educational places for those most like the dominant White majority. Nonetheless, increases in education levels and professional employment for race minorities can result from affirmative action policies and practices.

Can White-Majority Governments Be Made to Respond to Large Minorities?

U.S. political scientist David Canon notes that 'a central problem for representative democracy is to provide a voice for minority interests in a system ... dominated by the votes of the [White] majority' (1999, 1). One corrective, a controversial one that we discussed in chapter 4, was the creation of 'minority-majority' electoral districts. In effect, this was an affirmative action electoral mechanism that let African Americans and Hispanics be represented by 'one of their own' by crafting districts to have minority-majorities. This has ensured that U.S. governments have some African American and Hispanic legislators, which has the potential to make governments more responsive. But there is a huge 'race divide' in perceptions among voting rights experts regarding this sort of 'racial redistricting.' Some contend that it raises the spectre of apartheid and polarization in an electoral system that they believe should be colour-blind; others, that it is a form of affirmative recruitment that is essential for empowering large minorities such as African Americans and Hispanics.

The legitimacy and stability of these three settler states, and their status as representative democracies, depended on the achievement of minority enfranchisement. This is necessary if governments are to be responsive to minorities, albeit not a sufficient condition on its own. One result of the Civil Rights struggle in the United States was legislation – the Voting Rights Act (1965) and the Civil Rights Act (1964) – that focused on fair electoral processes so that African Americans would have an equal opportunity to vote if they so chose. But over the next two decades, it became clear that these laws were not enough. Hence in 1982, Congress amended the Voting Rights Act to incorporate a Supreme Court ruling that mandated that minorities ought to be able to 'elect representatives of their choice when their numbers and configuration permitted' (Canon 1999, 1). This focus on avoiding discriminatory *results* led to 'racial redistricting' – the redrawing of electoral boundaries to provide minority voters with *substantive* representation – that is, government responsiveness – by enabling them to choose 'one of their own' if they wished. This idea that African Americans need 'their own' to represent them has been strongly attacked, especially by White conservatives. No comparable program exists in either Australia or Canada. New Zealand, however, has always set aside four seats for Maori representation, though Maori members also are elected to other seats as well. In Norway, Indigenous Sami people have their own assembly.

In the debates over minority-majority districts, Whites, both supporters and opponents, tend to assume that there is a single, cohesive African American community with monolithic interests to represent. But Canon (1999, 3) claims that 'factions within the African-American community

produce candidates with different ideological backgrounds and different visions of the representation of racial interests.' Nonetheless, before
this approach was adopted, few African Americans were elected to
Congress and attention focused mainly on electing mayors and other
local politicians. No African Americans were elected from majority
White districts, especially in the South; and research about the 1980s and
1990s indicates that White legislators tended to ignore their African
American constituents even where they were 30 to 40 per cent of the
electorate in a district. Did more minority representatives in Congress
make government more responsive?

The ideological diversity among Black candidates and the 'Whiteness'
of Congress together meant that 'a centrist coalition of moderate White
and Black voters [has] the power to elect the Black candidate of their
choice' (Cannon 1999, 3) in many Black majority districts. This has promoted 'a politics of commonality.' As a result of this form of affirmative
action, more African American legislators have been elected, which is
what Congress and the Supreme Court intended. But those elected have
not promoted a 'politics of difference'; mainly, they have responded to
a coalition of Whites and Blacks supporting a 'politics of commonality.'[3]
Ironically, then, majority Black districts have been criticized by those
Blacks for whom a 'politics of difference' is the proper goal of Black
representation in Congress.

It is too early to tell whether the presidency of Barack Obama will be
a catalyst for substantial change in race politics in the United States. He
has inherited a White majority administration in which there have been
some gains on civil rights issues but whose institutions still have racist
values reflecting slavery and segregation embedded in them. The challenge is to separate the man from the institution, as Johnny Hill notes:
'Obama, with all of his multicultural roots does not represent movement
toward any notion of a post-racial society' (2009, 39). Rather, the hope is
that his presidency stands for the 'radical movement beyond the stag-
nant, rigid racial categories that informed much of America's segregated
past from slavery to Jim Crow' (Hill 2009, 107).

How President Obama translates his appeal into top-down policies
that will reduce inequalities for African Americans, Hispanics, and other
race minorities depends on the type of support he gets from his electoral
coalition of African Americans, Hispanics, Asians, and White liberals.
We earlier noted that a majority of (older) Whites voted for McCain in
the 2008 presidential election. Obama's election also revived White nationalist sentiments and the racial ugliness of the Tea Party rallies against

his policies and presidency. Building popular support for new civil rights initiatives or affirmative action legislation means that he has to keep the coalition together, which so far his cabinet and Supreme Court appointments have aimed at doing.[4]

Top-Down Change, Government Responsiveness, and Small Minorities

Indigenous people are small minorities in each of the settler states discussed in this book. So in this section, we focus on governments' attempts over more than a century to 'solve' their Indian or Aboriginal 'problem.' Regardless of when the attempts took place, until recently, governments have persistently acted as they saw fit, with no serious consultation or attempts at cooperation with those whom the changes were supposed to benefit. Most policies have intended to control the surviving Indigenous communities and keep them out of the way. Keep in mind here the contextual factors. In each country, Indigenous peoples are a very small minority. While they do not lack political resources, especially symbolic resources, they cannot generate mass movements of their own people. Given the importance of numbers in democracies, therefore, they must appeal to White conceptions of justice when legitimizing their claims and/or demanding self-government. Some have used threats of violence and direct action to gain the attention of governments, White citizens, and international agencies.

We focus first on Australian governments' top-down efforts to deal with Aboriginal peoples in the decades since the Second World War. Sarah Madison in *Black Politics* (2009) describes 'a history of policy failures.' But there are striking similarities among the policies adopted in the three countries, albeit at different times. Indeed, until governments became more responsive to Indigenous organizations and more willing to consider self-government, the history of all three was 'a history of policy failures.' We focus on Australia, however, because Indigenous policy there has become an issue that generates partisan divisions. As a consequence, perhaps, failure continues.

Historically, Australians considered their continent 'a White man's country,' and they considered Aboriginal peoples so 'primitive' that they surely would disappear as a result of fatal contact with superior Whites. As we discussed earlier, British colonizers conceptualized the continent as empty – *terra nullius*. And as late as the Second World War, Australian governments unabashedly defended the White Australia policy (Day 1996, 313). Japanese attacks on Northern Australia during the war[5] reinforced commitment to the policy. Why, then, did governments make Aboriginal peoples citizens and dismantle the White Australia policy in the two decades that followed?

The policy was actually *reinforced* right after the war, mainly because Australian governments feared a demographic time bomb from Asia. But there also were fears about the loyalties of Aboriginal people in the north, which faced Asia. During the war, many Aboriginal men entered the money economy, and though segregated from Whites, some six thousand had fought in defence of Australia. Like U.S. African Americans, after the war they were still barred from pubs, suffered bad living conditions and poorly-paid employment, and faced racist exclusions and casual violence (Day 1996, 262–3). The main trigger for change was international pressure; also, beginning in the 1960s, the example of the U.S. Civil Rights movement was available nightly on TV. The Labor government had granted the Commonwealth vote to those Aboriginals who had served in the war, but only if they already could vote in their state and had 'sufficiently developed the attributes of civilization as to be deemed capable of exercising the right to vote' (Day 1996, 365). 'Civilized' meant having abandoned 'tribal associations' – that is, having given up family ties. So, as in Canada and the United States, citizenship represented assimilation, and those enfranchised were expected to accept detribalization. Yet few were accepted by Whites, and most still lived on the margins of White communities.

Australian governments' attempts to 'solve' the Aboriginal 'problem' led to a policy of removing light-skinned children from their Aboriginal mothers to assimilate them into White society. This grab of the 'stolen generations' was done without consultation with Aboriginal leaders, and most White Australians who knew about it believed it was 'for the good of the children.' Indeed, this is the position that the former Prime Minister John Howard took when he refused to apologize. Non-British refugees from Europe also had been required to assimilate and abandon their languages and cultures, with the objective of preserving the homogeneity of the Australian nation. Top-down change involved not tolerating any differences that made White Australians uncomfortable.

Some basic civil rights also were granted to Aboriginal people in the 1960s, and all were enfranchised after 1962. But unlike White Australians, who are fined if they don't vote, Aboriginal citizens aren't required to register, and not much effort is made to get them registered. Citizenship did give Aboriginal people the legal right to purchase and drink alcohol, but it did not result in the return of Aboriginal land or in better health, housing, education, or employment. Moreover, once Aboriginal people had become citizens, many Whites – and governments – blamed them for their poverty and for other consequences of internal colonialism. Citizenship status did result in them becoming eligible for social benefits they previously were denied: maternity benefits, pensions, family allowances, and unemployment and sickness benefits (Morris 1997, 167).[6] But this also produced victim-blaming discourses. At the time, social benefits were considered rights of citizens according to Australia's ethos of economic egalitarianism, so denying them to Aboriginals once they were citizens could not be justified. Egalitarianism conflicted with a widespread belief that Aboriginal people were rorting (ripping off) the welfare system at White taxpayers' expense. Some White Australians claimed *they* were the victims, not Aboriginal people.

Despite the passage of Commonwealth laws that granted citizenship and some civil rights and that forbade race discrimination,[7] state practices that controlled Aboriginal peoples were not eliminated in Western Australia, Queensland, and the Northern Territory, where most of them live. Moreover, state officials, and those in the Northern Territory, kept land, natural resources, and even wages out of Aboriginal control. Though in 1981, South Australia returned land to the Pitjantjatjara and some symbolic landmarks were returned to traditional Aboriginal owners, governments in the three jurisdictions where most Aboriginal people live resisted returning land to them. Consequently, top-down Commonwealth legislation to remove race regimes was useless, and most Aboriginal people remained deprived and marginalized because of state practices, just as they had been before obtaining citizenship.

Rosalind Kidd, in *The Way We Civilize* (1997), reveals in stark detail the failed top-down practices of the Queensland government's Department of Aboriginal and Pacific Islander Affairs.[8] Official departmental documents show that between 1838 and 1988, the top-down policies and practices it employed actually *created* much of 'the Aboriginal problem.' State officials, missionaries, and Commonwealth officials acted from different ideological perspectives, and some were committed to ameliorating the awful conditions in which Aboriginal people lived; that said, the department's own records show that their efforts failed – indeed, only compounded the problem. The records reveal bungling, corruption, racism, arrogant optimism, and 'congenital failure.' Kidd (1997, xx) amply demonstrates that the failures resulted from the 'constant devising and implementing of supposedly more effective strategies.' Efforts to achieve change were constantly sabotaged by 'the conflicts and complexities arising from the sheer quantity and extent of official interventions.' Kidd's scholarship and personal integrity were attacked, but she ensured the survival of the files, which document her conclusion. She observes that each time government tried something new, it made things worse. This also was the pattern in Commonwealth Aboriginal policy for the Northern Territory, mainly because when governments changed, so too did the policies because of partisan polarization on Aboriginal issues.

Government bureaucracies borrowed policies and practices from one another, and as a result, failed policies were spread across jurisdictions and countries. Policies and practices tried in Queensland also were tried in the United States and Canada, with the important difference that in Australia until the 1960s, federalism assigned the 'problem' to the states, and to the Commonwealth only regarding the Northern Territory, whereas in Canada and the United States, federal governments were responsible. Input was rarely if ever sought from Aboriginal peoples – indeed, for many years there were no representative structures through which governments could consult them.

Why Did These Top-Down Approaches Fail?

Do all top-down government approaches fail when they involve small minorities? Certainly, 'responsiveness' to pressure from small minorities is removed from the equation, especially when communities are unrepresented and governments have no one within explaining what they need or want. In these situations, professional policy makers and deliverers of policy directives become surrogates and may even consider themselves the *victims*. In his comparison of U.S. and Canadian 'Indian' policies, Nichols (1998, xiv) provides some insights. He identifies five stages in government/Indigenous relations from 1513 to 1997: (1) tribal independence, and supremacy over Europeans; (2) Indian–White equality; (3) Indian dependency on White governments; (4) marginality, with Indian people at the fringes of White societies; and (5) the resurgence of cultural nationalism, economic recovery, and increased political activism and influence. At each stage, Indigenous people's capacity to express their needs and wants to White-dominated governments differed, as did the extent to which governments felt they must respond. Policy failures especially characterized stages 3 and 4.

In Australia, relations since early contact have been characterized by dependency and marginality. No treaties were signed, and there was little opportunity to experience equality or independence. The best situation existed in isolated parts of the Northern Territory, where communities experienced long periods of neglect. Starting in the 1990s, there were hopeful changes when the High Court ruled that in some cases, Aboriginal rights to land had been protected by the common law. While the instances were quite limited, the strategy of seeking legal rights seemed potentially effective.

Kidd (1997, 348) reports that in 1996, the Boridge Queensland government led 'a frenzied campaign to declare void a High Court decision that the [land] rights of the Wik people ...' may never have been extinguished.' The Howard federal government quickly legislated to undo the High Court's ruling. Top-down actions by state and federal governments explicitly supported the White majority's interests, notably those of pastoral and mining interests, some of which are international. The Boridge government also fought to keep its policy documents secret, in the same way that federal governments in North America fought to hide documents that showed their neglect of Indigenous communities' interests when they held their band or tribal resources in trust. The treatment of these small minorities was rarely positive until they became more confrontational, mobilized effectively across individual nations or tribes, and began to demand self-government and the recognition of Indigenous rights through legal action. (The existence of many treaties made the context different than in Australia.) The Red Power movement that paralleled the U.S. Civil Rights movement had positive outcomes in North America, as Nichols's analysis shows, which suggests that the former very poor relations were not inevitable just because the minority involved was small.

Until the 1970s, the dominant top-down policy in all three countries was coercive incarceration in residential schools, along with forced assimilation. Until the 1890s, U.S. governments viewed Indians as enemies to be defeated or exterminated. Ultimately, though, they too adopted an assimilation policy that incarcerated children in residential schools and banned Indigenous cultural and spiritual practices. The decision makers who came to power in the 1970s in these countries may well have been influenced by Hollywood westerns in which 'the good guys' (farmers, cowboys, the cavalry) fought 'the bad guys' (Indians and outlaws) to make the frontier safe for White settlement (women and children). In fact, Native American peoples were nearly eliminated in the U.S. West, with the survivors incarcerated on reservations that could not support them because they were too small and lacked the resources for self-sufficiency. This imposed dependency on government for the food needed to survive. Moreover, because some had resisted, they were portrayed as bloodthirsty enemies of peaceful settlers and civilizers. Among Whites, amnesia took hold regarding Indigenous people's dispossession and coercive education, as well as the suppression of Indigenous cultural and spiritual practices designed to weaken community solidarity.

During the First World War, Canada initially exempted non-citizen Indian men from military service, but many had already enlisted and some were overseas before the bureaucrats acted, leading to a policy reversal. By 1916, all male British subjects between twenty and forty-five were required to register, including Status Indians (Nichols 1998, 255). In Canada, Indigenous veterans were denied their share of postwar benefits, such as the 160 acres of land granted under the 1919 New Soldier Settlement Act. Similarly, in Australia, where Aboriginal men fought in the First World War and were eager that their bravery would be recognized, the government instead seized Aboriginal lands to provide settlement grants for White veterans.

When settler governments granted Indigenous people citizenship, they presented it as a benefit. But the recipients often saw it as a tool of assimilation. In 1920, for example, the Canadian government passed a bill mandating compulsory enfranchisement to resolve a conflict with the Six Nations Iroquois. After the bill passed, the Iroquois launched an international campaign claiming that they were a sovereign nation. A new government repealed the law. Then in the 1960s, another government again used the lure of citizenship to achieve assimilation. The White Paper Statement of the Government on Indian Policy (1969) revealed the government's plan to repeal the Indian Act and make Status Indians 'ordinary Canadians' by extinguishing their treaty rights. Native peoples joined together to fight this assimilation attempt, forming effective province-wide and pan-Canadian organizations and launching a wave of Indigenous mobilization that continues to this day and that focuses on gaining self-government and Indigenous rights.

In the United States, detribalization was a top-down initiative. In 1924, 'Indians' in the United States were 'rewarded' for their war effort with a law granting citizenship to all tribal people. But they were not required to abandon tribal membership, nor did they lose the federal benefits they were entitled to as 'Indians' (Nichols 1998, 270–1). As in African American communities, Indian leaders were divided: Should their goal be integration into White society as equals? Or should it be (re)building separate, self-sufficient nations and retaining traditional cultures? The federal government subdivided reservation lands by deeding allotments to individuals. (This policy is being advocated currently by some conservatives in Canada.) After becoming U.S. citizens, many sold their allotments, with the result that communal lands were lost, especially lands that were fertile or contained valuable resources. The granting of citizenship, which few Indians had sought, had legitimized the government's agenda of developing Indian lands, as well as assimilation. They had been turned into 'ordinary' citizens who could be treated the same as any other citizens.

Citizenship did open up access to valuable civil rights previously denied. For example, in Canada, it was illegal under the Indian Act for 'Indian' communities to hire lawyers to argue land claims in court. Such infringements of Indigenous peoples' civil rights, along with restrictions on their religious practices, and on their freedom of movement and association, ended once citizenship status was conferred, though the Indian Act remained. The attainment of citizenship in the 1960s laid the legal groundwork for contemporary political struggles.

Bureaucrats and legislators believed that the Indigenous 'problem' could be solved through enfranchisement, 'civilization,' and assimilative education. These policies, however, were disastrous for most Indigenous people, causing them great pain, loss, and suffering. As Kidd (1997, xx) writes about Queensland: 'If ... the state government has had almost total control over Aboriginal lives for a century, then it is the operations of state government which should be investigated to reveal the reasons for the disastrous conditions which persist for so many ... who were for so long their unwilling wards.'

A second example of failed top-down policies in the postwar era began in Western Australia in 1944. That state's government mandated citizenship for those Aboriginal people it deemed sufficiently 'civilized.' The Native Citizenship Rights Act (1944) required prospective citizens to prove 'they had adopted the manner and habits of civilized life, could speak and understand English, were not suffering from leprosy, syphilis or yaws, and were reasonably capable of handling their ... own affairs' (McGrath 1995, 256). Recipients had to carry a certificate to show they were exempted from laws that restricted the civil rights of Aboriginal peoples, including their freedom of movement. As in New South Wales and the Northern Territory, where similar policies prevailed, citizenship was provisional and could be suspended or cancelled if those granted it were found associating with tribal Aborigines. The children of these Aboriginal citizens also had to pass muster, since citizenship could not be inherited. Without a 'dog tag,' as Aboriginal people called the exemption certificates, they could not attain decent housing, education, or employment, which in turn made urban residency impossible. McGrath (1995, 256) concludes: 'You could be a citizen or an Aboriginal but not both.' These provisional citizens, however, were limited to inferior housing on the margins of White communities, to inferior education, health, and other services, and to mostly menial employment.

Conditional grants of citizenship also fractured solidarity among Aboriginal people, dividing those with light skins who had adopted European lifeways from darker-skinned, tribal Aborigines who maintained traditional ways. Queensland was the last state to enfranchise Aboriginal people and Pacific Islanders. Even then, the regulations gazetted in that state in 1966 continued to deny basic human rights to those who lived in Aboriginal communities, including reserves. Theoretically, they could vote, but 'the regulations governing their conduct treated them as prisoners and children ... [not] as citizens' (Chesterman and Galligan 1997, 172). State enfranchisement coincided with the 1967 constitutional referendum to empower the Commonwealth government to legislate about Aboriginal peoples. When the referendum succeeded, the constitution was changed and the Commonwealth franchise granted. But the complex and oppressive race regimes in each of the states have yet to be completely dismantled. In Queensland, Aboriginal citizens remained severely restricted until 1984, when some relaxation began. The referendum and the vote were tools that Aboriginal people needed in order to be included within the circle of Australian society; but they still lacked the tools to dismantle the race regimes that oppressed them.

In 1996, Lois (Lowitja) O'Donoghue, the first chair of the short-lived Aboriginal and Torres Strait Islander Commission (ATSIC) wrote: 'There have been two great themes to our struggle: citizenship rights, the right to be treated the same as other Australians, to receive the same benefits ... the same level of services; and Indigenous rights, the collective rights ... owed to us as distinct peoples and as the original occupiers of this land' (quoted in Chesterman and Galligan 1997, 193). For a small minority, the vote was symbolically important, though it was actually useful only where Indigenous people were concentrated in a few districts, mainly in the Northern Territory. Their struggle to attain collective rights has meant that polarized and White-dominated political parties and governments have had to be persuaded, which has required effective organization, which conservative governments have gone to some lengths to disrupt.

ATSIC was the first major government-supported organization through which Aboriginal people could express their needs and wants to governments. The Howard coalition government, from its first day in office, portrayed ATSIC as inefficient and financially unaccountable. Indeed, Howard closed it down in 2005, replacing it with a non-representative body, which it used to legitimize government's top-down policies. Katrina Ilford and Jan Muir (2004, 101–7) observe that Aboriginal leaders and supportive White Australians involved in the reconciliation movement have stated that no *meaningful reconciliation will occur without a body that provides Aboriginal people with effective political representation and participation*. Yet the Howard government also shut down the government-sponsored Council for Aboriginal Reconciliation in 2000. Government officials, including the prime minister, then felt free to declare Aboriginal communities and culture 'dysfunctional' and to insist that they be 'integrated into the real world economy.' The entrapped Aboriginal communities received no apologies and certainly no funding for healing in communities from which a generation of children had been stolen. Moreover, when a subsequent report about child sexual abuse in Aboriginal communities appeared, Howard used the opportunity to take control of some forty Aboriginal communities in the Northern Territory, in this way achieving *de facto* detribalization of Aboriginal lands, thereby opening them up to economic development.

New Approaches – Successes and Failures in Promoting Responsiveness

In recent decades, those struggling to deconstruct race regimes have developed new approaches to change – especially to reversing the consequences of the race oppression that states have sanctioned and administered. In this section we explore several examples of these new approaches. Some have failed, but others have succeeded in reversing some consequences of race regimes. Some approaches, such as *affirmative action*, are often viewed as *temporary* devices to undo the results of long-term race discrimination and oppression only until those individuals harmed directly by race regimes have 'caught up' or been compensated, or until a level playing field of equal opportunity has been created. Other approaches are more *permanent*, such as Canada's constitutional entrenchment of affirmative action for as long as minorities are disadvantaged.

New approaches to change also often differ in their objectives. In some cases the goal is to end the negative effects of race regimes – for example, to end the many deaths of Australian Aboriginal people while in police custody. Other approaches seek to go to the roots[9] of problems by changing the ground rules of societies and political systems – for example, by reforming the electoral system, which in all three states discussed in this book represses the numerical (or descriptive) representation of race minorities (see chapter 4). More radical approaches include creating new political units in which race minorities can enjoy *self-government* (e.g., Nunavut) because they become a majority in their own territory again. Another approach that *can* be radical, but often is not, involves truth and reconciliation commissions, whose goal is to achieve a deep understanding of what happened on which genuine reconciliation can be based. Of course, it often is not clear whether approaches considered radical by the White majority actually *are* radical in their outcomes. Some approaches merely reconstitute Whites' race advantage within a new discourse. Multiculturalism is a good example of an approach that is considered 'radical' by many of the White majority but that rarely has radical results for race minorities (see chapter 5).

Cooperative Approaches to Change – Aboriginal Sentencing Circles

A core idea in democratic theory is of a common *rule of law* – specifically, that the administration of the laws by police, courts, and bureaucrats should be even-handed and apply to all the same. As earlier chapters showed, a key feature of the 'race regimes' that oppressed non-Whites in settler societies was discrimination in the administration of justice – that is, use of the state to deliver unfair outcomes and to enforce unjust laws. In colonial Australia, for example, Aborigines could not testify in court even if they were the subject of the case – perhaps facing being hanged or imprisoned. Moreover, unfair treatment by the justice system seems to continue. As we showed in the Introduction, non-White people in all three countries are greatly overrepresented in the prison population. Non-Whites are often targets of police abuse, acts of racist violence, and excessive use of force. In all three countries, impartial reports such as the Report of the Australian Royal Commission into Aboriginal Deaths in Custody (1991) have shown that the institutions that are supposed to administer the laws fairly continue to victimize non-Whites at an alarming rate.

In the United States, an 1832 Supreme Court decision that Indian lands could only be passed or sold to the federal government and that Indian communities were to be treated as *domestic dependent nations* meant that state laws had no authority over those lands – only federal laws. This fostered a different relationship between the federal government and Indigenous communities in the United States than developed in Australia and Canada (Johnson 1999, 175–7). Criminal law in Canada is a federal jurisdiction, but its administration is a blend of federal and provincial responsibilities, which has made change complex. This contrasts with Australia and the United States, where the states control criminal law.

As we have seen, in the politics of race it is of profound importance who controls the police and justice systems, because of the disproportionate number of non-Whites in prison. After 1970, when Native American communities in the United States resumed governance responsibilities, arrest rates declined. In this same period, U.S. residential schools were closed and various Red Power movements promoted Indian justice systems and police forces. Where treaties with the federal government had been ratified, tribal justice systems and traditional peacekeeping approaches were revived. The Indian Service often undermined traditional institutions and leaders, however, which had deleterious effects on traditional justice systems. Where there are no ratified treaties (e.g., in California), Native Americans still face a justice system based on European legal practices and concepts of justice. Their traditional justice systems had been weakened and bypassed over the years; their survival and revival today means that those trying to develop policies to mitigate the disastrous consequences of contacts between Indigenous peoples and settler-society police and justice systems have useful resources.

No other aspect of the race regime of *internal colonialism* had such negative effects on Indigenous peoples as the justice systems of settler societies. In Australia, a policy of non-interference with Aboriginal customary law operated until 1835 as long as the crimes involved affected only Aborigines. But when Australia became an autonomous nation-state, a single justice system with one set of laws for all was established. To achieve this, judges adopted the legal doctrine of *terra nullius*, which held that Aboriginal peoples had no laws or principles of justice that Australian courts had to consider (Reynolds 1996, 74). Contrast this with the New Zealand Constitutional Act (1852), which stated (and still does) that Maori 'laws, customs and usages' would be maintained 'so far as they are not repugnant to the general principles of humanity' (Reynolds 1996, 80) . The New Zealand constitution limits the jurisdiction of White courts and magistrates in Aboriginal districts to 'giving effect' to Maori 'laws, customs and usages' (ibid., 80).[10]

Throughout their empire, the British adopted indirect rule and legal pluralism. But in Australia, they did not follow this approach because Aboriginal customary law was seen as involving 'lewd practices' that could not be incorporated into the new settler state's developing judicial system (ibid., 81). In essence, Australian Aborigines were seen as more 'primitive' than the peoples that Britain ruled elsewhere. Not until 1977 did the Australian Law Reform Commission consider the desirability of applying any part of Aboriginal customary law either to all Aborigines, or to those still living in tribal contexts (ibid., 83). Australia's international treaty obligations spurred the Commonwealth to pressure the states to recognize Aboriginal customary law, but the idea of one homogeneous system of laws persists.

Canada represents a midpoint between the American and Australian experiences. The notion of Indigenous peoples being *domestic dependent nations* was not accepted. Despite many ratified treaties, Indigenous communities were dealt with as wards of the federal government under the Indian Act, which imposed an inferior legal standing. Many First Nations activists and leaders in Canada have been inspired by the American experiment with self-government. Moreover, Canadian federalism already incorporates *legal pluralism*, with a different Civil Code in Quebec. Since the early 1990s, Justice Canada's new Aboriginal Justice Directorate has worked with Indigenous leaders to develop a *blended* judicial process that incorporates some Indigenous ideas and practices into the European-based Canadian system.

Rupert Ross (1996), an assistant Crown attorney responsible for criminal prosecutions in more than twenty remote Cree and Ojibway First Nations, has reported on a justice proposal developed in 1989 by the Sandy Lake First Nation that identifies as a serious gap the differences between Indigenous and non-Indigenous conceptions of wrongdoing. For non-Indians, an individual who commits a crime is by definition a bad person who must be punished. In Native communities, by contrast, a wrongdoing is either misbehaviour that requires teaching or an illness that requires healing. First Nations' proposals for judicial reform have led to a softening of the adversarial approach to judicial processes,[11] and to the development of community-based 'police committees' and sentencing circles that apply Indigenous values regarding justice, values that can then be incorporated into Canada's judicial system. These experiments with incorporating Indigenous processes and values have become part of a dialogue between Indigenous and European-origin people involved in the justice system. Note that the existence of a different judicial system in Quebec and in the Supreme Court had paved the way for this.

This blended system is controversial, even among Indigenous people. Some Indigenous women have been vocal critics of it, claiming that sentencing circles' emphasis on healing can cause serious problems when women and children who are victims of abuse and violence are expected to forgive, and continue to live with, those who have harmed them. They fear that when the emphasis is placed on healing and restoring community harmony, the judicial system will fail to protect those women and children who are at risk from further abuse, violence, even death. As Ross observes, victims who report their abuse to the Euro-Canadian system instead of accepting an Indigenous alternative may be ostracized, punished, and driven out of the community. Simply put, community courts are open to abuses, just like mainstream courts. To work for all, traditional justice must involve healers, teachers, and guides who are mindful of the problems of abuse.

Assessing Whether Top-down Approaches Produce Responsive Outcomes

How do we determine whether a top-down policy has a satisfactory outcome in terms of government responsiveness, especially when the views of White majorities and race minorities differ? Or when views differ among minorities? In this section we have chosen multicultural policies, practices, and discourses as our example for considering conflicting assessments of top-down policies. In Canada, multiculturalism is sanctioned by legislation and respect for its principles is embedded in the constitution. In Australia it involves some government practices and discourses aimed at legitimizing immigration by non-British, non–English-speaking (NES) and Asian migrants. In the United States, it involves mainly non-government discourses about race and ethnicity as well as practices maintained by education systems, museums, and other cultural institutions.

Multiculturalism was created as a policy in Canada in response to demands by White ethnic minorities, who felt excluded by a Liberal federal government's policy that Canada had been created by two founding nations – English and French. That is, it was not designed to respond to race bias. Nonetheless, some race minorities initially viewed multiculturalism favourably. But those who advocate anti-racist approaches view it with less favour – indeed, some believe that it *feeds* democratic racism. We will use these differences as a prism through which to consider whether top-down policies succeed or fail.

At its base, multiculturalism is a description of the diversity displayed by populations within settler societies, especially in contrast to the European ideal of one homogeneous nation per state. Multiculturalism also is an ideology that valorizes diversity. Frances Henry and her colleagues (1995, 328) define it as an ideology 'that holds that racial, cultural, religious, and linguistic diversity is an integral, beneficial, and necessary part of Canadian society and identity'; and 'a policy operating in various social institutions ... including the federal government.' The former president of the Canadian Political Science Association (CPSA), Vince Wilson (1993, 64), has defined multiculturalism as 'a doctrine that provides a *political framework* for the official promotion of *social inequality* and *cultural differences* as an integral component of the social order.' As Augie Fleras and Jean Leonard Elliot (1996, 320) have concluded: 'multiculturalism has an uncanny ability to mean different things to different people' within each settler state and especially across such states.

Fleras and Elliot (1996, 326ff) identify four main ways that multiculturalism is used (1) as an empirical description; (2) as an ideology or prescriptive statement extolling the virtues of diversity and promoting toleration of it; (3) as a policy of how state actors will 'accommodate' diversity; and (4) as the process through which state actors and elites in non-state institutions manage diversity. Analogies are often used to describe multiculturalism – a mosaic, a symphony orchestra, a tossed salad. The notion is that 'voices' come together while retaining their distinctiveness, thus creating new wholes more desirable than those assimilation would produce. Why would such an apparently desirable condition be resisted? Resistance to multiculturalism from those in the White majority who cling to their heritage and cultural dominance is understandable, but why do some race minorities reject it? Carl E. James (1996, 4–8) argues that a multicultural approach promotes values that are compatible with democratic racism. This he demonstrates by comparing multicultural values with the values that characterize anti-racism approaches – that is, approaches aimed at eliminating racism.

First Nations people resist multicultural policies because they experience their oppression as a consequence of internal colonialism. They don't consider themselves a race-minority group – they are the original inhabitants of the land. Moreover, they believe that race-minority immigrants also benefit from Indigenous dispossession, which results in a conflict of interests, not common cause. Like Québécois they resist being categorized as an 'ethnic' group, seeing themselves as founding nations. Hence, a number of groups suspect that multiculturalism is assimilationist.

Multiculturalism has different meanings and involves different policies in Australia and the United States. But in each country, there are both Whites and race minorities who criticize it. Some, like Wilson, contend that it is a framework in which *inequality* is accepted as part of the socio-political order to be explained as resulting from *cultural* differences. Thus, ethnic or race-based inequalities become consequences of minorities' traditional religious or cultural practices – which fits the logic of democratic racism. Some critics believe that the concept of multiculturalism weakens our capacity to recognize European-based, settler societies' problems with recognizing diversity, especially regarding race. Richard Day (2000) sees multiculturalism as a means by which settler-society elites 'manage' diversity by containing it within a centuries-old framework that valorizes Western European values, which posit one homogeneous nation in each state. Day traced Europeans' ways of thinking about diversity, beginning with the ancient Greeks, and shows how White settlers used such ways of thinking about diversity to justify dispossessing Indigenous peoples and extracting unpaid or cheap labour from many non-White peoples. These settlers racialized each group as 'others' to justify exploiting, oppressing, excluding, or incarcerating them. He also demonstrates how multicultural discourse and policy have perpetuated White elites' struggles to manage diversity without ever really coming to understand or accept its implications.

Day concludes that the logic of multiculturalism is part of nation-building projects in each country with knowledge of how Indigenous groups and migrants were repressed replaced with 'we were always multicultural.' Observing the process in Canada, he concludes: 'Let us not forget, that Canada is in fact an Empire formed through violent conquest – though this has been kept very quiet, supported first by a fantasy of voluntary "confederation," and now by one of voluntary "multiculturalism"' (222).

At some level, then, multiculturalism can be a fantasy that projects back into the past a harmonious mosaic of diverse groups living together voluntarily – which is certainly one reason why First Nations and francophones reject the discourse in Canada. It can block consideration of approaches that take diversity more seriously by recognizing its capacity for provoking conflict. It can also make it more difficult to deepen democracy beyond the numbers game according to which those made permanently small minorities by the facts of history can only gain what is just by persuading those who benefit from their dispossession and oppression. Moreover, approaches that are serious about diversity recognize differences that exist *within* race and ethnic minority communities – differences that affect individuals' life conditions as well.

American political scientist David Canon contends that in these settler nation-states, which are representative democracies, the big issue is how to provide a voice for those who will be minorities permanently and how a system dominated by the votes of Whites can be made responsive to those minorities. Those who recognize that their status as minorities is likely permanent may prefer a genuinely colour-blind society in which race is irrelevant, or they may prefer self-government in some form. For example, Black nationalists in the United States and Indigenous peoples in all three countries favour some kind of self-government. But will White majorities agree, especially if they also are expected to *pay* for governments and communities? As we've seen, the Reagan 'new federalism' enabled Native American communities to develop their capacities for governance. But the price to be paid for this right is high, because most of these communities cannot provide their members with employment, housing, education, or social services at a level close to that enjoyed by citizens in the surrounding White society. Unless land claims settlements provide significant resources and territories, self-government usually is synonymous with poverty.

Another option – perhaps more viable – is to use federalism to construct state jurisdictions in which, for example, Aboriginal people can constitute majorities. The Inuit-majority territory of Nunavut exists as a distinct political community, with a public government in which Inuit (currently) are a majority. Within that territory, the Inuit have a measure of autonomy on terms acceptable to the federal government, which acts on behalf of the White majority in the federation as a whole, and largely funds territorial governance. In this case, federalism has provided self-government, in that a new Territory has been created to form an Inuit majority government. Many critics observe that the Nunavut legislature's powers are limited and are subject to Ottawa's override. Others fear that Nunavut will never be viable economically without large transfers from the federal government. Inuit leaders, however, view the funding for Nunavut as rent owed to the Inuit for settlers' access to their lands and royalties owed for mineral and other resources. Perhaps the key to the so far successful self-government experiment is that, except for the resources to which the experiment permits access, few members of the White majority want the lands that Nunavut contains. The experiences of other First Nations suggest that the situation is different when desirable land and resources are involved, or when governments responsive to Indigenous majorities try to deny some rights to members of the White population. It is not clear whether most members of the majority of non-Indigenous Canadians view Nunavut in terms of their federal government paying rent and royalties on their behalf to Indigenous peoples, or whether they would support this policy if they did view it that way. So recognizing the cost of self-government may well be a crucial factor when it comes to majority support.

Canadian political scientist Alan Cairns (2000) has argued that the *separateness* and *autonomy* that Indigenous leaders and activists associate with self-government threatens to sever the bonds that make citizens prepared to support one another and to fund them when necessary – the bonds, that is, of being part of the same nation. He believes that the small size of most First Nations means they likely cannot 'go it alone' and that 'ordinary Canadians' and their leaders will not support fifty-plus territories like Nunavut. That is, he considers Indigenous dependency to be permanent and an insoluble condition. This limits the solutions to First Nations problems if we assume that many non-Aboriginal Canadians will refuse to help fund Indigenous communities if they consider them not part of Canada or if many Indigenous individuals reject their status as Canadian citizens.

Reynolds (1996) believes that Aboriginal sovereignty in Australia would entail an umbrella state of Aboriginal and Pacific Island peoples. But he recognizes that most White Australians would reject claims to an inherent right to self-government for which they would pay by means of rents, and corporations expect Australian governments to protect them from Aboriginal governments able to extract royalties for resources on their lands.

In contrast to Canada (where there is constitutional recognition of Indigenous rights) and the United States (where self-government by Native American tribes is well established), moral suasion centred on *reconciliation* is so far the most viable strategy in Australia. For example, the idea of a national apology – a 'Sorry Day' – emerged from a number of grassroots projects in a countrywide reconciliation movement, which involved groups of Whites and Aboriginal individuals discussing what they had experienced and trying to develop mutual understanding. In 1997, a national inquiry into the forced removal of Aboriginal and Torres Strait Islander children from their families (the 'stolen generation') published its findings in the report *Bringing Them Home*. One recommendation was for White Australians to acknowledge what had happened and apologize to avoid repetition. The former Howard government's refusal to apologize illustrated a denial of the need for understanding and reparation. In his opening address to the Reconciliation Convention in 1997, Prime Minister Howard argued that 'we must not join those who would portray Australia's history since 1788 as little more than a disgraceful record of imperialism, exploitation and racism.' Calling such a portrayal 'a gross distortion,' he urged Australians to be proud of what their (White) ancestors had achieved while 'acknowledging the blemishes in its past history' (cited in Cunneen and Libesman 2000, 147).

We might ask why so much had been invested in the reconciliation process, when the prime minister refused to apologize even for things that had clearly happened on his generation's watch. Howard and his sympathizers were demanding a common destiny for all Australians – on *their* terms. Howard *did* express 'deep and sincere regret' for injustices perpetrated by past generations ('Motion of Reconciliation Considered by Parliament,' *Sydney Morning Herald*, 12 May 2000, 13). But the creation of the overtly racist One Nation party to the right of Howard's coalition government made him reluctant to acknowledge how governments had harmed Indigenous people, especially if demands for reparations might surface.

Assessing Approaches: Multiculturalism and Anti-Racism

In this final section we focus on how anti-racist activists assess different approaches to the politics of race. The problems that top-down strategies encounter are resistance from the White majorities who elect governments, especially at the federal level, to give up their privileges; and lack of input from non-White minorities in shaping policies. This is why the reconciliation approach was so promising in the 1990s – it seemed to provide a moral basis for government-led approaches to change and to combine top-down with bottom-up approaches. Some sacrifice by White majorities might then be seen as the price of justice and future harmony. Indeed, a key theme of Barack Obama's 2008 campaign was his ability to bridge the chasm between Whites and Blacks so that each side could explain its real fears to the other, thus initiating understanding and reconciliation. Similarly, the Harper government's apology to the survivors of Canada's residential schools was matched by tangible redress for some of the damage done by former governments. In this final section, we explore perceptions of multiculturalism from the perspective of anti-racism activists.

Canadian scholar Carl James (1996, 3–8) unpacks the values and assumptions of multiculturalism and anti-racism, showing points of difference between them. Although not contextualized regarding large and small minorities, his exploration of these two approaches provides useful insights. In his comparison between the values underlying multiculturalism and those underlying anti-racism, he characterizes multiculturalism as *liberal* and thus compatible with top-down approaches in liberal societies. A key multicultural assumption is that (settler) societies are democratic and egalitarian and that they give citizens freedom of choice, freedom to access, and freedom to participate in whatever institutions/services they choose; another is that prejudice, racism, ethnocentrism, and anti-Semitism result from ignorance and lack of direct contact with those of different cultures, both of which can be solved by education and more contact. (This conflicts with evidence that where race-minority groups are large, White hostility is greatest regardless of the extent of contact and education.) Finally, in liberal multicultural thought, state institutions are considered neutral mechanisms through which all groups can express their interests.

In multiculturalism, 'culture' involves observable and easily communicated practices – dress, dance, food, art – and is viewed as static and internally monolithic. State practices informed by multiculturalism are also liberal, based on the assumption that providing everyone with the 'same treatment' constitutes equality. The values and behaviours of the majority group are the norm and are naturalized as neutral and value-free. The objective is getting people to 'tolerate' differences in 'cultures' – dine and dance – not on having minority values or behaviours accepted or adopted by the majority. It is assumed that the majority's values are best. Moreover, only some values of minorities can be 'tolerated,' and it is the majority that gets to decide which ones and to what extent. These liberal assumptions also fit with democratic racism.

Anti-racist approaches focus on individuals' experiences vis-à-vis power relations and the extent to which race-minority groups are present in social and political institutions. They view settler societies as stratified, with unequal distributions of power – especially political power – and resources. Access to power and opportunities is seen as limited by race and by other characteristics of oppression. Race is considered socially constructed and central to any analysis; racism viewed as an ideology woven through the fabric of society. That is, anti-racism does not focus on the role of settler states in the construction of race categories. The problem is deemed to be societal racism, not cultural differences, and not (primarily) states' racialist policies or failures to act. Culture is viewed as dynamic and open to many influences. Anti-racists contend that multiculturalism as a state policy closes minority communities, freezes cultural practices, and supports the power of traditional elites. They also contend that it is the majority group's actions, not those of minority cultures, that shape the life chances and conditions of race minorities. They reject the liberal idea that political institutions are neutral, and they view state actors as motivated by racist ideologies. They theorize that change must be predicated on individual empowerment through community-level, anti-racist activism that challenges power relations and social inequalities by demanding equal shares of power, the right to equal participation, and recognition of race-minority voices.

Anti-racists believe that societies and their institutions should change and that they eventually will be ready to do so. They support a bottom-up approach that focuses on empowering members of race minorities, and they view multiculturalism as inadequate for a number of reasons: it fails to recognize social stratification, inequality, and people's different starting points that are a consequence of their assigned racial or ethnic category; and it fails to recognize that social inequality and White privilege limit the 'choices' that non-Whites can make, besides denying them the capacity to participate. Anti-racist critics claim that identifying minority groups by race or culture ignores variations in power within minority communities. They also believe that emphasizing diversity as a historical fact ('we've always been multicultural') hides the dominance of the majority culture. Multiculturalism's fostering of individual 'choice' feeds into victim blaming against those who fail to 'make it' and who are then blamed for the choices they are claimed to have made. Anti-racists work to develop community-level actions to analyse social systems as they change, and to identify and challenge the stereotypes that race minorities have internalized. This consciousness-raising will help develop and communicate more viable self-images – for example, through Afro-centric education. Anti-racists also demand affirmative action for groups who have been held back to this day by past oppression and exploitation. Anti-racism brings deep-rooted ideas, attitudes, and stereotypes about 'others' to consciousness. Instead of pathologizing minority cultural practices, anti-racists explore them. This can increase conflict, but for understanding and achieving justice, it is preferable to superficial harmony. Anti-racist activism lets minority-group members challenge the status quo and promote change.

Conclusion

At its core, representative democracy is a matter of majority rule. Analyses of the income levels, housing, health, education, and employment of Whites versus non-Whites in these settler societies reveal the benefits of being part of the majority. If you are a White Australian, American, or Canadian, you are likely to have more money, to live in better housing, to be healthier and live longer, to be better educated, and to have a better job and a better self-image than if you are Indigenous, Aboriginal, Black, Hispanic, or a member of another race minority. The evidence of current benefit and privilege is clear. You can accept the victim-blaming ideas of democratic racism that attribute this to the laziness, backwardness, or cultural inadequacies of non-Whites; or you can try to believe that you are lucky, or work harder, or are superior to the non-White at the next desk or work station. But citizens of these settler societies must eventually face up to the facts of the matter. In the United States, with the election of Barack Obama, many people were forced to confront the racial myths underlying the idea of 'one America.' Though Obama tried to de-emphasize past race-based oppression and exploitation in his campaign, his election brought out many White Americans' worst fears that Blacks and other race minorities might seek revenge for how they had been treated.

In this chapter we have explored top-down approaches from the perspective of whether they were responsive to the stated needs and desires of race minorities large and small. We have seen that for many decades, top-down policies were bitter failures for small minorities, especially Indigenous people. Moreover, we saw that governments cannot be responsive if minorities lack effective, representative organizations that give voice to their needs and desires. Governments must take some responsibility for this, since the poverty and disadvantage of small minority communities make it very difficult for them to sustain national or even state/provincial organizations. For large minorities, developing ways to adapt the democratic electoral system to magnify their voices is a promising approach. For small minorities, the problem is much more difficult, since they have great difficulty attracting the attention of governments dominated by White voters.

Despite evidence of arrogant failure and wilful neglect, our discussions throughout the book point to effective bottom-up approaches such as the Civil Rights movement; and especially to cooperative approaches that link the efforts of governments and minority leaders, such as Canada's sentencing circles. The role of individual change agents in sparking cooperative ventures also should be noted. To succeed, however, requires coalitions in which groups pool their power and their resources. Without an effective electoral coalition, Obama likely would not have been elected president. And the many relationships built by the Civil Rights movement also contributed to that coalition. In the United States there is some evidence that a political party can be part of the coalition-building process. But in Australia the polarizing of Aboriginal policy making for partisan advantage has been a major setback for Aboriginal communities. We have made the case throughout this text that the embedded nature of race regimes in state and political institutions is a major problem for race minorities. But analysis in this chapter shows that there are some openings for change. All three settler societies still face major problems in dismantling democratic racism; and their record in top-down policy making is pretty dismal. In the past, failed policies were traded around from jurisdiction to jurisdiction; perhaps today the things that actually *can* make governments responsive and produce positive change also may be shared.

Discussion Questions

1 What role does democratic theory play in influencing how responsive governments are in these settler states to increasing racial equality?
2 What challenges or opportunities do elected race minorities face in White-dominated legislatures, courts, bureaucracies, and so on?
3 What are the rationales for affirmative action, and why is it often resisted as a mechanism for reducing White privilege?
4 Based on this chapter, what must those struggling to deconstruct race regimes in these settler states do to succeed?
5 What are the benefits of self-government for Indigenous and Aboriginal peoples in the three settler states?

7 'Back to the Future': Fragmented and International Race Formations

This chapter explores the racialization of Hispanics, contemporary Asians, and those victimized by Islamophobia. Hispanics[1] were racialized over the centuries as the United States expanded its territory to dominate the continent and the hemisphere. When it became a superpower, and especially when the Cold War ended and it became the sole superpower, it was drawn into conflicts around the world, which produced Islamophobia and the creation of a new race regime governing Asian Americans. This chapter focuses mainly on the recent construction of race formations in the United States, which is a powerful opinion leader imitated by the other two states. Thus, while the racialization of Hispanics was limited to the United States, Islamophobia has been imitated in Australia and Canada. The three cases considered show how governments racialize populations that are fragmented by race, religion, or national origin. The chapter also discusses the role played by international conflicts and foreign policy in creating new race formations and remaking old ones. The chapter ends with a brief exploration of the role played by the U.S. Census Bureau and similar bureaucratic agencies in making and remaking race categories reflecting the race theories of their governments.

Introduction and Overview

Racialization, the key concept in this chapter, was developed by U.S. race theorists to explain how new White and non-White groups have been incorporated into its race hierarchy, based originally on (mostly) Black slaves and White owners. The first census categorized people as 'free,' 'non-free,' and (taxpaying) Indians. The original race categories polarized the founding groups, creating this hierarchy, and subsequent racialization involved fitting new groups into the hierarchy. Despite the absence of slavery when they were officially founded, the Australian and Canadian governments also created race hierarchies in which 'Whiteness' was foundational, but with parallel, Aboriginal 'race regimes.' In the nineteenth century all three countries also developed a race regime that exploited Asian men as workers, allowing them few civil and no political rights, and that later excluded them *de facto* or by law. This regime sanctioned laws incarcerating thousands of Japanese Americans and expropriation of their property during the Second World War, as well as the coerced transfer after the war of many to Japan, including some born in the U.S. (Japanese Canadians had similar experiences.) In this chapter we will explore the postwar remaking of this race formation following the flight of many Asians from wars in Korea, Vietnam, and Cambodia to the United States. Recently, the success of Asians as students and professionals has made them the multicultural 'poster children'; as a result they nowadays are resented as competitors. This fear of Asian competition is invoked in one instalment of the *Back to the Future* movie trilogy, in which Michael J. Fox time travels to an Asian-dominated future and must take orders that his Asian boss sends him by videophone. This new racialization of Asians combines Americans' resentment of competition with their government's fear of military and economic dominance by China, Japan, and other Asian countries. This amounts to a recycling of the 'yellow peril' race trope of the nineteenth and twentieth centuries, except now it is directed against Asian Americans for their successes and the successes of countries from which they or their parents fled. Similarly, Islamophobia recycles Christian hostility toward Muslims dating from the Crusades. Indeed, current hostility is against anyone who 'looks Muslim.'

This chapter's broad theme is, once again, that 'states make race.' It explores how race is made and remade in multiple contexts and considers how states racialize groups that are marked not by skin colour but rather by language, ethnicity, faith, or national origin. We also show that governments often have been inconsistent in their treatment of such groups, which has made their relations with the dominant race hierarchy ambiguous or contradictory. Neither Hispanics nor Middle Easterners[2] share a common 'race' according to race theory as adopted by the U.S. government. So while usually they were treated as 'White' when they immigrated, in more recent contexts they have become 'non-White.' Moreover, while some individuals and families have been treated as Whites, these populations have been fragmented and their interests divided, since others in the group have been categorized as non-White. Politicians and bureaucrats acting for White majorities have dominated the category-making process, adapting earlier race regimes to fit new cases into the 'White'/'non-White' race dichotomy. In the resulting polarized race order, 'Whiteness' is the foundational category, with 'Black' as the primary 'non-White' category. Those who experience ambiguous race categorizations because they do not fit the bipolar race structure often fall in and out of 'Whiteness.' This was true with Mexican Americans after the United States annexed northern Mexico, and with Middle Easterners, some of whom went to the courts demanding that they be treated as Whites.

The chapter also explores how race categories are remade and how race ideas are recycled. To illustrate some of the mechanisms involved in the three cases, it examines the role of the U.S. Census Bureau in making and remaking race categories. Because 'those who are "White" dominate government [they] determine who is "non-White" or "other"' (Rodriguez 2000, 16). Nobles (2000) recounts how congressmen and presidents directed which race categories to include in the census to test various theories about 'race.' Until the 1960s, census enumerators applied the categories based on their perceptions of each person's 'race.' Since the civil rights 'revolution,' people have self-selected the category that best describes them. Yet as we will show, the categories remained grounded in their separate histories. Nobles (2000) and Rodriguez (2000) also show that 'non-White' communities have vested interests in these historic categories, because being included can grant access to programs intended to compensate for past discrimination. This suggests why the charter 'non-White' groups[3] resisted when Arab Americans sought re-classification as a 'race' (Rodriguez 2000), and why they resisted a movement that called for a 'mixed race' category. Meanwhile, Hispanics, who do not fit the dominant race framework, have resisted the Census Bureau's efforts to make them a 'race,' although the data indicate that they are racialized and suffer negative consequences as a result.

The Racialization of Hispanics

American scholars conceptualize *racialization* as a process by which new immigrant groups are fitted into the White/non-White race and power hierarchy.[4] The groups being racialized are conceptualized as immigrants, whereas Anglo 'Whites' ('Americans') are the 'host' group. This ignores Native Americans, who were America's original occupants, as well as Mexican Americans, who lived in territories that the United States annexed in the nineteenth century. As will be shown later, the diversity of their skin colour makes it difficult to fit Hispanics as a group into the bipolar race hierarchy. In this way, what seems to be a simple description of facts actually reflects ideological choices, embedded in the census categories. In the 1790 census, for example, Congress chose 'White' instead of 'free,' 'European,' or 'Christian' as the category for the 'host' group, making skin colour central to how groups were (and still are) classified and treated by governments. In 1900, when the Census Bureau substituted 'race' for 'color,' instructions to enumerators regarding how to classify people made it clear that skin colour remained basic to the official race ideology that underpinned the census categories. The centrality of 'White' and 'non-White' generated the bipolar framework that governments used to justify advantaging the dominant group while disadvantaging 'other races.' Having been racially fragmented by this framing of 'race,' 'Hispanics' were hard to categorize but easy to racialize in the sense of being subject to discrimination.

Racialization is conceptualized as part of discrimination against 'non-Whites' and as a means for negotiating where a new group will be placed in the existing race/power hierarchy. This accepts race-based discrimination and the superior status of 'Whites.' 'Critical to the racialization process was the belief that there always was some "other" group to which one was superior' (Roderiguez 2000, 18). This protected White supremacy by making it 'difficult [for racialized minorities] to understand and pursue ... common interests' so that 'Whites' could divide and rule. The concepts of 'racialization' and 'race regime' differ in two ways. Racialization assumes that all racialized groups are immigrants and ignores the government's role[5] in creating race/power hierarchies, which are maintained through legalized discrimination. Because there are few Hispanics in Australia and Canada, we cannot compare across the three countries. So instead, we will explore how Hispanics have been racialized in the United States over time and consider whether their varied treatment has constituted a coherent race regime.

According to the recent census, Hispanics are 15.8 per cent (48.4 million) of the U.S. population. That makes them the country's largest minority, exceeded only by 'non-Hispanic Whites' ('White Anglos'). On recent U.S. census forms, 'Hispanic' or 'Latino' (hereafter 'Hispanics') is listed as an 'ethnic' category; however, 'Hispanics' can also self-select their 'race' and country of origin. Because U.S. census forms have no 'mixed race' category, over 90 per cent of Hispanics are officially 'White.' But according to the American Community Survey, which has a 'mixed race' category, 54 per cent of them self-select as 'White,' while 40 per cent self-select as 'mixéd race.' The remainder self-identify as Black, Asian, Pacific Islander, or 'some other race.' Clearly, the 'Hispanic' group is fragmented by both official and self-selected ethnic and race categories, as well as by country of origin and legal status.

About 38 million Hispanics are U.S.-born or legal immigrants; about 11 million are undocumented.[6] While 64 per cent of Hispanics report originating in Mexico, some are descendants of the Mexican Americans who lived in the territories annexed by the United States in the nineteenth century. Spanish speakers have inhabited what is now the southern United States since the founding of St Augustine, Florida, in 1565. Thus, to portray all 'Mexicans' as immigrants let alone 'illegal' immigrants is to misrepresent the history of North America. The other 36 per cent of Hispanics originated in Puerto Rico (also annexed by the U.S.), Cuba, the Dominican Republic, Panama, Guatemala, or El Salvador. There also are small communities from the Spanish-speaking South American countries. Each national community is made up of diverse waves of immigrants and refugees and is fragmented by class, race, and ideology.

Comparative data about 'Hispanic' populations are rare, but we can provide brief sketches. In the late 1990s, the following reported experiencing 'some' or 'a lot' of discrimination in the judicial system, housing, employment, and education: 80 per cent of Mexicans, 74 per cent of Puerto Ricans, and 47 per cent of Cubans (Rodriguez 2000, 20). A 1997 survey by La Raza (cited in Rodriguez 2000, 23–5) reported that more Hispanics live in poverty than 'Whites' or 'Blacks'; that more are inadequately covered by health insurance and pension benefits; and that as a group they had lower rates of homeownership. That said, there were many differences within the 'Hispanic' category that related to colour, state of residence, and national origin. Moreover, discrimination likely has increased since these surveys now that some states have passed laws sanctioning discrimination purportedly against 'undocumented' immigrants – laws that have disproportionately affected the majority of Hispanics, who are U.S.-born citizens or legal immigrants.

The 2006 American Community Survey[7] reported that 25 per cent of Hispanic men had less than a grade eight education (compared to 6.7 per cent of all men surveyed). For Hispanic women, 23.3 per cent (compared to 6.3 per cent of all women) had less than grade eight. Also, 11.5 per cent of Hispanic men (compared to 30 per cent of all men) and 13 per cent of Hispanic women (compared to 26.2 per cent of all women) had a bachelor's degree or more. Median incomes for the year preceding the survey were $27,450 for Hispanic men (compared to $42,210 for all

Table 6
Origin and nativity of U.S. Hispanic resident population, 2008

Hispanic origin	Total resident population in the United States	Per cent born outside the United States	Per cent of US Hispanic resident population	Per cent of the US population
Mexican	30,746,270	37.0%	65.7%	10.1%
Puerto Rican	4,150,862	1.1	8.9	1.4
All Other Spanish/ Hispanic/Latino	1,777,278	13.6	3.8	0.6
Cuban	1,631,001	60.1	3.5	0.5
Salvadorean	1,560,416	64.7	3.3	0.5
Dominican	1,334,228	57.3	2.8	0.4
Guatemalan	985,601	69.4	2.1	0.3
Colombian	881,609	66.5	1.9	0.3
Spaniard	629,758	14.0	1.3	0.2
Honduran	607,970	68.6	1.3	0.2
Ecuadorian	590,602	66.4	1.3	0.2
Peruvian	519,349	69.3	1.1	0.2
Nicaraguan	351,704	63.3	0.8	0.1
Venezuelan	210,337	73.8	0.4	0.1
Argentinian	204,707	66.4	0.4	0.1
Panamanian	153,245	49.5	0.3	0.1
Chilean	127,747	62.5	0.3	<0.1
Costa Rican	121,655	59.8	0.3	<0.1
Bolivian	93,745	64.4	0.2	<0.1
Uruguayan	60,730	73.5	0.1	<0.1
Other Central American	43,352	60.8	0.1	<0.1
Other South American	21,945	58.0	<0.1	<0.1
Paraguayan	18,365	60.7	<0.1	<0.1
Total	**46,822,476**	**38.1**	**100.0**	**15.4**

Sources: Pew Hispanic Center Tabulations of the American Community Survey, Pew Hispanic Center, 2010. Statistical Portrait of Hispanics in the United States, 2008. http://www.pewhispanic.org/factsheets/factsheet.php?FactsheetID=58; U.S. Census Bureau. 2009. 'Annual Estimates of the Population by Sex, Race, and Hispanic Origin for the United States,' (NC-EST2008-03). American Statistical Abstract 2010. http://www.census.gov/compendia/statab/2010/cats/population/estimates_and_projections_by_age_sex_raceethnicity.html.

men); and $24,738 for Hispanic women (compared to $32,649 for all women). Clearly, Hispanics are now America's largest underclass. And with the lowest educational levels of any group, and little access to jobs leading to upward mobility, their status seems virtually permanent.

Hispanics are in the United States for different reasons: annexation, colonial rule, economic migration, and flight from civil wars and repression. How Hispanics have been treated has depended in part on whether they are considered 'White' or have been racialized. The undocumented refugees who are now the focus of White Americans' fears and anger are fleeing from economic exploitation, corruption, violence, civil disorder, and repression at home. But many millions more are legal immigrants. 'Mexicans' are the largest group of Hispanics; indeed, between 1820 and 1996 Mexico was America's second-largest source of legal immigrants (Gonzalez 2000, 97, Table 3). A caste-like race regime developed around the first groups of Mexican Americans that was later applied to Spanish-speaking immigrants from the Caribbean and Central America, who had darker skins. Darker-skinned undocumented refugees were detained and deported; usually, though, undocumented Hispanics with light skins were greeted warmly, hailed as anti-communists, and given generous help to settle.

The race hierarchy in the United States constructed and perpetuated a world that was polarized between the discrete categories of White and non-White. This made it difficult for U.S. governments to deal with racially diverse or fragmented groups. Until recently, 'Hispanics' did not appear as census category. As a result, most were counted as 'White' unless their features led enumerators to classify them as 'Black' or 'Asian.' For reasons discussed below, 'Mexican' appeared as a census category just once, in 1930 (Nobles 2000, 188).

Hispanics Incorporated by Annexation and Colonialism

The Monroe Doctrine of 'Americas for Americans' declared early on the U.S. government's intention to dominate the hemisphere by excluding European powers from trade and alliances. In 1845, the struggle to annex Texas, which focused on the defence of the Alamo, ignited popular fever for U.S. expansion. A new doctrine of *manifest destiny* combined expansion with race purity and fed that fever. Coined by John O'Sullivan, a magazine editor, Democratic Party publicist, and friend of presidents (Gonzalez 2000, 43), it 'meant the right to take over lands occupied by non-Whites.' O'Sullivan demanded that the United States expand into Mexico and Latin America; he also financed filibuster expeditions into Cuba (regarding filibusters, see below). Many annexationists were slave owners who were keen to expand slave territory, and many northerners believed that annexation was God's will.

Reflecting differences between Spanish and British colonial policies, Anglo-Americans believed in strict segregation, and many states passed laws prohibiting miscegenation. In Spain, however, long occupation by the Moors (dark-skinned Muslims) had led to many mixed marriages, especially in Andalusia, the southern region from which many coloniz- ers came. Intermarriage between White men and high-status Indian women was accepted in the Spanish colonies. Moreover, because more Indigenous people had survived European diseases, a significant *mestizo* or mixed-race population existed and was incorporated into the bottom of White societies. White Spanish Americans were minorities. By con- trast, 'American' (White) proponents of manifest destiny despised 'half- breeds' or 'mulattos,' believing that the White 'race' would be weakened if its 'purity' was lessened.[8] For White Americans, the ease with which they had seized land from non-Whites only proved their racial superior- ity. They considered Hispanics inferior regardless of their race, perceiv- ing them to be unsuitable as citizens in a democracy. Proponents of manifest destiny believed that the 'pure' Whiteness of 'Americans' made them superior and sanctioned their possession of the whole continent and that America's domination of the hemisphere was willed by God.

Between 1810 and 1860 there were fourteen attempted annexations of Mexican territories, and further attempts in Cuba, Nicaragua, and Honduras (Gonzalez 2000, 37–8). 'Americans' would move into a terri- tory and acquire land rights there – usually by promising to convert to Catholicism and by pledging loyalty to the Spanish Crown. In 1810, a group in West Florida 'resorted to a [new] form [when] … a band of … mercenaries … captured a town or territory and proclaimed their own republic' (Gonzalez 2000, 36). The Spanish called this sort of annexation by mercenaries filibustering (freebooting). When Anglo settlers declared the Republic of Baton Rouge, federal troops were sent to occupy the territory and the U.S. Congress subsequently incorporated it into Louisiana (which had been purchased from the French). The United States annexed the rest of West Florida during the War of 1812, at a time when the Spanish government was resisting an invasion by Napoleonic France and was unable to defend it. An 1836 filibuster first made Texas an independent republic. Then in 1845, over opposition from northern congressmen, it was annexed as a slave state. Still later, a filibuster in Hawaii forced the queen from her throne; soon after, the U.S. government annexed the islands.

General Ulysses S. Grant declared the 1848 war with Mexico 'the most unjust ever waged by a stronger against a weaker nation' (cited in Gonzalez 2000, 44). With 100,000 U.S. troops poised to occupy all of Mexico, a national controversy broke out regarding the wisdom of in- corporating so many racially mixed Mexicans, who it was feared would

threaten the supremacy of the White majority. Because of this controversy, annexation was limited to the less populated northern half of
Mexico – New Mexico, California, Utah, Nevada, parts of Arizona, and
more of Texas. The lands the United States acquired under the Treaty of
Guadalupe Hidalgo (1848) included the fertile territory between the Rio
Grande and Nueces rivers, equal in size to Massachusetts, New Jersey,
and Connecticut combined. Poet Walt Whitman spoke for most Americans: 'What has miserable, inefficient Mexico ... to do with the great
civilizing mission of peopling the New World with a noble race[?]'
(Takaki 2008, 164). Race theorists assured White Americans that when
two 'races' came into contact, the inferior was always overwhelmed.

The annexation of Mexican lands advantaged many White Americans
and European immigrants, who surged in. But 'with the conquered
lands came unwanted people.' Many Mexican Americans were as light-
skinned as the new settlers, and the treaty promised those who stayed
'the rights of citizens.' But Spanish-speaking, Catholic Mexican Americans were treated as foreigners in their own land. Newly arrived Americans 'routinely seized [Mexicans'] properties ... seizures ... upheld by ...
English-speaking courts the settlers installed' (Gonzalez 2000, 29–30).
Most Americans despised them for their mixed-race heritage. According
to a Mexican diplomat, 'descendants of ... Indians that we are, the North
Americans hate [and] depreciate us; even if they recognize the justice of
our cause, *they consider us unworthy to form with them one nation and one
society*' (cited in Takaki 2008, 165; our emphasis). Americans made no
distinction between Mexican Americans and Mexicans. The treaty may
have made the former citizens, but state laws controlled who could vote,
and whether they *could* vote, Americans soon outvoted them. Texas used
the same techniques as would exclude 'emancipated' African Americans
after Reconstruction was abandoned. In 1863 the *Fort Brown Flag* edito-
rialized: 'we ... oppose ... allowing an ignorant crowd of Mexicans to
determine ... political questions' (ibid., 166).

The 1848 treaty had guaranteed Mexican Americans' land rights, but
the U.S. Senate removed that clause before ratification, requiring them
to defend their titles in U.S. courts, which differences in language and
land-recording practices made difficult. In New Mexico, claims were
granted for just over 2 million acres but were denied for more than
33 million (ibid. 167). The claims process took on average seventeen
years, during which taxes still had to be paid. Most Mexican Americans
were dispossessed. After annexation, most Mexican Americans were
agricultural labourers or railway navvies or worked in the mines. They

'found themselves in a *caste labor system – a racially stratified occupational hierarchy'* (ibid., 173; our emphasis). Paid less than Whites, many fell into debt peonage – that is, enslavement to their employers for debts acquired for necessities.

When the United States defeated Spain in the Spanish-American War of 1898, it won control of Spain's overseas colonies, including Puerto Rico. The United States posed as a liberator while Congress passed the Foraker Act (1900), which declared the island to be U.S. territory. (The practice of outright annexation ended in 1898.) The Foraker Act gave the president the power to appoint a civilian governor and top administrators. A Puerto Rican House of Delegates was established, but Congress gave itself key powers over it, including the power to disallow legislation. Puerto Ricans had less self-government than they had enjoyed under Spanish rule – and just one non-voting delegate in the U.S. Congress. The United States also forbade commercial treaties with other governments, which meant that its companies held a monopoly on the island. Sugar companies gobbled up thousands of small, independent coffee plantations, forcing the former owners to become agricultural labourers (Gonzalez 2000, 60–1).

President Franklin Roosevelt gave the islanders the right to elect their own governors and President Truman introduced limited self-rule. But the Supreme Court subsequently ruled that Puerto Rico had not been properly 'incorporated' into the United States. So Congress had to grant citizenship expressly for the constitution to apply to Puerto Ricans and for them to be allowed to enter the mainland states. Nonetheless, Puerto Rico remains a colony without voting rights in Congress. And while some on the island want independence, its economic elite want statehood. The fact that the island remains highly profitable for U.S. corporations makes it hard to change the status quo. Yet by 2000, 2.8 million Puerto Ricans, many economically distressed, had migrated to the mainland for better lives. Just 3.8 million remained.

Racialization and Economic Exploitation

What made the U.S. government build its own equivalent of the Berlin Wall to keep Hispanics out? Gonzalez (2000, x–xi) contends that 'the US-Mexican border … [is] the epicenter of momentous changes in our hemisphere: by day, a constant stream of trucks head … south, carrying goods and capital to newly erected factories with nearly a million low-wage workers; by night the … unstoppable flood of people head[s] …

north in search of the U.S. wages that spell survival for the family ... left behind.' In recent decades, this situation has promoted unparalleled *legal* immigration from Mexico, Central America, and some South American countries, which has Latinized some of the largest U.S. cities (New York, Miami, Los Angeles) and states (California, New York, Texas, Florida). This has sparked fear among White Americans, especially regarding the possible impact of a growing Hispanic population on U.S. politics and perceived threats to the dominance of English speakers.

Few people ask *why* millions of Mexicans and other Hispanics head north. Most Americans know little about how their government built its empire, or how financiers and corporations created the recent massive waves of 'frightening' migrants. The underlying cause is the unequal relationship evident in two hundred years of wealth transfers from Latin or Hispanic countries to the United States. Gonzales (2000, xvii) claims that if Mexico and other Latin countries 'had not been ... pillaged by US capital ... millions of desperate workers would not now be coming here.' Moreover, once in the United States, Hispanics cannot easily move up, as other groups have. The U.S. economy is in decline, and free trade has resulted in the loss of millions of factory jobs of the sort that used to provide immigrants with upward mobility. Those jobs have been transferred to offshore countries and ironically to Mexico. Hispanics are stuck on the bottom rung of U.S. society, and their low participation in education has contributed to their racialization, as has the fact that many are undocumented. But racialization began in the nineteenth and early twentieth centuries, when 'Mexicans' were ascribed a caste-like racial status based on unskilled work. Though entitled to be citizens and in the country legally, they have become the second underclass in the United States.

The Immigration Act of 1917, which excluded Asians, encouraged the recruitment of Mexicans to harvest cotton, sugar beet, and vegetables. The Mexican population in the southwest grew rapidly, from 375,000 in 1900 to 1,160,000 in 1930 (Takaki 2008, 295). Like other immigrants, many were drawn to large cities, where many Mexican women worked in factories and the garment industry. But White-controlled unions kept Mexican men out of skilled work (e.g., as bricklayers). Consequently, few escaped a life of manual labour, and many protested their poor working conditions. Their experiences replicated the original caste-like racialization of Mexicans into the nineteenth century. Unlike the annexation-era Mexican Americans, few of the later immigrants were White. So in a deeply segregated America, *mestizo* agricultural workers from Mexico were categorized as 'non-White.'

Governments treated these legal Mexican immigrants inconsistently, which created more contradictions in their racialization. Because they were entitled to citizenship, the Alien Land Act (1913) did not apply to them. So Sikh men married Mexican women, who legally could purchase land. Few Mexican men, though, could afford to buy land. Mexicans were treated as 'coloured' when it came to access to services and public facilities, and Mexican children were limited to segregated schools. In fact, many children harvested crops with their parents and were un-schooled. This limited participation in education was systematically constructed by officials, who made sure those who did attend school learned to accept their place as 'not as good as a White man' (Takaki 2008, 303). They were trained to believe that their people had been imported 'to dig ditches' and were discouraged from attending high school.

Large increases in legal immigration frightened many Anglos, who saw Mexicans' high birth rates as threatening Whites' majority status. Mexicans were further racialized as 'foreign invaders' who would 'pollute' American's race purity. Whites demanded that Mexicans be excluded under the new immigration system. Indeed, the one-time appearance of 'Mexican' as a census category in 1930 facilitated the 're-patriation' of 400,000 Mexicans, most of whom were legal immigrants with children who were citizens. The category was removed before the 1940 census after pressure from the Mexican government and Mexican Americans, who saw it as a device to facilitate removals (Noble 2000). The Hispanic immigrants who arrived after the Second World War faced a racialization that was contradictory, multilayered, and caste-like.

Not until 1977, when the U.S. government's Office of Management and Budget issued *Statistical Directive No. 15* was a 'Hispanic' category added ('Latino' came later). In all statistical reporting to federal agencies, including the census, 'Hispanic' is defined as 'a person of Mexican, Puerto Rican, Cuban, Central or South American or other Spanish culture or origin, *regardless of race*' (cited in Nobles 2000, 81; our emphasis). This new *ethnic* category was a response to advice from Hispanic advisory committees as well as congressional and presidential pressures. The context had changed. Civil rights legislation had granted race minorities redress for discrimination, and Hispanics had to be counted as a group in order to benefit from this; they could not be fragmented and 'credited to' other race categories. But 'races' still were considered separate entities in the U.S. race theory that informed census categories. So while Hispanics were grouped together as an ethnic group, they still had to select one or several race categories. A third question was added in the 1980 census about Hispanics' countries of origin.

Racialization and Foreign Policy

Bankers, merchants, plantation owners, and speculators were the main proponents and beneficiaries of U.S. military, political, and economic dominance in Latin America. Many presidents claimed that U.S. domination had been ordained by nature or 'the Divine.' Annexation was replaced by a similar pattern of military incursion, political manipulation, economic penetration, and domination country by country, though the details and timing vary.[9] In this chapter we focus on Cuba because so many U.S. governments have fixated on it. We briefly outline multiple waves of immigrants and refugees, as well as the main U.S. incursions.

By 1994, one million Cubans lived in the United States. Until 1994, Cuban refugees had been given the red-carpet treatment by U.S. government agencies – the opposite of how despised and now hunted 'illegal' immigrants were being treated. But this treatment was not received by dark-skinned Cubans, Dominicans, or Haitians, whom U.S. authorities had forced to return to war-torn countries exploited by corrupt dictators. Why were Cubans routinely granted asylum and settlement support until 1994, whereas other Hispanics were denied entry? And why did the treatment of Cubans also change in 1994? Understanding this will let us see the connections between U.S. foreign policy and how Hispanics from different countries have been treated.

In the nineteenth century, the U.S. wanted Cuba. Presidents offered to buy it, and adventurers tried to take it by force. There were three filibuster expeditions between 1848 and 1851. Most of the combatants were North Americans, but a few Cubans and Spaniards joined, seeing profit in annexation.[10] Ultimately, American investment in and development of economic infrastructure proceeded without annexation. Railway construction brought thousands of Anglo engineers and mechanics. Then in the early 1870s, the ten-year War of Independence began, and thousands of Yankee settlers fled, along with thousands of Cubans. After the war, most of the Americans who had fled returned to the island, where they dominated sugar production. By 1890, 94 per cent of Cuba's sugar was going to the United States. Settlers from the United States established many other industries. The first wave of Cuban refugees were cigar makers, who settled in Miami and Tampa. By the 1880s, trade with Cuban was 25 per cent of U.S. world trade. U.S. economic penetration was so extensive that Cuba was a Spanish colony in name only.

The 1898 Spanish-American war brought President William McKinley and the U.S. military into conflict with Cuban patriots, who after thirty years of struggle expected acknowledgment of their provisional government as a war partner. The Americans faced 30,000 pro-independence troops on the verge of victory, so Congress renounced any intentions of the U.S. government to annex Cuba, and Cuban forces welcomed U.S. troops, who were there in theory to support their independence. But once on Cuban soil, the (mainly southern) military brass treated the (Black) Cuban soldiers with contempt, even barring them from Havana. The Cuban general was excluded from the surrender ceremony, and Spanish colonial authorities were left running the government. After the war, many new U.S. companies arrived, including the United Fruit Company, the symbol of American imperialism in the hemisphere.

The United States dominated Cuba without annexing it. It would send in troops to shore up its economic, financial, and political domination. When conflicts developed – with unhappy nationalists, peasants resisting loss of their land, or labourers demanding better working conditions – U.S. companies would call on Washington, which would send in Marines on the pretext that U.S. lives or property were being threatened. The United States helped dictators rise to power and supported their usually brutal regimes as long as American personnel and U.S. interests were secure. American bankers granted dictators unsound loans at high rates – money that usually went straight into overseas bank accounts. U.S.-owned plantations spread throughout the region, forcing millions off their lands. Some firms began moving labour among subject countries or annexed territories. When the Second World War cut off (acceptable[11]) European immigration, they hired Hispanics to work in the United States.

During the first military occupation, U.S. officials forced an amendment to Cuba's constitution that made it a protectorate of the United States. The Cuban elite, including naturalized Americans, gained from the protectorate. The United Fruit Company acquired 200,000 acres of land at bargain basement prices. By 1902, U.S. investment had doubled to $100 million. A second occupation (1906–9), which followed anticorruption protests, established a provisional government headed by General Magoon, who looted Cuba's treasury, turned public works into boondoggles, and gave rich concessions to his friends. U.S. troops returned in 1912 to put down a 'racially charged revolt by Black sugar workers' (Gonzalez 2000, 64). By then, nearly 10,000 Americans lived in Cuba and more than three-quarters of the land was foreign owned. In 1917, President Woodrow Wilson sent troops to help put down a rebellion against a U.S.-backed conservative president.

In the 1920s, with unemployment soaring, many Cuban workers immigrated to the United States. In Cuba, labour unrest produced Cuba's first modern dictator, who made his island hospitable to American investment again by crushing the labour movement. American bankers showered his government with loans. In 1933, President Roosevelt, determined to change the pattern, forced the dictator to resign. But when the United States couldn't control the provisional government it installed, which was engaging in radical change, U.S. officials urged the new Cuban army commander to stage a coup. (The 'revolution' lasted just 100 days.) The coup brought to power a new dictator, Batista, who after a period of progressive development presided over bloody repression, again forcing thousands of progressive Cubans into exile. This pattern continued. Fulgencio Batista, Cuba's longest-lasting dictator, was supported by a 'bizarre alliance of Wall Street investors, mobsters, and the Cuban managers of U.S. corporations' (Gonzalez 2000, 64). He ruled until 1959, when Fidel Castro displaced him and initiated the Cuban Revolution.

Between 1898 and 1959, Cubans who migrated to the United States were fleeing repression or civil unrest; or they were displaced peasants who had lost their land. Others were exiled labour activists and nationalists; or they were workers who had been imported by labour contractors. They received no special treatment. That changed in 1959, when members of the elite, who ran Cuba for the United States, fled to Miami. Many Americans caught up in anti-communism saw them as refugees from a communist takeover who should be treated as heroes. Between 1952 and 1980, people were categorized as 'refugees' only if they were fleeing from communist regimes. Under President Carter, Congress enacted the Refugee Act (1980), which defined a 'refugee' as someone who had suffered persecution or who had a 'well-founded fear of persecution based on race, religion, nationality, membership in a particular social group or political opinion' (cited in Gonzales 2000, 138). But before the act took effect, Ronald Reagan was elected and made anti-communism the core of his foreign policy for the Americas. Undocumented migrants who applied for political asylum would be placed in detention centres unless they were fleeing communism.

Those who fled from Cuba in the 1960s and 1970s were from upper- and middle-class families, light skinned, educated, and often highly skilled. U.S. governments provided extensive support, so that they became the most affluent and conservative Hispanic community in the United States. Later, though, starting in 1980 (with the Mariel boat people), the Cubans who fled were poorer, darker skinned, and less educated and skilled. When the American TV news showed some of the 125,000 Cubans entering over a four-month period, a racist backlash developed. Far from being anti-communist heroes, many of these Mariel refugees were convicts or mentally ill. They were incarcerated in mothballed military bases around the country like other Latino refugees. By 1994, one million Cubans were living in the United States.

By the early 1980s, Guatemala, El Salvador, and Nicaragua were all engulfed in civil wars, which had been fostered largely by U.S. policies and covert actions.[12] Threatened by right-wing death squads, refugees streamed into Mexico; by 1984, half a million people had entered the United States. The Salvadorean community in the United States increased tenfold between 1979 and 1983; many thousands of Guatemalans entered, most of them Mayan Indians fleeing their government's 'scorched earth' efforts to force them off their lands to permit 'development.' Many Nicaraguans also fled. We lack the space to detail each country's unique history, but the patterns are similar.

Racialized But Not a 'Race'

'Hispanics' constitute an aggregation of communities of diverse origins and characteristics united only by the fact that they speak Spanish. But they are treated as a single cohesive group when public policies are being applied to them. This has had both negative and positive repercussions. The 'Hispanic' minority has been constructed over a long period of time, and there have been many contradictions in terms of how successive governments treat Hispanics. Most significant is that, though 'Hispanics' have been racialized, they are not a race according to the race theory manifested in U.S. public policy. Most race theorists in the United States conceptualize 'races' as concrete entities that exist 'out there,' and that census takers observe and apply within official race categories. This differs from understandings of 'races' as socially constructed by those who create race categories and impose them through public policies. Remember that the key premise of this book is that *states make race*, but how they make (and unmake) race differs. Nobles (2000, 167) observes, for example, that in the U.S. 'legislative and administrative remedies for discrimination [also] are premised on the continued salience and stability of historical constructions of race identities.' So even when U.S. government institutions struggle to remedy race-based discrimination and oppression, the policies contained in those remedies remain based on historical 'race' categories. (By contrast, Canadian governments conflate race communities into a single category of 'visible minorities,' which they contrast to 'ethnic groups,' which are understood to be 'White.')

In the United States, Hispanics have been racialized and have experienced discrimination and oppression as a result since the 1840s. But they are not considered a 'race' according to the race ideas and categories sanctioned by U.S. government institutions. This is because 'for 179 years, the Census Bureau's mission ... was ... [to] define and ... distinguish who was "White" from who was "non-White" ... which meant who was "Black"' (Nobles 2000). Except in the 1930 census, Hispanics were not part of that history as a race category; rather, they were fragmented among the charter races. Thus they are officially an ethnicity.

Other groups too were racialized, usually immigrant groups associated with manual labour, or who were Catholic or non-Christian, or did not speak English, or had darker skins (such as southern Europeans). Ignatiev (1995) contends that the Catholic Irish already had been racialized in Ireland by the oppressive landlord and caste systems that the English imposed. Fighting their way into American 'Whiteness' meant losing some of their differences, and 'acting White,' which meant oppressing Blacks. Hispanics differ because they are the only large, racialized group that has remained an underclass for almost two centuries but that are not considered a race. Hispanics as a group are constantly growing in numbers as U.S. economic and foreign policies promote migration. Fragmented between 'White' and 'non-White,' many Hispanics have been excluded from the 'White' category, yet they are not considered a charter non-White 'race.' Mexicans, who are the largest fragment of Hispanics, have been locked into a caste-like relationship in the United States for more than a century, as manual labourers. Moreover, indicators such as repressive legislation and increased instances of residential segregation suggest that the societal climate is deteriorating for them, not improving.

Historically, 'Whiteness' meant speaking English, being Protestant, and not performing manual labour. Bodkin (2002) contends that Jews became 'White' only when Jewish intellectuals reconceptualized 'race' as applied to them as an ethnocultural identity. Ignatiev (1995) also theorizes 'race' as socially constructed, but he links race concepts to acts of oppression. He argues that 'Whiteness' gave the Catholic Irish a number of competitive advantages in racist America: they could sell their labour piecemeal, across occupations, and they could also negotiate their pay.

Also, their businesses were not limited to a segregated (Irish) market. Irish men (and later women) could vote and be elected. They could own land and buy houses. In the justice system, they would be judged by their peers. They could live anywhere they could afford and fund Catholic schools for their children's education. They could spend what they earned as well as will and inherit property. When we set Hispanics' life conditions and chances against these advantages of 'Whiteness,' we see how racialized they still are.

Islamophobia: Falling In and Out of 'Whiteness'

Some form of Islamophobia exists throughout the West, sanctioning discrimination against Muslims purportedly because of their faith. Some consider Islamophobia an updated version of older Western ideas with their origins in conflicts between European Christians and Muslims and Jews over control of the Holy Land. These ideas have variously resulted in the expulsion of the Moors, forced Christianization, and the expulsion, racialization, and ghettoization of Jews throughout Europe over many centuries. Colonizers would later apply the racial tropes thereby developed to Indigenous peoples in the 'New World.' Prejudice against Muslims, therefore, recycles ideas that have racialized the religious enemies of Christianity in the past.[13] But current Islamophobia takes different forms, varies between Europe and the United States, and also differs between the United States and Australia and Canada.

In Europe, according to Jocelyn Cesari (2011, 24), Islamophobia is hard to distinguish from anti-immigrant sentiments because most Muslims are recent immigrants and are marginalized socio-economically and excluded politically. In the United States, most Muslims are integrated as descendants of families who immigrated decades ago. Muslims in the United States are fragmented as a group by race, ethnicity, language, and national origins (which include more than fifty countries). They also vary regarding their visibility: many secular and observant Muslims wear no distinguishing clothing. Most followers of Islam in the United States are 'Arab American' or (more inclusively) 'Middle Eastern,' whereas in most European countries, Muslim immigrants come from previous colonies in North Africa and Asia. The United States historically has categorized some Middle Easterners as 'White' and so, even under old immigration rules, eligible for citizenship. U.S. race theory conceptualized some Middle Easterners as Aryans[14] or as descendants of Alexander the Great. But because Middle Easterners' features range from fair to dark, like Hispanics, they don't have a clearly defined place in the American racial order (Love 2009, 403), especially since their relationship with the fundamental White/Black race hierarchy has always been ambiguous. Most can 'pass' as White, and do so. Moreover, U.S. dependence on Middle Eastern oil has moderated any potential official mistreatment targeting those from the region. Islamophobia in the United States currently reflects geopolitical changes such as it becoming the world's only superpower since the collapse of the Soviet Union and its worsening relations with groups and governments in the Middle East. Especially since the 9/11 attacks, many Middle Easterners have 'fallen out of Whiteness' and have become targets of Islamophobia. Terror attacks are being attributed to 'Muslims' as a group, so anti-Muslim racism 'judge[s] Muslims *en masse* by the standard of their worse representatives' (Muscati 2003, 249). Islamophobia, therefore, differs where Muslims are marginalized and denied citizenship and is more complex where geopolitical factors shape how Muslims are perceived and treated.

In this section we focus mainly on Islamophobia in the United States, which is more extensive and complex than in Australia and Canada. We cannot compare Islamophobia systematically across the three White-majority countries because of the superpower status of the United States, its foreign policy, and the 9/11 attacks. As a global superpower, the United States has interests in most Muslim-majority countries and often clashes with them because of its foreign policy. Radical Islamists have targeted U.S. interests and military forces around the world. This links foreign and domestic policies and practices regarding Muslims. Australia was an ally of the United States in Iraq and Afghanistan and experienced a (smaller) 9/11-type attack in Bali. But Canadians have experienced no comparable attacks to date. Moreover, a Liberal government refused to participate in the Iraq War, and a Conservative government ended Canada's military participation in a NATO-led action in Afghanistan in 2011. Thus, while Islamophobia exists in all three countries, it differs in its nature and extent. The settlement patterns of people of Middle Eastern origins and Muslim faith in the three countries also differ. In Australia they resemble the European pattern, while the Canadian pattern resembles that in the United States.

We will discuss two conceptualizations of Islamophobia, which provide complementary insights. Stephan Sheehi (2011, 31–2) conceptualizes Islamophobia as a new 'ideological formation that has taken full expression since the collapse of the Soviet Union.' Exploring the ideas of neoconservative ideologues, he theorizes that Islamophobia 'facilitates American Empire' and sanctions policies and practices that under 'normal circumstances' would be deemed unconstitutional. Sheehi (2011, 33) focuses on two specific paradigms constructed by ideologues Bernard Lewis and Fareed Zakaria. They distil many Islamophobic tenets and 'amplif[y] mainstream hostility to Islam and its adherents' (Love 2009).

Erick Love (2009, 401) defines 'Islamophobia' in the United States as 'racialized bigotry, discrimination, policies and practices directed toward a range of groups, *Muslim and otherwise*' (our emphasis). Rooted in the 'linked and racialized history of ... Middle Eastern Americans' in the United States, Love shows that Islamophobia manifests itself as discriminatory state policies, bigotry, cultural stereotypes, and hate crimes against Muslims and those with Muslim-like appearance, who include Hindus, Sikhs, some Hispanics, and Jews and Christians from the Middle East. Some of these groups experience Islamophobia because their physical appearance resembles that of a stereotyped 'Muslim,' or because their clothing (e.g., a turban) is mistakenly thought to symbolize that faith, or because of symbols that believers wear, such as various forms of women's modest dress. Islamophobia distorts Islamic teachings to discredit Muslims and defame Islam, focusing especially on its purported oppression of women. But it also harms many people who practise other religions.

The Islamophobia that developed in the United States results from and contributes to a 'racial ideology ... based on socially constructed categories of phenotypical characteristics, or how individuals physically appear' (Love 2009, 412). Physical markers of appearance, especially skin colour, accent, and distinctive dress (turban or headscarf), make individuals resemble stereotypical 'Muslims.' Even today, those with no such characteristics can easily live in the White suburbs, passing as 'ordinary Americans.' Because most Americans see the world through a racial lens, with 'Whiteness' and 'Blackness' as that lens's basic terms, the state's treatment of Middle Easterners has always been ambiguous and has depended on individuals' features. So the Immigration Act of 1917 barred people from 'Arabia' as non-White, but classed as 'White' those from adjacent Muslim-majority countries (e.g., Iran) and allowed them to enter. Many Middle Easterners – including Arabs – who gained admittance succeeded in persuading U.S. judges that they were 'White' and thus entitled to become citizens under the Naturalization Act (1790). But other judges rejected such claims, and some Middle Easterners faced 'racism, [and] discrimination' because they did not resemble 'Whites' (ibid., 406).

Organized paradigms of Islamophobia emerged first in the 1990s and intensified after 9/11 because Americans blamed those attacks on

Muslims, Arabs, Middle Easterners, and anyone who looked like them. But Arabophobia had emerged earlier, after Israel humiliated the Arab nations in the Six Day War of 1967. Moreover, this Arabophobia was recycled from the 1970s oil crisis, which U.S. leaders blamed on Arab governments. The Iranian hostage crisis, throughout which the superpower United States was taunted daily by Islamist students, generated Islamophobia, given the Iranian Revolution's militantly Islamist nature. By the mid-1990s 'the racial stereotype that ... all terrorists must be Middle Eastern' was pervasive (ibid., 413). By the end of the Cold War, Middle Easterners and Islamists had replaced the Soviet Union and communism as the United State's global enemy 'other,' although this didn't happen spontaneously. Especially after 2001, Islamophobia reflected the linking by senior government figures and enemies of the United States' domestic and foreign policies.

Extensive literature exists about the U.S. government's milking of the public's Islamophobic reactions with massive civil rights infringements sanctioned by laws that Congress passed after the 2001 attacks – laws that gave sweeping powers to state agencies, especially to the Executive Branch. Some authors contend that the Bush White House substituted the 'war against terror' for anti-communism to frighten citizens who were reluctant to go to war in Iraq. Thus, a key characteristic of the enhanced security regime was racialized discrimination. Yet Middle Easterners[15] who do not differ from 'ordinary' (i.e., White) Americans physically or in their dress usually are not harmed by Islamophobia, because they are seen as White. Conversely, those who do differ physically or in their dress, or who come from suspect countries, have experienced surveillance, purportedly 'random' searches and 'voluntary' interrogations, or worse.

After 2001, many young Muslim Americans who felt alienated by their government's discriminatory actions began increasingly to assert their religious rights, which included enhancing their visible identity as Muslims – unlike their parents (Abdo 2005), who usually were secular or at least passed as 'ordinary Americans.' These young Muslims wore modest dress, attended mosque, joined Muslim student associations, and found partners through dating sites that promoted lives without alcohol, drugs, or premarital sex. They also demanded prayer rooms at their universities. These more visible identities have subjected this generation to more anti-Muslim hostility. Muslim migrants also experienced hostility. By 2007 there were 240,000 new Afghan refugees in the United States, many of whom resisted assimilation (Takaki 2008, 421).

Fear was widespread among Middle Eastern Americans after the 2001 attacks and some Afghans experienced attacks on their loyalty and on their persons directed against them both as Muslims and as Afghans. Nonetheless, some White Americans including some political figures spoke up against brutal attacks.

In Australia, Islamophobia is visible as racialized discrimination, with politicians sharply rejecting suggestions by some Muslim leaders that their religious values be accommodated. After the White Australia policy was rescinded, some Middle Easterners were admitted as legal immigrants and categorized as 'White.' Early immigrants from the region were often Christians – from Lebanon, for example. Later groups, many of them refugees from war zones, were Muslim. In any case, Islamophobic re/actions often mistake who is Muslim, as for example in the case of attacks about modestly dressed Lebanese women on a popular beach – women who were Christian. Controversies about mosque building also have been reported. When a Muslim cleric in 2005 demanded that *sharia* law courts be established, intense Islamophobia was evident among members of the Howard cabinet. In this case, Islamophobia blamed an undifferentiated 'Islamic culture' for having undemocratic values and for oppressing women. Commonwealth Treasurer Costello declared: 'There is only one law in Australia ... If you prefer Sharia law ... go to another country.' Education Minister Nelson insisted that 'if people don't want to ... live by Australian values ... they can clear off' (cited in Ghobadzedeh 2010, 313). The Howard government, which previously had rolled back women's rights and courted the Christian right with faith-based social programs now declared that Australian democracy required strict separation between religion and the state. Previous Labor governments' commitments to multicultural accommodation were clearly dead. By promoting Islamophobia, the Howard government blunted any censure for the civil rights abuses of Aboriginal Australians and the harsh treatment of refugees.

Islamophobia was also evident in Canada immediately after the 9/11 attacks. But a different context lessened some of its impact. A debate about the possibility of private arbitration under *sharia* law in Ontario is revealing. Asked to extend the opportunity for private arbitration under the Arbitration Act of 1991, which had let orthodox Jewish participants arbitrate under a religious legal code, the McGuinty Liberal government appointed Marion Boyd, a well-known feminist and former attorney general, as a one-woman commission of inquiry. Because the key issue was how the provision could affect Muslim women, Boyd held hearings with most Muslim women's organizations, with mainstream feminist groups, and with more than two hundred individual Muslim women. Boyd's report was cautiously supportive, largely because faith-based arbitration systems already existed for fundamentalist Jews with few problems. A broader debate was promoted by ex-Muslim activists from Britain and elsewhere, who were determined to deny any official standing for *sharia* law in any Western country. Ontario Premier Dalton McGuinty eventually decided to end any private religious arbitration in Ontario, removing the multicultural accommodation already in place. Since the duty to provide such accommodation is constitutional in Canada, however, the issue could reappear before the courts.

Ghobadzedeh (2010) contends that the fact that multicultural accommodation is constitutionally entrenched in Canada muted the impact of Islamophobia – without, however, eliminating it. Intense debates in Quebec about how far governments must go to provide 'fair accommodation' have indicated as much. Moreover, Canadians often disagree with U.S. foreign policies. For example, Canadian governments stayed out of the Vietnam War and the war in Iraq; and many Canadians, especially in Quebec, have sympathy for the Palestinians. But it was the high-profile case of Maher Arar that most weakened Islamophbia. Arar is a telecommunications engineer and a Canadian citizen, born in Syria, who in 2002 was detained by U.S. authorities while in transit in New York returning from a family vacation in Tunisia, where his wife was born. After denying him access to legal and Canadian consular representation, U.S. officials sent him to Syria, where he was tortured for nearly a year. Led by his wife, Monia Mazigh, a highly educated and visibly observant Muslim, a campaign to free him succeeded. On his return, a government inquiry blamed the U.S. government and some cooperative Canadian security officers for what happened to Arar. No evidence was found that he had any links to terrorism. Arar received $10.5 million compensation from the Canadian government and now teaches college. The U.S. government still claims that he has links to terrorists, however, and keeps him and his family on a no-fly watch list. (At the time of writing, *Arar v. Ashcroft* is proceeding through the U.S. courts.)

The Arar case made many (White) Canadians suspicious of Islamophobic abuses by state officials, and sympathy developed for Arar and his wife. How to balance state officials' need to provide security, with the protection of Canadians' basic rights under the Charter of Rights and Freedoms, remains a matter of debate and some conflict. The Arar case, and the fact that Canada has suffered no terrorist event attributable to Muslims, may have made many unwilling to tolerate Islamophobic government actions. Yet many such actions have been taken by federal governments against vulnerable Muslims and their communities. Natasha Bakht's *Belonging and Banishment: Being Muslim in Canada* (2008) identifies other issues and cases such as the Harper Conservative government's apparent unwillingness to assist former child soldier Omar Khadr, a Canadian citizen incarcerated in Guantánamo. The federal government has also used surveillance techniques developed in the United States. One example relates to the treatment of the Somali community. At first, Canada received Somalis as Black refugees from a small, war-torn African country. They experienced race-based discrimination, but some have accessed higher education, and strong community leadership has developed despite clan divisions. Since 2011, however, Somalis increasingly have been framed as Muslims and as potential terrorists by Conservative ministers and the security services under their direction. Unlike the Arar case, this treatment of a Black Muslim community has received little publicity, so many White Canadians continue to believe that Islamophobia is largely a U.S. or European problem. As elsewhere, problems of mistaken identity are common since acts motivated by Islamophobia sometimes have targeted non-Muslims and non-Muslim religious buildings.

New Views of Asians: Immigrant Poster Children or Eternal Foreigners?

In this last case, we discuss how 'Asians' currently experience 'race.' In legal terms, there are few similarities to the race regimes of the nineteenth and early twentieth centuries. More than a century and a half ago, the U.S. Congress passed the Chinese Exclusion Act (1882) during an economic depression. This was the first law to prohibit the entry of aspiring immigrants because of their nationality (Takaki 2008, 7). Currently, Asian Americans can enter and become citizens in all three countries. While some Asians descend from nineteenth-century immigrant communities, most are recent immigrants or refugees, who often fled from anti-communist wars (Korea, Vietnam, Cambodia) or have been displaced by economic exploitation or civil disorder and violence. In the United States, they are categorized by the pan-ethnic identity of 'Asians'; while in Canada, they usually are folded into the category of 'visible minorities.' In Australia, the door admitting them is only half open: most Asian immigrants are professionals who entered as students and have been allowed to stay because of their skills and because their language facility gives Australian enterprises better access to Asian markets. Asian Americans are more affluent, with higher achievement in education and professional employment than other non-White groups.

After the Second World War, changes in immigration laws affected 'Asians' in all three countries. Currently, there are about 15 million people of full or partial Asian heritage. That is 5 per cent of the U.S. population. About 8.7 per cent of Australians are Asians (1.7 million), and about 11 per cent of Canadian residents (3 million). Asians are Canada's fastest-growing visible minority group. These data have been gathered, however, by census bureaux, whose definitions of 'Asian' vary.[16] This again makes systematic comparisons difficult.

In the United States, Asians are now the 'poster children' for immigrant and refugee groups. Unlike the nineteenth-century Chinese, many Asians entering the country today are highly educated or come from educated families. Usually, though, they must still do unskilled work until they have learned English and re-established their credentials. Their families are committed to education, however; and their children are raised to focus on acquiring a strong education and a well-paid professional job. From the outside, they represent everything that is positive about hard work and self-reliance. In Canada, a 'business class' for immigrants has allowed many wealthy Chinese, especially from Hong Kong, to acquire a Canadian passport. Many Asian refugees have been anti-communist supporters of the West.

That Asians enjoy a relatively positive image and are upwardly mobile does not prevent them from being racialized. The large numbers of Asian students on university campuses are seen as unfair competition by White society – especially by White children's parents – and not as the result of Asian students' intelligence and hard work. Asian families' commitment to education is threatening to Whites; Asian students are seen as overachievers 'taking places away' from 'regular Americans' or 'ordinary Canadians.' Universities in Australia profit by admitting students from Asia and charging them high fees,[17] and this has accentuated the threat perceived in that country. In popular culture, the old 'yellow peril' trope is being recycled, with Asians being projected as foreigners whose loyalty cannot be trusted and who would support Asian governments. But does this result in discriminatory actions by governments?

Starting with the Reagan administration, U.S. governments have pitted Asian Americans against African Americans and Hispanics, whom they portray as welfare bums who succeed only through affirmative action.

Asian immigrants in the United States have been widely viewed as pulling themselves up by their bootstraps to success without relying on 'society' (i.e., White taxpayers) for support. This discourse has been used to delegitimize affirmative action programs. For example, in California (where Whites fear becoming a minority), a 1996 proposal to end affirmative action statewide – misleadingly named the California Civil Rights Initiative (Proposition 209) – was approved by 54 per cent of those voting. Yet exit polls showed that 25 per cent of those who voted for the initiative *supported* affirmative action (Takaki 2008, 403); they had been confused by the initiative's title. Eliminating affirmative action was justified by Asian Americans' success and their purported 'overrepresentation' on campuses. After 1996, university attendance declined sharply among African Americans from 15 to 5 per cent, and among Hispanics from 8 to 2 per cent. Similar dynamics have not developed in Australia or Canada, mainly because neither country has quota-based affirmative action programs and because Canada's employment and pay equity programs benefit disadvantaged Whites (e.g., women and people with disabilities) as well as race minorities. This has created a stronger support base that makes it harder to pit racial groups against one another.

As the U.S. economy experiences difficulty competing, especially with China, the negative implications of the Asian American 'bootstrap' success story have become evident. Anxieties about domination by Asian countries have always been part of the Australian national psyche, because of its location and because of Japanese attacks during the Second World War. But anxieties are especially strong in the United States because its international economic, political, and military power is being challenged by rising economies and potential military opponents. In his account of the reracialization of Asian Americans, Wu (2002) cites evidence from popular and high culture that reveals these fears. One example is Samuel Huntington's *The Clash of Civilizations* (1996) and the many imitators it has stimulated. Huntington's ideas, however, are retooled versions of those in Madison Grant's *The Passing of the Great Race* (1917) and Lothrop Stoddard's *The Rising Tide of Color Against White World-Supremacy* (1920).

Is there evidence of racialized discrimination by state authorities against Asian Americans? In all three countries, people of Japanese descent were interned during the Second World War, their civil rights having been denied by governments that did not protect them or their property. Wu (2002, chapter 3) argues that Asian Americans will always be treated as perpetual foreigners, who will never really assimilate and whose loyalty Whites will never rely on. In 1988 the U.S. Congress approved legislation providing reparations to internment camp survivors. But Asian Americans in the military continue to face suspicion, racial slurs, and sometimes exclusion. It took a long legal struggle for Bruce Yamashita, a third-generation American from Honolulu, to win his commission in the Marines in 1994. Moreover, many White Americans so fear the decline of the United States that governments again likely would suspend Asians' rights, treating them like the foreign enemies that many Whites believe they are.

Conclusion

In this chapter we have explored three race formations that connect domestic and foreign policies. We have shown that how governments 'make race' has changed, though earlier race tropes and ideas are always being recycled. The fears of the White majorities who still dominate the three states are increasingly evident in politics and in popular and high culture as the possible loss of majority status looms. Apartheid-era South Africa showed how much state violence and corruption of government institutions were needed for a White minority to dominate a non-White majority. Especially in the United States and in the international arena, evidence of declining White power makes some increasingly determined to preserve their political and economic dominance. Whether we will learn to create multiracial societies in which racialization is not a tool of oppression and dominance is the big question for future generations.

Discussion Questions

1 How did racialization affect different waves of Hispanics
  in the United States?
2 What was the role of census bureaux in the construction
  of race categories?
3 Can President Obama exert substantial influence on his government
  when it comes to improving conditions for race minorities?
4 Explain the rise of new race formations like Islamophobia.
5 Why is comparing race regimes across countries so difficult?

8 Basic Concepts for Understanding the Politics of Race

Introduction

In this chapter we discuss the main concepts used in the book. The definitions often differ from those in dictionaries, which are written from the perspective of those in power. In studying the politics of race, you learn there are no simple definitions, nor do ordinary dictionaries or encyclopedias help. There are specialized encyclopedias specifically about race issues, but the concepts related to the politics of race are hotly contested; also, the meanings vary in different countries and change over time as groups struggle to control what words used to describe or categorize them mean. So to understand what the words used in this book mean, you need to know when and where the words were used (their *context*), as well as who used them, in order to understand which frame was used that shaped their meaning.

This entries in this chapter are in alphabetical order. Many concepts are complex, with multiple and contested meanings that change over time and place. Some concepts, such as 'race regime,' are original to this book. The book has explored the following race regimes: internal colonialism, slavery, Whites-only nationalism, segregation, and democratic racism.

Affirmative action

This term relates to policies aimed at reversing the effects of historical patterns of oppression experienced by disadvantaged race minorities, as well as other groups, such as women and people with disabilities. For example, because the former race regimes of slavery and segregation excluded African Americans from citizenship and did not create a level playing field, affirmative action policies provide an advantage – a 'leg up' – to compensate for those currently disadvantaged because of those historic exclusions. An example would be providing qualified members of disadvantaged race minority groups some preference in employment or education. States vary in how they administer these policies; usually, though, they are seen as temporary and are intended to last only until the effects of past and present race-based oppression or discrimination have been erased.

What the various affirmative action policies and practices usually have in common is that they go beyond equal opportunity guarantees, which make current discrimination illegal (ensuring a level playing field *now*). Instead, affirmative action policies address the current dis-crimination experienced because of prior collective oppression by giv-ing preferential treatment to qualified members of the disadvantaged minorities.

Apartheid

This term, which means 'apartness,' in Afrikaans, refers to South Africa's segregation regime, which envisioned total separation of the different races in all areas of life, though this never happened in practice because White South Africans had non-Whites as servants and Blacks worked in the mines that produced much of South Africa's wealth. This policy was based on racialist ideas and the desire to maintain the purity of White blood. South Africa's Nationalist government formally institutionalized the apartheid system in 1948. It was deconstructed as a race regime in the early 1990s when a multirace, multiparty convention drafted a provisional constitution and the first elections based on a universal franchise occurred. Nonetheless, elements remain, especially in Whites' economic dominance and residential segregation.

Assimilation

This is the process whereby minorities become similar to majorities by surrendering their own cultural identity, voluntarily or forcibly. The most common methods have involved the physical removal of young children to be raised by majority culture parents or institutions; and coercive education in which minority group children are forcibly edu-cated in schools that disparage their cultures, forbid their languages, punishing them for speaking them, and promote the majority's culture and language.

Backlash

This is a hostile, and sometimes violent, reaction to policies and practices that governments adopt (or sometimes just propose) to end oppression. When state institutions try to dismantle race regimes and undo the effects of state racism, backlash is reflected in demands that the status quo not be disturbed and that everyone be 'treated equally.' Many reactions to change – actual and potential – feed democratic racism.

Citizenship/Citizen

In theory, citizens have full rights and 'share both in the ruling and being ruled' (Chesterman and Galligan 1997, 1) in a country. Historically, *citizenship* was a status and identity enjoyed by relatively few inhabitants of a country. Moreover, many groups – women, foreigners, servants, slaves, people of a different race – were denied citizenship in earlier purported democracies. Those who are not citizens of a country are *denizens* who usually cannot vote or hold office.

In the 1950s the British scholar T.H. Marshall conceptualized citizenship as a political and legal status with three aspects: *civil rights*, including freedom of movement, speech, association, assembly, and belief, and the right to own property; *political rights*, including the right to vote, to run for office, to lobby, demonstrate, go to court, state your views, and participate in the political process; and *social rights*, including access to education and social services on the same basis as others in the community. The race regimes in all three countries discussed in this book have denied non-Whites all or some of these rights and entitlements.

African Canadian activist Glenda Simms (1993, 334) posited that citizenship is a matter of identity as much as of rights. For example, most Canadians (and foreigners) assume that Canada as a nation is White and European; thus, non-Whites can be excluded culturally, even though they have legal rights. Simms contends that racism constructs 'non-Whites,' 'immigrants,' and 'visible minorities' as less than 'Canadian.'

Second-class citizenship refers to situations where non-Whites have legal rights as citizens but are not included in the national identity.

Citizenship rights. See Citizenship.

Civil disobedience

A form of political action whereby citizens deliberately break what they consider an unjust law, non-violently. They are prepared to accept the penalty for their actions. See also *non-violent non-cooperation*.

Civil rights. See *Citizenship*.

Civil society

Political scientists long defined politics as involving mainly the state and its institutions. According to liberal theory, however, much politics takes place *outside* the state in organizations and activities that are described as civil society. These range from traditional organizations such as churches, unions, professional associations, and media to organizations that foster mass participation, such as political parties, voluntary associations, lobby groups, and various movements. Civil society is where both the values that support democracy and the prejudices that maintain racism develop.

Civilized/Primitive /Savage

These concepts are part of the race theories that Europeans developed and applied in order to justify dispossessing Indigenous and other non-White peoples whom they dominated while colonizing them. The categories were hierarchical, with 'civilized' people (read 'Whites') deemed superior to those categorized as 'primitive' and 'savage.' This superiority was deemed justification for 'Whites' ruling non-Whites. The schema ignores the fact that numerous civilizations (Chinese, Japanese, Hindu, etc.) were created by non-Whites. See also *social Darwinism*.

Colonialism

The current politics of race in settler countries are the result of conquest of non-White peoples and exploitation of their lands from the sixteenth century to the twentieth by European nations that were technologically advanced regarding warfare, industrial production, and financial transactions. That process we call colonialism. Colonialism took two forms. The first was the domination of distant countries. French colonists mainly engaged in trade; Spanish colonists exploited resources such as gold; Britain settled lands using free emigrant or convict labour for resource extraction and agricultural production to feed its industrial-izing cities. In each case, new forms of production were introduced, new systems of power relations were imposed, and new patterns of inequal-ity established privileges for the White colonizers while oppressing the non-White, dominated population. These patterns would persist for generations. Some colonizers enslaved conquered peoples; others imported slaves, mainly from Africa, to work the land.

A second form of colonialism developed when Europeans (convicts, peasants thrown off their lands in Europe, orphans, fortune hunters) settled in the colonized countries, and the settler states imposed systems of internal colonialism.

Colonizers saw colonized people as different in physical appearance, beliefs, ways of life, and culture. These people were viewed as barely human. According to Markus (1994), racist ideas[1] (including the belief in White superiority) developed to justify the dispossession and exploi-tation of colonized people, who were classified as 'savages' or 'primi-tive.' This book focuses on three White, settler states formed within the British Empire, which applied British concepts of racial superiority to justify oppressing and exploiting Indigenous peoples, often seen as 'dying races' that would disappear as a result of 'fatal contact' with more advanced people. Other colonists believed that Indigenous peoples were so low on the ladder of evolution that it would take them generations to become 'civilized.' Consequently, racialists saw colonial-ism as part of 'the White man's burden' to 'civilize' the non-Whites they now dominated.

Colonialism operated at many levels, from the level of *cultural racism* (the idea that Whites are superior because of how they live) to the level of state actions. The supplanted nations lost political control and eco-nomic self-sufficiency, resulting in relations of dependence on the state and civil society institutions. Indigenous languages, customs, religions, knowledge, and political systems were repressed or destroyed. Children often were removed from their parents, supposedly 'for their own good,' to be assimilated via adoption or coercive schooling. The ideologies that justified colonialism assumed human inequality, and those ideologies survive in the laws, popular imagination, culture, and knowledge sys-tems of these societies to this day. Racialist ideas, passed down from one generation to the next, have become embedded in the state institutions in each settler society.

Internal colonialism. Most colonies were acquired by invasion. This conquest often was facilitated by the diseases that Europeans carried with them, to which Indigenous peoples lacked immunity. (Note that in

Asia, Europeans more often died from disease than those they sought to rule.)

In North America, Indigenous peoples were sometimes treated as allies when European colonizers were in economic and military competition with each other and needed Indigenous peoples' support. Ultimately, though, Indigenous peoples were forcibly removed from their land and incarcerated on small reserves or missions. In the early frontier days especially, deliberate efforts were sometimes made to exterminate them.

Internal colonialism involved British and (later) settler-state control over internal colonies or reserves maintained by violence (or the threat of violence) and bureaucratic[2] action. After initially being segregated, the surviving Indigenous communities experienced systematic efforts to assimilate their children and eradicate their culture. Indigenous peoples were usually excluded from the dominant economy. Their labour was exploited, and they were denied political and civic rights. Racialist ideas justified internal colonialism.

Colony

An area of land settled or conquered by a distant state and controlled by it.

Cultural racism

While force and state action were important in establishing race regimes, cultural racism also offered powerful instruments for persuading both the colonizers and those they colonized that racialism was justified. The belief in White superiority was embedded in virtually all aspects of colonial culture, from religious sermons and scientific works to songs, stories, plays, and books. 'Art,' for example, meant only European cultural forms – symphonies, opera, and framed paintings. Racist doctrine held that 'primitive' people were incapable of 'true art' or 'real music.' Their creative expressions were merely folklore or crafts. Cultural racism persisted long after race regimes were stripped of their legal sanctions.

Democracy

Traditionally, this term meant a political system based on rule by the people. In Greek, *demos* meant 'the people.' Thus, *democracy* meant 'rule by the people.' But who 'the people' are differs from place to place and from era to era. *Representative* democracy differs from *direct* democracy. In the latter, all citizens (but not all people) share in making the laws, with the administrators chosen by lot. In representative democracies, those who are citizens have the right to vote in elections for representatives (i.e., legislators). In some representative democracies there are elements of *direct* democracy, such as the ballot initiatives and referenda found in some U.S. states that let citizens put questions on the ballot to be voted on in a referendum provided enough registered electors sign on. In some representative democracies, citizens can recall their representatives if they can persuade enough other citizens.

Democratic racism

This is an ideology that combines two apparently conflicting sets of values: the democratic egalitarian values of justice and fairness; and racialist ideologies, attitudes, and assumptions that sanction White rule. Democratic racism is also a race regime and is discussed in detail under that heading. See Henry and her colleagues (1997, 13–17).

Deskilling. See *Skill discounting*

Discrimination

Actions taken on the basis of prejudice. Prejudice is the belief that race stereotypes – negative images of race minorities – are true. *Official discrimination* involves state actions taken on the basis of prejudice, such as the denial of political rights.

Disease

In all three settler societies discussed in this book, colonial invasion and Whites' settlement was facilitated by the many diseases the Europeans carried such as measles and smallpox to which Indigenous peoples had little or no immunity. Thus, for example, the number of Indigenous people in what is now the United States dropped from an estimated more than five million in 1492 to less than half a million by the late nineteenth century (Thornton 1987). This was partly a result of violence, but it was also from the effects of diseases brought by Europeans and from poor conditions on reserves and at missions.

Equality-seeking movements

These are movements of people who have mobilized to achieve the
changes needed to become equal in rights and status to others in the
society. In the United States, for example, the Civil Rights movement –
active in the 1960s and 1970s – worked to resist race-based segregation.
The Red Power movement in the same period involved Indigenous
peoples in both the United States and Canada seeking land rights, self-
government, and respect for their cultures and spiritual practices.

Ethnicity

This word is rooted in the Greek *ethne* or *ethnos*, meaning 'others' or
'heathens' (i.e., not Greeks) (Day 2000, 52ff). *Ethnos* was the opposite of
polis – the political community in which Greeks lived. Herodotus, the
ancient Greek historian, developed a system of rules and categories
regarding the different kinds of 'others' that Greeks encountered. In this
sense, he was the founder of ethnography, which is the study of 'uncivilized' peoples by 'civilized' people. Later, ethnology came to mean the
study of those who were neither Jews nor Christians. Ethnicity was
attributed to those whom Greeks classified as inferior, because they
were 'barbarians.'

The equating of ethnicity with inferiority was embedded in Western
ways of thinking and adopted by Western philosophers and theolo-
gians. Max Weber claimed that race and ethnicity were largely synonymous, and theories of ethnicity often involve the belief that it is inherited
(Guibernau and Rex 1997, 15–26). Anthony Smith (cited in ibid., 27)
contends that ethnicity underlies European conceptions that nations are
'human populations with shared ancestry, myths, histories and cultures'
and that they have links to 'a specific territory and a sense of solidarity.'
Ethnicity was substituted for race after the Second World War, during
which millions died in the name of racial purity. The concept of 'tribe'
also came under attack during the wave of decolonization that followed
the Second World War. The term 'ethnic group' was substituted for
'tribe'; similarly, 'ethnic discrimination' replaced both 'racism' and 'trib-
alism.' To avoid this confusion of concepts we use 'race' in discussions
of characteristics associated in settler societies with non-White skin
colour and other physical characteristics. Note, however, that anti-
Semitism and Islamophobia, which we describe as racial formations,

target people because of their faith although in most cases Jews and Muslims are described as having distinctive physical characteristics.

Federalism

A way of organizing a state into two levels of government, which divide decision-making power (sovereignty) vertically. Each level of government interacts directly with citizens, and each has final authority over citizens in some fields (jurisdictions). These fields are specified in a written constitution, which is adjudicated by the highest court in each country. Australia, Canada, and the United States are all federations. The significance of federalism for the politics of race is the subject of chapter 4.

Filibusters

Rebellions by American mercenaries intended to facilitate U.S. annexations of territory. Between 1810 and 1860 there were 14 attempted annexations of Mexican territories, and multiple attempts in Cuba, Nicaragua, and Honduras (Gonzalez 2000, 37/8). Initially, 'Americans' moved into a territory and acquired land rights, usually by promising to convert to Catholicism and pledging loyalty to the Spanish crown, as was required to become citizens. But in 1810, a group in West Florida 'resorted to a [new] form [when] ... a band of ... mercenaries ... captured a town or territory and proclaimed their own republic' (Gonzalez 2000, 36). Because the Spanish called those who undertook such acts *filibusteros* (freebooters), their 'rebellions' were called *filibusters*. Filibusters also were used in the Pacific, to annex Hawaii. Once (White) manhood suffrage was established in the 1830s, it became easy to drum up political support for such American 'settlers' or 'pioneers' whose rights were portrayed as being infringed upon by non-Whites, or Spanish-speakers. The term 'filibuster' is also used to describe procedures in the U.S. Senate when a senator speaks non-stop to make a point or prevent a bill from passing.

Genocide

The deliberate extermination of a people because of its race, ethnicity, or faith; or because it occupies land those who exterminate wish to occupy. *Cultural genocide* is the attempt to eliminate a people's culture –

including its language, customs, and religious/spiritual practices – by force, by law, by removing children and coercively educating them, and/or by bureaucratic regulations.

Gerrymandering

This involves setting the boundaries of an electoral district in such a way that one party or candidate of a particular race is always elected because the votes of other parties or race candidates are diluted. Though historically a *negative* mechanism used against non-White candidates, more recently it has been used positively to create minority-majority districts. Also referred to as *racial redistricting*, and *vote dilution*.

Govern/Government

'Govern' means to rule with authority; to conduct the affairs of a country (Hawkins 1979, 347). *Government* involves activities conducted within specialized institutions, including: courts, legislatures, executives, the civil service, the military, and the police. Government also identifies the institutions through which governing occurs and the people who govern.

Ideology

Ideology is a set of beliefs, perceptions, assumptions, and values that provide members of a group with an understanding of and explanation for their world. It also provides a framework for 'organizing, maintaining and transforming relations of power and dominance in society' (Henry et al. 1997, 13). A parallel term is 'framing.' See also *democratic racism* and *social Darwinism*.

Imperialism

A complex system involving the economic activities in the colonies of a European country, in which the transportation of products (rice, cotton, sugar) from the colony to the metropolitan (colonizing) country generates wealth for the latter's citizens based on the exploitation of the labour of the colonized. The form of imperialism developed by Europe between the fifteenth century and the 1960s also involved slavery and the presence of White settlers.

Institution

A set of structures that persist over time and the ideas that legitimize them. For example, the House of Commons, the Supreme Court, the U.S. presidency, and so on are all political institutions. Ideological formations such as nationalism can also be institutionalized. Usually, an institution's form has been developed over many years and has been legitimized by ideas that explain how and why they operate.

Invasion

Entering a territory you do not own and where you are not wanted, using force or the threat of force.

Legislature. See *State.*

Manifest destiny

A doctrine coined in 1845. Initially, it referred to U.S. government efforts to annex, purchase, or acquire lands for expansion, which were justified by the claim that the United States was 'exceptional' in terms of its origins and the nature of its government ('born in liberty,' 'the shining city on a hill,' and so on). It posited that westward expansion and the removal and eventual incarceration of Indians was justified in the name of liberty and democracy. Thus, America's manifest destiny was to expand across the continent and for Anglos to rule lands occupied by non-Whites. As America's goal was to expand its dominance spreading democracy far and wide, the scope of the concept was broadened to include domination of more lands and incorporation of more peoples.

Minority-majority districts. See *gerrymander.*

Monroe Doctrine

This was promulgated in 1823 by President James Monroe, who declared 'America for Americans.' It was issued at a time when many Latin American countries were struggling for independence and when the U.S. government was concerned about preventing other (i.e., European) powers from taking over Spain's colonies. The doctrine signalled that the United States intended to dominate North and South America. Munroe stated that the U.S. government would consider further efforts by European countries to colonize land or interfere in the Americas as acts of aggression against the United States. He also promised that the United States would not interfere with any European colony in the hemisphere that was not seeking independence, nor would it interfere in European affairs. From the beginning, the doctrine has been an important plank of American foreign policy; presidents as recent as Ronald Reagan have invoked it.

Multiculturalism

Multiculturalism takes different forms in each settler society. It is used to describe a condition of historical or current social diversity. Multicultural ideology valorizes cultural diversity. As government policy, it endorses or promotes increasing the presence of diverse groups in society, to be achieved, for example, through immigration from non-European source countries. Multiculturalism is also an approach to managing diversity in institutions – for example, a museum may increase its displays about minority groups; and students from minority cultures may demand to be taught things about cultures other than the one that is dominant in their society. Though multiculturalism is used to describe state policies that manage conflicts among diverse groups, it should be distinguished from anti-racist approaches.

Nation/Nationalism/Nation-State

These are hotly contested concepts (Guibernau 1999, 13). The dominant meaning of *nation* comes from European experiences from the seventeenth century to the present, during which modern nation-states were built that in theory were to be culturally homogeneous. Most Western theorists conceptualize a nation as 'a human group conscious of forming a community, sharing a common culture, attached to a clearly demarcated territory, having a common past and a common project for the future and claiming the right to rule itself' (ibid., 14).

A nation is also conceptualized as 'an imagined political community' (Anderson 1983) marked by a 'deep, horizontal comradeship.' This, even though nations are marked by internal inequality, exploitation, and oppression. Anthony Marx (1998) argues that in settler states there is a White 'comradeship' fostered by race supremacy, since these new nations were and remain imagined by White settlers as White (men's) nations. White solidarity and racialism were used to build new settler nations.

The doctrine of *nationalism* holds that a group claiming to be a nation has the right to be self-governing, either by having its own state (see below); or through autonomy in a federal state; or through some other arrangement involving some autonomy concerning culture. Also, nationalism is a sentiment held by people who feel they are members of a nation because they identify with its symbols and share its main characteristics. Thus, nationalism is an ideology that includes principles of inclusion and exclusion that identify insiders and outsiders.

The term *nation-state* relates to European experiences that have joined nations with states in ways that legitimize claims to a territory and elites' claims to dominate a territory. According to Max Weber, a state is 'a human community that (successfully) claims the *monopoly of the legitimate use of physical force* within a given territory' (Gerth and Mills 1991, 78). A nation-state is a modern political institution that Europeans created and then exported around the world through colonialism and imperialism. European theory assumes that the creation of nation-states – nation building – involves cultural homogenization (Guibernau 1999, 14). This can be by peaceful means where the peoples within the state's claimed territory share a common language, faith, and history. But often nation building has also involved majorities repressing minority languages and cultural or religious groups.

Anthony Marx (1999) posits that a homogeneous nation is almost always a goal in the politics of race. In theory, nations can be 'civic' – that is, they can be based on shared political values instead of shared blood; but in practice, national solidarity in European nation-states is usually based on ethnicity. Settler societies, which were built through immigration, resorted to race superiority and White dominance as the basis of solidarity. This resulted in *Whites only nationalism*, whereby solidarity was built by privileging otherwise divided Whites over non-Whites. Marx's example is the United States, in which northern and southern Whites were united after the Civil War and Reconstruction through a Whites-only nationalism, which itself was based on denying all non-Whites citizenship. Australia and Canada also developed versions of Whites-only nationalism.

Non-violent non-cooperation. See *Civil disobedience.*

Oppression

Iris Young (1990, 9) theorizes that oppression has five aspects: exploitation, marginalization, powerlessness, cultural imperialism, and violence.

Though their effects are systematic, oppression is not an on/off, all-or-nothing thing. Thus, people can experience some but not all aspects of oppression. Young also theorizes that people can be oppressed in some ways, but also oppress others when different aspects are considered.

Exploitation, according to Young, is a steady process whereby the results of the labour of one social group are transferred to the benefit of another group (ibid., 49). An example is slavery, where the results of the work of unpaid Black slaves generate wealth for White owners and their families. Another example is sharecropping, where free Blacks and others work the land for a 'share' of the crop, with the profits going to the landowner. Two others are the poorly paid work of Asian 'coolies,' who built the railways, mines, and roads that opened up the West for Whites to develop for profit; and of Hispanics, who toiled on farms, plantations, and ranches so that White landowners could prosper. In all of these examples, the workers were stigmatized – that is, they were framed as uneducated, lazy, unskilled, and so on, which made it legitimate to exploit their work.

Marginalization, again according to Young (1990, 53), occurs when 'a whole category of people is expelled from useful participation in social life and thus potentially subjected to material deprivation and even extermination.' Usually, those who have been marginalized are racially marked by physical characteristics. One horrible example of marginalization was the killing of around six million Jews by the Nazis between 1930 and 1945. But many groups – the elderly, those with disabilities, and especially Indigenous/Aboriginal peoples – have also been marginalized. For example, Australia developed a welfare state, but its Aboriginal people were denied the right to benefit from the resulting programs until the states grudgingly extended them citizenship in the 1960s. Even afterwards, they remained marginalized and subject to 'the often arbitrary and invasive authority of social service providers and ... administrators' (ibid., 54). They were marginalized, too, by being denied the right to participate politically, and they remain stigmatized.

The *powerless* lack power or authority even in the limited sense in which it exists in modern, representative democracies (ibid., 56). The powerless must always take orders but never get to give them and can never avoid obeying them. Many theories confuse not being powerful with being powerless; actually, those two states are different. Those who are powerless have no resources of status, respectability, and so on, to use as defences against other aspects of oppression. Examples of powerlessness are a Black youth who goes into a store to buy a sweater and is automatically suspected of shoplifting; or a Black man driving a nice car who is arrested for theft or pursued as a criminal. In both examples, powerlessness can be linked to race. *Some* Blacks have *some* power in situations in which they are known (e.g., when they are seen as professionals who are Black); but when their role is not known, the stigma of being Black (or Asian, Hispanic, or Indian) makes others assume that they are the stereotypes being used against them, and collectively they lack the social power to change this.

Cultural imperialism arises in settler societies when the culture, language, and other lifeways of the dominant founding English-speaking groups become universalized or naturalized as 'the norm.' All other cultures, languages, and lifeways are stereotyped as the 'other' – that is, as foreign, alien, and inferior. Young (1990, 59) contends that the dominant group 'reinforces its position by bringing the other groups under the measure of its dominant norms.' Even if 'others' assimilate by adopting the norms of the dominant majorities, minorities remain marked as different if their physical characteristics distinguish them.

Some minorities experience *violence* that the police refuse to take seriously. Historically, Black men in the United States have been lynched to make other Blacks accept their inferior position. Women are raped; gays are bashed; old people and children are battered. Vulnerable, marginalized minorities are killed and abused by partners, caregivers, employers, supervisors, and strangers. Young contends that 'violence is systemic [oppression] because it is directed against members of a group simply because they are members of that group' (ibid., 62). Furthermore, the dominant majority tolerates violence, as do many state officials. Fear of unpredictable violence makes those who are threatened by it change their behaviour, which exacerbates their marginalization.

These multiple faces of oppression often work together.

Political rights. See *Citizenship.*

Power

Some people in the settler society – usually the dominant White elites – have the power to force obedience to policies that achieve *their* aspirations and satisfy *their* needs. Political power rests in some sense on the threat of physical coercion. But power also has an ideological element – if we think we ought to obey others because they are superior to us, those others have power over us. Power, then, is a relationship between those who are privileged and those who are disadvantaged.

Prejudice

This involves the prejudging of groups based on stereotypes or false images. Prejudice results in a dislike of others based on faulty generalizations and irrational and unfounded assumptions. It affects people's ability to treat members of stigmatized groups fairly and impartially.

Race

Our assumption in this book is that race is socially constructed and that those who construct and transmit race ideas, or who act on them, assume that certain physical characteristics – notably skin colour, hair type, or facial features – indicate intellectual, moral, and cultural inferiority (Henry et al. 1997, 4). Race is the most complex concept we deal with in this book, as well as the most frequently contested. Moreover, approaches to understanding race differ over time and with place. So we briefly outline the two main approaches.

One approach sees 'a race' as a group of people linked by common origins, conceptualized historically as sharing common blood. 'Race' entered the English language in the sixteenth century. Up until the early nineteenth century, it referred mainly to common features assumed to reflect shared descent. For example, the concept of the Anglo-Saxon 'race' was used to describe 'the English.' Thus, in this period, 'race' was synonymous with 'nation.' Until the eighteenth century, the main ideas for explaining physically different groups came from the Old Testament and from both Greek and modern philosophy (see *multiculturalism*). Physical differences were considered part of God's plan; as caused by environmental differences like climate; or as resulting from different ancestry. In each usage, 'race' meant common descent. After the mid-nineteenth century, however, race doctrines emerged, influenced by slavery and modern science. Racialists who endorsed White rule claimed there was a single scientifically correct definition of 'race' and that it prioritized physical differences such as skin colour. Race came to be seen as an inherited cluster of physical and cultural differences.

By the early nineteenth century, colonization had greatly increased Europeans' knowledge of human differences, and this led them to theorize about the broad varieties they encountered. They conceptualized differences as constituting distinctive *types* – that is, original forms that existed independent of climate or other physical differences. This *pre-Darwinian* view considered human 'types' to be permanent. So 'race' came to designate 'types' of people with distinct physical constitutions and mental capacities, and this led to a revival of the ancient Greeks' distinction between themselves, who were civilized, and barbarians, who were not. This typology formed the core of the pre-Darwinian doctrines.

Darwin posited that 'types' were not permanent, and his theories led to new interpretations of human differences. Darwin saw these as a result of the inheritance of different characteristics. (The mechanism remained unknown for some time.) According to Darwin, 'races' were subcategories of the human species and had developed when members of that species were isolated from other human groups. He insisted, however, that all people were of the same species and could reproduce and that their differences were superficial. His theory of natural selection (1859) has been (mis)used by racialists – for example, by proponents of *social Darwinism*. Science now considers classifications based on the wide variety of physical variations to be of little value. In this sense, 'race' has no relevance.

Race has been used in other ways. Physical anthropologists used to speak of a human race. Others have made multiple attempts to construct typologies that divide the human species into categories based on physical differences. All such schemas have failed, and over the past fifty years, it has become clear that no meaningful taxonomy or classification schema is possible. Many groups cannot be fitted into categories, and physical anthropologists cannot agree on where boundaries should be drawn or even on how many groups there are. There have also been non-European classification systems. For example, North America's Indigenous people used a four-type classification system – Red, White, Black, Brown – but arranged these types in a circle to avoid the belief that one was superior.

In the past, governments defined 'race' in many different ways when applying laws that privileged or disadvantaged people. In developing legal definitions, they emphasized characteristics that they believed distinguished between 'races.' When settler states sought to prevent some types of people from immigrating, they usually devised tests that bureaucrats could apply based on inspection of physical characteristics. When officials who registered the birth of a baby had to fill in its 'race,' some definition had to be used. Often, the rules that countries followed for assigning people to race categories ran counter to knowledge of genetic inheritance. Current pressures for 'colour-blind' classification reflect concerns that governments should no longer sanction categories discredited by science. Nonetheless, race continues to have an impact on politics, racialist ideologies persist that defend White rule, and people still act on racist beliefs.

The use of 'race' as a synonym for 'nation' or 'ethnic group' began in the nineteenth and early twentieth centuries. Since the Second World War, 'ethnic group' and 'ethnicity' have often been used where race used to be. However, 'nation' or 'ethnic group' is now used to describe White minority populations, whereas 'race' is still used to describe non-Whites. So 'race' now increasingly identifies people who are *socially defined* as a group because of *physical* markers such skin pigmentation, hair texture, eye shape, or stature. Most social scientists today use race only in this sense of a social group defined by some visible physical characteristics. This does not accord with earlier uses; furthermore, there are major differences across countries, which is evidence that these classifications are social constructions. For example, in Brazil and Canada, Hispanics are usually classified as 'White,' while in the United States, some are classified as people of colour. Clearly, race labels vary in their content and meaning at different times and in different places. Socially constructed 'races' are not genetic subspecies. Not all societies construct social races. Race and racism go hand in hand, and unless states 'make race,' races are not relevant aspects of political power.

Race regimes

This concept is compatible with the state-focused, institutionalist approach reflected in this book. We understand race-based discrimination and oppression to be consequences of ideas, discourses, and laws embedded in state institutions by past governments. Hence a race regime is a *political system* with three distinct parts:

- *Structures.* Institutions through which those in power construct, administer, and change or restructure race regimes. They include legislatures, bureaucracies, political parties, police, courts, and prison systems.
- *Discourses or ideas.* Ideologies, including specific systematic racialist doctrines such as social Darwinism and democratic racism. Also, constitutions, laws, and regulations that establish categories to which

people are assigned according to some constructed race schema, and that state how they should be treated in different contexts.

- *Power relationships.* Such as those existing between citizens and denizens;[3] between rulers or elites and those whom they rule; between the elites and the masses; between slaves and free people; between the oppressors and the oppressed; between the exploiters and the exploited; between voters and representatives; and between the dominant and powerful and those who are subordinate, less powerful, or powerless.

A race regime involves state institutions and governments treating some people in a country (or who wish to enter) differently in terms of rights and benefits because of their 'race,' which we conceptualize as a category assigned to them because of their physical characteristics, which are often combined with ethnicity, culture, or religion. 'Race' also determines their legal status as 'Indians,' slaves, free settlers, citizens, or denizens. Governments may establish several different race regimes simultaneously or over time.

Racialism / Race discrimination / Systemic racism

These three relate to the belief in the superiority or inferiority of a particular group based on characteristics constructed as racial, such as skin colour, hair, and eye shape. Behavioural traits are also often attributed to a person's purported race. *Racialism* is the active expression of racism; it aims to deny members of racialized groups equal access to rights as well as scarce and valued resources.

Race discrimination is based on perceived negative attributes, characteristics, and deficiencies of *groups* (i.e., rather than individuals) and operates in such a way that individuals are denied opportunities or rewards for reasons unrelated to their own capabilities, industry, and merit. They are judged on their membership in an identifiable group to which negative traits have been assigned – traits perceived as attributable to race.

The term *systemic racism* has come into popular use in recent decades to describe the discriminatory nature and operations – intentional or not – of governments, large organizations, or entire societies. (The term *institutional racism* is also used.) This term suggests that discrimination is not always the result of intentional acts by individuals with negative attitudes. Rather, the term points to a complex system of factors that are discriminatory in their *effect*.

Racialization

In American race theory, this is the process whereby new immigrant groups struggle to fit into the White/non-White race hierarchy, which associates non-Whites with manual labour. Groups struggling to be categorized as 'White' are seen as accepting the race-based system of discrimination. Rodriguez (2000, 18) writes that 'critical to the racialization process was the belief that there always was some "other" group to which one was superior.' This protected White supremacy by making it 'difficult [for racialized minorities] to understand and pursue … [their] common interests,' which allowed 'Whites' to divide and rule.

'Racialization' and 'race regimes' differ in several ways. Racialization theory assumes that all racialized groups are immigrants; race regimes involve Indigenous groups as well. Racialization theory is about a *process* that in the United States historically applied to some 'White' groups (Irish Catholics, Jews). The race regime approach pays more attention to the roles played by government institutions in creating race hierarchies and the laws, practices, and ideas they use to maintain legalized discrimination. The notion of a power contest among groups to determine racialization neglects the role of race theories as applied by immigration officials, census officials, judges, and so on.

Racism

Up until the late 1960s, racism was conceptualized as a doctrine, dogma, ideology, or set of beliefs. Always the core element, however, was that 'race' determined a person or group's culture and that such cultural attributes were inherited. This buttressed claims of racial superiority and inferiority. In the 1960s, the word's use expanded to include practices and attitudes as well as beliefs. Racism now refers to any factors that produce racial discrimination.

Reconciliation Movement

Australia's Aboriginal peoples and sympathetic Whites have met, usually locally, to explore what happened during the invasion and settlement of the continent. Based on the movement popularized by the South African Truth and Reconciliation Commission, the Reconciliation movement is predicated on the belief that decades of violence and anger can be healed if everyone learns what happened and accepts responsibility for what their forefathers and mothers did, so that they can be reconciled through forgiveness. The movement has increased contact between Aboriginal peoples and Whites and has increased knowledge of the abuses the former suffered over many years. Some, however, perceive the goal as having Aboriginals become reconciled to White rule.

Red Power Movement

In the 1960s and 1970s, many Indigenous peoples in North America engaged in activities focused on gaining greater autonomy for their communities as well as greater respect for their traditional cultures. While different views and goals were involved, these groups and their activities collectively were referred to as the Red Power movement.

Rule of law

A basic principle of the democratic legal system in all three countries discussed in this book. The premise is that everyone in the territory, including those in government, is subject to the same laws. In fact, Indigenous people and often other non-Whites are subject to different laws.

Second-class citizenship. See *Citizenship.*

Segregation

This involves spatial separation or distance between groups who live in a common territory. It can be *de facto* (by common practice) or *de jure* (by law), as with the race regimes of apartheid in South Africa, 'Jim Crow' separation in the United States, and more locally administered regimes in Australia and Canada.

There is distinction between voluntary and imposed segregation. *Imposed* segregation is always negative. But some groups want to maintain a distinct way of life and choose *voluntary* separation. It may not be easy to determine whether segregation is voluntary or imposed, since dominant groups often claim that imposed segregation (e.g., in 'homelands') is voluntary. Some pariah groups find a measure of protection against hostility and discrimination in externally imposed segregation, which, however, limits their life chances.

Self-government

This became the goal of many North American Native communities in the 1970s and 1980s because it seemed to them that representative democracy would always place them at the mercy of governments elected by White majorities. It followed that only some form of self-government within their own territories would produce governments responsive to their needs. Current debates over land and resource claims involve attempts to conceptualize exactly what the right to self-government will mean in practice.

Settlement/Settler

This usually means peaceful entry onto and improvement of lands by hard work. European laws and philosophies legitimized dispossession of Indigenous peoples on the grounds that Europeans used land better or 'properly' – that is, by building permanent dwellings and fences and by engaging in agriculture that 'improved' it. It was assumed that Indigenous peoples were unable to use the land 'properly' even when they had built permanent structures and had fenced and farmed their lands. Thus, 'settlement' was associated with European occupancy and enhancements. A *settler* is 'a person who goes to live permanently in a previously unoccupied land; a colonist' (Hawkins 1979, 743). Note the bias in this definition. In North America and Australia, colonists rarely entered land that was empty, since Indigenous nations and peoples had settled it before they were pushed out, concentrated on reserves, or died of imported diseases, violent conflict, and so on.

Skill discounting/deskilling

The devaluation and lack of recognition of foreign credentials, including education (degrees and diplomas), professional training, apprenticeships, work experience, and other work-related skills that immigrants bring with them (see Esses et al. 2007, 114–18).

Slavery

This exists when a person is subject to another's right of ownership with the consequence that forced, unremunerated labour is imposed. In the

United States, slavery was a race regime, with southern state governments upholding the rights of slave owners. Slaves were excluded from
any kind of participation in politics or civil rights. They were forced to
work on plantations, in mines, or in houses as domestic servants or as
artisans. Racist doctrines were used to justify subjecting them to
inhuman conditions.

In 1807 the British Empire ended the legal slave trade on its territories;
in 1833, 800,000 slaves were freed in Britain and its colonies. In the
United States, most slaves were freed during the Civil War by the Emancipation Proclamation of 1863. After slavery was abolished, however,
racism did not disappear. Instead, a segregation race regime was developed to keep the 'races' apart and to justify the continuing exploitation
of Black workers.

Social Darwinism

A race doctrine based on a distorted account of Darwin's theory of
evolution. Social Darwinists believed that the races and nations that
dominated colonies were 'the fittest' and that those conquered had lost
because of their inferiority. They had been doomed by contact with more
advanced people. This developed into scientific racism, which permeated popular culture, educational texts, sermons, and political culture.

Social rights. See *Citizenship.*

Sovereign/Sovereignty

In European political philosophy, a *sovereign* is a supreme, all-powerful
leader. *Sovereignty* is the absolute power to rule. European theorists
believed that the power to rule or govern must be absolute and undivided in order to avoid civil war (internal disorder), and that ultimately
sovereign power rests on fear of violence or coercion. Thomas Hobbes
wrote in 1651 that the power to punish (police power), the judicial
power (the power to judge), and the legislative power (the power to
make decisions) all must be in the same hands and that people only obey
those they fear. Federal political systems challenge this by dividing
sovereignty between two levels of government. The U.S. theory of
limited government challenges it by separating state powers as John
Locke prescribed.

State

A set of institutions through which a society's elites govern a territory and its occupants, mainly by monopolizing the legitimate use of force. The main institutions of a state are as follows:

- *Legislatures*. Structures for making rules and for allocating material and symbolic resources. In representative democracies, legislatures are elected by the citizens.
- *Bureaucracies*. Structures for implementing decisions and administering policies. These operate by applying rules and regulations to all cases in the same way, thereby routinizing power.
- *Police and prisons*. Structures that apprehend those deemed to have broken laws and that enforce adjudications, taking coercive steps if needed.
- *Courts and judicial systems*. Structures for adjudicating disputes, applying laws, and deciding about jurisdictions between governments.
- *The military*. A structure for exercising force legitimately against perceived external enemies and internal threats of disorder.

Those who control these institutions constitute the government of a society and its inhabitants. See also *federalism*.

Supplanting societies

An alternative term for *settler societies*, one that emphasizes that the societies created by European settlers *supplanted* the Indigenous communities that occupied the territories before the European arrival.

Systemic discrimination

This concept recognizes that inequality is built into institutions in ways that often are invisible both to those who dominate and to those who are dominated. It involves any action that has a *result* that disadvantages or privileges people because of their membership in stigmatized or privileged groups, regardless of the intent of those who have designed or who run the institution in question.

Terra nullius

A European legal doctrine which held that if a land was empty in the sense that there were no organized governments evident, colonizers did not need to sign treaties with or buy land from individual Indigenous owners. The concept was a core political myth in Australia and elsewhere (British Columbia), where imperialists and settlers held that the mere presence of 'some people' on the land did not mean there were organized governments.

Underground Railway

In the decades after slavery was abolished in Canada, but before it was abolished in the United States, many slaves sought to escape by leaving the United States. The exit routes, guides, and safe houses were collectively known as the Underground Railway.

Visible minority

This is the Canadian government's official description of race minorities. Visible minorities are persons 'other than Aboriginal persons ... who are non-Caucasian in race or non-White in colour.' This includes Chinese, South Asians, Blacks, Arabs and West Asians, Filipinos, Southeast Asians, Latin Americans, Japanese, and Koreans. It does not include people with observable disabilities. Critics see the term as imposed on non-Whites by the state, or on minorities by a dominant group. Widely used by media and academics, it has become part of multicultural discourse. Related terms are 'people of colour,' 'racialized minorities,' and 'race minorities.'

Whites-only nationalism. See nationalism.

Appendix A
The Facts of the Matter

1. Aboriginal Peoples in Canada

1.1 Mortality

Life expectancy of Registered Indian men (2001): 70.4 years
Life expectancy of all Canadian men (2001): 77.0
Life expectancy of Registered Indian women (2001): 75.5
Life expectancy of all Canadian women (2001): 82.1

Source: Indian and Northern Affairs Canada (2004).

Mortality rate of infants born to First Nations mothers (2001): 7.2 per
  1,000 births
Mortality rate of infants born to all Canadian mothers (2001): 5.2 per
  1,000 births

Source: Indian and Northern Affairs Canada (2004).

1.2 Population and Representation

Aboriginal Identity population (2006): 1,172,785 (3.8 per cent of the
  Canadian population)
North American Indian (single response) population (2006): 69,025
  (2.2 per cent of the Canadian population)
Inuit (single response) population (2006): 50,480 (0.2 per cent of the
  Canadian population)

Métis (single response) population (2006): 389,785 (1.2 per cent of the
    Canadian population)
Registered Indian population (2006): 623,780 (2.0 per cent of the
    Canadian population)
Visible minority (other than Aboriginal peoples) population (2006):
    5,068,090 (16.2 per cent of the Canadian population)

Source: Statistics Canada (2008); see also Statistics Canada (2006a).

Total number of Aboriginal senators since Confederation: 15 (2 Inuit,
    4 Métis, 9 First Nations)
Current number of Aboriginal senators (April 2010): 6 (1 Inuit, 1 Métis,
    4 First Nations)
Number of Aboriginal members of House of Commons since Confed-
    eration: 28 (5 Inuit, 15 Métis, 8 First Nations)
Current number of Aboriginal members of the House of Commons (July
    2011): 7 out of 308

Source: Library of Parliament Canada (2010a, 2010b, 2011).

1.3 Health

In 2002–3, 14.5 per cent of First Nations adults living on-reserve reported
    having been told by a health care professional that they have diabetes.
In the same period, the incidence of diabetes among all Canadians was
    4.3 per cent.

Source: Health Canada (2008).

The rate of tuberculosis among Aboriginal people in Canada (2008):
    28.2 per 100,000.
The rate of tuberculosis among non-Aboriginal, non–foreign-born
    people in Canada (2008) was 0.6 per 100,000.

Source: Public Health Agency of Canada (2009a).

Percentage of Canadians who are HIV positive who self-identified as
    Aboriginal (2007): 21.4

Percentage of new HIV infections diagnosed in Canadians who self-identify as Aboriginal (2005): 9

Source: Public Health Agency of Canada (2009b).

Percentage of Aboriginal women among Aboriginal people with HIV: 45.1
Percentage of Aboriginal women among Aboriginal people with AIDS: 24.6
Percentage of non-Aboriginal women among non-Aboriginal people with HIV (1998 to June 2003): 19.5
Percentage of non-Aboriginal women among non-Aboriginal people with AIDS (1998 to June 2003): 8.5

Source: Public Health Agency Canada (2007); Boulos, Yan, Schanzer, Remis, and Archibald (2006); Canadian Institute of Child Health (2006).

1.4 Socio-Economic

Median yearly income of Aboriginal Canadians (2006): $16,796
Median yearly income of Registered Indians (2006): $14,146
Median yearly income of all Canadians (2006): $25,618
Unemployment rate for Aboriginal Canadians (2006): 14.8 per cent
Unemployment rate for Aboriginal Canadians on reserve (2006): 24.7 per cent
Unemployment rate for non-Aboriginal Canadians (2006): 6.3 per cent

Source: Statistics Canada (2006b); Indian and Northern Affairs Canada (2001); Luffman and Sussman (2007); Hull (2008).

1.5 Education

In 2001, 38 per cent of all Aboriginal people in Canada were post-secondary graduates. In 2006, this figure increased to 44 per cent, among whom:
• 14 per cent had trade credentials,
• 19 per cent had a college diploma, and
• 8 per cent had a university degree (up from 6 per cent in 2001).

Source: Policy Research Initiative (2008).

Percentage of Aboriginal people who have not completed high school
(2006): 34
Percentage of all Canadians who have not completed high school (2006):
15

Source: Statistics Canada (2008).

1.6 Incarceration and the Justice System

At the end of March 2007, Aboriginal people comprised 17.0 per cent of
federally sentenced offenders though the general Aboriginal population is only 3.8 per cent of the Canadian adult population.

Source: Correctional Service of Canada (2009); Trevethan, Shelley, and Rastin
(2004).

Percentage of the federal offender population who self-identify as
Aboriginal (2007–8): 17.3
Percentage of Aboriginal federal offenders who were under the age of
30 (2007–8): 49.4
Percentage of non-Aboriginal offenders who were under the age of 30
(2007–8): 38.6

Source: Public Safety Canada, Portfolio Corrections Statistics Committee (2008);
Michelle Mann (2009).

Median age of Aboriginal federal offender at admission (2008): 31 years
Median age of non-Aboriginal federal offender at admission (2008):
33 years

Source: Public Safety Canada, Portfolio Corrections Statistics Committee (2009).

1.7 Juveniles

Rate of Aboriginal youth charged in Canada (2003): 64.5 per 10,000
Rate for non-Aboriginal youth charged in Canada (2003): 8.2 per 10,000

Source: Policy Research Initiative (2008).

1.8 Language and Culture

Percentage of Inuit who speak an Aboriginal language well enough to converse (2006): 69

Percentage of Métis who speak an Aboriginal language well enough to converse (2006): 4

Percentage of First Nations who speak an Aboriginal language well enough to converse (2006): 29

Percentage of First Nations on reserve who speak an Aboriginal language well enough to converse (2006): 51

Percentage of First Nations off reserve who speak an Aboriginal language well enough to converse (2006): 12

Source: Statistics Canada (2008).

For more information on visible minorities in Canada, Statistics Canada's portal on Ethnic Diversity and Immigration is a good starting point: http://www.statcan.gc.ca/subject-sujet/theme-theme.action?pid =30000&lang=eng&more=0.

2. American Indian and Alaska Native, Black, and Hispanic People in the United States

2.1 Mortality

Life expectancy for all Americans (2006): 77 years

Life expectancy for White Americans (2006): 78.2 years

Life expectancy for Black Americans (2006): 73.2 years

Life expectancy for American Indians and Alaska Natives (1999–2001): 74.5 years.

Source: U.S. Bureau of the Census (2010b); Indian Health Service (2006).

Mortality rate for infants born to all American mothers (2005): 6.7 per 1000 births

Mortality rate for infants born to White mothers (2005): 5.7 per 1000 births

Mortality rate for infants born to Black mothers (2005): 13.7 per 1000 births

Mortality rate for infants born to American Indian and Alaska Native mothers (2005): 8.1 per 1000 births

Source: National Center for Health Statistics (2010).

2.2 Population and Representation

Black population of the United States (2009): 39,641,000 (12.9 per cent of Americans)

American Indian and Alaska Native population of the United States (2009): 3,151,000 (1.0 per cent of Americans)

Hispanic origin population of the United States (2009): 48,419,000 (15.8 per cent of Americans)

White, non-Hispanic population of the United States (2009): 199,851,000 (65.7 per cent of the United States)

Source: U.S. Bureau of the Census (2010b). Note that people reporting multiple, Asian, Native Hawaiian, and other Pacific Islander races are not included in these totals.

U.S. House of Representatives

Members of the U.S. House of Representatives who are African American (December 2010): 41 (approx. 7.8% of the 111th Congress, i.e. House and Senate)

Members of the U.S. House of Representatives who are Native American or Alaska Native (December 2010): 1

Members of the House of Representatives who are Hispanic (December 2010): 28 (approx. 5.4 per cent of the Congress)

U.S. Senate

Members of the U.S. Senate who are African American (December 2010): 1

Members of the U.S. Senate who are Native American or Alaska Native (December 2010): 0

Members of the U.S. Senate who are Hispanic (December 2010): 1

Source: Manning (2010). *Membership of the 111th Congress: A Profile.* Congressional Research Service.

2.3 Health

Percentage of Americans who have been diagnosed with diabetes (2006): 7.8

Percentage of White Americans who have been diagnosed with diabetes (2006): 6.6

Percentage of Hispanic Americans who have been diagnosed with diabetes (2006): 10.4

Percentage of Black Americans who have been diagnosed with diabetes (2006): 11.8

Percentage of American Indians and Alaska Natives who have been diagnosed with diabetes (2006): 16.5

Source: Centers for Disease Control and Prevention (2010).

HIV/AIDS rate for Americans of all races (2007): 21.1 per 100,000
HIV/AIDS rate for White Americans (2007): 9.2 per 100,000
HIV/AIDS rate for Hispanic Americans (2007): 27.7 per 100,000
HIV/AIDS rate for Black Americans (2007): 76.7 per 100,000
HIV/AIDS rate for American Indians and Alaska Natives (2007): 12.8 per 100,000

Source: Centers for Disease Control and Prevention (2009).

2.4 Socio-Economic

Percentage of all American families below the poverty level (2008): 9.5

Percentage of White families below the poverty level (2008): 6

Percentage of Black families below the poverty level (2008): 21.3

Percentage of American Indian and Alaska Native families below the poverty level (2008): 21.4

Percentage of Hispanic families below the poverty level (2008): 18.5

Source: U.S. Bureau of the Census (2010a).

Unemployment rate of White Americans (2008): 5.4 per cent
Unemployment rate of Black Americans (2008): 10.1 per cent
Unemployment rate of American Indians and Alaska Natives (2008): 5.6
    per cent

Source: Austin (2009); U.S. Bureau of the Census (2010b).

Median household income of all American households (2008): $61,355
Median household income of Black households (2008): $40,174
Median household income of Hispanic households (2008): $40,566
Median household income of American Indian and Alaska Native
    Households (2008): $37,815

Source: U.S. Bureau of the Census (2010b); Centers for Disease Control and
Prevention (2009).

2.5 Education

Percentage of all Americans who have not completed high school (2007):
    14.3
Percentage of White Americans who have not completed high school
    (2007): 9.4
Percentage of Black Americans who have not completed high school
    (2007): 17.2
Percentage of Hispanic Americans who have not completed high school
    (2007): 39.7
Percentage of American Indians and Alaska Natives who have not
    completed high school (2007): 19.7

Source: Snyder and Dillow (2009); DeVoe, Darling-Churchill, and Snyder
(2008).

Percentage of all Americans who have completed an associate's or
    bachelor's degree (2007): 27.5
Percentage of White Americans who have completed an associate's or
    bachelor's degree (2007): 29.8
Percentage of Black Americans who have completed an associate's or
    bachelor's degree (2007): 21.8

Percentage of Hispanic Americans who have completed an associate's or bachelor's degree (2007): 15.6

Percentage of American Indians and Alaska Natives who have completed an associate's or bachelor's degree (2007): 18.1

Source: Snyder and Dillow (2009); DeVoe, Darling-Churchill, and Snyder (2008).

2.6 Incarceration and the Justice System

Imprisonment rate of American men (2008): 952 per 100,000
Imprisonment rate of White American men (2008): 487 per 100,000
Imprisonment rate of Black American men (2008): 3,161 per 100,000
Imprisonment rate of Hispanic American men (2008): 1,200 per 100,000
Imprisonment rate of American Indians and Alaska Natives (both sexes) (2008): 921 per 100,000

Source: Minton (2009); Sabol, West, and Cooper (2009).

Imprisonment rate of American women (2008): 68 per 100,000
Imprisonment rate of White American women (2008): 50 per 100,000
Imprisonment rate of Black American women (2008): 149 per 100,000
Imprisonment rate of Hispanic American women (2008): 75 per 100,000
Imprisonment rate of American Indians and Alaska Natives (both sexes) (2008): 921 per 100,000

Source: Minton (2009); Sabol, West, and Cooper (2009).

Number of active federal judges, 30 April 2010: 761
Number of active federal judges who are White, 30 April 2010: 607 (79.8 per cent)
Number of active federal judges who are Black, 30 April 2010: 85 (11.2 per cent)
Number of active federal judges who are Hispanic, 30 April 2010: 59 (7.8 per cent)
Number of active federal judges who are American Indian or Alaska Native, 30 April 2010: 0 (0 per cent)

Source: Federal Judicial Center (2010).

2.7 Juveniles

Percentage of juveniles in residential placement who are White (2006): 35

Percentage of juveniles in residential placement who are Black (2006): 40

Percentage of juveniles in residential placement who are American Indian or Alaska Native (2006): 2

Percentage of juveniles in residential placement who are Hispanic (2006): 20

Source: Sabon, West, and Cooper (2009).

3. Aboriginal Peoples in Australia

3.1 Mortality

Life expectancy of Indigenous men, 2005–7: 67.2 years
Life expectancy of non-Indigenous men, 2005–7: 78.7 years
Life expectancy of Indigenous women, 2005–7: 72.9 years
Life expectancy of non-Indigenous women, 2005–7: 82.6 years

Source: Australian Bureau of the Census (2009a, 2010).

Mortality rate of infants born to Indigenous mothers: 12.7 per 1,000 births
Mortality rate of infants born to non-Indigenous mothers: 4.4 per 1,000 births.

Source: Australian Bureau of Statistics (2009a).

3.2 Population and Representation

Aboriginal and Torres Strait Islander population, 2006: 455,031
Indigenous people as percentage of all Australians, 2006: 2.3 per cent

Source: Australian Bureau of Statistics (2009b).

As of 2010, there were no Aboriginal or Torres Strait Islander representatives in either the House of Representatives or the Senate of Australia.

3.3 Health

Rate of diabetes among Indigenous people (2004–5): 6.4 per cent
Rate of diabetes among non-Indigenous people (2004–5): 3.8 per cent

Source: Australian Bureau of Statistics (2008).

High blood pressure among Indigenous people 25–54 (Northern Territory and Queensland), 2006: 27 per cent
High blood pressure among non-Indigenous people 25–54 (Northern Territory and Queensland), 2006: 9 per cent

Source: Wang et al. (2005). See also Thompson et al. (2009).

Age-standardized HIV/AIDS rate among Indigenous men (2004–6): 10.8 per 100,000
Age-standardized HIV/AIDS rate among non-Indigenous men (2004–6): 10.1 per 100,000
Age-standardized HIV/AIDS rate among Indigenous women (2004–6): 2.2 per 100,000
Age-standardized HIV/AIDS rate among non-Indigenous women (2004–6): 1.4 per 100,000

Source: National Centre in HIV Epidemiology and Clinical Research (2008).

3.4 Socio-Economics

Indigenous unemployment rate (2006): 15.6 per cent
Non-Indigenous unemployment rate (2006): 5 per cent

Source: Australian Bureau of Statistics (2008a).

Median weekly income for Indigenous Australians (2006): $362
Median weekly income for non-Indigenous Australians (2006): $642

Source: Australian Bureau of Statistics (2008b).

3.5 Education

Non-Indigenous people who have not completed year 12 of school
(2006): 51 per cent
Indigenous people who have not completed year 12 of school (2006):
77 per cent

Source: Australian Bureau of Statistics (2008b).

Non-Indigenous people who have completed vocational training, trade
certification, or a college or university degree (2006): 46.8 per cent
Indigenous people who have completed vocational training, trade
certification, or a college or university degree (2006): 24.7 per cent

Source: Australian Bureau of Statistics (2008b).

3.6 Incarceration and the Justice System

Incarceration rate of non-Indigenous Australians (2006): 129.2 per 100,000
Incarceration rate of Indigenous Australians (2006): 2,255.5 per
100,000

Source: Australian Institute of Criminology (2008).

Indigenous youth, aged 10–17, under a juvenile justice suspension
(2005–6): 44.4 per 1,000
Non-Indigenous youth, aged 10–17, under a juvenile justice suspension
(2005–6): 2.9 per 1,000

Source: Australian Bureau of Statistics (2008b, 2010).

3.7 Juveniles

Rate of Indigenous children who were subject to a child protection
substantiation, Australian Capital Territory (2005–6): 56.8 per 1,000

Rate of non-Indigenous children who were subject to a child protection substantiation, Australian Capital Territory (2005–6): 10.9 per 1,000
Rate of Indigenous children who were subject to a child protection substantiation, Northern Territory (2005–6): 15.2 per 1,000
Rate of non-Indigenous children who were subject to a child protection substantiation, Northern Territory (2005–6): 3.2 per 1,000

Source: Australian Bureau of Statistics (2008b).

3.8 Language and Culture

Percentage of Indigenous people who speak an Indigenous language at home (2006): 12.1
Percentage of Indigenous people under 14 years of age who speak an Indigenous language at home (2006): 10.3
Percentage of Indigenous people over 45 years of age who speak an Indigenous language at home (2006): 13.07
Percentage of Indigenous people living in major cities who speak an Indigenous language at home (2006): 1.25
Percentage of Indigenous people living in very remote areas who speak an Indigenous language at home (2006): 56.26

Source: Australian Bureau of Statistics (2006c).

Appendix B
Resources for Further Research

Australia

Australian Bureau of Statistics: http://www.abs.gov.au

Department of Immigration and Citizenship: www.immi.gov.au

Australian Human Rights Commission site on Aboriginal and Torres Strait Islander Social Justice: http://www.hreoc.gov.au/social_justice/index.html

Australian Museum: Indigenous Australia site contains historical and current information: http://australianmuseum.net.au/Indigenous-Australia

National Library of Australia e-resources on Aboriginal and Torres Strait Islander peoples: http://www.nla.gov.au/app/eresources/item/1541?id=1541&loaditem=true

Canada

Statistics Canada: http://www.statcan.gc.ca

Metropolis Canada: an international network for comparative research and public policy development on migration, diversity, and immigrant integration: Canada.metropolis.net

Indian and Northern Affairs Canada: http://www.ainc-inac.gc.ca

Library and Archives Canada portal for Aboriginal Peoples: http://www.collectionscanada.gc.ca/aboriginal-peoples/index-e.html

Black History Month: http://www.collectionscanada.gc.ca/black-history/index-e.html

Ethno-Cultural Groups: http://www.collectionscanada.gc.ca/ethno-cultural/index-e.html

United States

United States: http://www.census.gov

Pew Hispanic Center: A PewResearchCenter Project: http://www
.census.govpewhispanic.org

PBS: Race – The Power of an Illusion (website to accompany the
California Newsreel documentary): http://www.pbs.org/race

Library of Congress portal for American Indian History: http://www
.loc.gov/topics/content.php?subcat=2

Library of Congress portal for African-American History: http://www
.loc.gov/topics/content.php?subcat=12

Library of Congress portal for Immigration and Ethnic Heritage: http://
www.loc.gov/topics/content.php?subcat=16

Notes

Preface

1 We use 'non-Whites' because these states largely used skin colour as the marker that privileged those of European descent and that disadvantaged others. Each state created complex categories, to which they assigned various non-Whites. For specific groups, we use the term common in that country.

Introduction: The Politics of Race in Three Settler States

1 Many authors place quote marks around race to indicate that it is a problematic term. The fact that we do not doesn't mean we believe 'race' is a biological phenomenon. Our view – discussed below – is that all racial categories have been constructed by those who hold power in a society. All bolded words in the text are defined and discussed in chapter 8.

2 There are many such settler states, especially in the Americas, including Argentina, Venezuela, and Mexico. They were originally settled by the Spanish or Portuguese (Brazil). In some of these states – Mexico, for example – mestizo people are the majority; others, such as Argentina, are White settler states.

3 This is the principal theme of Anthony Marx's *Making Race and Nation: A Comparison of the United States, South Africa, and Brazil* (1998). Though we acknowledge our intellectual debt to Marx, our analysis differs from his in major ways, as we note.

4 *Sydney Morning Herald,* 27 May 2000, 10. http://www.smh.com.au.

5 Data from Gerald Friesen, 'The LaFontaine-Baldwin Essay,' reprinted in the *Globe and Mail,* 27 March 2002.

6 The diseases of colonization include these: first, diseases such as measles and smallpox, to which Indigenous peoples had little immunity and from which many died; second, violent deaths from contact and the processes of dispossession; third, starvation from life on reserves without access to traditional food sources; fourth, deaths resulting from cultural loss, including from alcoholism and other self-destructive behaviours; and finally, deaths resulting from various forms of abuse within Indigenous families directly related to the loss of parenting skills among the generations raised in residential schools.

7 Methodological differences mean that these data cannot be compared with those from 2000 in the first edition.

8 These data are incomplete so should be used cautiously.

9 Demographic changes – increases in the numbers of young people – are one reason.

10 The data reported come only from states with significant AI populations and Alaska Natives (about 60 per cent of the AI population in the United States). Also, they exclude Native Hawaiians.

11 'All races' includes Whites but not Hispanics. Sources: National Centre for Health Statistics, Indian Health Services Statistics, U.S. Census Bureau, Federal Judicial Center documents, Department of Justice – Bureau of Justice Statistics, National Centre for Juvenile Justice. See Appendix for website directions.

12 Includes Barack Obama, the current president.

13 Documentaries on U.S. race terrorism of show a picture of a lynched Black man with a sign attached saying 'This n——r voted.'

14 The presence of one or several Blacks or Indigenous people in positions of power does not negate the statistical picture. But it does allow critics of anti-racist analysis to undercut that picture by suggesting that whatever barriers exist could be overcome if only stigmatized minorities tried harder. The idea of equal opportunity – that 'any African American or Indian can be president if they just try hard enough' – is inconsistent with the statistical profiles. So in this book we will consider how and whether President Obama's election should change our analysis. While change is happening – at least in the United States – negative reactions since his election, especially the Tea Party protests, reveal that many Whites are deeply troubled and angry about his election and that they believe he is destroying 'their' country. Polls have reported that almost 25 per cent of those who identify as Republicans think Obama 'may be the anti-Christ' and that his election signals the end of the world.

15 The United States has no standard birth certificate, nor do most states, which devolve that power to country or parish authorities. President Obama, the son of a Kenyan exchange student, spent some of his childhood in Indonesia, where his mother did development work.

1. Foundational Race Regimes

1 European nationalist theorists distinguished between 'historic' nations, which 'had' states or were entitled to them; and 'inferior' nations, which, according to the leaders of the historic nations, would disappear under the domination of the historic nations.

2 Britain experimented with legal pluralism – the Scots, for example, have retained their own code of law. Britain also used indirect rule, under which Indigenous rulers continued to enforce their own laws, while Europeans in the territory were governed by British law. The idea of applying law to individuals rather than to territories was not, however, acceptable to the *rule of law* thesis, which posited one code of law per state.

3 An autonomous community with shared values.

4 An *ideology* is a set of beliefs, assumptions, perceptions, and values that provide a group with a coherent understanding and explanation of their world.

5 *Power* has different meanings. We use it here to mean *the capacity to make people do things they would not otherwise do or do not wish to do.* That capacity comes primarily from having a monopoly on the instruments of coercion – police, laws, prisons, the military, and so on. Ultimately, physical force – that is, the ability to kill and coerce – is the basis of political power in the state. The use of violence is evident in these foundational race regimes.

6 While he was a military leader, Jackson had fought to expel 'Indian' nations from territories wanted by Whites for settlement. When the U.S. Supreme Court declared the Cherokee 'a definite political community over which the laws of Georgia had no legal force' (Remini 1966, 148), Georgia rejected their claim to national autonomy and Jackson refused to use his presidential power to enforce the Court's decision. In 1830, Congress passed the Indian Act and the military removed eastern Indian nations forcibly to west of the Mississippi. The forced migration of the Cherokee ('the Trail of Tears') resulted in many deaths. Most Americans supported Jackson.

7 What is now the United States and Canada.

8 The outcome of the war was a settled boundary between the United States and the British in Canada, which ended the value of Indian allies to either.

9 The influence of French colonialism is limited, though the presence of francophones in Quebec shaped Canadian federalism, which somewhat affected internal colonialism.

10 Georgia, for example, passed a law forbidding Whites to reside among 'Indians' without a licence, and 'Indians' were forbidden to leave their reservations.

11 In the Americas, many nations used their lands 'properly' even by European standards by fencing and farming it. European ideology as advanced by Locke in his *Second Treatise of Government* (1690) has ignored the agricultural traditions of many Indigenous nations. Locke made fencing and cultivating land (removing it from the common) central to the concept of property, which, he argued, the modern state was established by contract to protect.

12 In Canada, the Department of Indian Affairs is older than the country itself. In both Canada and the United States, such departments originated within the military.

13 After the High Court found that some Aboriginal land rights had survived, the Commonwealth government legislated to eliminate those common law rights and assigned responsibility for land issues to the states, which resisted any restoration.

14 Pre-modern slavery in Europe was not based on race in terms of skin colour. The term *slave* derived from 'Slav: since Slavs – considered a separate "race" despite white skins – were long victims of European slavery' (Ball 1998, 31). Slavery, though, fell into disuse as a major economic system in the eighth century. It was revived in the Americas after Columbus 'discovered' them in 1492. Spanish colonizers enslaved Indigenous peoples, millions of whom died. Spanish religious scruples, the vulnerability of 'Indians' to European diseases, and the fact that Indigenous slaves were familiar with their territory and could call on relatives to help them escape, led to the substitution of Africans as slaves.

15 There is a distinction between labour slavery, under which owners can command a person's labour, and chattel slavery, under which the person is owned and can be bought and sold. Slaves in the United States were usually chattel slaves (Ball 1999). In parts of what became the United States after the Louisiana Purchase, while it was still under French rule, the *Code Noir* specified rights for slaves – rights that were lost after the territory became part of the United States.

16 The slave trade was run by the London-based Royal Africa Company, secured by King Charles II in 1672. The British Crown profited from

'chattel slavery,' which the British substituted for 'freehold slavery,' whereby a worker could not be forced to leave his/her place.

2. Subsequent Race Regimes – Segregation and Whites-Only Nationalism

1 Britain included England, Wales, Scotland, and Ireland; the latter two remained Catholic. The real colonial power was England, however, though many Welsh and Scots were employed by the great companies through which British imperialism proceeded. Many Irish peasants and Scots, Welsh, and English workers were transported as convicts or recruited as settlers to build colonies.

2 England's experiences with its colonies in Ireland strongly shaped its later colonial ventures. As a result of constant resistance and rebellions by the indigenous Catholic Irish, the English authorities developed legal and military strategies to compel submission and obedience. The same resistance resulted in propaganda, which included descriptions of the Irish peasants as 'savage' and 'uncivilized,' to justify brutal forms of coercion. See Howard Mumford Jones, *O Strange New World: American Culture, The Formative Years* (New York: Viking, 1967).

3 Before Confederation, slavery existed in some British colonies and in New France. By 1867, however, slavery had been abolished. None of the colonies that became part of Canada were 'slave societies' in the sense that slavery was central to them; several were 'societies with slaves.'

4 'Jim Crow' was a character in the minstrel shows performed in the American South by Whites in blackface. Such characters debased African Americans by portraying them as ignorant, 'primitive,' and fit only for segregation and service.

5 See chapter 4 for a discussion of the post–Civil War survival of slavery.

6 The Ku Klux Klan and other vigilante groups were formed to re-enforce social distance between the races and to maintain White dominance. They did so through violence (threatened or real) and other forms of intimidation. Lynching continued into the 1960s as a means of maintaining segregation and White power.

7 It was illegal in some places for African Americans to own land. Indeed, 'sharecropping,' under which African American families worked White-owned land, receiving in return little more than seed, food, and primitive shelter, perpetuated the substance of a slave life for generations.

8 The Canadian government's 'official' description of visible minorities is persons 'other than Aboriginal persons who are non-Caucasian in race or

non-white in colour.' Specifically, this includes Chinese, South and Southeast Asians, Blacks, Arabs and West Asians, Filipinos, Latin Americans, Japanese, and Koreans (*The Daily* 2005, 2). In this book we use *non-Whites* and *visible minorities* interchangeably.

9 Governor Arthur had experience in the treatment of slaves in British Honduras. His idea for a reserve for the Tasmanians on the northeast coast reflected British colonial policy in Canada and in southern Africa's Cape Colony (McGrath 1995, 319).

10 In Australia, unlike in North America, there was a severe imbalance between the sexes. As a consequence, coerced miscegenation (rape) was endemic, which resulted in many 'half-breeds.' Because of under-population and the fear of Asian invasion, assimilated, light-skinned Aboriginal people were considered valuable.

11 So important was race purity that the Commonwealth government passed the Sugar Bounty Act (1901) and other legislation to subsidize industries that were unable to compete with goods produced by cheap non-European labour elsewhere. 'Buy white sugar' was a 'White Australia' policy.

12 So northern Italians would be admitted, but southerners excluded.

13 André Siegfried, a French observer, wrote *The Race Question in Canada* (1907), in which 'races' referred to the French and the British.

3. Immigration Policy and Multiculturalism

1 This happened, for example, in Florida, Louisiana, Texas, New Mexico, California, Alaska, and Hawaii. Misrepresentations included White Americans migrating to Hawaii and agitating for its monarch to be overturned and for Hawaii to be annexed. In Texas, Americans first promoted Texan independence from Mexico; only after that did they promote union with the United States. In fact, the United States developed into an aggressive colonial power both within and outside North America.

2 Liberal theorists such as Locke legitimized this by theorizing that 'ownership' involved intensive land use such as the building of fencing and permanent dwellings and the undertaking of plough agriculture.

3 Citizenship and Immigration Canada (2010).

4 Arizona's immigration law sparked huge rallies. It requires local state and law enforcement officials to question people about their immigrant status if there is reason to suspect they are in the country without proper documentation. The same law makes it a crime to be in the state illegally.

5 The Leadership Conference on Civil Rights (LCCR) is a rights-based coalition founded in 1945 by A. Phillip Randolph. This coalition, along with the NAACP, was the principal lobby group for the 1964 Civil Rights Acts. Its membership includes groups and organizations across the political, social, and labour spectrums. When the Voting Rights Act was renewed in 1975, the NAACP opposed the inclusion of an amendment to prohibit discrimination against language minorities. Latino groups were left to fight on their own to get language rights covered by the Voting Rights Acts, and this soured their relations with the African American membership (Walton and Smith 2003, 122).

6 From the White House's Web page on immigration.

7 For the data in this paragraph, we relied on Waslin (2009, 40–6).

8 This was the mantra for a vocal minority of Whites – mostly men – at McCain/Palin rallies during the primaries. While often heard on direct feeds (CPAC) and in the film about Obama's campaign, the clips that the news media reported rarely included it. This was also true for reporting on the Tea Party rallies, in which Obama was delegitimized as president for his skin colour or for his purportedly foreign birth ('birthers') or Muslim faith.

9 In this discussion, we rely on Bannerji's (2000, ch. 1) comparison of Canadian and American multiculturalism. She cites a number of American anti-racist activists and scholars who were hostile to multiculturalism in the 1980s.

10 See Jayasuriya (1997, 60). In this section, we rely on Jayasuriya's text.

11 See Betts (1991, 12). Australians actually weren't 'unduly generous,' but conservative critics turned arrivals of non-White refugees, mostly from Asia, into high-profile examples of faulty policy. Unless otherwise noted, we rely on Jupp (2002), who notes that (White) Australians have an historic fear of being invaded by 'Asian hordes.'

12 Howard was being pressed in this by the overtly racist One Nation party.

13 The two groups eventually were lumped together administratively when the Commonwealth government created a ministry that combined immigration and Aboriginal affairs – 'a ministry of other people,' some observed.

14 Anti-terrorism Act, http://www.cbc.ca/news/background/cdnsecurity.

15 The Anti-terrorism Bill, which expired in 2007, contained a five-year sunset clause requiring the Attorney General and the Minister of Public Safety and Emergency Preparedness to report annually as to whether provisions

contained in the original Anti-Terrorism Act should be maintained. That sunset clause would last through to 2012. See 'The Anti-terrorism Act: Parliamentary Review of the Anti-terrorism Act,' at http://www.justice. gc.ca/antiter/home-accueil-eng.asp.

16 Numerous articles discuss these High Court cases involving detained asylum seekers. The most accessible is Gelber (2004).

4. Federalism and Electoral Systems: Mechanisms of the Politics of Race

1 African American men gained the *legal* right to vote after the Civil War; all women gained it in 1920. But except during Reconstruction (1870s), most Black men couldn't exercise that right until the late 1960s because the states, which controlled the federal franchise, imposed exclusionary tests and poll taxes. Violence also played a role, in that lynching and other acts of violence were used against those who tried to vote.

2 In the nineteenth century, Pierre-Joseph Proudhon (1809–65) developed a socio-economic theory of federalism. As a response to the effects of industrialization in Europe, and as a means to fulfil the (failed) French Revolution's promises of equality, he advocated the decentralization of power in society and the economy by making workers self-governing producers. This had little impact on British accounts of federalism.

3 This paragraph relies in part on Walton and Smith (2003, 13, 14, Box 1.3).

4 *Gerrymandering* began in British elections when districts were designed to produce a majority for a particular party. In the United States, it was used to prevent African American majorities.

5 In 2007 the new Florida governor, Charlie Christ, persuaded the state's Executive Clemency Board to restore the right to vote to most felons who had served their sentences.

6 Status Indians are those First Nations peoples for whom the British (later federal) government assumed responsibility because they had signed treaties. This left out the Métis, a people formed by French/First Nations intermarriage during the fur trade era, until they too were recognized as having 'Indigenous rights' under the constitution. As we discuss in the text, the Inuit were ruled to be 'Indians' by the Supreme Court but now are understood to be a separate Indigenous community.

7 Both names offend the groups they signify. 'Indian' repeats Columbus's mistaken belief that he had found India. Most Indigenous communities prefer the collective name 'First Nations' or their individual nation name. 'Eskimo' is a derogatory term used to identify the 'Inuit.' 'Indian tribe' is accepted usage in the United States but not in Canada. Wher-

ever possible, we use the terms that Indigenous peoples use when referring to themselves.

8 Also, there are a few wealthy communities whose leaders, to avoid
sharing, have denied the right of return to those women and children who
have been excluded by the Indian Act's sex-discriminatory provisions.

9 Like Quebec with French, Nunavut established Inuktitut as the language
of government. It also established a consensual form of government with
no political parties.

10 The Northern Territory was granted some self-government, with a
unicameral legislature and some representation in the Commonwealth
Senate. But the Commonwealth government can disallow its legislation.

11 Because Aboriginal people are a large minority in the Northern Territory,
the Commonwealth government could divide the territory to create a new
federal unit with an Aboriginal majority, giving many Aboriginal people
more self-government. The Commonwealth government also controls the
terms of the territory's accession to statehood. When it offered the territory
less than equal statehood, its voters rejected that offer in a referendum.

12 In contrast to Canada, where appeals to Britain persisted until 1949, the
Australian High Court was established at the time of federation as the
final appeal court.

13 Australia's first-past-the-post, single-member electoral system only partly
explains why no Aboriginal person has ever been elected to Australia's
House of Representatives, which is the lower house of parliament. Neither
governing party seems to view electing racial or ethnic-minority members
as a high priority.

5. The Politics of Race: Contexts and Bottom-Up Approaches to Change

1 Hispaniola is now Haiti and the Dominican Republic.

2 Estimates (e.g., Thornton 1987) are that up to five million died in what are
now the United States and Canada. There is much controversy over how
many Indigenous people died from disease (i.e., instead of deliberate killing). There is evidence that in the nineteenth century, diseases sometimes
were deliberately introduced by Europeans, as was alcohol. Some Indigenous authors claim that a Holocaust occurred between 1592 and 1890.
Similar controversies exist in Australia.

3 Pinderhughes discusses this in her presidential address to the American
Political Science Association (APSA) meetings.

4 There are predictions – often used as scare tactics – that these settler states
will have non-White majorities in the near future. The most realistic

scenario is a non-White majority composed of Latinos and African Americans. But since the two combined currently constitute only 20 to 25 per cent of the U.S. population, their combined numbers won't exceed 50 per cent nationally in the near future, though they could do so in several states. In Canada and Australia, such predictions relate only to a few cities, such as Toronto and Vancouver. Neither country has a combined non-White population that could exceed 50 per cent within the next century. The fears that such scare tactics promote are now central to the politics of race.

5 Some are recruited as tokens and then manipulated and used against their communities. This is especially evident when governments promoting multicultural policies must also promote the formation of ethnic groups that bureaucrats can consult. Government policy is rarely changed as a consequence.

6 Ryan (1976) explains that family instability results from poverty and affects poor White families too, but not middle-class African Americans.

7 See Malcomson (2000).

8 Du Bois eventually resigned from the NAACP because it wouldn't support Pan-Africanism. He joined the Communist Party and grew increasingly disillusioned with the NAACP's pursuit of integration. Whites supported the two institutions for complex and often contradictory reasons. Some staunch segregationists supported Tuskegee, viewing it as an institution that would sustain segregation. But most supporters were northerners motivated by moral or spiritual values – for example, the White ministers who participated in civil rights marches in the 1960s.

9 Wingfield and Feagan (2010, 19) describe two White racial frames: hard and soft. Hard racial framing is overtly racist commentary in public as encountered in language or in negative evaluations of people of colour. Soft racial framing involves little overtly racist commentary but is manifested in colour-blind discourses, language, or behaviour.

10 In addition to the article by Lewis-Beck, Tien, and Nadeau (2010), the data we cite are all from http://www.cnn.com /Election/2008/results, accessed 4 May 2010. The breakdowns by race and sex are from CNN's Election Day exit polls.

6. Top-Down Approaches and Democratic Responsiveness

1 They also are regionally organized at the federal level, especially in Canada.

2 The absence of party discipline and the U.S. separation-of-powers system make this conception of representation/responsiveness both plausible and

easily observed. In parliamentary systems, representatives are limited by party discipline in their ability to respond to voters.

3 Canon (1999, 314): 'A politics of commonality strives to provide equal protection of the laws without special treatment for any single group, while a politics of difference calls for proper remedies for previous discrimination and exclusion.'

4 Ifill (2009, 256) observes that many African American politicians at the state level saw their careers boosted after Obama's victory.

5 Recognition of the poor treatment of Aboriginals made some in government fear that those in the north might join the Japanese if they invaded, as happened in some British colonies in Asia. Military occupation of the Northern Territory was the response.

6 Most benefits are regulated by state governments, so what Aboriginals received varied.

7 The Commonwealth government passed the Racial Discrimination Act in 1975, using the constitution's external affairs power, which allows it to legislate a treaty obligation.

8 Government bureaucracies are notoriously secretive, but Kidd (1997) gained access to the department's records covering 150 years of regulating Aboriginal and Pacific Island peoples between 1840 and 1988. Kidd's revelations caused a scandal – not because of what government bureaucrats had done, but because the text uncovered the brutal race regimes using the records of the department itself.

9 *Radical* means 'to go to the roots,' though it has taken on other connotations.

10 The New Zealand settler government withdrew from these principles for a period, but the size, military strength, and success of Maoridom preserved the basic relationship. That the Maori were seen as more 'civilized' than Aborigines was reflected in the Australian constitution, which provided for the desired joining by New Zealand and which recognized Maori citizenship, granted in 1893.

11 European adversarial legal systems originated in trial-by-combat processes in the Middle Ages. Capitalist values have also shaped their competitive nature.

7. 'Back to the Future': Fragmented and International Race Formations

1 After the practice of the U.S. census, we use 'Hispanic' or 'Latino' to identify Spanish-speaking populations generally. Otherwise, 'Mexican American' identifies those who lived in annexed territories; 'Mexican' or

'Chicano(a)' designates migrants from Mexico. Other Spanish-speaking groups are identified according to their place of origin.

2 The term 'Middle East' may offend because of its colonial origins, but we use it for brevity. We discuss its relationship to 'Arab' and 'Muslim' in Section Two.

3 'Asian' or 'Pacific Islander,' 'Black' or African American, and 'Native American.'

4 Our discussion of 'racialization' relies on Rodriguez (2000, 16–18).

5 State governments play key roles in constructing race regimes.

6 An estimated two million of the undocumented arrived in the United States as children.

7 In the 2000 census, the question was: 'Is this person Spanish/Hispanic/Latino.'

8 Many American race theorists believed, incorrectly, that 'mulattos' were weaker than, and died earlier than, either parent. They persuaded Congress to include a 'mulatto' category in the census to prove it and to justify strict segregation (Nobles 2000).

9 An early displacement involved detaching a province from Columbia to build the Panama Canal. This produced a sizeable Panamanian community in the United States.

10 Our discussion of Cuba relies on Gonzalez (2000).

11 Discriminatory quota laws stayed in place, and thousands of desperate Jewish refugees fleeing Nazi terror were denied entry to the United States and Canada.

12 Despite widespread support for annexations and economic policies in Mexico and the Caribbean, many Anglo-Americans reject U.S. policy in Central America.

13 Race tropes are also present in non-Western civilizations, such as the Han Chinese and the Japanese.

14 A theory of a light-skinned 'Aryan race' developed in the mid-nineteenth to twentieth centuries. Aryans were believed to speak an archaic Indo-European language linking them to Europeans, and to have settled ancient Iran and northern India.

15 Middle Easterners' official status as Whites meant that the FBI categorized hate crimes against them as 'anti-White,' which fed Islamophobia (Love 2009).

16 U.S. statistics use a racial definition of Asia, so they exclude Siberia and West and Central Asia, categorizing the inhabitants of those regions as White. Canadian statistics define 'Asian' geographically (i.e., pan-continent). Australian statistics include Northeast, Central, and South Asian ethnic groups as 'Asian' but exclude the others.

17 This trend is emerging in Canada. Reaction so far is against
   'overrepresentation.'

8. Basic Concepts for Understanding the Politics of Race

1 Racism exists apart from colonialism, and vice versa. Moreover, racism
   also exists in non-European countries such as China; and it existed before
   European contact.
2 Actions against Indigenous peoples were often taken quietly, through
   regulations developed by bureaucrats, rather than through laws or courts.
3 Denizens live in a country without the right to become citizens.

References

Abdo, Genieve. 2005. 'Islam in America: Separate but Unequal.' *Washington Quarterly* 2814 (Autumn): 7–17.

Abu-Laban, Yasmeen, and Christina Gabriel. 2002. *Selling Diversity*. Peterborough: Broadview.

Abu-Laban, Yasmeen, and Judith A. Garber. 2005. 'The Construction of the Geography of Immigration as a Policy Problem: The United States and Canada Compared.' *Urban Affairs Review* 40, no. 4 (2005): 520–61.

Acton, Lord. 1907. *Historical Essays and Studies*. Edited by J.N. Figgis and R.V. Laurence. London: Macmillan.

Alfred, Gerald R. 1995. *Heeding the Voices of Our Ancestors: Kahnawake Mohawk Politics and the Rise of Native Nationalism*. Oxford: Oxford University Press.

Anderson, Benedict. 1983. *Imagined Communities: Reflections on the Origin and Spread of Nationalism*. Ithaca: Cornell University Press.

Aristotle. *The Politics*. Edited by E. Barker. 1946. New York: Oxford University Press.

Backhouse, Constance. 1999. *Colour-Coded: A Legal History of Racism in Canada*. Toronto: University of Toronto Press.

Bakht, Natasha. 2008. *Belonging and Banishment: Being Muslim in Canada*. Toronto: TSAR.

Ball, Edward. *Slaves in the Family*. New York: Ballantine, 1998.

Ballot Initiative Strategy Center. 2010. Immigration. http://www.ballot.org/pages/immigration. Accessed 23 April 2010.

Bannerji, Himani. 2000. *The Dark Side of the Nation*. Toronto: Canadian Scholars' Press.

Beresford, Quentin, and Marilyn Beresford. 2006. 'Race and Reconciliation: The Australian Experience in International Context.' *Contemporary Politics* 12, no. 1: 65–78.

Berlin, Ira. 1998. *Many Thousands Gone: The First Two Centuries of Slavery in North America.* Cambridge, MA: Belknap.

Betts, Katharine. 1991. 'Australia's Distorted Immigration Policy.' In *Multicultural Australia: The Challenges of Change.* Edited by David Goodman, D.J. O'Hearn, and Chris Wallace-Crabbe. Newham: Scribe.

Blackmon, Douglas A. 2009. *Slavery by Another Name: The Re-enslavement of Black Americans from the Civil War to World War II.* New York: Doubleday.

Bodkin, Karen. 2002. *How Jews Became White Folks.* New York: Scholarly Books.

Boyco, John. 1995. *Last Steps to Freedom: The Evolution of Canadian Racism.* Winnipeg: Watson and Dwyer.

Breton, Raymond. 1986. 'Multiculturalism and Canadian Nation-Building.' In *The Politics of Gender, Ethnicity, and Language in Canada.* Vol. 4. Edited by Alan C. Cairns and Cynthia Williams. Royal Commission on the Economic Union. Toronto: University of Toronto Press.

Cairns, Alan C. 2000. *Citizens Plus: Aboriginal Peoples and the Canadian State.* Vancouver: UBC Press.

Calliste, Agnes, and George J. Sefa Dei. 2000. *Anti-Racist Feminism: Critical Race and Gender Studies.* Halifax: Fernwood.

Camarota, Steven A. 2010. 'An Examination of Minority Voters' Views on Immigration.' Backgrounder, Centre for Immigration Studies, February. http://www.cis.org. Accessed 15 May 2010.

Canon, David T. 1999. *Race, Redistricting, and Representation.* Chicago: University of Chicago Press.

Catt, Helena. 1999. *Democracy in Practice.* London and New York: Routledge.

CBC News. 2010. 'Arizona Immigration Law Sparks Huge Rally.' http://license.icopyright.net/user/viewFreeUse.act?fuid=ODIwNzA5MA %3D%3D. Accessed 3 March 2011.

CBSA. 2011. 'Information for People Detained under the Immigration and Refugee Protection Act.' http://www.cbsa-asfc.gc.ca/publications/pub/ bsf5012-eng.html. Accessed 30 June 2011.

Cesari, Jocylyne. 2011. 'Islamophobia in the West: A Comparison between Europe and the United States.' In *Islamophobia: The Challenge of Pluralism in the 21st Century,* ed. John L. Esposito and Ibrahim Kalin. Oxford: Oxford University Press.

Chappell, Louise, John Chesterman, and Lisa Hill. 2009. *The Politics of Human Rights in Australia.* Melbourne: Cambridge University Press.

Chesterman, John, and Brian Galligan. 1997. *Citizens without Rights: Aborigines and Australian Citizenship.* Sydney: Cambridge University Press.

Citizenship and Immigration Canada. 2008. News Release: Government of Canada Announces New Funding for Research on Immigration and

Diversity. http://www.cic.gc.ca/english/department/media/releases/ 2008/2008–01–07.asp. Accessed 23 April 2010.

– 2010. Canadian Visa Offices. http://www.cic.gc.ca/english/information/ offices/missions.asp. Accessed 23 April 2010.

Cottrol, Robert J., Raymond T. Diamond, and Leland B. Ware. 2003. *Brown v. Board of Education*. Lawrence: University Press of Kansas.

Cowlishaw, Gillian, and Barry Morris, eds. 1997. *Race Matters: Indigenous Australians and 'Our' Society*. Canberra: Aboriginal Studies Press.

Cunneen, Chris, and Terry Libesman. 2000. 'An Apology for Expressing Regrets?' *Meanjin* 59: 145–61.

Day, David. 1996. *Claiming a Continent: A History of Australia*. Sydney: Angus and Robertson.

Day, Richard. 2000. *Multiculturalism and the History of Canadian Diversity*. Toronto: University of Toronto Press.

Department of Immigration and Citizenship (Australia). 2009. Fact sheet 82 – Immigration Detention. Media: Fact Sheets. http://www.immi.gov.au/ media/fact–sheets/82detention.htm. Accessed 23 April 2010.

Dyck, Noel. 1997. *Differing Visions: Administering Indian Residential Schools in Prince Albert, 1867–1995*. Halifax and Prince Albert: Fernwood and Prince Albert Band Council.

Eddy, John, and Deryck Schreuder, eds. 1988. *The Rise of Colonial Nationalism*. Sydney: Allen and Unwin.

Edwards, Rebecca. 1997. *Angels in the Machinery: Gender in American Party Politics from the Civil War to the Progressive Era*. Oxford: Oxford University Press.

Esses, Victoria M., Joerg Diez, Caroline Bennet-Abuayyash, and Chetan Joshi. 'Prejudice in the Workplace: The Role of Bias against Visible Minorities in the Devaluation of Immigrants' Foreign-Acquired Qualifications and Credentials.' *Canadian Issues* (Spring 2007): 114–18.

Ferejohn, John A., and Barry R. Weingast, eds. 1997. *The New Federalism: Can the States Be Trusted?* Stanford: Hoover Institution Press.

Fleras, Augie, and Jean Leonard Elliot. 1996. *Unequal Relations: An Introduction to Race, Ethnic and Aboriginal Dynamics in Canada*. 2nd ed. Scarborough: Prentice Hall Canada.

Frankenberg, Ruth. 1993. *White Women, Race Matters: The Social Construction of Whiteness*. Minneapolis: University of Minnesota Press.

Friesen, Gerald. n.d. 'The LaFontaine-Baldwin Essay.' Reprinted in the *Globe and Mail*, 7 March 2002.

Frymer, Paul. 1999. *Uneasy Alliances: Race and Party Competition in America*. Princeton: Princeton University Press.

Garcea, Joe. 2006. 'Provincial Multiculturalism Policies in Canada, 1974–2004: A Content Analysis.' *Canadian Ethnic Studies* 38, no. 3: 1–20.

Gelber, Katharine. 2004. 'High Court Review 2004.' *Australian Journal of Political Science* 40, no. 2: 307–22.

Gellner, Ernest. 1983. *Nations and Nationalism.* Ithaca: Cornell University Press.

Gerth, H.H., and C. Wright Mills. 1991. *From Max Weber.* Originally published 1948. New York: Norton.

Ghobadzedeh, Naser. 2010. 'A Multiculturalism–Feminism Dispute: Muslim Women and the Sharia Debate in Canada and Australia.' *Commonwealth and Comparative Politics* 48, no. 3: 301–19.

Gilroy, Paul. 1987. *'There Ain't No Black in the Union Jack': The Cultural Politics of Race and Nation.* London: Hutchinson.

Gonzales, Juan. 2000. *Harvest of Empire: A History of Latinos in America.* New York: Penguin.

Green, Donald. 1999. 'The Contextual Nature of American Indian Criminality.' In *Contemporary Native American Political Issues.* Edited by Troy R. Johnson. Walnut Creek: Altamira.

Greer, Allan, and Ian Radforth. 1992. *Colonial Leviathan: State Formation in Mid-Nineteenth-Century Canada.* Toronto: University of Toronto Press.

Griffin, John D., and Brian Newman. 2008. *Minority Report: Evaluating Political Equality in America.* Chicago: University of Chicago Press.

Guibernau, Montserrat. 1999. *Nations without States: Political Communities in a Global Age.* Cambridge, MA: Polity.

Guibernau, Montserrat, and John Rex, eds. 1997. *The Ethnicity Reader.* Oxford: Polity.

Hanchard, Michael, and Erin Aeran Chung. 2004. 'From Race Relations to Comparative Racial Politics: A Survey of Cross-National Scholarship on Race in the Social Sciences.' *Du Bois Review* 73, no. 3: 319–43.

Hawkins, Freda. 1991. *Critical Years in Immigration.* Montreal and Kingston: McGill-Queen's University Press.

Hawkins, Joyce, ed. 1979. *Oxford Paperback Dictionary.* Oxford: Oxford University Press.

Hawthorne, Lesleyanne. 2007. 'Foreign Credential Recognition and Assessment: An Introduction.' *Canadian Issues* (Spring): 3–13.

Henry, Frances, Carol Tator, Winston Mattis, and Tim Rees. 1995. *The Colour of Democracy: Racism in Canadian Society.* Toronto: Harcourt Brace Canada.

– 1997. *The Colour of Democracy: Racism in Canadian Society.* 2nd ed. Toronto: Harcourt Brace Canada.

Hill, Johnny Bernard. 2009. *The First Black President: Barack Obama, Race, Politics, and the American Dream.* New York: Palgrave Macmillan.

Hueglin, Thomas O., and Alan Fenna. 2006. *Comparative Federalism: A Systemic Inquiry.* Toronto: University of Toronto Press.

Ifill, Gwen. 2009. *The Breakthrough: Politics and Race in the Age of Obama.* New York: Anchor.

Ignatiev, Noel. 1995. *How the Irish Became White.* New York and London: Routledge.

Ilford, Katrina, and Jan Muir. 2004. 'Dealing with Unfinished Indigenous Business.' *Australian Journal of Public Administration* 63, no. 4: 101–7.

Isaac, Annette. 2008. 'Connection and Disconnection: Leadership of Women of Colour in NAC, 1995–2003.' Paper presented at the Canadian Political Science Association Annual Conference, Vancouver, 4–6 June.

Jakubowski, Lisa Marie. 1997. *Immigration and the Legalization of Racism.* Halifax: Fernwood.

James, Carl E., ed. 1996. *Perspectives on Racism and the Human Services Sector: A Case for Change.* Toronto: University of Toronto Press.

Jayasuriya, Laksiri. 1997. *Immigration and Multiculturalism in Australia.* Nedlands: School of Social Work and Social Administration, University of Western Australia.

Johnson, Troy R. 1999. 'Part IV: Law and Justice.' In *Contemporary Native American Political Issues.* Edited by Troy R. Johnson. 175–79. Lanham: Rowman and Littlefield.

Jupp, James. 2002. *From White Australia to Woomera: The Story of Australian Immigration.* Cambridge: Cambridge University Press.

Kidd, Rosalind. 1997. *The Way We Civilize: Aboriginal Affairs – The Untold Story.* St Lucia: Queensland University Press.

Krog, Antjie. 1998. *Country of My Skull: Guilt, Sorrow, and the Limits of Forgiveness in the New South Africa.* New York: Three Rivers.

Kymlicka, Will. 1995a. *Multicultural Citizenship: A Liberal Theory of Minority Rights.* Oxford: Oxford University Press.

– 1995b. *The Rights of Minority Cultures.* Oxford: Oxford University Press.

Lawson, Steven F., and Charles Payne. 1998. *Debating the Civil Rights Movement, 1945–1968.* Langham: Rowman and Littlefield.

Lewis-Beck, Michel S., Charles Tien, and Richard Nadeau. 2010. 'Obama's Missed Landslide: A Racial Cost?' *PS: Political Science and Politics* 43, no. 1: 69–73.

Locke, John. 1924[1690]. *Second Treatise of Government.* New York: Everyman's Library.

Love, Erik. 2009. 'Confronting Islamophobia in the United States.' *Patterns of Prejudice* 43, nos. 3–4: 401–25.

Maddison, Sarah. 2009. *Black Politics: Inside the Complexity of Aboriginal Political Culture*. Crows Nest: Allen and Unwin.

Malcolmson, Scott L. 2000. *One Drop of Blood: The American Misadventure of Race*. New York: Farrar Straus Giroux.

Manning, Jennifer, E. Membership of the 111th Congress: a Profile. Congressional Research Service. 7-5700. http://www.senate.gov/CRSReports/crs-publish.cfm?pid=%260BL)PL%3B%3D%0A. Accessed 8 July 2011.

Markus, Andrew. 1994. *Australian Race Relations, 1788–1993*. St Leonards: Allen and Unwin.

Marx, Anthony W. 1998. *Making Race and Nation: A Comparison of the United States, South Africa, and Brazil*. Cambridge: Cambridge University Press.

McClure, Daniel M. 2008. 'Restricted Authority.' *Political Research Quarterly* 61, no. 4 (2008): 671–85.

McGrath, Ann, ed. 1995. *Contested Ground: Australian Aborigines under the British Crown*. St Leonards: Allen and Unwin.

McKissack, Patricia C., and Frederick L. McKissack. 1996. *Rebels against Slavery: American Slave Revolts*. New York: Scholastic.

Morris, Barry. 1997. 'Racism, Egalitarianism, and Aborigines.' In *Race Matters: Indigenous Australians and 'Our' Society*. Edited by Gillian Cowlishaw and Barry Morris. 177–89. Canberra: Aboriginal Studies Press.

Moynihan, D.P. 1967. 'The Negro Family.' Reprinted in *The Moynihan Report and the Politics of Controversy*. Edited by L. Rainwater and W.L. Lancy. Cambridge, MA: MIT Press.

Mulcare, Daniel. 2008. 'Restricted Authority: Slavery Politics, Internal Improvements, and the Limitation of National Administrative Capacity.' *Political Research Quarterly* 61, no. 4: 671–85.

Muscati, Sina Ali. 2003. 'Reconstructing "Evil": A Critical Assessment of Post-September 11 Political Discourse.' *Journal of Muslim Minority Affairs* 23, no. 2: 249–67.

National Conference of State Legislatures. 2006. 'Immigrant Policy: Ballot Initiatives Affecting Immigrants: Past and Present.' Issues and Research: Immigration: Immigrant Policy Project Ballot Initiatives. 8 January. http://www.ncsl.org/IssuesResearch/Immigration/ImmigrantPolicyProjectBallotInitiatives/tabid/13122/Default.aspx. Accessed 16 April 2010.

National Immigration Forum. 2007. 'Backgrounder: Immigration Law Enforcement by State and Local Police.' http://www.immigrationforum.org. Accessed 15 May 2010.

Nichols, Roger. 1998. *Indians in the United States and Canada: A Comparative History*. Lincoln: University of Nebraska Press.

Nobles, Melissa. 2000. *Shades of Citizenship: Race and the Census in Modern Politics*. Stanford: Stanford University Press.

Noël, Lise. 1994. *Intolerance: A General Survey*. Translated by Arnold Bennett. Montreal and Kingston: McGill-Queen's University Press.

Ozolins, Uldis. 1993. *The Politics of Language in Australia*. Cambridge: Cambridge University Press.

Pickus, Noah, and Peter Skerry. 2007. 'Good Neighbors and Good Citizens.' In *Debating Immigration*. Edited by Carol M. Swain. Cambridge: Cambridge University Press.

Pinderhughes, Dianne. 2009. 'The Challenge of Democracy: Explorations in American Radical Politics.' *Perspectives on Politics* 7, no. 1: 3–11.

Reynolds, Henry. 1996. *Aboriginal Sovereignty: Three Nations, One Australia?* Sydney: Allen and Unwin.

Richards, Leonard L. 2000. *The Slave Power: The Free North and Southern Domination, 1780–1860*. Baton Rouge: Louisiana State University Press.

Riker, William. 1964. *Federalism: Origin, Operation, Significance*. Boston: Little Brown.

– 1975. 'Federalism.' In *Handbook of Political Science*. Edited by Fred Greenstein and Nelson Polsby. 93–172. Reading: Addison Wesley.

– 1987. *The Development of American Federalism*. Boston: Kluwer.

Rodriguez, Clara E. 2000. *Changing Race: Latinos, the Census, and the History of Ethnicity in the United States*. New York and London: New York University Press.

Rosenblum, Marc R. 2009. 'Immigration and U.S. National Interests.' In *Immigration and Refugee Policy in a Post-9/11 World*. Edited by Terri E. Givens, Gary P. Freeman, and David L. Leal. New York: Routledge.

Ross, Rupert. 1996. *Returning to the Teachings: Exploring Aboriginal Justice*. Toronto: Penguin.

Ryan, William. 1976. *Blaming the Victim*. New York: Vintage.

Schram, Sandford F. 2002. 'United States of America.' In *Handbook of Federal Countries 2002: A Project of the Forum of Federations*. Edited by Ann L. Griffiths. 342–57. Montreal and Kingston: McGill-Queen's University Press.

Senese, Phyllis H. 2000. 'Weeds in the Garden of Civic Nationalism.' In *Nation, Ideas, Identities: Essays in Honour of Ramsay Cook*. Edited by Michael D. Behiels and Marcel Martel. 113–29. Toronto: Oxford University Press.

Sheehi, Stephen. 2011. *Islamophobia: The Ideological Campaign against Muslims*. Atlanta: Clarity.

Siegfried, André. 1907. *The Race Question in Canada*. London: Eveleigh Nash.

Simms, Glenda. 1993. 'Racism as a Barrier to Canadian Citizenship.' In *Belonging: The Meaning and Future of Canadian Citizenship*. Edited by William Kaplan. 333–48. Montreal and Kingston: McGill-Queen's University Press.

Sinclair-Chapman, Valeria, and Melanye Price. 2008. 'Black Politics, the 2008 Election, and the (Im)possibility of Race Transcendence.' *PS: Political Science and Politics* 41 (October): 739–45.

Smallacombe, Sonia. 2000. 'On Display for Its Aesthetic Beauty: How Western Institutions Fabricate Knowledge about Aboriginal Culture Heritage.' In *Political Theory and the Rights of Indigenous Peoples*. Edited by Duncan Ivison, Paul Patton, and Will Sanders. 152–62. Cambridge: Cambridge University Press.

Stasiulis, Daiva, and Nira Yuval-Davis, eds. 1995. *Unsettling Settler Societies: Articulations of Gender, Race, Ethnicity, and Class*. London: Sage.

Steinman, Erich. 2005. 'Indigenous Nationhood Claims and Contemporary Federalism in Canada and the United States.' *Policy and Society* 24, no. 1: 98–123.

Swain, Carol M., ed. 2007. *Debating Immigration*. Cambridge: Cambridge University Press.

Takaki, Ronald. 2008. *A Different Mirror: A History of Multicultural America*. New York: Little, Brown.

Thompson, Debra. 2008. 'The Politics of Race.' *Canadian Journal of Political Science* 41, no. 3: 525–47.

Thornton, R. 1987. *America Indian Holocaust and Survival*. Norman: University of Oklahoma Press.

van den Berghe, Pierre L. 1978. *Race and Racism*. London: Wiley.

Walton, Hanes, Jr, and Robert C. Smith. 2003. *American Politics and the African American Quest for Universal Freedom*. New York: Longman.

Wang, Zaimin, Sabina Knight, Andrew Wilson et al. 2006. 'Blood Pressure and Hypertension for Australian Aboriginal and Torres Strait Islander People' *European Journal of Cardiovascular Prevention and Rehabilitation* 13, no 1: 438–43.

Waslin, Michelle. 2009. 'The Latino Community Since 9/11.' In *Immigration Policy and Security*. Edited by Terri E. Givens, Gary P. Freeman, and David L. Leal. New York: Routledge.

Williams, Kim M. 2003. 'From Civil Rights to the Multiracial Movement.' In *New Faces in a Changing America*. Edited by Loretta I. Winters and Herman L Debosse. Thousand Oaks: Sage.

Wilson, V. Seymour. 1993. 'The Tapestry Vision of Canadian Multiculturalism.' *Canadian Journal of Political Science* 26 (December): 645–69.

Wingfield, Adia Harvey, and Jorge R. Feagin. 2010. *Yes We Can? White Racial Framing and the 2008 Presidential Campaign*. New York: Routledge.

Wroe, Andrew. 2008. *The Republican Party and Immigration Politics*. New York: Palgrave Macmillan.

Wu, Frank H. 2002. *Yellow: Race in America beyond Black and White*. New York: Basic.

Young, Iris Marion. 1990. *Justice and the Politics of Difference*. Princeton: Princeton University Press.

Statistical References: Canada

Boulos, D., P. Yan, D. Schanzer, R.S. Remis, and C.P. Archibald. 2006. 'Estimates of HIV Prevalence and Incidence in Canada, 2005.' Public Health Agency of Canada. *Canada Communicable Disease Report* 32, no. 15: 165–74. http://www.phac–aspc.gc.ca/publicat/ccdr–rmtc/06vol32/dr3215a–eng .php. Accessed 3 July 2011.

Canadian Institute of Child Health. 2006. *The Health of Canada's Children: A CICH Profile*. 3rd ed. Ottawa: Canadian Institute of Child Health. http://www.cich.ca/Publications_monitoring.html#Profile3. Accessed 3 July 2011.

Correctional Service of Canada. Aboriginal Initiatives Branch. 2009. *Aboriginal Initiatives*. http://www.csc-scc.gc.ca/text/prgrm/abinit/who-eng.shtml. Accessed 3 July 2011.

Health Canada. 2008. *Healthy Canadians: A Federal Report on Comparable Health Indicators 2008*. Cat. no. H21–206/2008E–PDF. Ottawa. http://www.hc-sc. gc.ca/hcs-sss/pubs/system-regime/index-eng.php. Accessed 3 July 2011.

Hull, Jeremy. 2008. 'Aboriginal Youth in the Canadian Labour Market.' *Horizons* 10, no. 1: 40–4. http://policyresearch.gc.ca/doclib/Horizons_ Vol10Num1_final_e.pdf. Accessed 3 July 2011.

Indian and Northern Affairs Canada. 2001. 'Comparison of Socio-Economic Conditions, 1996 and 2001: Registered Indians, Registered Indians Living on Reserve, and the Total Population of Canada.' Cat. no. R32–163/2001E– PDF. Ottawa: Minister of Indian Affairs and Northern Development. http://dsp-psd.pwgsc.gc.ca/Collection/R32-163-2001E.pdf. Accessed 3 July 2011.

– 2004. *2004 Basic Departmental Data*. Cat. no. R12–7/2003E. Ottawa: Minister of Indian Affairs and Northern Development. http://www.ainc-inac.gc.ca/ ap/index-eng.asp. Accessed 3 July 2011.

Library of Parliament Canada. 2010a. 'House of Commons: Biographical Information: Inuit, Métis, or First Nation Origin.' PARLINFO v.2.10.0.

Library of Parliament. 1 February. http://www2.parl.gc.ca/Parlinfo/
Compilations/Parliament/Aboriginal.aspx?Menu=HOC–Bio&Role=
MP&Current=False&NativeOrigin=&Role=MP. Accessed 3 April 2010.

– 2010b. 'Senate: Biographical Information: Inuit, Métis, or First Nation
Origin.' PARLINFO v.2.10.0. Library of Parliament. 1 February. http://
www2.parl.gc.ca/Parlinfo/Compilations/Parliament/Aboriginal.aspx?
Role=Senators. Accessed 3 April 2010.

– 2011. Inuit, Métis Or First Nation Origin. http://www.parl.gc.ca/Parlinfo/
Compilations/Parliament/Aboriginal.aspx?Role=Senators&Current=True&
NativeOrigin. Accessed 25 June 2011.

Luffman, Jacqueline, and Deborah Sussman. 2007. 'The Aboriginal Labour
Force in Western Canada.' *Statistics Canada: Perspectives on Labour and Income.*
8 (January): 13–21.

Mann, Michelle. 2009. 'Good Intentions, Disappointing Results: A Progress
Report on Federal Aboriginal Corrections.' Ottawa: Office of the
Correctional Investigator. http://www.oci–bec.gc.ca/rpt/oth–aut/oth–
aut20091113–eng.aspx. Accessed 27 April 2010.

Noël, Alain, and Florence Larocque. 2009. 'Aboriginal Peoples and Poverty in
Canada: Can Provincial Governments Make a Difference?' Paper presented
at the annual meeting of the International Sociological Association Research
Committee, Montreal, 20 August.

Policy Research Initiative. 2008. 'Aboriginal Youth in Canada: Emerging
Issues, Research Priorities, and Policy Implications.' Workshop report,
Government of Canada Policy Research Initiative. Cat. no. PH4–50/2009E–
PDF. Ottawa: Policy Research Initiative.http://www.horizons.gc.ca/page
.asp?pagenm=2009-0005_01. Accessed 3 July 2011.

Public Health Agency of Canada. Centre for Infectious Disease Prevention and
Control. 2007. 'HIV/AIDS epi updates.' November. Ottawa. http://www.
phac-aspc.gc.ca/aids-sida/publication/epi/epi2007-eng.php. Accessed
3 July 2011.

– 2009a. 'Tuberculosis in Canada 2008 – Pre-Release.' http://www.
publichealth.gc.ca/tuberculosis. Accessed 3 July 2011.

– 2009b. 'HIV and AIDS in Canada: Surveillance report to December 31,
2008.' Ottawa. http://www.phac-aspc.gc.ca/aids-sida/publication/
survreport/2008/dec/index-eng.php. Accessed 3 July 2011.

Public Safety Canada. Portfolio Corrections Statistics Committee. 2008.
'Corrections and Conditional Release Statistical Overview.' Cat. no. PSI–
3/2008E. Ottawa: Public Works and Government Services Canada.
http://www.publicsafety.gc.ca/res/cor/rep/_fl/2008-04-ccrso-eng.pdf.
Accessed 3 July 2011.

– 2009. 'Corrections and Conditional Release Statistical Overview.' Cat. no. PS1–3/2009E. Ottawa. http://www.publicsafety.gc.ca/res/cor/rep/2009-ccrso-eng.aspx. Accessed 3 July 2011.

Statistics Canada. 2006a. 'Immigration in Canada: A Portrait of the Foreign–Born Population.' Cat. no. 97–557–XIE. Ottawa. http://www.statcan.gc.ca. Accessed 3 July 2011.

– 2006b. 'Census of Population.' Cat. no. 97–560–XCB2006031. Ottawa. http://www.statcan.gc.ca. Accessed 3 July 2011.

– 2008. 'Aboriginal Peoples in Canada in 2006: Inuit, Métis, and First Nations, 2006 Census.' Cat. no. 97–558–XIE. Ottawa. http://www.statcan.gc.ca. Accessed 27 June, 2011.

– 2011. Education Chart 9. Postsecondary Educational Attainment by Aboriginal Identity, Population Aged 25 to 54, 2006. http://www.statcan.gc.ca/pub/89-645-x/2010001/education-eng.htm. Accessed 27 June 2011.

– The Daily. 2005. Study: Canada's visible minority population in 2017. http://www.statcan.ca/Daily/English/050322/d050322b.htm. Accessed 8 July 2011.

Trevethan, Shelley, and Christopher J. Rastin. 2004. 'A Profile of Visible Minority Offenders in the Federal Canadian Correctional System.' Research report no. R–144. Ottawa: Research Branch, Correctional Service of Canada. http://www.csc-scc.gc.ca/text/rsrch/reports/r144/r144-eng.shtml#/LinkTarget24681. Accessed 3 July 2011.

Statistical References: Australia

Australian Bureau of Statistics. 2006a. 'Ancestry.' 2006 Census of Population and Housing – Fact Sheets, 2006. Cat. no. 2914.0. http://www.abs.gov.au/AUSSTATS/abs@.nsf/mf/2914.0. Accessed 4 July 2011.

– 2006b. 'A Picture of the Nation: The Statistician's Report on the 2006 Census.' Cat. no. 2070.0. http://www.abs.gov.au/ausstats/abs@.nsf/mf/2070.0. Accessed 4 July 2011.

– 2006c. 'Population Characteristics, Aboriginal and Torres Strait Islander Australians.' Cat. no. 4713.0. http://www.abs.gov.au/ausstats/abs@.nsf/mf/4713.0. Accessed 4 July 2011.

– 2007. 'Population Distribution, Aboriginal and Torres Strait Islander Australians, 2006.' Latest Issue: 15 August 2007. http://www.abs.gov.au/ausstats/abs@.nsf/Latestproducts/4705.0Media%20Release12006?opendocument&tabname=Summary&prodno=4705.0&issue=2006&num=&view. Accessed 27 June 2011.

– 2008. 'The Health and Welfare of Australia's Aboriginal and Torres Strait Islander Peoples, 2008.' Cat. no. 4704.0. http://abs.gov.au/AUSSTATS/abs@.nsf/mf/4704.0. Accessed 4 July 2011.
– 2009. 'Causes of Death, Australia, 2008.' Cat. no. 3303.0. http://www.abs.gov.au/AUSSTATS/abs@.nsf/mf/3303.0. Accessed 4 July 2011.
– 2009a. 'Experimental Life Tables for Aboriginal and Torres Strait Islander Australians, 2005–2007.' Cat. no. 3302.055.003. http://www.abs.gov.au/aus-stats/abs@.nsf/mediareleasesbytitle/C65F4C150DD0497ACA2575BE002656BC?OpenDocument. Accessed 4 July 2011.
– 2009b. 'Experimental Estimates and Projections, Aboriginal and Torres Strait Islander Australians, 1991–2021.' Cat. no. 3238.0. http://www.abs.gov.au/AUSSTATS/abs@.nsf/mf/3238.0. Accessed 4 July 2011.
– 2009c. 'Deaths, Australia, 2008.' Cat. no. 3302.0. http://www.abs.gov.au/ausstats/abs@.nsf/mf/3302.0. Accessed 4 July 2011.
– 2009d. 'Prisoners in Australia, 2009.' Cat. no. 4517.0. Accessed 4 July 2011.
– 2010. '2009–10 Year Book Australia.' Cat. no. 1301.0. http://www.abs.gov.au/ausstats/abs@.nsf/mf/1301.0. Accessed 4 July 2011.
Australian Institute of Criminology. 2008. 'Australian Crime: Facts and Figures 2008.' http://www.aic.gov.au/publications/current%20series/facts.aspx. Accessed 4 July 2011.
Department of Immigration and Citizenship. 2009. 'Immigration Update: 2008–2009.' http://www.immi.gov.au/media/publications/statistics/immigration-update/update-jun09.pdf. Accessed 4 July 2011.
National Centre in HIV Epidemiology and Clinical Research. 2008. *Bloodborne Viral and Sexually Transmitted Infections in Aboriginal and Torres Strait Islander Peoples: Surveillance Report 2008.* Sydney: National Centre in HIV Epidemiology and Clinical Research, University of New South Wales.
Steering Committee for the Review of Government Service Provision. 2009. 'Overcoming Indigenous Disadvantage: Key Indicators 2009.' Canberra. http://www.pc.gov.au/gsp/reports/indigenous/keyindicators2009. Accessed 4 July 2011.
Thompson, Neil, et al. 2009. 'Overview of Australian Indigenous Health Status, December 2010.' Australian Indigenous Health Info Net. http://www.healthinfonet.ecu.edu.au/health–facts/overviews. Accessed 27 April 2010.
Wang, Zaimin, et al. 2006. 'Blood Pressure and Hypertension for Australian Aboriginal and Torres Strait Islander People.' *European Journal of Cardiovascular Prevention and Rehabilitation* 13, no. 3: 438–43.
Willis, Matthew. 2008. 'Reintegration of Indigenous Prisoners: Key Findings.' *Trends and Issues in Crime and Criminal Justice* 364. Australian Institute of

Criminology. http://www.aic.gov.au/en/publications/current%20series/tandi.aspx. Accessed 4 July 2011.

Statistical References: United States

Austin, Algernon. 2009. 'High Unemployment: A Fact of Life for American Indians.' Economic Policy Institute, 9 December. http://www.epi.org/economic_snapshots/entry/high_unemployment_a_fact_of_life_for_american_indians. Accessed 27 April 2010.

Centers for Disease Control and Prevention. 2009. 'HIV Surveillance Report, 2007.' Vol. 19. Atlanta. http://www.cdc.gov/hiv/topics/surveillance/resources/reports. Accessed 4 July 2011.

– 2010. 'Prevalence of Diagnosed and Undiagnosed Diabetes in the United States, All Ages, 2007.' Diabetes Public Health Resource. http://www.cdc.gov/diabetes/pubs/estimates07.htm#1. Accessed 15 April 2010.

DeVoe, Jill Fleury, Kristen E. Darling-Churchill, and Thomas D. Snyder. 2008. 'Status and Trends in the Education of American Indians and Alaska Natives: 2008.' NCES 2008–084. Washington: Department of Education, Institute of Education Sciences.

Federal Judicial Center. 2010. 'Biographical Directory of Federal Judges: Research Categories.' http://www.fjc.gov/history/research_categories.html. Accessed 23 April 2010.

Indian Health Service. 2006. *Facts on Indian Health Disparities*. http://www.ihs.gov/PublicAffairs/IHSBrochure/Files/DisparitiesFacts-Jan2006.pdf. Accessed 4 July 2011.

Jefferys, Kelly, and Randall Monger. 2008. 'U.S. Legal Permanent Residents: 2007.' Annual Flow Report. Office of Immigration Statistics Policy Directorate, Department of Homeland Security. http://www.dhs.gov/xlibrary/assets/statistics/publications/LPR_FR_2007.pdf. Accessed 18 July 2011.

Minton, Todd. 2009. 'Jails in Indian Country, 2008.' NCJ 228271. Washington: Bureau of Justice Statistics, U.S. Department of Justice.

National Center for Educational Statistics, 2007. Digest of Education Statistics, 2007. http://nces.ed.gov/pubsearch/pubsinfo.asp?pubid=2008022. Accessed 7 July 2011.

National Center for Health Statistics. 2009. 'Health, United States, 2010: With Special Feature on Medical Technology.' Centers for Disease Control, Hyattsville. http://www.cdc.gov/nchs/hus.htm.

Sabol, William J., Heather C. West, and Matthew Cooper. 2009. 'Prisoners in 2008.' NCJ 228417. Washington: Bureau of Justice Statistics, U.S. Department of Justice.

Sickmund, Melissa, T.J. Sladky, and Wei Kang. 2008. 'Census of Juveniles in Residential Placement Databook.' Office of Juvenile Justice and Delinquency Prevention. http://www.ojjdp.gov/ojstatbb/ezacjrp. Accessed 4 July 2011.

Snyder, Thomas D., and Sally A. Dillow. 2010. 'Digest of Education Statistics, 2009.' NCES 2010–013. Washington: National Center for Education Statistics, U.S. Department of Education. http://nces.ed.gov/pubsearch/pubsinfo.asp?pubid=2010013. Accessed 4 July 2011.

U.S. Bureau of the Census. 2007. 'Race and Hispanic Origin of the Foreign-Born Population in the United States: 2007.' American Community Survey Reports. ACS–11. http://www.census.gov/prod/2010pubs/acs-11.pdf. Accessed 4 July 2011.

– 2009. 'The Foreign-Born Labor Force in the United States: 2007.' American Community Survey Reports. ACS–10. http://www.census.gov/prod/2009pubs/acs-10.pdf. Accessed 4 July 2011.

– 2010a. State and County QuickFacts: USA. http://quickfacts.census.gov/qfd/states/00000.html. Accessed 23 April 2010.

– 2010b. The 2010 Statistical Abstract: The National Data Book. http://www.census.gov/compendia/statab. Accessed 17 April 2010.

Index

Note: The letters t and f following a page number denote table and figure, respectively.